German History from the Margins

EDITED BY
Neil Gregor, Nils Roemer,
and Mark Roseman

GERMAN HISTORY FROM THE MARGINS

German History from the Margins

Edited by
Neil Gregor, Nils Roemer,
and Mark Roseman

INDIANA UNIVERSITY PRESS

Bloomington and Indianapolis

This book is a publication of
Indiana University Press
601 North Morton Street
Bloomington, IN 47404-3797 USA

http://iupress.indiana.edu

Telephone orders   800-842-6796
Fax orders   812-855-7931
Orders by e-mail   iuporder@indiana.edu

Library of Congress Cataloging-in-Publication Data

German history from the margins / edited by Neil Gregor, Nils Roemer, and Mark Roseman.
p. cm.
Includes bibliographical references and index.
ISBN 0-253-34743-2 (cloth : alk. paper)
1. Germany—Ethnic relations. 2. Minorities—Germany—History—19th century. 3. Minorities—
Germany—History—20th century. I. Gregor, Neil, date. II. Roemer, Nils H. III. Roseman, Mark.
DD74.G36 2006
305.800943′09034—dc22
2005029147

1 2 3 4 5   11 10 09 08 07 06

Contents

Contents

Acknowledgments

This volume has its origins in a conference on "German History from the Margins" held at the University of Southampton, UK, in collaboration with the German History Society. We gratefully acknowledge the generous financial support provided by the Thyssen-Stiftung as well as by the German History Society, the British Academy, the Royal Historical Society, and the Hartley Institute and Vice Chancellor's Fund at the University of Southampton itself. Not all the original participants could be included here (and a number of new contributions have been added), but we would like to thank all paper givers for the stimulating discussions that provided the impetus for this volume. Thanks, too, to our contributors for their patience and willing cooperation in the subsequent editorial process. We would like also to acknowledge all those who make the University of Southampton such a stimulating place to pursue an interdisciplinary conversation on matters of German history and culture. Finally, we would like to thank Indiana University Press for taking on this project and for providing such excellent editorial support.

N.G., N.R., M.R., Southampton/Bloomington, May 2005

GERMAN HISTORY FROM THE MARGINS

Introduction

Neil Gregor, Nils Roemer, and Mark Roseman

I

Why a collection approaching German history "from the margins"? It would be disingenuous to claim that German historiography has remained trapped in the corridors of power, its gaze wedded to the view from the center. More than thirty years ago, in the wake of the student revolutions of the late 1960s, historians of modern Germany assumed the moral and political challenge of writing a counterhistory from below. The working-class or female subjects of these studies were not marginal in numerical terms, but, deprived of economic and cultural power, they lacked access to the dominant organs of representation.[1] The new research gave voice to the silent, the dispossessed, or the persecuted. Something of that empathetic embrace of the excluded can be found in the essays presented here, even if it is not the present volume's principal concern.

Though interest in the German working class as revolutionary subject waned in the late 1970s and 1980s, the attention devoted by historians to marginal groups only grew. When the focus shifted from class conflict to the place of ethnic, religious, and other minorities, Germany's relations with its minorities seemed often peculiarly characterized by conflict, exclusion, and intolerance.[2] Historians demonstrated how from *Kulturkampf* to *Kristallnacht* a variety of outsider groups came to be castigated as enemies inside the gates, with the center repeatedly defining itself in negative terms against the deviant, the dangerous, and the outlawed.[3] For some historians, it was indeed Germany's inability to integrate and absorb its diverse communities that produced the extremes of nationalism and racism. The weakness of the nation and the strength of nationalism stood in close relation. Viewed from this particular perspective, Germany was in thrall to its margins, even as it tried to suppress or incorporate them.[4] Nowhere else in the Western world did the coercive and exclusionary impulses of modern society find more horrific expression than in the Third Reich's policies toward Jews, gypsies, the handicapped and other foreign bodies in the "People's community."[5]

Yet the last few years have seen a paradigm shift in German historiography. Increasingly, Germany's margins have figured in a way that cannot be encompassed by a "lachrymose history" of suppression, segregation, and murder. Until the Nazi era, as much recent scholarship has emphasized, discourses of coercion and exclusion always coexisted with more open dialogues and encounters.[6] Indeed, the language and terms of national identity were subject to interpretation and debate, with minorities themselves frequently claiming to define their own place in the national community.[7] As a consequence, we now recognize that the margins were less dominated by the center and more constitutive of German identity than the conventional paradigm allows. The aim of the present volume is to introduce and explore these new ways of thinking about minorities and outsiders in modern German history.

II

What does it mean to write history from the margins? The metaphor of the margin does not seek to define specific sociological categories, even those as contested as race, class, or gender. Rather, as a spatial analogy, the image of the margin alerts us to the presence in society of groups that are somehow excluded, separate or distanced from the political or cultural center. It invites and facilitates comparisons, prompting us to think across the changing experience of minority groupings in different places and at different moments in the German past. It also reminds us that minorities and majorities constrained and shaped each other's spaces within the nation. While the center defined what was marginal, the margins encroached upon and redefined the territory of the center. Minority groups existed not only as outsiders, as inhabitants of a distinct space in which they lived out their own histories (though on terms frequently dictated by the dominant culture)—they also engaged the center and thereby altered its contours and character. Approached from the perspective of the margins, the center appears less homogenous and finite, more fluid and tenuous. Both sides—the dominant and the dominated, the central and the marginal—remained not only internally heterogeneous but also mutually implicated. It was Fritz Stern who long ago observed that uncertainty with regard to the question "What is Jewish?" mirrored a similar uncertainty concerning the question "What is German?"[8] And as Stephen Aschheim has recently argued in respect of Jews' relationship to their German fellow citizens, they were co-constitutive.[9]

For understandable reasons, theorists of nationalism or nation building have emphasized the dissolution of differences rather than their reproduction or continued significance. In Benedict Anderson's classic study, the emergence of a public sphere in which the nation could first be imagined was an essential precondition for the making of a nation; with the development of national awareness and subsequent state formation, individuals and groups came to associate themselves with a larger community of people whom they had never met.[10] Ernest Gellner's 1983 account argued that the formation of a nation requires central power, standardized language and education, and a common culture.[11] In both Anderson's and Gellner's formulations nationalism, under the slogan of the universal, functions as a powerful agent that coerces and melts regional, social, or religious differences into the harmony of the whole.

Anderson and Gellner contributed enormously to the understanding of the making of a nation and its culture, but their interpretations tend to understate the ongoing presence both of diversity within the nation and of competing visions of what the nation might be. Moreover, in common with many theoretical treatments of nationalism, they tended to see contemporary invocations of the nation as descriptive, rather than essentially prescriptive accounts. When Gottlieb Fichte, Heinrich Heine, Leopold von Ranke, or Richard Wagner engaged the question "What is German?" after all, their contributions described an ambition, rather than a state of affairs—an acceptable desire, perhaps, but hardly a historical reality. Even as a more strident national agenda washed over Germany in the era of Wilhelm II, regional cultures and identities were dampened but far from drowned.[12]

If theorists of nationalism have acknowledged the ongoing presence of difference only imperfectly, how far have the grand narratives penned by historians of Germany since the Second World War incorporated issues of marginality? There was until well into the postwar period a deep-rooted and surprisingly persistent tradition of history writing that took the homogeneity of the nation, and the identity of both author and reader with that nation, for granted. Gerhard Ritter's multivolume "Sword and Scepter" study of modern Prussian/German history remains the outstanding example.[13] Interested in the exercise of state power, diplomacy, and warfare, Ritter acknowledged the presence of diverse forces and interests in German society only insofar as he rued the presence of "selfish private and class goals" or "partisan strife." Identity, inasmuch as it mattered, was determined simply by subject status. Ritter was typical of a generation writing in the immediate postwar era which sought to explain not ethnic conflict and genocide but expansionism and military aggression—his analysis correspondingly focused on the evolution of military-civil relations rather than on interactions between the state and minorities or on ideologies and cultures of exclusion.

Ritter's account of a healthy "Prussian" history corrupted by the short-term historical accident of Hitler gave way in the 1960s and 1970s to far more critical narratives in which Nazism figured as the culmination of, not an aberration from, long-term developments in German history. Curiously, though, Ritter's critics displayed the same tendency to ignore issues of marginality as Ritter himself. Arguing on the same terrain as those whose arguments they sought to supplant, and thus partially determined by the very narratives they sought to subvert, theories of a German "Special Path" operated with much the same understanding of a largely homogenous state and society, the latter divided only by relatively simple class interests.[14] Indeed, as late as 1987, Hans-Ulrich Wehler felt able to introduce the first part of his four-volume social history of modern Germany with a methodological statement which ignored issues of gender. The presence of a multitude of foreigners, minorities, and discriminated outsiders living among and alongside the German people was acknowledged in passing but then also essentially ignored.[15] Such groups intruded into Wehler's narrative only infrequently and then very briefly, their encounters with society at large going untraced. With his focus on the evolution of state and administration, economy, and culture (the latter understood in terms of institutions such as churches and universities rather than identities, rituals, or beliefs) and on the intersection between those three spheres, Wehler argued, in any case, that the hallmark of modernity was growing uniformity. If the space for difference in the eighteenth century had been characterized by the presence of segmented, regionally diverse local societies, "one of the fundamental development processes of the nineteenth and also the twentieth centuries lay precisely in the fact that from this social diversity a homogenized national society with continuous class and strata boundaries and clear borders with the outside was to emerge."[16]

Despite substituting the ideas of Michel Foucault for Wehler's Weberian analysis and depicting the onward march of modernity in much more critical terms, Detlev Peukert painted a similar picture of homogenization. For Peukert, one of the most systematic and theoretically sophisticated enunciators of the new, more somber sensibility of the post-'68 era, the margin marked the boundary of the "modern project," the front line of the bureaucratic and discursive construction, regulation, and destruction of "otherness." Here, the historian could observe the *Gleichschaltung* of particularity or non-conformity—the smoothing outs involved in the colonization of lifeworlds (*Kolonisierung der Lebenswelten*).[17] In tandem with this change in sensibility, historians often shifted the spotlight from the working class to new groups of outsiders—to youth, for example, or to those classed as mentally ill or asocial by bureaucrats, doctors, and other elites—and increasingly also to ethnic minorities. But whilst in such writing the margin attained new significance as an index of modernity, the underlying narrative, as before, was of increasing uniformity imposed by the center.

Nonetheless, in the 1980s the growing body of empirical research into the different communities resident within Germany's (changing) borders started to influence the broad picture painted by historians of modern Germany. Thomas Nipperdey's magisterial three-volume study of nineteenth- and early twentieth-century German history marked a major advance in incorporating the findings of such research into a more general narrative.[18] In the English-speaking world, James Sheehan argued around the same time that "the essential character of the German past and the German present [is] its diversity and its discontinuity, its richness and fragmentation, fecundity and fluidity." Rather than try to shoe-horn everything into a single story, he suggested, "we must try instead to follow the many different histories that coexisted within German-speaking central Europe, histories that led Germans towards and away from one another, at once encouraging them to act together and making such common action virtually impossible."[19]

Germany's history, whether in the eighteenth or twentieth centuries, was never the history just of Germans. Sheehan observed that in 1762 "Germany," in the form of the Holy Roman Empire, contained a significant number of non-Germans: "Flemings and Walloons in the Austrian Netherlands, Italians in the south, Czechs in Bohemia and Slovenes along the southern frontier."[20] We might add that among those who considered themselves Germans, local, regional, religious, and cultural identities remained complex and fragmented.[21] This was just as true for both West and East Germany in the 1950s and 1960s. In the post-1945 era Germany was still characterized by the presence of border regions with complex national, ethnic, linguistic, and cultural identities. Moreover, a significant residual population of displaced persons and resettled former collaborators ensured the presence of many different non-German residents from Eastern Europe.[22] As such groups left or were absorbed into the mainstream they were supplanted by growing numbers of Italian, Greek, and Turkish migrant workers in the West and Vietnamese workers in the East.[23] Adding to the picture of postwar diversity were the large numbers of American, British, and Russian troops, providing further opportunities for Germans to define and redefine themselves through encounters with the foreign "other" on home soil.[24] Perhaps even more important, but often ignored in this context, was the presence of millions of ethnic Germans who fled westward in 1945, were expelled in 1946, or slowly trickled into West Germany in the 1950s and 1960s. Here was a group of individuals only recently vaunted by National Socialism as the advance guard in its project to Germanize eastern territory; now they found themselves demoted to marginal outsiders in the shrunken borders of the Federal Republic, ensuring that Germans' encounters with themselves, never mind with others, remained as complex as ever.[25]

The presence of such groups suggests that Wehler and Peukert are wrong to see modernity as necessarily reducing diversity. The arrival of the expellees was testimony precisely to the destructive ferocity of modern warfare and its capacity to generate refugee movements of unprecedented scale. Such con-

stituent elements of modernity as globalization, colonization, and decoloniza-
tion have been at the heart of many other stories of modern migration movements and of encounters with difference. Even where modernity has had a
homogenizing aspect, as for example in the trend to secularization, we need
to bear in mind the striking breadth and depth of historical spaces in which
diverse cultures of religiosity long continued to flourish. The presence of such
cultures remained a constituent feature of German life until at least the
mid-twentieth century.[26] Narratives of bureaucratization or the "colonization
of life-worlds" often underestimate the continued presence of spheres into
which these processes intruded only very imperfectly. Our volume proceeds
from the assumption that German history was still highly diverse in the twentieth century, and that relationships between majorities and minorities, cores
and peripheries, centers and margins remained as complex as ever.

Just around the time Nipperdey and Sheehan wrote their general histories,
enormous challenges to received ways of conceptualizing centeredness and
diversity in German history were beginning to emerge. Most obviously, German reunification opened up new perspectives both on the history of the
German nation and more broadly on continuities and discontinuities in German history.[27] It reinforced the conservative calls, already evident in the *Historikerstreit*, for a rediscovery of the nation and for renewed emphasis on the
national question in German history. But this call for a recentering of German history coexisted, sometimes paradoxically, with conservative challenges
to the idea that modern German history was dominated by racism and intolerance. In the wake of the *Historikerstreit*, there have been many attempts to
see reunification as the moment of closure in relation to working through the
moral legacies of National Socialism.[28]

There are clearly some siren voices for whom a "recentering" of German
history implies little more than an opportunity to reassert older narratives
of healthy national traditions disrupted only by the contingent short-term accident of National Socialism. But attempts to rediscover the more positive
traditions of tolerance and pluralism in Germany's past have not been restricted to the right. German museums of Jewish culture and some historians
of German Jewry have begun to foreground a set of German-Jewish encounters which are not best understood simply as preconditions or rehearsals for
the Holocaust. These developments have been hotly contested, and, as the
debates surrounding the Jewish Museum in Berlin show, accompanied by protracted disputes. Some have argued that the creation of such a museum forms
part of a process by which Germans are being encouraged to invent for themselves a fictitious past in which Jews and other Germans lived happily together.[29]

In reality, however, the rediscovery of diverse traditions involves something
more complex than a simple process of "normalization" in the pursuit of conservative agendas. It demonstrates the centrality of minority experiences to

the act of reimagining the nation in the changed contemporary era. Moreover, this post-reunification reappraisal has itself taken place in the context of a more diffuse set of interactions between postmodern thought and its critics. As the postmodern challenge to the idea of a master narrative filtered into the history profession, it encouraged a new set of writings about ethnic and religious groups that emphasized the diversity and multiplicity of voices. This approach has resulted in stimulating reappraisals of the interrelationships between Jews, Catholics, and Protestants, of the interaction between local, provincial, and national identities, of the degree of cosmopolitanism and the place of culture in Wilhelmine Germany, and many other themes.[30] A number of the key voices in this reappraisal are represented in the present volume.

Volker Berghahn has recently pointed out the danger in allowing the nation to dissolve into a series of margins, disconnected localities, or pluralistic encounters and in forgetting the role of the "center"—in the form of states, institutions, and other hegemonic structures—in shaping encounters between majorities and minorities or between different cultural groups.[31] As Berghahn argues, we need to make sure we are not constructing a partial and misleading reading of the forces which have shaped modern German history. Indeed, in other disciplines, where postmodernism as a theoretical mood advanced more quickly, there has now been a reaction against its decenteredness, resulting not least in a move to "put the state back in." Borders, for example, have long been sites for interrogating the complexity of human identities, but recent work on their anthropology has begun to reemphasize the role of the state in shaping and interacting with ethnic identities.[32]

In short, the question of how far, and in what direction, we can and ought to reconceptualize identities and relationships in modern German history remains open. Three key areas remain the subject of debate: the strength, authority, and appeal of German political structures; the degree of homogeneity in German society; and the level of intolerance in German nationalism. Encounters between the state and its minorities, between majority and minority cultures, and between members of different marginal groupings offer excellent prisms through which to explore such themes. To all of these things, and to their implications for one another, the present volume has a contribution to make.

III

Covering the period between the formation of the Second Empire and the consolidation of the Federal Republic, the volume seeks to illuminate relationships between different ethnic, religious, and social groups, and—sometimes—the relationship of these to the German state, from a variety of perspectives. The emphasis is particularly on ethnic and religious minorities, but also on the way those minorities negotiated or were fractured by the fault lines of region, gender, and class. All of the contributors are in some way interested in questions of continuity and discontinuity with the radical policies of exclusion pursued by the Nazis. For this reason the editors chose within the limited confines of the volume to restrict post-1945 coverage to the Federal Republic and not to introduce the rather different questions raised by the imposition of the Soviet Communist model on East Germany. Whilst all the contributions are alive to relationships between discourse and identity, within that shared broad sensitivity the editors have deliberately encouraged a diverse range of approaches. Some explore particular sets of texts or debates, others focus on behaviors and interactions between social groupings, others look at political parties as they expressed or reacted to ethnic groupings, and still others consider state policies directed at the margins.

In common with a small number of other scholars in the last few years, Till van Rahden and Yfaat Weiss look at a fascinating and important characteristic of the *Kaiserreich* and Weimar years—the degree to which minorities were able to adopt nationalist discourses of identity to legitimate and articulate their own relationship to the Reich. In this case, the two scholars look at the way Jewish intellectual and communal elites responded to the discourse of the *Stamm* or tribe—this is van Rahden's topic—or in Weiss's paper, the new scientific discourse of race.

Till van Rahden surveys the way in which over a lengthy period Jews came to redefine and reevaluate the definition of identity they had originally adopted during the battle over emancipation. The emancipation view that Jews could be adequately characterized as German citizens of Jewish faith was losing its credibility. For one thing, Jews were divided between liberal and Orthodox communities and thus somewhat polarized by their faith. For another, the level of observance was declining, so that, as one ironic voice put it, Jews and Christians were now distinguished by the days on which they did *not* go to worship. A purely religious self-definition was thus no longer so compelling. In an age of *völkisch* understandings, and with the strong Jewish sense of history that had emerged in mid-century, the notion of the *Stamm* or tribe came to seem an attractive and plausible way of defining what it was to be Jewish. In this way, Jews could portray themselves as a component part of the German nation just like the other regional *Stämme*, thus laying claim to a kind of ethnic identity that did not challenge the equally strong sense of being German.

This essay thus also reminds us that the way in which Jews perceived and defined their identity evolved over time. It shows too the role of key intellectual communal elites well versed in wider national discussion and education—some of them, like the philosopher, psychologist, and university professor Moritz Lazarus, a cofounder of the *Lehranstalt für die Wissenschaft des Juden-*

thums in Berlin, with a sophisticated understanding of the voluntaristic character of national identity to rival that of Ernst Renan or, in our times, Benedict Anderson.

In "Identity and Essentialism: Race, Racism, and the Jews at the Fin de Siècle," Yfaat Weiss similarly pursues the complex and varied responses of Jewish intellectuals to the mainstream discourse around them, in this case to the concept of race that was increasingly prevalent in the social sciences in early twentieth-century Germany. Of course, as George Mosse argued long ago and Yfaat Weiss reminds us, racial "science" in the early twentieth century was often not explicitly antisemitic.[33] As scientists, social scientists, or medical professionals, Jews were invited or tempted to adopt the new language of race themselves. Yet there was always a discriminatory potential in its use. With her powerful opening metaphor of "Red Peter," the humanized ape in Kafka's "A Report to an Academy," Weiss shows us that much as they were tempted to be scientific observers, Jews found themselves at the same time the object of racial categorization. It was, as she argues, therefore no accident that some of the most systematic early critics of racial theory were the Jewish scholars Franz Boas and Franz Oppenheimer.

Nevertheless, the notion that the essence of a people might lie in its blood proved extraordinarily tempting to Jewish thinkers. In part this resulted from a natural impulse of minorities to seek essentialist explanations for their cultural differences. Moreover, even thinkers of the caliber and sophistication of Martin Buber did not see the explosive negative potential of racial theories, and found themselves forced to retract or redefine their earlier statements as their dangerous implications became all too apparent. This was not a problem just for Jews, as Weiss points out, since W. E. B. Du Bois too could not escape the idea that blacks might have common inherited characteristics other than simply the color of their skin.

Van Rahden's intellectuals, coining the concept of *Stamm*, and Weiss's Jewish scientists, helping to bring the language of race into Jewish self-understanding, have a certain tragic irony to them. But to concentrate on this irony is to argue with hindsight and to ignore one of the essays' most striking conclusions, corroborating recent work by Celia Applegate, Alan Confino, and Mark Hewitson: local, regional, religious, and ethnic groups made use of the language of nationhood and race as a way of articulating their own interests and identities.[34] Nationalism, as Margaret Lavinia Anderson wrote recently, is less powerful than we once thought, but at the same time broader.[35] The dream of a homogenous nation coexisted with the fact that a variety of groups utilized the nationalist vocabulary in different ways. Yet juxtaposing the two essays, with their very different vocabularies of *Stamm* and race, shows us also that the particular discourses were not exclusive or universal even with respect to particular minorities.

In Helmut Walser Smith's and Eric Kurlander's essays, the margin figures not only as social metaphor but also as geographical boundary, with both authors examining the relationships between majority and minority ethnic groupings in Germany's border regions. Germany, of course, had extensive borders with a variety of different countries and languages. For the most part the border regions were characterized by the linguistic, ethnic, and confessional complexities that resulted from centuries of population movement and interstate conflict. In many cases the position of the frontier posts was contested and indeed subject to revision several times during the period under review. So the boundaries were important laboratories for Germany's ethnic and confessional relationships.

Helmut Walser Smith joins that small number of younger scholars reviving research on what has, since the Second World War, been one of Germany's more underresearched territories—the former Prussian east.[36] Focusing on three particular groups—the Masures, Cassubians, and Prussian Lithuanians—Smith takes as his subject the unexpectedly rich and complex relationships crossing ethnic and religious boundaries. In particular, he seeks to illuminate the way religion itself could act as a bridge between languages and ethnicities and establish, in James Clifford's words, "cosmopolitan competencies—the arts of crossing, translation and hybridity." Each of these groups saw confessional ties that crossed or counteracted linguistic and ethnic bonds. The Masures, despite a Polish language, heritage, and customs, were nevertheless tied by their Protestantism to their German counterparts and were fiercely loyal to Prussia; the same was true of the Prussian Lithuanians. The Cassubians, with a distinct Slavic dialect, formed an even more complex group, since they were internally divided by confession and also in their wider loyalties.

But beyond this comparatively straightforward story of confessional allegiances fracturing linguistic and ethnic boundaries, Smith shows the more intricate and complex allegiances that could emerge. The Masurians, though loyal Protestants, enjoyed a particular corporeal piety that established bridges to Catholic neighbors by allowing them to celebrate specifically Catholic festival days and make pilgrimages to sites of Catholic miracles. Mixed marriages were common at least until the mid-nineteenth century. Threatening to disrupt the established denominations in the second half of the century were the new ecstatic sects such as the *Gemeinschaftsbewegung* that swept up Protestants but also some Catholics in Prussian Lithuania and Masuria.

At the same time Smith acknowledges that these complexities and allegiances were living on borrowed time. In the 1870s such hybrids and contacts still found sympathetic intellectuals to document and support them—pastors learning dialects to cater to their flock or tolerating dual-language services, lexicographers, and ethnologists. But from the *Kulturkampf* onward, German Protestant church leaders began to aggressively promote the Germanization of Christian services. Under this onslaught, the old hybrids began to dissolve and, by the First World War, much of this world had disappeared.

For his part, Eric Kurlander examines the relationship between ethnic minorities and German liberalism in two border regions—Schleswig-Holstein and Alsace-Lorraine. Kurlander reminds us that it was Germany's marginal groups—the Danes in Schleswig-Holstein, the (ethnically German) Alsatians, and indeed the Jews in almost all regions—who were the most ardent defenders of liberalism's universal promise. Long after mainstream liberalism in Germany had moved to *völkisch* values, minority groups clung to the old-style principles, which alone could guarantee their independence. Until the First World War, they continued to find conversation partners in the mainstream liberal parties. But after the war, those liberal parties increasingly sought to combat their weakness on the left by subscribing to the values of the *völkisch* right.

At the same time the regions under review show marked differences. At least until the First World War, Schleswig-Holstein saw a series of seemingly paradoxical alliances. It was the *völkisch* liberals, with their strong sense of ethnic affinity with the Nordic peoples, who were more tolerant of the Danes' claim to cultural self-representation, while more universalist liberals worried that any separate ethnic grouping would undermine the universal character of the polity. These paradoxical stances reinforce Till van Rahden's argument that the challenge of accommodating sub-groups and identities was never an easy one for universalists. They also show the particular situation in Schleswig-Holstein, where the Danes, unlike Jews and Poles, could call on a great deal of ethnic sympathy from *völkisch* ideologues. And indeed right through to the Nazi seizure of power *völkisch* liberals would continue to see scope for expressions of Danish identity within Germany (and for German self-determination in the now Danish area of north Schleswig).

In Alsace-Lorraine, which joined the German Reich in 1871, there was no significant ethnic minority. Ninety-six percent of the inhabitants were German speakers. But the republican inheritance from their years under French revolutionary rule created a very distinct political identity among the Alsatians. The more signs emerged after 1871 of illiberal tendencies within the German Reich, the more an Alsatian particularism emerged to preserve the republican-universalist spirit. Instead of German nationalism, the "clerical-autonomist" Anselme Laugel concluded, it was "liberty, holy and fecund liberty that one must invoke and thanks to liberty Alsace [was] proud to continue producing men who know to take up in her name the word among nations and express her eternal truths in forms familiar to her genius." This explains why it was that Alsatians largely welcomed French troops with open arms in 1918, despite their cultural and linguistic affiliations with Germany. Even though resentment of the Third Republic's rule grew after 1918, a racialist majority never developed as it did in Schleswig-Holstein.

On one level, then, Smith and Kurlander remind us of the sheer ethnic, confessional, and linguistic diversity of nineteenth- and early twentieth-century Germany and in particular of the ethnic complexities in the border regions. But at the same time they offer with striking clarity an inversion of the once familiar picture of cosmopolitan liberals providing a veneer of openness and perspective to the narrow provincialism of ordinary folk in the provinces. For Smith, the unexpected story in East Prussia is rather the way a "modest, limited, rooted cosmopolitanism," transacted in forms of piety and patterns of commerce, was wiped out in the intensifying conflict between Germanizing civil servants and clergymen, on the one hand, and self-consciously Polish intellectuals in the other. For Kurlander, similarly, the underlying story is the increasingly *völkisch* tones of Germany's liberals, dismissing the plaintive reminders from Alsatian Germans, Schleswig Danes, and (as Kurlander has added elsewhere) Silesian Jews[37] that there had once been a universalist liberal conversation in the provinces.

In different ways, Winson Chu and Frank Bösch also identify fractures running against the more familiar ethnic grain, but in this case their subject is not the ties that bind different ethnicities, but rather the regional and particular sub-groupings that challenge our sense of the solidarity of German nationalism and conservatism.

Chu offers us the unfamiliar story of regionalism and division among the Germans of Poland after 1918. As he reminds us, the German minorities to be found in the newly reformed Polish state after the First World War had a threefold provenance. In the west were the formerly Prussian border regions, whose German speakers had until 1918 been part of Prussia, later the German empire, and had been accustomed to being the dominant players in the region. This grouping could not adjust to its new-found subordination and in that respect its situation was similar to that of a second grouping, the German speakers in the south in Silesia and Galicia, formerly part of the Austrian empire. Finally, the east and northeast of Poland were home to ethnic Germans formerly under Russian rule, who hoped that the new Polish state would demonstrate a greater toleration of their ethnicity than had their Russian lords.

Chu's principal concerns are the shifting dynamics that prevented these different groups from forming a united front within Poland. Despite common interests in opposing real and imagined Polish suppression of their ethnic identities, the Germans in the east were resentful of their better-supplied counterparts in western Poland, who enjoyed the lion's share of covert aid from a Weimar Republic keen to see its eastern boundaries revised. After the Nazis came to power, however, the relationship changed, with the eastern Germans enjoying increasing prominence within Poland's German minority. This was partly a question of demographics—as the German minority in the west declined, the number of ethnic Germans in Congress Poland grew rapidly. But even more significant was the Nazis' different hierarchy of value. Unlike the limited territorial revisionism of the Weimar Republic, which had given priority to the western Poles, the Nazis' support for Germandom wherever it was to be found provided greater rhetorical, administrative, and financial momentum to the formerly Russian Germans. The result was that despite a broad acceptance of Nazism, the latent regional divisions within the German minority in Poland did not disappear until 1939. Minority leaders were able to synthesize prevailing ideological considerations with these concrete interests, often in ways quite frustrating to their Reich caregivers. Indeed, Nazi support for the ethnic Germans in eastern Poland served to deepen rather than bridge regional divisions.

Frank Bösch too offers an unexpected take on "marginality" within the German ethnic mainstream, this time looking at a group that at first sight seems at the very heart of the German establishment, and certainly one located as far from the German borders as it was possible to get. The Guelphic conservatives in Hanover have been largely ignored by historians of German conservatism, in favor of Prussian elites and Catholic conservatives of the southwest. As Bösch argues, this itself reflects the Guelphs' increasing sense of marginality after the incorporation of the kingdom of Hanover into Prussia in 1866.

Bösch shows the striking persistence of Guelph identity over a full century of post-Hanoverian history. Ministers from the Guelph party (DHP, later DP) played prominent roles in Lower Saxon politics until well into the post-WWII period. This persistence belied a recurrent pattern whereby the party gained major impetus from the moments of national reorganization (1871, 1918, and 1945) but then declined during the stable years of the *Kaiserreich*, Weimar, and the Federal Republic. A well-connected network of local notables, from the grand aristocrats of Hanover down to lawyers and local pastors, kept the movement's identity alive, while nevertheless making economic and social use of whatever regime was in place. Perhaps the most interesting point for our purposes is the mixture of continuity and discontinuity in the rhetoric which accompanied the Guelphs' assertions of independence. After 1866, the movement saw itself as struggling against the overweening Prussian monarchy. In 1918, its anti-Prussianism was more anti-Bolshevik than anti-monarchist. Absorbed (but not dissolved) reasonably uncomplainingly into the Nazi movement, it emerged after 1945 embodying the "safe" patriotism of regionalism and old monarchical traditions, without the rejected mantle of nationalism. In each case, the existing infrastructure of local notables was sufficiently credible to bring new generations of supporters on board.

While almost all of our contributors are interested in discourse, Gideon Reuveni and Katharine Kennedy are explicitly concerned with the politics of texts. Both look at establishment efforts in the *Kaiserreich* and the Weimar

Republic to control what the public read and at the images of minorities that were presented to them. Reuveni and Kennedy emerge with answers that reveal unexpected ambiguities and openness in contemporary discourse.

Kennedy's focus is the reading texts designed for grades five to eight in Germany's elementary schools. As she delved into the texts, her principal discovery was an unexpected absence: she did not find the negative stereotypes and demons she had expected. Rather, a diverse set of texts existed (for the different denominational schools), each of which in themselves had a tendency to ignore diversity. In part, this is a reminder of the institutionalized pluralism of Germany's public school system—in which, until 1933, Catholic, Protestant, and some Jewish elementary schools existed side by side—and in which the states retained local responsibility. Beyond that, there was a generic tendency to ignore, rather than demonize, difference. Thus each promoted an imaginary homogenous, harmonious Germany, but the precise content varied from book to book according to the population for whom it was primarily intended. The main religious communities were able to shape the texts for their particular schools, and tended to avoid the contentious issues of difference. The states also varied somewhat in their choice of texts. Even socialism barely figured as a bugbear, though there were several Prussian texts from the *Kaiserreich* extolling the kaiser's deeds for the workers.

It is only in Nazi Germany after 1935 and particularly in wartime revisions to the textbooks that we find radical discontinuity, the elimination of diversity, the stifling of positive support for Christian denominations, and the increasingly rabid denunciations of brutal Communists and devious Jews. As Kennedy notes, the writers of Nazi textbooks had been educated in the *Kaiserreich* and Weimar, so that the post-1933 schoolbook culture cannot simply be detached from the preceding era. Nevertheless, Kennedy urges caution in creating a teleology of German intolerance.

Like Kennedy's, Gideon Reuveni's interest lies as much in what he did not find in the texts as what he did find. His expectations had been fashioned by the well-established historical interpretation of the German *Kaiserreich*, of which Shulamit Volkov has been one of the most prominent advocates, that antisemitism became its generic anti-modernist "code," a pervasive and emotive shorthand for opposition to industrialization, urbanization, socialism, and democracy.[38] Reuveni investigated the equally encapsulating and symbolic movement against "trash and smut" in literature and the war on alcohol. Enjoying the support of a panoply of voluntary groups and official bodies, the movement sought to combat threats as heterogeneous as pornography, homosexuality, internationalism, and capitalism. Yet Reuveni discovered the remarkable fact that from the *Kaiserreich* into the Weimar years, antisemitism barely figured in this campaign. In contrast, antisemitism featured prominently in the debates about animal protection in Germany—when animal welfarists attacked Jewish ritual slaughter as inhumane, cruel, and torturous—as well as in the fight against department stores.

One conclusion Reuveni draws from this is that much work on antisemitism has focused rather narrowly on the literature of the antisemites themselves, a perspective that has encouraged circular conclusions about the *Kaiserreich*. The silence on Jews he uncovered is remarkable, particularly given the apparent overlaps in anti-modernist sentiment between the antisemitic movement, the campaign against pulp writings, and the movement against alcoholism. Placed alongside his analysis of the antisemitism in the debates about animal protection and the battle against department stores, his finding challenges common wisdom. To account for the striking differences, Reuveni's explanation draws on what he calls "consumer" and "producer" discourses, different contexts of meaning and explanation, in only one of which the Jews figured centrally. In the consumer discourse, of which the campaign against trash or smut was an example, the vulnerable groups in society were seen as the masses, the uneducated, women, and other suggestible individuals. In this discourse, Jews were not seen as a particular threat; on the contrary, as upholders of high culture they figured, if at all, as holders of virtue. It was in the "producer discourse," which dealt more directly with division and conflicts among the bourgeois classes, that Jews became targeted.

Like Kennedy, therefore, Reuveni reminds us of the "openness" and multifaceted character of public discourse. Particular views function as "tropes" within a given context and set of connotations. This discourse can be powerful and reinforcing, but it is contextually located and not as generic as a mindset or mentality (if such a thing as a mindset indeed really exists, independent of given contexts).

Historians have long been conscious both of the mutual constitutiveness of gender and ethnicity, and of the ways in which debates about sex regularly resonate with deeper anxieties about the nation, its purity, and its violability. It is now a commonplace that in every patriarchal society, racism involves thinking about the sexuality of the women of the racial other. In the case of Jewish men, research has shown how attribution of gender worked in highly complex and paradoxical ways. On the one hand, as Erik Erikson observed long ago, there existed the apelike and predatory sexuality stereotyped by Adolf Hitler. But there was also the widely perceived feminization of Jewish men, enunciated first so powerfully by Otto Weininger.[39] And if racial stereotypes were overlaid with gender, so studies over the last two decades have shown how far National Socialist gender policy was imbued with racism.[40]

Most historiography has emphasized Nazism's sexually conservative side, seeing it as a reaction to the liberal, and by extension "Jewish," sexual culture of a putatively permissive and decadent Weimar era. Yet as Dagmar Herzog demonstrates in line with a growing body of stimulating and persuasive scholarship on sex in the Third Reich, the regime contained a multitude of competing voices on this issue which reflected the broader presence of diverse conservative, Christian, radical, and atheistic contingents within the regime.[41] Both conservative and "liberal" voices on sexual behavior drew on antisemitic constructions of sexual theory and behavior during the Weimar era, but what was most striking about Nazi advocates of pre- and extramarital heterosexual activity was their tendency to reproduce much the same arguments as those "Jewish" sexual reformers whose activities they consistently damned. In doing so, moreover, they tapped into a deep vein in German society which sought the pleasures of a less conservative sexual culture and which found "Jewish" ideas of sexual freedom highly appealing. As Herzog has argued more extensively elsewhere, the era of sexual repression against which the radicals of 1968 reacted was not, as they thought, the era of fascism itself, but the period of the 1950s in which Christian, conservative sexual norms were reasserted *against* the behavioral patterns encouraged by the Third Reich.[42] What Herzog also underlines in this piece, however, is that competing and contradictory constructions of Jewishness were at the core of German debates about correct or permissible sexual behavior. While Katharine Kennedy emphasizes the radical simplifications and polarizations of Nazi rhetoric, Herzog points to how fluid discursive tropes could be even within the Third Reich, and indeed how that which counted as Jewish was also of central importance to non-Jewish Germans.

Atina Grossmann's essay too explores the intersections of ethnicity and gender, focusing on what she calls the "desperately over-determined" issue of gendered encounters and sexual activity amongst Jewish DPs and Germans in the 1945–49 period. She notes the astonishing fact that far from being *judenrein*, Germany contained a Jewish population which was characterized at a rough estimate by "a birth rate 'higher than that of any other population' in the world." To support this reproductive behavior, Jewish women, whose privileged access to scarce resources gave them considerable purchasing power, enlisted a variety of medical, nannying, and other services from the German population. Using a rich array of sources and exploring the issues from a variety of perspectives, Grossmann's essay delineates the complex brew of collective self-assertion, revenge, opportunism, and simple human attraction that lay behind the baby boom and the set of interactions around it.

What distinguishes this essay from the others in the volume is the strange interregnum in German history it describes. Germany itself was powerless, and the DPs' situation shaped as much by international forces—Allied occupation policy, British policy toward Palestine, U.S. policy on immigration in general and American Jewish pressures in particular, Zionist demands and actions to deliver Jews to Palestine for the establishment of a state of Israel—as by any decisions made by Germans themselves. Many of the assumptions made elsewhere about relationships between centers and peripheries do not apply here; indeed, those relationships were radically reversed. Not only the survivors in the camps were displaced, but also the power structures in which they negotiated and acted. And as Grossmann so vividly shows, these shifts in power reached into the most intimate of spheres. But though taking place in a strange interregnum, the forging of relationships between Germans and DPs had a certain character of rehearsal, and in that sense Grossmann's essay marks a bridge to the last section of this book. The interactions between DPs and Germans were of course dominated by past experiences, often impelled by nothing more than short-term opportunism, and laden with spoken and unspoken resentments. Nevertheless, for the Germans they could also represent a first rehearsal, under Allied tutelage, of a different performance of self, one that laid claim to a dignified German inheritance of toleration and openness, part of a wider Christian tradition of respecting one's neighbor.

Continuing this story, Heide Fehrenbach and Karen Schönwälder look at the Federal Republic's approach to its minorities. Like the authors of earlier essays, both identify the complexity of the relations between center and margins—but this time in the self-conscious space of the post-Holocaust era. Fehrenbach's essay concerns a group whose small size might have made it invisible to a larger public were it not for its symbolic value, namely the mostly illegitimate children of African American GIs and German women. Much scholarly research has dwelled on the coerced sex experienced by German women at the hands of Soviet soldiers in and around Berlin, but as Fehrenbach reminds us, the occupation era led to a much wider variety of sexual interactions, most of which were consensual, between Germans and others.[43] In readjusting their neuroses concerning sex, race, and nationhood, many Germans focused in particular on relationships between white German women and black American soldiers.[44] Here, as in relation to the DPs, West Germans had an early postwar opportunity to explore questions of race after the Holocaust. Since antisemitism was, at least in public discourse, largely taboo, postwar discussion of race was increasingly framed in terms of the distinctions between blackness and whiteness. The term *Mischling*, for example, survived into the postwar period—but now used exclusively to describe children of white German women and foreign men of color.

Drawing on older mentalities of anti-black racism learned in the colonial period and the Nazi era and confirmed in their apparent legitimacy by the occupiers' own attitudes to their black troops, West Germans were able to recode their attitudes to difference and rescue them into the democratic era, albeit on the basis of highly reordered taxonomies of race. A federal German census of children fathered by occupation troops sought to classify paternity in terms of nationality (American, British, French, etc.) with one exception, "colored," a non-national category that showed how the issue of race was now being reduced to the distinction between black and white. To have separately listed Jewish fathers in such a context, even assuming such information had been available, would have been unthinkable. Race—and here Germany was following the evolution of American social science in the 1930s and '40s—was now a matter of color. As Fehrenbach shows, debates during the late 1940s and 1950s on the adoption and integration of the children these relationships produced provide an excellent opportunity to map changing West German attitudes to race and difference in the 1950s and 1960s.

Karen Schönwälder's subject is the Federal Republic's approach to "guest workers" in the early 1970s, and in particular the abrupt November 1973 reversal of a previously liberal recruitment policy. Until now, historians have been agreed that successive German governments blithely pursued short-term labor-market objectives without recognizing or confronting the implications for long-term immigration. Up to 1973, it is argued, huge numbers of guest workers were imported under the naive assumption that they were there only for the short haul. Then, reeling from the 1973 oil crisis, the government introduced a unilateral stop, seemingly unaware of the obvious consequence, namely, that labor migrants already in Germany, recognizing that they would not be readmitted on a subsequent occasion, were now unlikely to leave. Using a wealth of recently released records, Schönwälder demonstrates that all these assumptions about government policy are false.

On the one hand government was indeed well aware of the potential long-term implications of labor migration, and had long been concerned enough to seek alternatives. In economic terms, there was a growing worry that future social costs might outweigh the benefits of expanding the labor force. Perhaps more influential was the explosion of anxiety that followed the murder of Israeli athletes at the Munich Olympics in summer 1972. The widespread concern, fanned by the *Bildzeitung,* that foreign workers might bring terror onto German soil drew on traditional linkages between the alien and the frightening. But in this case such fears had a postwar twist, since the public outrage was linked to calls for better protection of Germany's Jews, and fears about the impact of the Olympics on international perceptions of Germany. More than a year before the 1973 ban, consensus had thus been reached in government circles that a change in policy was required.

On the other hand, as Schönwälder also clearly demonstrates, the authorities were so trapped between competing domestic and international priorities that concerted action was not forthcoming until the oil crisis, and even afterward a coherent policy proved elusive. There was deep ambivalence among contemporaries as to what kind of society Germany should be. Many in government circles shared the view that Germany could not absorb too many migrants from other cultures. They were worried about inflaming German racism and undermining the SPD's support in future elections. Yet at the same time, in the 1972–73 period, Interior Minister Genscher made a number of gestures in the direction of acknowledging that West Germany had become a land of immigration and the SPD too presented itself as the advocate of a more social and liberal approach, in tune with the character of the Federal Republic. Legal measures to restrict the rights of migrants sat uneasily with this image. The FRG also did not want to alienate those foreign partners for whom the temporary export of labor was an important economic fact, but who—as Yugoslavia—would be offended by moves to settle their citizens permanently in Germany. Together, these contradictory concerns prevented clear steps before 1973 and afterward led to the policy of *rückkehrorientierte Integration* (integration oriented toward departure), a term so absurd it can hardly be translated.

In sketching out different facets of the FRG's evolving responses to minorities in its midst, both Fehrenbach and Schönwälder bring out a distinctive feature of the postwar period, namely, the enormous international symbolism that interactions between center and margin had acquired. When West Germans looked at the "other," they did so supremely conscious of the gaze of outsiders looking in at them. Of course, the Nazis, too, had been conscious of world opinion on the Jewish question, but this awareness had increasingly lost its power to restrain brutal actions, or had at most prompted irrational efforts to use Jews as hostages to prevent Germany's "Jewish" enemies from acting against it. In the postwar period, the "stain" of Nazi Germany was so profound that presenting a liberal image, or at least avoiding an illiberal one, became imperative for successive German administrations, and a major policy factor. This was one, though far from the only, factor promoting a progressive liberalization of public attitudes on race and ethnicity, in which inherited assumptions from Nazi and pre-Nazi Germany gradually faded from public discourse.

West Germany nevertheless struggled with the idea of a diverse and multiethnic society. Older racial assumptions enjoyed a continued half-life. At government level, such assumptions now appeared less as overtly defended claims of racial difference than packaged as fears about adverse popular reactions. In Fehrenbach's account we see health and welfare officials supposedly worried about the psychological impact on mixed-race children or their mothers of living in a non-pluralistic society. In Schönwälder's, we find Willy Brandt and his government anticipating popular protest against proposed government policies on permanent immigration. Only in the 1990s, after the fall of the Berlin Wall, did a more concerted—though thoroughly contested—discussion about a new citizenship law take place, and only in 2000 were the citizenship rights of the guest workers and their families finally acknowledged.

In his concluding paper, Geoff Eley reviews some of the key questions raised by this volume and offers an agenda for future research. Reminding us of the striking discontinuities in form, self-definition, and territorial extent of the German nation over the last 150 years, Eley begins with a lengthy account of the stages and processes by which the nation—in Germany and elsewhere—nevertheless came in the late nineteenth and twentieth centuries to acquire a "self-evidentness" that went beyond formal citizenship and entered the interstices of private identities and public life. This provides the context for his underlying question, namely the degree to which we can and should recognize a "centeredness" in modern German history.

In examining the relationship of margin and center, Eley illustrates again how versatile and complex the metaphor of the margin can be. In his discussion of the margin as *spatial* metaphor, Eley reminds us, for example, of the ways in which local and provincial identities become "sutured" to an idea of the nation. Turning to the idea of the margin as a metaphor of "cultural condition," Eley looks at the relationship between National Socialism and the many groups it sought to enlist in, or eradicate from, the racial community. He underscores the value of recent work on the power of the Nazi notion of racial community but argues that it has overstated the degree to which different communities and groupings were subject to the Nazis' totalizing impulses. Ultimately, Eley's purpose is to balance historical interest in the margins with a continued sense of the sources of cohesion, unity, or hegemony in modern German history. The point is that the "centeredness" of the national can be understood only through examining the co-constitutiveness of the margins. Finally, Eley uses the notion of centeredness (though here the apposition is perhaps less with marginality than with fragmentation) in a third way, namely as a yardstick by which to measure the historiography of modern German history. For Eley, National Socialism remains the central organizing question of modern German history.

It may seem odd, then, that only one contributor to the present volume, Dagmar Herzog, deals exclusively with the Nazi era. Of course, all the other essays have a great deal to say that is relevant to understanding the origins and impact of the Nazis' monstrous project, not least with reference to the rhetorics of inclusion and exclusion, to processes of identity formation and articulation, and to the homogenizing ambitions and practices of state institutions. But the decision to pursue these issues outside the period of the Third Reich itself is a sign of the somewhat paradoxical way in which Nazism and the Holocaust have shaped current historiographical debates and the questions posed by this volume. On the one hand, the moral framework underlying almost all of the contributions does indeed derive ultimately from the challenge that Nazism and the Holocaust have bequeathed to contemporary scholars. In that sense, all avenues of enquiry lead directly or indirectly from Auschwitz. On the other hand, if this volume is shaped by one overarching hypothesis, it is that while National Socialism continues to set the ultimate reference point for interest in the margins, the questions to which our post-Holocaust sensibility gives rise are beginning to take us down roads which do not, necessarily, lead us back to Auschwitz. In short, attuned to the importance of the ways in which modern nations incorporate and respond to their minorities, we are rediscovering the complexity, diversity, and openness of German history's traditions.

Notes

1. On the enormous literature on workers and class, see Wolfgang Schmierer, *Von der Arbeiterbildung zur Arbeiterpolitik: Die Anfänge der Arbeiterbewegung in Württemberg, 1862-1878* (Hannover: Verlag für Literatur und Zeitgeschehen, 1969); Hugo Eckert, *Liberal-oder Sozialdemokratie? Frühgeschichte der Nürnberger Arbeiterbewegung* (Stuttgart: E. Klett, 1968); Klaus Tenfelde, *Sozialgeschichte der Bergarbeiterschaft an der Ruhr im 19. Jahrhundert* (Bonn-Bad Godesberg: Neue Gesellschaft, 1977); Jürgen Kocka, *Klassengesellschaft im Krieg: Deutsche Sozialgeschichte, 1914-1918* (Göttingen: Vandenhoeck und Ruprecht, 1973); Hans Mommsen and Ulrich Borsdorf, eds., *Glück auf, Kameraden! Die Bergarbeiter und ihre Organisation in Deutschland* (Cologne: Bundverlag, 1979); Mary Nolan, *Social Democracy and Society: Working-Class Radicalism in Düsseldorf, 1890-1920* (Cambridge: Cambridge University Press, 1981); and W. L. Guttsman, *Workers' Culture in Weimar Germany: Between Tradition and Commitment* (New York: Berg, 1990). For introductions to the literature on women, see Richard J. Evans, *The Feminist Movement in Germany, 1894-1933* (London: Sage, 1976); Ute Gerhard, *Verhältnisse und Verhinderungen: Frauenarbeit, Familie und Rechte der Frauen im 19. Jahrhundert* (Frankfurt am Main: Suhrkamp, 1978); Karin Hausen, ed., *Frauen suchen ihre Geschichte* (Munich: C. H. Beck, 1983); John C. Fout, ed., *German Women in the Nineteenth Century: A Social History* (London: Holmes and Meier, 1984), with a comprehensive English-language bibliography; Ute Frevert, *Frauen-Geschichte: Zwischen Bürgerlicher Verbesserung und neuer Weiblichkeit* (Frankfurt am Main: Suhrkamp, 1986); and Lynn Abrams and Elizabeth Harvey, eds., *Gender Relations in German History: Power, Agency, and Experience from the Sixteenth to the Twentieth Century* (Durham, N.C.: Duke University Press, 1997).

2. Influential texts in an extraordinarily diverse field include, on Germany and its Jews, Peter Pulzer, *The Rise of Political Anti-semitism in Germany and Austria* (New York: Wiley, 1964); Shulamit Volkov, *The Rise of Popular Anti-modernism in Germany: The Urban Master Artisans, 1873-1896* (Princeton, N.J.: Princeton University Press, 1978); William Hagen, *Germans, Poles, and Jews: The Nationality Conflict in the Prussian East, 1772-1914* (Chicago: University of Chicago Press, 1980); and Wolfgang Benz and Werner Bergmann, eds., *Vorurteil und Völkermord: Entwicklungslinien des Antisemitismus* (Freiburg: Herder, 1997); on eugenics and race, Hans-Walter Schmuhl, *Rassenhygiene, Nationalsozialismus, Euthanasia: Von der Verhütung zur Vernichtung "lebensunwerten Lebens," 1890-1945* (Göttingen: Vandenhoeck und Ruprecht, 1987); and Paul Weindling, *Health, Race, and German Politics between National Unification and Nazism, 1870-1945* (Cambridge: Cambridge University Press, 1989); on other ethnic and social minorities, Hagen, *Germans, Poles, and Jews;* Hans-Ulrich Wehler, "Polenpolitik im Deutschen Kaiserreich," in *Krisenherde des Kaiserreichs, 1871-1918: Studien zur deutschen Sozial- und Verfassungsgeschichte* (Göttingen: Vandenhoeck und Ruprecht, 1979); and Detlev J. K. Peukert, *Grenzen der Sozialdiszi-*

plinierung: Aufstieg und Krise der deutschen Jugendfürsorge von 1878 bis 1932 (Cologne: Bund-Verlag, 1986). On Protestant nationalism and the marginalization of Catholics, see Horst Zillessen, ed., *Volk, Nation, Vaterland: Der deutsche Protestantismus und der Nationalismus* (Gütersloh: Gütersloher Verlagshaus G. Mohn, 1970); and Arlie J. Hoover, *The Gospel of Nationalism: German Patriotic Preaching from Napoleon to Versailles* (Stuttgart: F. Steiner, 1986).

3. On exclusion and citizenship, see Andreas K. Fahrmeier, *Citizens and Aliens: Foreigners and the Law in Britain and the German States, 1789-1870* (New York: Berghahn, 2000); and Dieter Gosewinkel, *Einbürgen und Ausschliessen: Die Nationalisierung der Staatsangehörigkeit vom Deutschen Bund bis zur Bundesrepublik Deutschland* (Göttingen: Vandenhoeck und Ruprecht, 2001). On violence toward the other, see Richard J. Evans, *Tales from the German Underworld* (New Haven, Conn.: Yale University Press, 1998); and Dirk Walter, *Antisemitische Kriminalität und Gewalt: Judenfeindschaft in der Weimarer Republik* (Bonn: Dietz, 1999).

4. See Harold James, *A German Identity, 1770 to the Present Day* (New York: Routledge, 1989); and Stefan Berger, *Germany: Inventing the Nation* (London: Arnold, 2004).

5. For recent syntheses of Nazi policy toward Jews, see Saul Friedländer, *Nazi Germany and the Jews: The Years of Persecution, 1933-1939* (London: Phoenix Giant, 1997); and Peter Longerich, *Politik der Vernichtung: Eine Gesamtdarstellung der nationalsozialistischen Judenverfolgung* (Munich: Piper Verlag, 1998). On gypsies, see Michael Zimmermann, *Rassenutopie und Genozid: Die nationalsozialistische "Lösung der Zigeunerfrage"* (Hamburg: Christians, 1996); and Guenter Lewy, *The Nazi Persecution of the Gypsies* (Oxford: Oxford University Press, 2000). On euthanasia, see Michael Burleigh, *Death and Deliverance* (Cambridge: Cambridge University Press, 1994); and Götz Aly, Peter Chroust, and Christian Pross, *Cleansing the Fatherland: Nazi Medicine and Racial Hygiene* (Baltimore: Johns Hopkins University Press, 1994). On the Nazis' black victims, see Reiner Pommerin, *Sterilisierung der Rheinlandbastarde: Das Schicksal einer farbigen deutschen Minderheit, 1918-1937* (Düsseldorf: Droste, 1979); and Clarence Lusane, *Hitler's Black Victims: The Historical Experiences of Afro-Germans, European Blacks, Africans, and African Americans in the Nazi Era* (New York: Routledge, 2002). The breadth of the Nazi assault on difference emerges anew from Robert Gellately and Nathan Stoltzfus, eds., *Social Outsiders in Nazi Germany* (Princeton, N.J.: Princeton University Press, 2001).

6. On Jewish-Christian relations, an early example of a more differentiated approach is Uriel Tal, *Christians and Jews in Germany: Religion, Politics, and Ideology in the Second Reich, 1870-1914* (Ithaca, N.Y.: Cornell University Press, 1975). More recently, see Till van Rahden, *Juden und andere Breslauer: Die Beziehungen zwischen Juden, Protestanten und Katholiken in einer deutschen Großstadt von 1860 bis 1925* (Göttingen: Vandenhoeck und Ruprecht, 2000); the essays in Helmut Walser Smith, ed., *Protestants, Catholics, and Jews in Germany, 1800-1914* (Oxford: Berg, 2001); and Thomas Weber, "Anti-semitism and Philo-semitism among the British and German Elites: Oxford and Heidelberg before the First World War," *English Historical Review* 118 (2003): 86-119. On Catholics' place in Germany, see (as well as essays in Smith, above) Thomas Mergel, *Zwischen Klasse und Konfession: Katholisches Bürgertum im Rheinland* (Göttingen: Vandenhoeck und Ruprecht, 1994); Raymond Chien Sun, *Before the Enemy Is within Our Walls: Catholic Workers in Cologne, 1885-1912* (Boston:

Humanities, 1999); and Jonathan Sperber, *The Kaiser's Voters: Electors and Elections in Imperial Germany* (New York: Cambridge University Press, 1997). Emphasizing cosmopolitanism and tolerance in the *Kaiserreich* more generally is Margaret Lavinia Anderson, *Practicing Democracy: Elections and Political Culture in Imperial Germany* (Princeton, N.J.: Princeton University Press, 2000).

7. Again Jewish history has been in the vanguard here. For an early example, see Peter Gay, *Freud, Jews, and Other Germans: Masters and Victims in Modernist Culture* (Oxford: Oxford University Press, 1979). A key recent essay is Steven E. Aschheim, "German History and German Jewry: Boundaries, Junctions, and Inter-dependence," *Leo Baeck Institute Year Book* 43 (1998): 315–22. For other religious minorities, see Helmut Walser Smith, *German Nationalism and Religious Conflict: Culture, Ideology, Politics, 1870–1914* (Princeton, N.J.: Princeton University Press, 1995); Heinz-Gerhard Haupt and Dieter Langewiesche, eds., *Nation und Religion in der deutschen Geschichte* (Frankfurt am Main: Campus, 2001); and Hartmut Lehmann and Michael Geyer, eds., *Religion und Nation / Nation und Religion: Beiträge zu einer unbewältigten Geschichte* (Göttingen: Wallstein, 2004). The reappraisal of the relation-ship of religious and ethnic minorities with nation overlaps with sophisticated recent attempts to rethink that between locality, region, and nation; see Celia Applegate, *A Nation of Provincials: The German Idea of Heimat* (Berkeley: University of California Press, 1990); Celia Applegate, "A Europe of Regions: Reflections on the Historiog-raphy of Sub-national Places in Modern Times," *American Historical Review* 104, no. 4 (1999): 1157–82; Alon Confino, *The Nation as a Local Metaphor: Württemberg, Imperial Germany, and National Memory, 1871–1918* (Chapel Hill: University of North Carolina Press, 1997); Nancy R. Reagin, "Recent Work on German National Identity: Regional? Imperial? Gendered? Imaginary?" *Central European History* 37, no. 2 (2004): 273–89; and Charlotte Tacke, *Denkmal im sozialen Raum: Nationale Symbole in Deutschland und Frankreich im 19. Jahrhundert* (Göttingen: Vandenhoeck und Ruprecht, 1995).

8. Fritz Stern, *Gold and Iron: Bismarck, Bleichröder, and the Building of the Ger-man Empire* (New York: Knopf, 1977), 471.

9. Aschheim, "German History and German Jewry."

10. Benedict Anderson, *Imagined Communities: Reflections on the Origin and Spread of Nationalism*, rev. ed. (London: Verso, 1991).

11. Ernst Gellner, *Nations and Nationalism* (Oxford: Blackwell, 1983).

12. Maiken Umbach, ed., *German Federalism: Past, Present, Future* (Houndmills, Basingstoke, Hampshire: Palgrave, 2002); Confino, *Nation as a Local Metaphor;* and Abigail Green, *Fatherlands: State-Building and Nationhood in Nineteenth-Century Ger-many* (Cambridge: Cambridge University Press, 2001).

13. Gerhard Ritter, *Staatskunst und Kriegshandwerk: Das Problem des Militarismus in Deutschland*, vol. 1, *Die altpreussische Tradition (1740–1890)* (Munich: Oldenbourg, 1954), and subsequent vols.

14. The classic statement of this position remains Hans-Ulrich Wehler, *The Ger-man Empire, 1871–1918* (Oxford: Berg, 1985), first published in German as *Das deutsche Kaiserreich, 1871–1918* in 1973.

15. Hans-Ulrich Wehler, *Deutsche Gesellschaftsgeschichte*, vol. 1, *Vom Feudalismus des Alten Reiches bis zur Defensiven Modernisierung der Reformära, 1700–1815* (Mu-nich: C. H. Beck, 1987).

16. Wehler, *Deutsche Gesellschaftsgeschichte,* vol. 1 (3rd ed., 1996), 124.

17. Detlev J. K. Peukert, *Inside Nazi Germany: Conformity, Opposition, and Racism in Everyday Life* (New Haven, Conn.: Yale University Press, 1987); and Peukert, *Grenzen der Sozialdisziplinierung;* see also Frank Bajohr, Werner Johe, and Uwe Lohalm, eds., *Zivilisation und Barbarei: Die widersprüchlichen Potentiale der Moderne: Detlev Peukert zum Gedenken* (Hamburg: Christians, 1991).

18. Thomas Nipperdey, *Deutsche Geschichte, 1800–1866: Bürgerwelt und starker Staat* (Munich: C. H. Beck, 1984); Thomas Nipperdey, *Deutsche Geschichte, 1866–1918,* vol. 1, *Arbeitswelt und Bürgergeist* (Munich: C. H. Beck, 1990); and Thomas Nipperdey, *Deutsche Geschichte, 1866–1918,* vol. 2, *Machtstaat vor der Demokratie* (Munich: C. H. Beck, 1992).

19. James J. Sheehan, *German History, 1770–1866* (Oxford: Oxford University Press, 1989), 1.

20. Sheehan, *German History,* 15.

21. Confino, *Nation as a Local Metaphor;* Applegate, *Nation of Provincials.*

22. David Rock and Stefan Wolff, eds., *Coming Home to Germany? The Integration of Ethnic Germans from Central and Eastern Europe in the Federal Republic since 1945* (New York: Berghahn, 2002). On Jewish DPs, see Angelika Königseder and Juliane Wetzel, *Waiting for Hope: Jewish Displaced Persons in Post–World War II Germany* (Evanston, Ill.: Northwestern University Press, 2001). On Jewish life in postwar Germany, see Michael Brenner, *After the Holocaust: Rebuilding Jewish Lives in Postwar Germany* (Princeton, N.J.: Princeton University Press, 1997); Micha Brumlick, ed., *Jüdisches Leben in Deutschland seit 1945* (Frankfurt am Main: Jüdischer Verlag bei Athenäum, 1986); and Y. Michal Bodemann, ed., *Jews, Germans, Memory: Reconstructions of Jewish Life in Germany* (Ann Arbor: University of Michigan Press, 1996).

23. Karen Schönwälder, *Einwanderung und ethnische Pluralität: Politische Entscheidungen und öffentliche Debatten in Großbritannien und der Bundesrepublik von den 1950er bis zu den 1970er Jahren* (Essen: Klartext, 2001); Karen Schönwälder, Rainer Ohliger, and Triadafilos Triadafilopoulos, eds., *European Encounters: Migrants, Migration, and European Societies since 1945* (London: Ashgate, 2003); and Ulrich Herbert and Karin Hunn, "Guest Workers and Policy on Guest Workers in the Federal Republic: From the Beginning of Recruitment in 1955 until Its Halt in 1973," in *The Miracle Years: A Cultural History of West Germany, 1949–1968,* ed. Hanna Schissler (Princeton, N.J.: Princeton University Press, 2001), 187–218.

24. Maria Höhn, *GIs and Fräuleins: The German-American Encounter in 1950s West Germany* (Chapel Hill: University of North Carolina Press, 2002); Heide Fehrenbach, *Race after Hitler: Black Occupation Children in Postwar Germany and America* (Princeton, N.J.: Princeton University Press, 2005); and Norman Naimark, *The Russians in Germany: A History of the Soviet Zone of Occupation, 1945–1949* (Cambridge, Mass.: Belknap Press of Harvard University Press, 1995), 1–30.

25. On the expellees see, for example, Albrecht Lehmann, *Im Fremden ungewollt zuhaus: Flüchtlinge und Vertriebene in Westdeutschland, 1945–1990* (Munich: C. H. Beck, 1993); and Dierk Hoffmann, Marita Kraus, and Michael Schwartz, eds., *Vertriebene in Deutschland: Interdisziplinäre Ergebnisse und Forschungsperspektiven* (Munich: Oldenbourg, 2000).

26. Olaf Blaschke, ed., *Konfessionen im Konflikt: Deutschland zwischen 1800 und*

25

1970; Ein zweites konfessionelles Zeitalter (Göttingen: Vandenhoeck und Ruprecht, 2002).

27. See, for example, Reinhard Alter and Peter Monteath, eds., *Rewriting the German Past: History and Identity in the New Germany* (Atlantic Highlands, N.J.: Humanities, 1997).

28. On the *Historikerstreit*, see Charles S. Maier, *The Unmasterable Past: History, Holocaust, and German National Identity* (Cambridge, Mass.: Harvard University Press, 1988). On post-1989 debates, see Stefan Berger, *The Search for Normality: National Identity and Historical Consciousness in Germany since 1800* (Oxford: Berghahn, 2003), part 2; and Berger, *Germany.*

29. See Jack Zipes, "The Contemporary German Fascination for Things Jewish: Toward a Minor Jewish Culture," in *Re-emerging Jewish Culture in Germany: Life and Literature since 1989,* ed. Sander L. Gilman and Karen Remmler (New York: New York University Press, 1994), 15–45; Sabine Offe, *Ausstellungen, Einstellungen, Entstellungen: Jüdische Museen in Deutschland und Österreich* (Berlin: Philo, 2000); and Ruth Ellen Gruber, *Virtually Jewish: Reinventing Jewish Culture in Europe* (Berkeley: University of California Press, 2002).

30. See the references above in notes 6 and 7 as well as the survey of recent work in Matthew Jefferies, *Imperial Culture in Germany, 1871–1918* (Basingstoke: Palgrave Macmillan 2003).

31. Volker R. Berghahn, "The German Empire, 1871–1914: Reflections on the Direction of Recent Research," *Central European History* 35, no. 1 (2002): 76–77.

32. Thomas M. Wilson and Hastings Donnan, "Nation, State, and Identity at International Borders," in *Border Identities: Nation and State at International Frontiers,* ed. Thomas M. Wilson and Hastings Donnan (Cambridge: Cambridge University Press, 1998), 1–30; and John Borneman, *Belonging in the Two Berlins: Kin, State, Nation* (Cambridge: Cambridge University Press, 1992).

33. George L. Mosse, *Toward the Final Solution: A History of European Racism* (Madison: University of Wisconsin Press, 1985).

34. Applegate, *Nation of Provincials;* Confino, *Nation as a Local Metaphor;* and Mark Hewitson, *National Identity and Political Thought in Germany: Wilhelmine Depictions of the French Third Republic, 1890–1914* (Oxford: Clarendon, 2000).

35. Margaret Lavinia Anderson, "Reply to Volker Berghahn," *Central European History* 35, no. 1 (2002): 85.

36. See Mathias Niendorf, *Minderheiten an der Grenze: Deutsche und Polen in den Kreisen Flatow (Złotów) und Zempelburg (Süepólno Krajenskie), 1900–1939* (Wiesbaden: Harrassowitz, 1997); Robert Traba, ed., *Selbstbewußtsein und Modernisierung: Sozialkultureller Wandel in Preußisch-Litauen vor und nach dem Ersten Weltkrieg* (Osnabrück: Fibre, 2000); Andreas Kossert, *Masuren: Ostpreußens vergessener Süden* (Berlin: Siedler, 2001); Andreas Kossert, *Preußen, Deutsche oder Polen? Die Masuren im Spannungsfeld des ethnischen Nationalismus, 1870–1956* (Wiesbaden: Harrassowitz, 2001); and Richard Blanke, *Polish-Speaking Germans? Language and National Identity among the Masurians since 1871* (Cologne: Böhlau, 2001).

37. Eric Kurlander, "Nationalism, Ethnic Preoccupation, and the Decline of German Liberalism: A Silesian Case Study, 1898–1933," *The Historian* 65, no. 1 (2002): 95–121.

38. Volkov, *The Rise of Popular Anti-modernism;* and Shulamit Volkov, "Anti-Semitism as a Cultural Code: Reflection on the History and Historiography of Anti-Semitism in Imperial Germany," in *Leo Baeck Institute Year Book* 23 (1978): 25–46.

39. For recent work on Jewish sexuality, see Sander L. Gilman, *Difference and Pathology: Stereotypes of Sexuality, Race, and Madness* (Ithaca, N.Y.: Cornell University Press, 1985); George L. Mosse, *Nationalism and Sexuality: Respectability and Abnormal Sexuality in Modern Europe* (New York: H. Fertig, 1985); Sander L. Gilman, *Jewish Self-Hatred: Anti-Semitism and the Hidden Language of the Jews* (Baltimore: Johns Hopkins University Press, 1986); Sander L. Gilman, *The Jew's Body* (New York: Routledge, 1991); and Julius H. Schoeps and Joachim Schlör, eds., *Antisemitismus: Vorurteile und Mythen* (Munich: Piper, 1995).

40. Gisela Bock, *Zwangssterilisation im Nationalsozialismus: Studien zur Rassenpolitik und Frauenpolitik* (Opladen: Westdeutscher Verlag, 1986); and G. Czarnowski, *Das kontrollierte Ehepaar: Ehe und Sexualpolitik im Nationalsozialismus* (Weinheim: Deutscher Studienverlag, 1991).

41. On the range of Christian voices, see Richard Steigmann-Gall, *The Holy Reich: Nazi Conceptions of Christianity, 1919–1945* (Cambridge: Cambridge University Press, 2003).

42. Dagmar Herzog, "Desperately Seeking Normality: Sex and Marriage in the Wake of War," in *Life after Death: Approaches to the Cultural and Social History of Europe during the 1940s and 1950s,* ed. Richard Bessel and Dirk Schumann (Cambridge: Cambridge University Press, 2003), 161–92.

43. See also the essay by Atina Grossman in this volume.

44. See also Höhn, *GIs and Fräuleins;* Maria Höhn, "Heimat in Turmoil: African-American GIs in 1950s West Germany," in Schissler, *Miracle Years,* 145–63.

One

Germans of the Jewish *Stamm*

Visions of Community between Nationalism and Particularism, 1850 to 1933

Till van Rahden

I

Nation-building engenders anxieties about the nation's margins, and this is especially true in times of national unification. Once the initial wave of unifying enthusiasm has faded, debates about the relationship between national unity and diversity intensify. Even if there is little specifically German about this dynamic, Imperial Germany's first decade serves as a graphic example of the phenomenon. Although the foundation of the new empire in 1871 provided answers to some longstanding questions about the shape and meaning of the German nation-state, recent scholarship has reminded us of the contested and open-ended nature of the "Germany" that emerged.[1]

In November 1879, one of the leading German ideologues of his time, the historian Heinrich von Treitschke, threw his weight behind the growing anxiety about the place of Jews within the nation. "It cannot be denied that there are numerous and powerful groups among our Jews," Treitschke claimed in an article that triggered the so-called Berlin debate on antisemitism, "who definitely do not have the good intention to become simply Germans." Rejecting a pluralist conception of nationhood, Treitschke warned that unless "our Jewish fellow-citizens make up their minds to be Germans without reservation," an "era of German Jewish mixed culture" would "follow after thousands of years of Germanic morality."[2] As is well known, Treitschke's antisemitism sparked a polemical debate about diversity and difference in the newly founded *Kaiserreich* and forced prominent Jewish intellectuals, including Heinrich Graetz, Hermann Cohen, and Ludwig Bamberger, to publicly defend a right to be different.

Among these Jewish intellectuals, no one developed a more fundamental critique of Treitschke than the anthropologist cum philosopher Moritz Lazarus (1824–1903). The son of a merchant and a rabbinical scholar, he served as a professor in Bern from 1860 to 1866 and taught at the Prussian War Academy from 1868 to 1872, after which he held an honorary professorship of philosophy at the Friedrich Wilhelm University in Berlin. In both 1869 and 1871, Lazarus served as president of the liberal Jewish synods of Leipzig and Augsburg. Because he was a prolific writer in scholarly journals and the press as well as a gifted public speaker, he had established himself as a respected figure among German Jews and in liberal culture. On the occasion of his seventieth birthday, in 1894, the high-brow journal *Nord und Süd* praised him as one "of the few German philosophers alive" whose work had reached not only a scholarly audience but the "educated public," too. In short, whatever Lazarus said, it mattered among Jews and other Germans.[3]

Lazarus's essay *Was heißt national?* can be read not only as a carefully crafted dissection of Treitschke's essentialist and ethnic understanding of German nationhood but also as an attempt to substantiate a universal right to be different in an age of nationalism. Although Lazarus had originally delivered his critique of Treitschke as a lecture at the annual general assembly of the Berlin *Hochschule für die Wissenschaft des Judentums* in December 1879, he published his speech as a widely circulated pamphlet, which liberal politicians and intellectuals recognized as a major contribution to the debate over the meaning and future shape of German nationalism.[4]

Lazarus drew both on his own earlier work and on carefully selected contemporary scholarship on national identity, including an article titled "On the Concept of the Nation" by Gustav Rümelin, the president of the University of Tübingen and a leading statistician of his time. Out of these materials Lazarus now developed an understanding of nationhood that I would like to characterize as radically voluntaristic, pluralistic, and processual. This line of reasoning allowed him to reject as unsubstantiated Treitschke's demand that Jews should become "Germans without reservation." Citizens did not belong to a national community because they had ceased to be different, but precisely because they had preserved their particular identities in an age of national unity. The tension between national unity and particular identities could not be reconciled, but only balanced and preserved by rearticulating it on a higher plane. The "German nationality we are aspiring to," Lazarus argued, is incompatible with "any felony against inherited traditions and any felony against universal human principles." In contrast to Treitschke's call for radical assimilation, Jews who wanted to be "perfect and highly able Germans" in fact "had the duty" to preserve both "the intellectual peculiarity they possessed as a tribe and the inherited virtue and wisdom they possessed as a religion."[5]

Clearly, Lazarus considered Jews a tribe, i.e., a *Stamm*, as well as a religious group. Yet whereas we are familiar with the latter concept, the term "tribe" sounds quaint at best or part and parcel of a racist or *völkisch* vocabulary at worst. Concern about the term "tribe" has a respectable tradition that goes back at least to the immediate post-Holocaust era. In 1955, Helmuth Plessner, like Lazarus a philosopher and anthropologist, noted that the use of the term "tribe" was "painful and distressing." The term, Plessner argued, had been "difficult to grasp historically" to begin with, and after many years of propaganda it had even acquired the connotation of "race," a concept steeped in blood.[6] Moreover, as specialists in the history of German antisemitism will point out, the term "tribe" played a prominent role in antisemitic discourse throughout the nineteenth century. One of numerous nineteenth-century liberal critics of Jewish emancipation, the Königsberg historian Friedrich Schubert, for example, argued in 1835 that Jews could never become equal members of the German nation because they were an alien "Asiatic tribe."[7] Indeed, in the course of the Berlin debate on antisemitism Treitschke himself argued that Judaism was the "national religion of an originally [*ursprünglich*] foreign tribe."[8]

Yet what then are we to make of Moritz Lazarus's use of the term *Stamm?* Did the celebrated scholar suffer a momentary lapse of reason when he argued that German Jews constituted a tribe? What I will argue is that, in fact, Lazarus invoked the term because it was a central concept in German debates about national unity and diversity between the mid-nineteenth century and the late 1920s. By exploring the place of the term "tribe" at critical junctures and intersections of German Jewish and German history, I would like to pursue three themes. First, what vision of community did German Jews try to develop once the concept of an "individual Mosaic confessionalism," which had predominated throughout the emancipation era (and found a belated echo in the title of the "Central Association of German Citizens of the Jewish Faith," established in 1893), had begun to erode in the face of growing secularization and increasing religious and political pluralization among German Jews?[9] Second, how did Jewish intellectuals attempt to balance the tension between equality before the law in an age of national unity and a right to preserve a specifically Jewish particularity after the emancipation-era argument that Jews were a *Konfession* just like any Christian denomination had become contestable? Third, I would like to draw attention to the way we conceptualize the relationship between the particular and the universal, between different groups and a space in which they negotiate their terms of coexistence. This question will open up a discussion that not only is of interest for German Jewish history but may help us rethink our understanding of the age of nation-states, especially the way we conceptualize the tension between particularism, nationalism, and universalism.

II

In nineteenth-century Germany, Jewish identities changed dramatically. Until the late eighteenth century, religion had encompassed almost every aspect of Jewish life and had provided a seemingly self-evident framework for a vision of a unified Jewish community. By the mid-nineteenth century, however, it had become a divisive factor. Unity of theological doctrine and religious discipline was lost once and for all, opening the way to incertitude, retreat, and possibly disengagement. By 1900, three competing visions of Judaism existed: Reform, Orthodox, and Conservative. The Reform movement proposed a new understanding of Judaism as it historicized and thereby relativized both the Halacha and the oral and liturgical traditions. Its insistence on the importance of the individual's faith eroded the authority of religious law. At the center of the rabbinical assemblies of the 1840s was the question of how to transform national-religious aspects of Judaism into a civic "confessionalism." Central elements of Judaism, such as the Messianic idea and eschatological hopes, were stripped of national and ethnic connotations and reconfigured in universally human terms.[10]

By the 1840s, the conflict between Orthodoxy and Reform had become so bitter that it threatened to paralyze communal life. The Geiger-Tiktin debate in early 1840s Breslau, for example, seemed to indicate the imminent breakup of Germany's second largest Jewish community. By the late nineteenth century, although Reform, Orthodoxy, and Conservatism had developed a peaceful coexistence of sorts, a unifying religious vision of what it meant to be Jewish had ceased to exist. In fact, several Jewish intellectuals argued that any attempt to ground a common Jewish identity on religion could lead to the disintegration of the Jewish community. Surveying the religious landscape of late nineteenth-century Germany, the chair of the Dresden Jewish community, Emil Lehmann, argued, "in both religions what in the eyes of one observer constitutes divine revelation and history, is for another holy lore, legend, symbol, and for a third a mythology. The distance between them is so wide . . . , that it is no more possible to speak of a unified religion among Christians, Catholics, or Protestants than it is among Jews. The Christian who believes in miracles is much closer on this point to the Jew who believes in miracles than the liberal is to the orthodox Jew."[11]

By 1900, moreover, the number of Jews had increased who lived as *Staatsbürger jüdischen Unglaubens*, literally "citizens of Jewish irreligion," as Sigmund Freud liked to remark sarcastically. True, some who publicly eschewed religious rituals continued to practice their devotions privately, especially in the context of family life.[12] Yet around the turn of the century numerous observers noted that synagogues were often empty because most Jews only turned up on the high holidays, living as "synagogal day-flies," to borrow a phrase from the Breslau Zionist Aryeh Maimon. In a popular early twentieth-century joke, a self-confessed "enlightened" Jew let it be known that he had "no sympathies for any ritual aspects of our religion. Of all the Jewish holidays the only one I keep is the Grünfeld concert"—Grünfeld being a famous pianist of the time.[13] Such a decline of public forms of religious observance raised the question of how to define a sustainable conception of Jewish identity, when many contemporaries believed that the only remaining difference between Jews and Christians was that the former no longer attended synagogue on Saturdays whereas the latter no longer attended church on Sundays.

While the importance of religious visions of community declined, German Jews' ethnicity, embedded in the term *Stamm*, became increasingly important.[14] True, when faced with antisemitism many Jews continued to emphasize that they had long ceased to be an ethnic group—a *Volk*, that is—and stressed instead that they, just like Catholics or Protestants, were a religious community. Yet Jews from all walks of life and from different conflicting religious and political camps used the concept of *Stamm*, literally "tribe," or *Stammesbewußtsein*, literally "tribal consciousness," to articulate a vision of community that was based on the idea of a common descent rather than religion and therefore transcended religious and political divisions within the Jewish community. Already in 1869, the Viennese rabbi Adolf Jellinek (1821–93), who was considered one of the most eloquent Jewish preachers of his time in Central Europe, claimed that Jews were one of the Habsburg Empire's numerous *Stämme*.[15] Balancing what he believed to be the universalistic mission of Jews and their particularistic right to be different, Jellinek asserted that "[the Jew] is particularistic enough, stable enough, subjective enough not to be absorbed by other people; he is however also sufficiently universalistic, enthusiastic, progressive and objective not to persist in insolent and rigid isolation. . . . The Jewish *Stamm* is therefore truly chosen for its mission."[16]

One reason why so many invoked the concept of *Stamm* was its very vagueness. It provided the lowest common denominator between those Jews who considered themselves a religious community and those who thought of themselves as an ethnic group, a nation, or even a "race." In 1901, for example, Heymann Steinthal, the linguist, philosopher, and close collaborator of Lazarus, urged Jews to put aside religious quarrels lest they provoke "deadly divisions" among themselves. Although deeply religious himself, Steinthal extended his hand to those *Stammesgenossen* who were convinced that they could live "without any traditional elements not only of ceremony but also of faith." Rather than focus on religious divisions, Jews of all warring factions should remember their common "semitic blood and temperament." As Ivan Kalmar has recently pointed out, Steinthal's argument is ambiguous, possibly even contradictory: "When Steinthal speaks about the Jews," the anthropologist notes, "I hear a powerful voice grounding the Jewish—and the German—experience in the purely intellectual concept of *Völkerpsychologie;* but I also hear here and there a smaller voice that takes pride in the Jews as a Semitic *Stammesgemein-schaft.*"[17]

Others to whom racial concepts would have been anathema used the term *Stamm* and the concepts of religion or denomination in the same breath. In the *Israelitische Wochenschrift*, a widely read Jewish weekly close to the Conservative movement, a self-confessed "truly faithful German of the Jewish Faith" urged Jews in 1887 to fight antisemitism "out of respect for their religion and their *Stamm.*"[18] Although Walther Rathenau felt practically no affiliation with Judaism as a religion, the industrialist and combative intellectual used the term. "I am a German of the Jewish tribe," he wrote in his call "To Germany's Youth" of 1918: "My people is the German people, my home is the German lands, my confession is the German faith."[19] Even liberal Jews, who, like Emil Lehmann, rejected the term because they feared that it could hardly be distinguished from ethnic, or worse, racial visions of community, developed a conception of Jewish identity that was remarkably similar—even if Lehmann emphasized common historical experiences rather than common descent. In 1891, Lehmann, the veteran fighter for the emancipation of Saxony's Jews who had played a leading role in the founding of the *Deutsch-Israelitischer Gemeindebund*, argued that Jews had long ceased to be a *Volks-stamm*, literally a national or ethnic tribe, nor were they a religious group in any meaningful sense, but that they had become a "community of suffering" instead.[20] Looking back on more than a century of internal debates over the nature of the Jewish community, the philosopher Julius Guttmann (1880–1950) noted that the "consciousness of community" (*Gemeinschafts-bewußtsein*) among German Jews had been radically transformed. In the *K.C.-Blätter*, the monthly of the liberal and anti-Zionist Jewish student organizations, the son of the Breslau Reform rabbi Jakob Guttmann argued that within the context of a "modern cultural sphere" even those who eschewed any form of Jewish religiosity continued to embrace a "feeling of a tribal community" (*Gefühl der Stammesgemeinschaft*). Such a "communal spirit" should not be confused with the "mystical voices of blood." Instead a "consciousness of tribal bonds" reflected the "community of fate and memories, which reach into the innermost aspects of life," as well as "that unspoken sense of belonging that arises where an individual simply grows up in a community [*Lebens-gemeinschaft*], rather than having to first gain his place through personal qualities and achievements."[21]

During the Weimar Republic, the notion that Jews constituted neither a religious nor a national community was even more widespread than in late Imperial Germany. In the immediate postwar era, Benno Jacob (1862–1945) noted that the majority of German Jews rejected the modern idea of a territorial Jewish nation. Invoking a diasporic, rather than a nationalistic, conception of Jewishness, the liberal rabbi argued that "we consider ourselves to be of one tribe with all Jews of the world." In 1932, no lesser figure than the director of the Central Association of German Citizens of the Jewish Faith, Ludwig Holländer, answered the question "Why we are and shall remain Jews" by pointing out that he did not consider Jews a religious community. According to Holländer, the heritage of a common history was the key element of German Jewish identity. Precisely because they belonged to the German people, Jews should be as proud of their "tribal history" as "any other German tribe." At the end of the Weimar Republic, the vaguely Zionist *Jüdisches Lexikon* reviewed this semantic tradition and noted that "in the last decades" the concept of "tribal community had become a much used designation for the Jewish community or the Jewish people." Unlike the concept of a religious community, the term "tribe" emphasized, the encyclopedia concluded, the "aspect of common descent and history"—a definition that is almost identical with constructivist definitions of ethnicity, if we substitute the term "idea" for the term "aspect."[22]

Probably the term "tribe" was especially attractive for those Jewish associations that are usually considered as part of the "organizational renaissance" of German Jewry of the 1880s and 1890s. For want of a better term one might call these associations post-traditional, insofar as they consciously reflected their distance from premodern forms of Jewish community-building. In order to bridge divisions between different factions of German Jews, they claimed to be "neutral" in questions of internal Jewish politics. All these associations freely borrowed from a conception of Jews as a community of common descent rather than faith. A perfect example of this trend is the German chapter of the Independent Order of B'nai B'rith, founded in 1882. Its members attempted to develop an understanding of German Jewry that would allow it to gain members from all parts of the Jewish community. According to the lodge's pledge, it aimed "to foster the spiritual and moral character of our tribe." As Louis Maretzki, its president of many years, emphasized, all educational activities of the lodge were in accordance with the "moral character of our tribe." In 1895, Maretzki explained that the work of the lodge should contribute to the "social and ethical progress of our tribe" and serve "as a wake-up call for Jewish consciousness," especially among those "Israelites who live without any contact with the spiritual life of our tribe."[23]

It was this broad resonance and wide appeal of the concept that some leading German Zionists tried to tap when they attempted to fashion a specifically Western European brand of Zionism that would appeal not just to faithful followers but to members of the liberal majority of German Jews. In an article in the movement's leading journal, the weekly *Die Welt: Zentralorgan der zionistischen Vereinigung*, the sociologist Franz Oppenheimer (1864–1943) argued in February 1910 that "we West Europeans," among whom he included American Jews, had an altogether different relation to Zionism than "East Europeans": the latter had a *Volksbewußtsein*, the former a *Stammesbewußtsein*. Tribal consciousness, he emphasized, "is a matter of the past; it exists when individuals subscribe to the idea that they descend from a nation," literally a *Volkstum*, that is just as "glorious and noble" as the nation "whose citizens they are now." *Stammesbewußtsein*, in short, was the consciousness of "common descent, of common blood, or at least of an erstwhile common *Volkstum*, of a common history with all its memories of suffering and joy." The "national consciousness" of Eastern European Jews, in contrast, was "a matter of the present: [based on] the commonality of language, of customs, of economic and legal ties, and of spiritual culture [*geistige Kultur*]." Unlike Western European Jews, who belonged to the national communities of the countries in which they lived, Eastern European Jews were indeed a people without a land who could hardly wait to go to Palestine. Among Jews in Western Europe, however, there were very few who considered themselves part of a Jewish nation; notwithstanding some "young hotspurs . . . who are throwing the baby out with the bath water; a few who, so to speak, have already packed up to leave for Palestine." Rather than present themselves as a national movement, Zionists in Germany should reach out to all Jews who preserved some form of tribal consciousness.[24] Oppenheimer, who had successfully outlined plans for cooperative settlements in Palestine at the Basle Zionist Congress of 1903, hit a raw nerve, and his article triggered much soul-searching among German Zionists. It is probably impossible to assess how typical his stance was among the run-of-the-mill members of the movement. Yet the very fact that members of the Zionist leadership who subscribed to a nationalistic conception of Jewishness felt obliged to prove Oppenheimer wrong perhaps indicates that he expressed a common sentiment.[25]

After the turn of the century, the Central Association of German Citizens of the Jewish Faith attempted to provide a home for members of all factions among German Jews. Against this background it made perfect sense for its leaders to fall back on the rhetoric of a "tribal community." In March 1913, in response to the Oppenheimer controversy among German Zionists, Eugen Fuchs (1856–1923), one of the founding members of the Central Association, invited all those Zionists to join for whom "Jewish Nationalism means no more than a catchword to describe the historical community that has brought us together for hundreds and thousands of years, . . . a loyalty to our past," in short, the idea of a "tribal community."[26] Once antisemitism became an ever-increasing threat during the second half of the First World War, Fuchs, who was now head of the Central Association, explicitly considered himself to be part of this community. Given his "Jewish descent" and his "Jewish upbringing," Fuchs noted in the *Neue Jüdische Monatshefte* in 1917, he was a "Jew on account of religion and of tribe." In contrast to the issue of tribal belonging, Fuchs emphasized that the "national question" was "not a question of being but reflects an act of volition," thus building on Lazarus's voluntaristic concept of the nation. His "tribal heritage," Fuchs concluded, did not separate him from German Christians, "just like a Friesian peasant's tribal heritage does not separate him from a Rhenish industrial worker or a Berlin proletarian."[27]

III

As the last quotation indicates, the rhetoric of a tribe was part not just of a German Jewish discussion about the nature of Jewish identity but also of a broader debate that took place between the mid-nineteenth century and the late 1920s about the relationship between national unity and cultural diversity in German political culture. The more that German Jews considered themselves as a tribal community rather than simply a religious community, the more questionable became a certain conception of the relationship between the universal and the particular that had been at the heart of debates about Jewish emancipation between the late eighteenth century and the late 1860s. Critics of Jewish emancipation asserted that Jews could not become part of the German nation because of their foreign nationality. Those who supported legal emancipation, such as the editor of the *Deutsches Staats-Wörterbuch*, Johann Bluntschli (1808–81), emphasized that the "antagonism of nationality" had become irrelevant, because Jews had ceased to be a "separate people." They were, Bluntschli argued in 1860, no longer "strangers to the land, but natives of Germany, no longer alien to our nation, but national companions," literally *Volksgenossen*.[28]

According to those who supported legal emancipation, Jews, too, could both be full members of the nation and enjoy a right to be different. As long as Jews considered themselves to be a religious rather than a national community they should be allowed to assert their peculiarity just like members of Christian communities. Although many mid-nineteenth-century liberals argued that both the state and civic virtue rested on a religious foundation, it was not the state's business to decide which specific religion this should be. In a religiously neutral state, Jews should therefore enjoy the same right to be different as members of Christian denominations. The entry on "Jewish Emancipation" in the 1846 edition of the famous *Staats-Lexikon* edited by Rotteck and Welcker reflected the more general pro-emancipation turnaround among German liberals of the 1840s. "It is generally agreed in the modern age," argued the Holzminden notary Karl Steinacker (1801–1947), that church and state "must exist alongside one another as independent communities, if one is not either to suppress freedom of conscience or conversely end up in a theocracy."[29] According to Steinacker, the state could ask its citizens to be religious "because the supreme civic virtue and any reasonable will can be expected only from a morally and religiously purified and ennobled mind." The state, however, should exercise no influence on the citizens' specific religious persuasion lest it limit the freedom of conscience: "The question of which religion best serves the public weal," the author concluded, "cannot but remain unanswered because the state itself has no means to decide" it. The right to religious difference finds its own limit at the point at which the highest purpose of the state, namely to defend the rights of its citizens, is called into question. The state may limit the freedom of conscience of individual faith communities only when their "religious beliefs contain teachings whose pursuit would endanger the state," i.e., ran counter to the rule of law.[30] At the heart of the emancipatory contract, therefore, stood a quid pro quo: Jews could enjoy the same right to be different as Christians, as long as and only if they transformed national-religious aspects of Judaism into a civic "confessionalism."

Once many German Jews considered themselves to be part of a "tribe" rather than a religious community, the tension between equality before the law in an age of national unity and a right to be different had to be reconceptualized and renegotiated. After the 1870s, the emancipation-era arguments about religious diversity and the neutrality of the state had to be recast in more universal terms to include a right to be culturally and ethnically different, too. In this context, the concept of *Stamm* was particularly attractive to Jews because it was also well established in general political discourse, expressing a legitimate form of cultural and ethnic difference.[31]

Whereas many nineteenth-century German nationalists believed the peculiar character of German national unity to be based on tribal diversity, there was considerable disagreement on the question of whether the process of national unification would ultimately require the dissolution and blending of all tribes or whether German national unity required the continuous diversity of tribes. The author of the article "Volk—Volksstamm" in the 1819 edition of the Brockhaus encyclopedia emphasized that nations were based on "small parts of a whole," called *Volksstämme*. Just as the "Hebrew nation" had emerged from the blending of twelve tribes, so that no member of the Hebrew nation could remember the tribe from which he descended, "our German nation," too, had emerged from "many tribes, such as the Alemani, the Swabians, the Franks, [and] the Saxons." In the course of time there had been so much mixing with other "tribes" that no member of the German nation could prove which tribe he descended from originally. Clearly, the author implicitly argued that true national unity was only possible after a dissolution of tribal identities through mixing.[32]

The debates in the Frankfurt National Assembly of 1848 throw considerable light on the question of how the tension between unity and diversity should be balanced in a future German nation-state. The vast majority of deputies supported a middle course between a centralized nation-state and a loose confederation of independent states. The Frankfurt debates of 1848 reveal the centrality of the concept of tribe for mid-nineteenth-century nationalism and indicate that it would be misleading to equate the language of "tribal peculiarities" with dynastic loyalties. Deputies from the right as well as the left agreed that the "most dangerous form" of all particularisms, namely "dynastic particularism," had to be overcome.[33] At the same time, even a few democratic deputies, who were most inclined to support a centralized nation-state, argued that tribal diversity was a form of "healthy particularism."[34]

From the mid-nineteenth century not just Jews but other Germans, too, began to argue that Jews were part of the general tribal diversity. When, in 1842, the Prussian secretary of the interior asked provincial governors whether they supported a single legislation for Prussian Jews, the Breslau provincial governor endorsed almost full equality before the law. Given the high quality of the Prussian judicial system, it was possible to grant to "confessors of all religious faiths, the descendants of all tribes" all freedoms they might need for their "civic and moral progress as well as their intellectual uplift."[35] The idea that the German nation consisted of several tribes and that nationalists should respect diversity emerged most clearly in the context of the Berlin debate on antisemitism, especially in Theodor Mommsen's acerbic rejoinder to Treitschke. Mommsen, a leading liberal intellectual of his time, argued that the German nation "is based . . . on the cohesion and the blending of different German *Stämme*," of which Jews were one "no less than the Saxons, Swabians, or Pomeranians." Rather than denying this "diversity," the public should "take delight in it."[36] Walter Rathenau was probably referring to Mommsen's wording when he argued, in 1916, in a letter to Wilhelm Schwaner, the leader of the reformist *Volkserzieher-Bewegung*, that the German nation was based on the idea of "race." "My people," he asserted, "are the Germans, and nobody else." To Rathenau, Jews were "a German tribe, just like the Saxons, the Bavarians, or the Wendish."[37]

Through the concept of *Stamm*, then, the public could imagine the national community both as a united people and as a plurality of tribes. Such a pluralistic understanding of national unity stood in contrast to an older tradition, in which diversity had been conceptualized as the coexistence of dynastic principalities. In September 1918, when Max Warburg, the Hamburg banker and advocate of Jewish civil rights, gave a speech to the *Deutsche Gesellschaft für Völkerrecht* on what political reforms should be introduced in Germany to allow for a reconciliation between the nations, he also built on the concept of *Stamm*. His principal demand was to turn the German Reich into a federal state, because it provided the "ideal political structure for states made up of many tribes."[38] This liberal, anti-dynastic tradition found its most prominent expression in the preamble to Weimar Germany's constitution of 1919. Whereas the 1871 constitution of Imperial Germany had asserted that it was based on "an eternal union" of princes, the *Weimarer Reichsverfassung* based its legitimacy on the fact that it was a constitution agreed upon by "the German people united in its tribes."[39] "The new Reich and its laws have no intention," Gerhard Anschütz emphasized in his commentary on the constitution, "of suppressing the 'tribes'—these natural branches of the German people—and of extinguishing their peculiarities." At the same time, according to this liberal teacher of public law, the tribes had "nothing to do with those arbitrary formations of dynastic politics, the individual states nowadays known as *Länder*."[40]

IV

This leads back to the question of how we can conceptualize the relationship between the particular and the universal. With this sketch of the history of the term "tribe" in mind, I can return to Moritz Lazarus's ambitious attempt to analyze the tension between nationalism and particularism and its implications for relations between Jews and other Germans.

In his 1879 address, Lazarus contrasted his radically voluntaristic, pluralistic, and processual understanding of the nation to an essentialist and objective concept of the nation. Although his argument should be viewed against the backdrop of a larger contemporaneous central European discourse that emphasized the contractual nature of nations, Lazarus's contribution is remarkable for its sophistication.[41] According to Lazarus, no nation whatsoever was based on objective criteria, such as morals and manners, geography or citizenship, religion or descent, not even on the comparatively soft criterion of language. Any "genealogical" classification of humanity missed the "true nature of nationality," because nations could only be understood "as the result of the mind and the intellect," literally of *Geist*.[42] A "nation," he argued—two years before Ernest Renan famously defined it as a "daily plebiscite"—was rooted not in "objective circumstances" but only in "the subjective conviction of its members, who all consider themselves to be a nation."[43] Any form of essentialist understanding of the nation could not do justice to the fact that it was the result of historical contingency. Nations are never given, but forever in the making. The *Volk*, Lazarus argued, results from the "mental and intellectual volition of individuals" who belong to it. It is not that members "are a nation," but, in fact, that they "perpetually create it."[44] Because the nation never "exists" but is forever in the making, any search for a foundational moment, the hour of national birth, was futile. Instead a nation creates itself in a never-ending chain of "acts of self-formation," literally *Bildungsakten*.[45]

If the nation was not based on any objective criteria, there could be no objective answer to the question of national belonging. According to Lazarus all those belonged to a nation who consciously and voluntarily participated in these national "acts of self-formation." Jews had been involved in the "last, [and] highest act of self-formation of the German people," the Franco-German war of 1870-71, as well as other "national projects": "We have proven ourselves on the battlefield," Lazarus noted, "we have deliberated in parliaments, we have served as city magistrates, have cured and nursed in hospitals, [and] we have taught at universities."[46]

Lazarus's radically voluntaristic and processual understanding of nationhood allowed him to reject as unsubstantiated Treitschke's demand that Jews become "Germans without reservation." If citizens belonged to a national community not because they had ceased to be different, but precisely because they remained different, the tension between national unity and particular identities could not be reconciled, but only balanced and preserved by rearticulating it on a higher plane. It is in this context that we can begin to make sense of Lazarus's argument that the "German nationality" he was aspiring to was incompatible with "any felony against inherited traditions and any felony against universal human principles."[47] According to Lazarus, therefore, Jews who wanted to be "perfect and highly able Germans" were obliged to preserve "the intellectual peculiarity they possessed as a tribe."[48]

What I have tried to argue, in summary, is not only that the concept of "tribe" played a prominent role in German Jewish debates about identity as well in general political discourse in nineteenth- and early twentieth-century Germany; more importantly, the concept's vagueness notwithstanding, the term served as a key element in answering two challenges of the postemancipatory era. The first challenge was how German Jews could develop an overarching vision of community that was neither national nor religious in the face of growing secularization and increasing religious and political pluralization among German Jews. The more successfully Jews answered this first challenge, the more pressing the second challenge became: how Jews could defend a right to be different after the emancipatory quid pro quo argument (that Jews could enjoy the same right to be different as Christians as long as, and only if, they transformed national-religious aspects of Judaism into a civic "confessionalism") had become contestable. In response, arguments from the emancipation era about religious diversity and the neutrality of the state were recast in more universal terms to include a right to be culturally and ethnically different, too. In this context, the concept of *Stamm* was particularly attractive to German Jews because it was well established in general German political discourse, expressing a legitimate form of cultural and ethnic difference.

What I would like to draw attention to is the way we conceptualize the relationship between the particular and the universal, between different groups and a space in which they negotiate their terms of coexistence.[49] The gradual establishment of the rule of law opened the public sphere, the state, and the nation to contestation and debate. These became ever-changing arenas in which competing claims of communities were articulated and possibly, but not necessarily, accommodated. No less than Catholics or Jews, members of the Protestant middle class and others whom we might consider as the bearers of "true" nationhood or civic virtue asserted a right to be "different." In relation to the public sphere, the state, or the nation—in relation to the universal, in other words—not just some communities, but all were "minorities"—even if some minorities were more equal than others.

This is not to claim that power did not matter in these sometimes dialogical, sometimes profoundly antagonistic negotiations. Within higher echelons of the government, the military, and the universities, Protestants enjoyed a virtual monopoly on positions of power. A serious consequence of government discrimination against Jews and Catholics was that both communities found it more difficult than Protestants to voice their concerns and grievances, to advance their claims to Germanness and to civic virtue, and to articulate their right to be different. However, if discrimination disadvantaged Jews and Catholics, it did not silence them, as attested by the Center Party's considerable success in national elections and by the prominent role of Jews in city councils and in middle-class associations.[50] What I am interested in here, in short, is complicating Theodor Herzl's ex cathedra answer to the question of how bonds of national belonging are made and unmade. "Who belongs and who does not belong," Zionism's founding father had argued, "is decided by the majority; it is a question of power."[51]

Nor am I suggesting that the public sphere, the state, or the nation was neutral. Whenever nineteenth-century Jews, Protestants, or Catholics publicly pursued an interest that was of concern to their community, they simultaneously advanced a specific vision of how the tension between unity and diversity, between the universal and the particular, should be balanced. An irreconcilable tension lay at the heart of the nineteenth-century nation.[52] On the one hand, civic community and nation were understood as homogenous entities that could be traced back to a common past. On the other hand, such representations of the universal were constituted in a perpetual series of controversies and debates in which citizens asserted their visions of individual and communal selfhood. Protestants did not enjoy a monopoly on defining what it meant to be German, nor were they more nationalistic than other Germans. Protestant claims such as that of court chaplain Adolf Stoecker that Germanness *was* Protestant, his talk of a "Holy Protestant Empire of the German Nation," were just that: *claims*, and are probably best understood as another way of saying that his vision of the nation was different than that of Catholics or that of Jews.[53] Such a claim, indeed, mirrors similar arguments by Catholic ideologues such as Ignaz Döllinger, who had argued in 1848 that Catholics were the "true bearers and representatives of German nationhood," or, in fact, by Jewish intellectuals such as Lazarus, who claimed that Jews were the "most venerable head" of the German nation.[54] In the context of German history, such negotiations and contestations among competing conceptions of the German nation continued until the suspension of the rule of law in January 1933—and resumed after the destruction of the "Third Reich" in May 1945. Nationalist dreams of a nation, one and indivisible, should not distract us from the fact there were competing, possibly antagonistic visions of that very national unity. Just as the particular is not a fact but rather a "production," which is never complete, the universal may best be conceived as an ever-changing arena, as "'in-between' spaces" that are "produced in the articulation of cultural differences."[55]

Notes

1. Most recent studies have therefore focused on the intersection of nationalism with other visions of community, such as religion and regionalism: Heinz-Gerhard Haupt and Dieter Langewiesche, eds., *Nation und Religion in der deutschen Geschichte* (Frankfurt am Main: Campus, 2001); Helmut Walser Smith, *German Nationalism and Religious Conflict: Culture, Ideology, Politics, 1870–1914* (Princeton, N.J.: Princeton University Press, 1995); Helmut Walser Smith, ed., *Protestants, Catholics, and Jews in Germany, 1800–1914* (Oxford: Berg, 2001); Gerd Krumeich and Hartmut Lehmann, eds., *"Gott mit uns": Nation, Religion und Gewalt im 19. und frühen 20. Jahrhundert* (Göttingen: Vandenhoeck und Ruprecht, 2000); Hartmut Lehmann and Michael Geyer, eds., *Religion und Nation / Nation und Religion: Beiträge zu einer unbewältigten Geschichte* (Göttingen: Wallstein, 2004); James Edward Bjork, "Neither German nor Pole: Catholicism and National Ambivalences in Upper Silesia, 1890–1914" (Ph.D. diss., University of Chicago, 1999); Kevin Charles Cramer, "The Lamentations of Germany: The Historiography of the Thirty Years' War, 1790–1890" (Ph.D. diss., Harvard University, 1998); Celia Applegate, *A Nation of Provincials: The German Idea of Heimat* (Berkeley: University of California Press, 1990); and Celia Applegate, "A Europe of Regions: Reflections on the Historiography of Sub-national Places in Modern Times," *American Historical Review* 104, no. 4 (1999): 1157–82.

2. Heinrich von Treitschke, "A Word about Our Jewry" (1880), in Paul Mendes-Flohr and Jehuda Reinharz, eds., *The Jew in the Modern World: A Documentary History*, 2nd ed. (Oxford: Oxford University Press, 1995), 343–45 (the translation has been modified slightly). The so-called "Berlin Debate on Antisemitism" has yet to receive a monographic treatment. For recent analyses see Ulrich Sieg, "Bekenntnis zu nationalen und universalen Werten: Jüdische Philosophen im Deutschen Kaiserreich," *Historische Zeitschrift* 263 (1996): 609–39, especially 611–21, as well as Klaus Holz, *Nationaler Antisemitismus: Wissenssoziologie einer Weltanschauung* (Hamburg: Hamburger Edition, 2001), 165–247. Unsurpassed to this day: *Der Berliner Antisemitismusstreit*, ed. Walter Boehlich (Frankfurt am Main: Insel, 1965). For more recent evaluations, see Uffa Jensen, *Gebildete Doppelgänger: Bürgerliche Juden und Protestanten im 19. Jahrhundert* (Göttingen: Vandenhoeck und Ruprecht, 2005); and *Der "Berliner Antisemitismusstreit," 1879–1881: Eine Kontroverse um die Zugehörigkeit der deutschen Juden zur Nation; Kommentierte Quellenedition*, im Auftr. des Zentrums für Antisemitismusforschung, ed. Karsten Krieger (Munich: Saur, 2003).

3. Moritz Brasch, "Der Begründer der Völkerpsychologie: Eine Studie zu Moritz Lazarus' 70. Geburtstag," *Nord und Süd: Eine deutsche Monatsschrift* 70 (September 1894): 339. On Lazarus generally: Ludwig Stein, "Moritz Lazarus," in *Biographisches Jahrbuch und deutscher Nekrolog*, ed. Anton Bettelheim, vol. 8 (Berlin, 1905), 124–34;

Richard M. Meyer, "Nachruf Moritz Lazarus," *Zeitschrift des Vereins für Volkskunde* 13 (1903): 320–24; Elke Natorp, "Art. Moritz Lazarus," *Neue Deutsche Biographie*, vol. 14 (Berlin: Duncker und Humblot, 1985), 11–13; Ingrid Belke, introduction to *Moritz Lazarus und Heymann Steinthal: Die Begründer der Völkerpsychologie in ihren Briefen, Bd. 1*, by Moritz Lazarus (Tübingen: Mohr Siebeck, 1971), xiii–lxxx; Ivan Kalmar, "The *Völkerpsychologie* of Lazarus and Steinthal and the Modern Concept of Culture," *Journal of the History of Ideas* 48 (1987): 671–90; and Matti Bunzl, "Völkerpsychologie and German-Jewish Emancipation," in *Worldly Provincialism: German Anthropology in the Age of Empire*, ed. H. Glenn Penny and Matti Bunzl (Ann Arbor: University of Michigan Press, 2003), 47–85.

4. Ingrid Belke, "Liberal Voices on Antisemitism in the 1880s: Letters to Moritz Lazarus, 1880–1883," *Leo Baeck Institute Year Book* 23 (1978): 61–87; and Michael A. Meyer, "Great Debate on Anti-Semitism: Jewish Reactions to New Hostility in Germany, 1879–1881," *Leo Baeck Institute Year Book* 11 (1966): 148.

5. Moritz Lazarus, *Was heißt national? Ein Vortrag von Prof. Dr. M. Lazarus, mit einem Vorwort von Isid. Levy* (Berlin: Philo Verlag, 1925), 46. Lazarus was building on Gustav Rümelin, "Über den Begriff des Volkes," in *Kanzlerreden* (Tübingen: Mohr, 1907), 68–90, originally published in 1872; on Rümelin see Siegfried Weichlein, "'Qu'est-ce qu'une nation?' Stationen der deutschen statistischen Debatte um Nation und Nationalität in der Reichsgründungszeit," in *Demokratie in Deutschland: Chancen und Gefährdungen im 19. und 20. Jahrhundert: Festschrift für Heinrich August Winkler*, ed. Wolther von Kieseritzky and Klaus-Peter Sick (Munich: C. H. Beck, 1999), 71–90, especially 77–78.

6. Helmuth Plessner, epilogue to *Kleine Geographie des deutschen Witzes*, by Herbert Schöffler (Göttingen: Vandenhoeck und Ruprecht, 1961), 97.

7. Friedrich Schubert, *Handbuch der Allgemeinen Staatskunde in Europa*, vol. 1 (Königsberg: Bornträger, 1835), 161–62, quoted in Brian E. Vick, "Conceptions of Nationhood among the 1848–1849 Frankfurt Parliamentarians" (Ph.D. diss., Yale University, 1997), 148 n. 14.

8. Heinrich von Treitschke, "Noch einige Bemerkungen zur Judenfrage," in Boehlich, *Der Berliner Antisemitismusstreit*, 86.

9. I owe the phrase "individual Mosaic confessionalism" to Jacob Toury, "Die Revolution von 1848 als innerjüdischer Wendepunkt," in *Das Judentum in der Deutschen Umwelt, 1800–1850*, ed. Hans Liebeschütz and Arnold Paucker (Tübingen: Mohr Siebeck, 1977), 369.

10. Andreas Gotzmann, "Zwischen Nation und Religion: Die deutschen Juden auf der Suche nach einer bürgerlichen Konfessionalität," in *Bürger, Juden, Deutsche: Zur Geschichte von Vielfalt und Differenz seit dem späten 18. Jahrhundert*, ed. Andreas Gotzmann, Rainer Liedtke, and Till van Rahden (Tübingen: Mohr Siebeck, 2001), 241–62; generally see Michael A. Meyer, *Response to Modernity: A History of the Reform Movement in Judaism* (Oxford: Oxford University Press, 1988).

11. Emil Lehmann, "Die Aufgaben der Deutschen jüdischer Herkunft (1891)," in *Gesammelte Schriften* (Berlin: Hermann, 1899), 360. See also Heymann Steinthal, "Die Stellung der Semiten in der Weltgeschichte," in *Juden und Judenthum: Vorträge und Aufsätze*, ed. Gustav Karpeles (Berlin: Poppelauer, 1906), 105–25, especially 124 (originally published in *Jahrbuch für jüdische Geschichte und Literatur* 4 [1901]: 46–69).

12. See especially Marion A. Kaplan, "Redefining Judaism in Imperial Germany: Practices, Mentalities, and Community," in *Jewish Social Studies* 9 (2002): 1–33.

13. Sigmund Freud, quoted in Michael Brenner, "Religion, Nation oder Stamm: Zum Wandel der Selbstdefinition unter den Juden," in Haupt and Langewiesche, *Nation und Religion*, 588; Arye Maimon, *Wanderungen und Wandlungen: Die Geschichte meines Lebens* (Trier: Arye-Maimon-Institut für Geschichte der Juden, 1998), 29; and Alexander Moszkowski, *Der jüdische Witz und seine Philosophie: 399 Juwelen echt gefaßt* (Berlin: Eysler, 1922), 51.

14. Given how frequently German Jews invoked the concept of *Stamm* in the imperial and Weimar period, it is puzzling to find scholars who argue that "German Jews therefore abandoned the idea of a German nation comprising different *Stämme*, just as they abandoned the idea of Judaism as a *Stamm*" in the mid-1870s; see, e.g., Silvia Cresti, "German and Austrian Jews' Concept of Culture, Nation, and Volk," in *Towards Normality? Acculturation and Modern German Jewry*, ed. Rainer Liedtke and David Rechter (Tübingen: Mohr Siebeck, 2003), 280.

15. Adolf Jellinek, *Der jüdische Stamm: Ethnographische Studien* (Vienna: Herzfeld und Bauer, 1869); see "Die Reichen," *Allgemeine Zeitung des Judenthums* 34 (1870): 570, 572.

16. Jellinek, *Der jüdische Stamm*, 66, quoted in Marsha L. Rozenblit, "Jewish Identity and the Modern Rabbi: The Cases of Isak Noa Mannheimer, Adolf Jellinek, and Moritz Güdemann in Nineteenth-Century Vienna," *Leo Baeck Institute Year Book* 35 (1990): 116. Although Rozenblit's critique of historians who consider Jellinek a forerunner of Zionist nationalism and racism is well taken, she fails to do justice to the polyvalent meanings of the term *Stamm* when she argues that Jellinek understood the "Jewish people . . . in solely religious terms" (116). Probably Jellinek was familiar with the important place of the term in contemporaneous political discourse within the Habsburg Empire and German-speaking Central Europe. It is particularly important, in respect to Jellinek, that the term *Volksstamm* in article 19 of the so-called "December constitution" of the Cisleithanian half of the Habsburg Empire of 1867 occupied a prominent position, regardless of the fact that the imperial court of Vienna classified Jews not as a *Volksstamm* but as a *Konfession* until the disintegration of the Habsburg empire. See Gerald Stourzh, "Galten die Juden als Nationalität Altösterreichs," *Studia Judaica Austriaca* 10 (1984): 73–116; and Gerald Stourzh, *Die Gleichberechtigung der Nationalitäten in der Verfassung und Verwaltung Österreichs 1848–1918* (Vienna: Verlag der Österr. Akad. d. Wiss., 1985).

17. Steinthal, "Die Stellung der Semiten," 124–25; Ivan Kalmar, "Steinthal, the Jewish Orientalist," in *Chajim H. Steinthal: Sprachwissenschaftler und Philosoph im 19. Jahrhundert = Chajim H. Steinthal: Linguist and Philosopher in the 19th Century*, ed. Hartwig Wiedebach and Annette Winkelmann (Leiden: Brill, 2002), 135; see also Cornelie Kunze, "H. Steinthal über Juden und Judentum im Kontext des aufkommenden Antisemitismus," in ibid., 153–70.

18. "Noch eine Stimme über Lazarus' Broschüre," *Israelitische Wochenschrift* 18 (1887): 99.

19. Walther Rathenau, "An Deutschlands Jugend," in *Gesammelte Schriften, vol. 6: Schriften aus der Kriegs- und Nachkriegszeit* (Berlin: Fischer, 1929), 99.

20. Lehmann, "Die Aufgaben der Deutschen jüdischer Herkunft (1891)"; on Lehmann, see Ismar Schorsch, *Jewish Reactions to German Antisemitism, 1870–1914*

(New York: Columbia University Press, 1972), especially 24. I would like to thank Cornelia Hecht for calling Emil Lehmann's essay to my attention.

21. "[D]ie bis in das Innerste des Lebens hineinreichen," as well as the "Selbstverständlichkeit einer Lebensgemeinschaft, in die der Einzelne nur hineinzuwachsen braucht, statt sie sich erst durch persönliche Fähigkeiten und Leistungen erringen zu müssen." Julius Guttmann, "Der Begriff der Nation in seiner Anwendung auf die Juden," in *K.C.-Blätter: Monatsschrift der im Kartell-Convent vereinigten Korporationen* 4 (1914), no. 4: 79, 76.

22. N. Samter, *Was thun? Ein Epilog zu den Judentaufen im 19. Jahrhundert*, Hg. Verein für jüdische Geschichte und Literatur (Breslau: Th. Schatzky, 1900), 44–45; "Ost und West," *Ost und West* 1 (1901): 1; quoted in Michael Brenner, *The Renaissance of Jewish Culture in Weimar Germany* (New Haven: Yale University Press, 1996), 29; and Max Joseph, "Stammesgemeinschaft," in *Jüdisches Lexikon*, ed. Georg Herlitz, vol. 4, no. 2 (Berlin: Jüdischer Verlag, 1930), 628–29. Generally, see George L. Mosse, *Germans and Jews: The Right, the Left, and the Search for a "Third Force" in Pre-Nazi Germany* (Detroit: Wayne State University Press, 1987), 107–108; Steven E. Aschheim, *Brothers and Strangers: The East European Jew in German and German-Jewish Consciousness, 1800–1923* (Madison: University of Wisconsin Press, 1982), 97; Derek J. Penslar, *Shylock's Children: Economics and Jewish Identity in Modern Europe* (Berkeley: University of California Press, 2001), 135–37; and Jacob Toury, *Die politischen Orientierungen der Juden in Deutschland: Von Jena bis Weimar* (Tübingen: Mohr Siebeck, 1966), 143.

23. Andreas Reinke, "'Eine Sammlung des jüdischen Bürgertums': Der unabhängige Orden B'nai B'rith in Deutschland," in Gotzmann, Liedtke, and van Rahden, *Bürger, Juden, Deutsche*, 322–23; see also Jacob Borut, "Vereine für jüdische Geschichte und Literatur at the End of the Nineteenth Century," *Leo Baeck Institute Year Book* 41 (1996): 89–114, especially 92.

24. Franz Oppenheimer, "Stammesbewußtsein und Volksbewußtsein," *Die Welt: Zentralorgan der zionistischen Vereinigung* 14, no. 7 (February 18, 1910): 139–40.

25. Steven Aschheim, in fact, in his nuanced discussion of the controversy, considers Oppenheimer "typical" of the first generation of German Zionists; Aschheim, *Brothers and Strangers*, 96–98. For a recent summary of the debate see Yfaat Weiss, "'Wir Westjuden haben jüdisches Stammesbewußtsein, die Ostjuden jüdisches Volksbewußtsein': Der deutsch-jüdische Blick auf das polnische Judentum in den beiden ersten Jahrzehnten des 20. Jahrhunderts," *Archiv für Sozialgeschichte* 37 (1997): 157–78.

26. Eugen Fuchs, "Referat über die Stellung des Centralvereins zum Zionismus in der Delegierten-Versammlung vom 30. März 1913," in *Um Deutschtum und Judentum: Gesammelte Reden und Aufsätze, 1894–1914* (Frankfurt am Main: Kauffmann, 1919), 241.

27. Eugen Fuchs, "Glaube und Heimat," in *Um Deutschtum und Judentum*, 252–53 (originally published in *Neue Jüdische Monatshefte* 1, no. 22 (1917), 629–41); see also Avraham Barkai, "Between *Deutschtum* and *Judentum*: Ideological Controversies inside the Centralverein," in *In Search of Jewish Community: Jewish Identities in Germany and Austria, 1918–1933*, ed. Michael Brenner and Derek J. Penslar (Bloomington: Indiana University Press, 1998), 74–91, especially 78; and "Jüdische Feldgraue für die Einigkeit der Juden," in *Im Deutschen Reich* (April 1918): 173, quoted

in Greg Caplan, "Militärische Männlichkeit in der deutsch-jüdischen Geschichte," *Die Philosophin*, no. 22 (2000): 85–100, especially 93–94.

28. Johann Bluntschli, "Juden: Rechtliche Stellung," in *Deutsches Staats-Wörterbuch*, ed. J. C. Bluntschli and K. Brater, vol. 5 (Stuttgart: Expedition des Staats-Wörterbuchs, 1860), 443–44.

29. Karl Steinacker, "Emancipation der Juden," in *Das Staats-Lexikon: Encyclopädie der sämmtlichen Staatswissenschaften für alle Stände*, ed. Carl von Rotteck and Carl Welcker, vol. 4 (Altona: Hammerich, 1846), 318 (translated by the editors). Friedrich Wilhelm Carové, a leading Hegelian of his time, advanced a similar argument. In 1844, he advocated Jewish emancipation not only as a means of making Jews full members of society, but also as a way of enabling them to continue to develop their own life as Jews; see Carové, *Über die Emanzipation der Juden, Philosophie des Judentums und jüdische Reformprojekte zu Berlin und Frankfurt a. M.* (Siegen: Friedrich, 1845), quoted in Shlomo Avineri, "A Note on Hegel's Views on Jewish Emancipation," in *Jewish Social Studies* 25, no. 2 (1968): 145–51, especially 151.

30. Steinacker, "Emancipation," 319–21.

31. For recent thoughtful discussions of how central the idea of a diversity of *Stämme* was in nineteenth-century German nationalism, see especially Abigail Green, *Fatherlands: State-Building and Nationhood in Nineteenth-Century Germany* (Cambridge: Cambridge University Press, 2001), 267–97, especially 270–73; and Dieter Langewiesche, *Nation, Nationalismus, Nationalstaat in Deutschland und Europa* (Munich: C. H. Beck, 2000), 143, 154, 159, and 164. My own reading differs from that of Green and Langewiesche in two ways. First, by emphasizing that tribal identities were closely tied to dynastic loyalties they miss the often antidynastic tendencies in the language of *Stämme*. Not only was the identification of dynastic and tribal identities "tenuous," because the "boundaries of *Stamm* and state seldom coincided"—as Green herself admits (270)—but, more importantly, tribal identities were "portable fatherlands" and thus independent of dynastic citizenship. A Bavarian, e.g., could move to Berlin and legally acquire Prussian citizenship. Thus, he would cease to be a Bavarian citizen, but could continue to consider himself a member of the Bavarian *Stamm*. Second, Green and Langewiesche seem to suggest that the idea of tribal diversity was important between the 1830s and the late 1860s and became irrelevant after the foundation of the German Empire in 1871, whereas I emphasize that the concept of *Stamm* remained central to German nationalism—although this phenomenon is often discussed under the rubric of Heimat-ideology (see, e.g., Green, *Fatherlands*, 330).

32. "Art. Volk—Volksstamm," in *Conversations-Lexicon oder encyclopädisches Handwörterbuch für gebildete Stände*, vol. 10 (Leipzig: Brockhaus, 1819), 371.

33. Schüler (Jena), in *Stenographischer Bericht über die Verhandlungen der Deutschen constituirenden Nationalversammlung zu Frankfurt am Main*, ed. Franz Wigard, vol. 7 (Frankfurt am Main, 1848; reprint, Munich: Moos, 1988), 4898, quoted in Irmline Veit-Brause, "Partikularismus," in *Geschichtliche Grundbegriffe*, vol. 4 (Stuttgart: Klett, 1978), 748. See also Dan S. White, "Regionalism and Particularism," in *Imperial Germany: A Historiographical Companion*, ed. Roger Chickering (Westport: Greenwood, 1996), 131–55.

34. Buss (Freiburg), in *Stenographischer Bericht*, vol. 7, 4894, quoted in Veit-Brause, "Partikularismus," 749.

35. "Die Regierung Breslau, Abteilung des Innern, an den Minister des Innern, Grafen von Arnim. Die Rechtsverhältnisse der Juden im Regierungsbezirk. Die geplante Regulierung der Verhältnisse der Juden," in *Die Juden und die jüdischen Gemeinden Preußens in amtlichen Enquêten des Vormärz, Teil 1: Die Enquête des Ministeriums des Innern und der Polizei über die Rechtsverhältnisse der Juden in den preußischen Provinzen, 1842–1843*, ed. Manfred Jehle (Munich: Saur, 1998), 275.

36. Theodor Mommsen, "Auch ein Wort über unser Judentum," quoted in Boehlich, *Der Berliner Antisemitismusstreit*, 212.

37. Rathenau to Schwaner, August 18, 1916, BA Koblenz, NL Rathenau, Bd. 6, Bl. 52, quoted in Helmuth F. Braun, "'Höre, Israel!' Antisemitismus und Assimilation," in *Die Extreme berühren sich: Walther Rathenau, 1867–1922*, ed. Hans Wilderotter (Berlin: Argon, 1993), 323.

38. Warburg Papiere, Archiv der Hamburger Warburg Bank, Jahresbericht 1918, Akte 161a, Anlage 21, quoted in Werner T. Angress, "Kurt Hahn und Max M. Warburg als Berater des Prinzen Max von Baden vor und während seiner Amtszeit als Reichskanzler," in *Geschichte und Emanzipation: Festschrift für Reinhard Rürup*, ed. Michael Grüttner, Rüdiger Hachtmann, and Heinz-Gerhard Haupt (Frankfurt am Main: Campus, 1999), 240.

39. Gerhard Anschütz, *Die Verfassung des deutschen Reichs vom 11. August 1919*, 14th ed. (Berlin: Stilke, 1932), xii; see also 2.

40. "Es liegt dem neuen Reiche und seinem Recht fern . . . die 'Stämme,' diese naturwüchsigen Gliederungen des deutschen Volkes . . . unterdrücken und ihre Besonderheiten auslöschen zu wollen." Anschütz, *Die Verfassung des Deutschen Reichs*, 32f.; see also Wilhelm Heile, *Stammesfreiheit im Einheitsstaat* (Berlin: Fortschritt, 1919); and Willibalt Apelt, *Geschichte der Weimarer Verfassung* (Munich: Biederstein, 1946), 127–31. Because of its democratic and antidynastic preamble, the constitution was a favorite target of conservative criticism; see Fritz Hartung, "Stammesbewußtsein," in *Politisches Handwörterbuch*, vol. 2, ed. Paul Herre (Leipzig: Koehler, 1923), 723; and Axel von Freytag-Loringhoven, *Die Weimarer Verfassung in Lehre und Wirklichkeit* (Munich: Lehmanns, 1924), 50–55.

41. Recent scholarship on nineteenth-century nationalism is increasingly questioning the dichotomy between a Western model of a voluntaristic and civic nationalism and an Eastern European model of an essentialist and ethnic nationalism; see, e.g., Brian C. J. Singer, "Cultural versus Contractual Nation: Rethinking Their Opposition," *History and Theory* 35, no. 3 (1996): 309–37; Patrick Weil, *Qu'est-ce qu'un français? Histoire de la nationalité française depuis la Révolution* (Paris: Grasset, 2002); and Weichlein, "'Qu'est-ce qu'une Nation?'" 86.

42. Lazarus, *Was heißt national?*, 23.

43. Lazarus, *Was heißt national?*, 24. Here, my reading of Lazarus's essays differs from that of other scholars. Both Matti Bunzl ("Völkerpsychologie and German-Jewish Emancipation," 75–78) and Ulrich Sieg ("Bekenntnis zu nationalen und universalen Werten," 615) argue that in *Was heißt national?*, too, Lazarus views language as the basis of a nation. Contrary to Bunzl and Sieg, I believe that *Was heißt national?* constitutes a break with Lazarus's earlier work, in which he had indeed argued that common nationality could only be established through language. Looking back on his earlier work, Lazarus acknowledges the "deep significance of language as a characteristic feature of nationality." At the same time he rejects the notion "that this and

this alone expresses the nature of nationhood and can determine the borders of the nation. The true nature and the actual essence of nationhood can only be conceived from the intellect [*Geist*]." Lazarus, *Was heißt national?*, in *Treu und frei: Gesammelte Reden und Vorträge über Juden und Judentum* (Leipzig: winter 1887), 64. Although the question lies beyond the scope of this paper, it may be worthwhile to consider Lazarus's essay as a foundational text for constructivist conceptions of the nation. Max Weber's famous dictum that "a common language is insufficient in sustaining a so-called sense of national identity" might well echo Lazarus's argument. Max Weber, *Economy and Society* (Berkeley: University of California Press, 1978), 395 and 922, quoted in Sung Ho Kim, "Max Weber's Liberal Nationalism," *History of Political Thought* 23, no. 3 (2002): 439. (Kim mentions only Renan as an influence on Weber; ibid., 445–46). As Siegfried Weichlein has argued, Renan's essay "Qu'est-ce qu'une Nation?" builds on Lazarus as well as other central European intellectuals; Weichlein, "'Qu'est-ce qu'une Nation?'" 84–85.

44. Lazarus, *Was heißt national?*, 24.

45. Ibid., 37.

46. Ibid., 37.

47. Ibid., 46.

48. Ibid., 48.

49. The following reflections address the controversy concerning which ideas among the concepts and debates of cultural studies and postcolonial studies may be of use to the study of German Jewish history. See David N. Myers, "'The Blessings of Assimilation' Reconsidered: An Inquiry into Jewish Cultural Studies," in *From Ghetto to Emancipation: Historical and Contemporary Reconsiderations of the Jewish Community*, ed. David N. Myers and William V. Rowe (Scranton, Pa.: University of Scranton Press, 1997), 17–35; Sander L. Gilman, "The Frontier as a Model for Jewish History," in *Jewries at the Frontier: Accommodation, Identity, Conflict*, ed. Sander L. Gilman and Milton Shain (Urbana: University of Illinois Press, 1999), 1–25; Jonathan Boyarin and Daniel Boyarin, eds., *Jews and Other Differences: The New Jewish Cultural Studies* (Minneapolis: University of Minnesota Press, 1997); Jonathan Judaken, "Mapping the 'New Jewish Cultural Studies,'" *History Workshop Journal* 31 (2001): 269–77; and Till van Rahden, "Jews and the Ambivalences of Civil Society in Germany, 1800 to 1933—Assessment and Reassessment," *Journal of Modern History*, 77 (2005): 1024–1047.

50. Stefanie Schüler-Springorum, *Die jüdische Minderheit in Königsberg/Preussen, 1871–1945* (Göttingen: Vandenhoeck und Ruprecht, 1996); Jan C. Palmowski, "Between Dependence and Influence: Jews and Liberalism in Frankfurt am Main, 1864–1933," in *Liberalism, Anti-Semitism, and Democracy: Essays in Honour of Peter Pulzer*, ed. Henning Tewes and Jonathan Wright (Oxford: Oxford University Press, 2001), 76–101; and Till van Rahden, *Juden und andere Breslauer: Die Beziehungen zwischen Juden, Protestanten und Katholiken in einer deutschen Großstadt von 1860 bis 1925* (Göttingen: Vandenhoeck und Ruprecht, 2000).

51. Theodor Herzl quoted in Leo Strauss, "Preface to Spinoza's Critique of Religion (1965)," in *Jewish Philosophy and the Crisis of Modernity: Essays and Lectures in Modern Jewish Thought*, ed. Kenneth Hart Green (Albany: State University of New York Press, 1997), 141. The statement is in Joseph Adler's introduction to Theodor Herzl, *The Jewish State (Der Judenstaat)*, trans. Harry Zohn (New York:

Herzel Press, 1970), 34. It is followed by some very tough-minded comments on the perils of assimilation and upward mobility for "a minority that was but recently despised" (35).

52. Homi K. Bhabha, "Dissemination: Time, Narrative, and the Margins of the Modern Nation," in *The Location of Culture* (London: Routledge, 1994), 145–46.

53. The phrase was coined by Adolf Stoecker in "Zur sozialen Frage," *Neue Evangelische Kirchenzeitung*, 27 January 1871, quoted in Walter Frank, *Hofprediger Adolf Stoecker und die christlichsoziale Bewegung* (Berlin: Hobbing, 1928), 32–33. See also R. Laurence Moore, "Insiders and Outsiders in American Historical Narrative and American History," *American Historical Review* 87, no. 2 (April 1982): 390–412. Moore quotes an "essay by the Reverend S. M. Campbell written in 1867. . . . 'This is a Christian Republic, our Christianity being of the Protestant type,' he wrote. 'People who are not Christians, and people called Christians, but who are not Protestant, dwell among us; but they did not build this house. We have never shut the door against them but if they come, they must take up with such accommodations as we have'" (396–97). The essay is S. M. Campbell, "Christianity and Civil Liberty," in *American and Presbyterian Theological Review* 5 (1867): 390–91.

54. *Acta et decreta sacrorum conciliorum recentiorum, quae ab episcopis Germaniae, Hungariae et Hollandiae ab a. 1789 usque ad a. 1869 celebrata sunt* (Collectio Lacensis, vol. 5), ed. Gerhard Schneemann (Freiburg: Herder, 1879), quoted in Rudolf Lill, *Die ersten deutschen Bischofkonferenzen* (Freiburg: Herder, 1964), 34; and Lazarus, *Was heißt national?*, 65.

55. Bhabha, *Location of Culture*, 1–2.

Two

Identity and Essentialism
Race, Racism, and the Jews at
the Fin de Siècle

Yfaat Weiss

> It is very desirable, therefore, that we should employ the
> same weapons as our opponents—that is to say, the weap-
> ons of anthropology, sociology, and natural science—to
> investigate the social value of the Jews.
> —Ignatz Zollschan, *Jewish Questions*

Honoured Members of the Academy!

You have done me the honour of inviting me to give your Academy an account of the life I formerly led as an ape.

I regret that I cannot comply with your request to the extent you desire. It is now nearly five years since I was an ape, a short space of time, perhaps, according to the calendar, but an infinitely long time to gallop through at full speed, as I have done, more or less accompanied by excellent mentors, good advice, applause and orchestral music, and yet essentially alone, since all my escorters, to keep the image, kept well off the course. I could never have achieved what I have done had I been stubbornly set on clinging to my origins, to the remembrance of my youth. In fact, to give up being stubborn was the supreme commandment I laid upon myself; free ape as I was, I submitted myself to that yoke. In revenge, however, my memory of the past has closed the door against me more and more. I could have returned at first, had human beings allowed it, through an archway as wide as the span of heaven over the earth, but as I spurred myself on in my forced career, the opening narrowed and shrank behind me; I felt more comfortable in the world of men and fitted it better; the strong wind that blew after me out of my past began to slacken; today it is only a gentle puff of air that plays around my heels; and the opening in the distance, through which it comes and through which I once came myself, has grown so small that, even if my strength and my will power sufficed to get me back to it, I should have to scrape the very skin from my body to crawl through. To put it plainly, much as I like expressing myself in images, to put it plainly: your life as apes, gentlemen, insofar as something of that kind lies behind you, cannot be farther removed from you than mine is from me. Yet everyone on earth feels a tickling at the heels; the small chimpanzee and the great Achilles alike.[1]

I

With these words Franz Kafka opened his story "A Report to an Academy," which first appeared in the October–November 1917 issue of the periodical *Der Jude*, edited by Martin Buber.

The report is a scientific lecture given by "Red Peter" about his former life as an ape. The topic of the lecture is the process of *Menschwerdung;* at the end of a journey that begins with his capture in Africa, and culminates in his being tamed at Hamburg's Hagenbeck Zoo, the chimpanzee hero becomes a human being. In Kafka's story, the ape appears to go through a "civilizing process" that is simultaneously one of rapid degeneration.[2]

The universal nature of Kafka's writing generates an effect of timelessness on the one hand, as well as a strong sense of presentiment. In "A Report to an Academy," the ape-mimic has an uncanny knack of coming up with basic expressions which will be reformulated decades later in the framework of postcolonial theory. Following some of Homi K. Bhabha's early insights, the ape demonstrates in "A Report to an Academy" the way colonial discourse encourages the subject to imitate the ruler's values, customs, and institutions. Clearly, the results are not perfect replications. Instead, they will inevitably be distorted and sometimes rather threatening.[3] A straightforward examination of the ape, however, reveals that this imitation conceals both mockery and threat, or, as Bhabha puts it, "that mimicry is at once resemblance and menace."[4]

The imitation that lies at the heart of "A Report to an Academy" touches a central nerve regarding the relationship between rulers and ruled, exposing the ambivalence of attraction and repulsion between the two partners—the victor and the vanquished, the man and the ape. What constitutes the center of Kafka's ironic study is the central "scientific" prism used when determining relations of power and control between subjugators and the subjugated. The ape, who investigates the laboratory studying his "civilizing process," can serve as metaphor for the position of Western Jews of that same period. Jews became willing and active partners or collaborators in the scientific cultures of their countries, an area in which "mimicry," i.e., the copying and taking on board or internalization of an accepted scientific tradition, constituted the only possible model. But this science, whose hypotheses they shared, at the same time also examined—sometimes directly, but mainly indirectly—how the Jews themselves fitted into the same society and how well they were able to integrate into it. This simultaneity required reflexivity regarding the character of the scientific tools in question.[5]

Kafka's short story, much like his less well-known tale "Investigations of a Dog,"[6] makes reference to, and disagrees with, the generally accepted scientific views of his period. Kafka's ironic contribution to the pivotal nature-nurture debate on the relative influence of heredity and the environment pokes fun at all essentialist views of the Jews, as well as all attempts to establish any link between their characteristics and their ethnic origin and birthplace.

What "A Report to an Academy" actually does is to compare and contrast the position of the observer with that of the participant. Red Peter—the man-ape—is the object of research. Through him science investigates the "civilizing process." However, when Red Peter is invited to deliver his lecture at the Academy, he fails to maintain this approach. As he gives his address, using the language and the accepted scientific tools of his period, he does so from the position of an observer, thereby eliding the clear-cut observer/participant distinction.

In the historical context of the story's publication, in Buber's *Der Jude*, this dual perspective of observer and participant sheds light on the internal contradictions that characterized European Jews' involvement in the scientific discussions of the period. As men of science they were observers, but at the same time as Jews they constituted a permanent subject of discussions about environment and heredity, ethnic origin and culture, assimilation and essence. Kafka's approach predates anthropology's self-awareness of the fine line between the observer's position and that of the participant. It anticipates both the critical anthropological awareness of the observer position in general, and the postcolonial awareness of the contexts of "knowledge and power" (in Foucault's terms), or, as Kafka, through Red Peter, puts it:

> And so I learned things, gentlemen. Ah, one learns when one has to; one learns when one needs a way out; one learns at all costs. . . . With an effort, which up till now has never been repeated, I managed to reach the cultural level of an average European. In itself that might be nothing to speak of, but it is something insofar as it has helped me out of my cage and opened a special way out for me, the way of humanity.[7]

All that Red Peter, the "subjugated" participant-observer, wants is "to stand up,"[8] but the reader is made to enter the secret of the price that Peter has paid for this achievement.

II

The turn of the twentieth century was characterized by the emergence and strengthening of race as a scientific paradigm. In time, this occurred in relatively well-established disciplines such as anthropology, as well as in new ones like sociology. These developments were of twofold significance from the Jewish perspective. In the long term they would provide the lexicon of terms, and would to a large extent dictate the discourse used, in the exclusion of the Jews from the surrounding society. But in the short term, and, somewhat ironically, many years before the lexicon of exclusion and destruction came into being, this development created a system of concepts which imposed itself on the discourse of Jewish identity in Central Europe. Jews found themselves in the position of "participant observers" in a scientific discourse dominated by racist assumptions. It was exactly that discourse, which in decades to come constituted the bedrock of racist insights—scientific and popular alike—that would bring about their exclusion as European Jews and lead to their persecution and murder.

This essay discusses how concepts and ideas from Western scientific discourse came to permeate the discourse of European Jewish identity. Many scientific frames related to this discourse: biology, medicine, sociology, anthropology, and racial hygiene. The scientific debate, and its shift to discourses of identity, was mostly conducted in German. Even where this was not the case, there was always a reference to Germany and to the German academic world as the source of knowledge and wisdom. In this way, the debate crossed the boundaries of the nation-state that were accepted in the writing of history generally and of Jewish history specifically.

I will single out a limited number of the scientific debates of the period that connected directly with the question of Jewish identity. Firstly, I will explore the involvement of Jewish academics in developing racist research hypotheses. This will be done in the context of the anthropological and sociological discussions at the turn of the twentieth century that asked whether there were firm connections between ethnic origin, heredity, environment, and culture. In the light of the scientific prestige of racist research hypotheses, I shall examine whether, and to what extent, Jewish academics showed any special sensitivity to them arising from their membership in a particular ethnic group which was itself the target of racist attacks.

A second set of questions revolve round the relationship between nationalism and science. There were undoubtedly mutual interconnections between the rise of German nationalism and the emergence of scientific hypotheses postulating the primacy of race. At the same time Jewish intellectual discourse looked for what it considered objective criteria for defining Jewish national identity.[9] German, moreover, was the intellectual language of nascent Zionism. In this context I will scrutinize the biologistic metaphors used by Zionism in its early days—primarily the "blood relationship" as a key component of the "idea" of genealogy, i.e., the generational continuum—and I will explore the relationship between Zionism and racism.

Finally, the use of genealogy and blood as markers in the process of demonstrating the Jewish national subject, and the discussions about a mandatory nexus between genetic relationship, geographic origin, and culture, served to create a nexus between the generational continuum and the territory of origin. Two concepts were decisive here: genealogy and blood. Together they tried to constitute the Jewish national subject. The embeddedness of genealogy, geographic origin, and culture made clear that generational continuity and territory of origin were inextricably linked. I shall discuss the relationship between return and essentialist thinking, and call into question the interpretation that sees the use of the metaphors taken from the scientific racist discussion at the turn of the century as inevitably leading to racism and chauvinism.

III

"Race" and "culture" were major concepts in both academic and public debates at the turn of the twentieth century. However, these could still be debated without reference to Jews or antisemitism. As George Mosse has argued,

> Not all social Darwinism was dedicated to their [the Jews'] destruction. Indeed, this science of race in general tended to reject anti-Semitism . . . there is no warrant for the claim to see in the German and English doctrine of "racial biology and hygiene" the immediate forerunner of the Nazi policy against the Jews.[10]

The intellectual challenge posed by the issue of the Jews' participation in these discussions thus lies in the gap between the significance of these discussions at the time and their examination from a later vantage point, and in the relationship between this discourse and the discourse of Jewish identity. An examination of anthropological discourse, and in particular of developing sociological discourse, offers a good starting point.[11]

The German Sociological Association held its first conference in 1910, in Frankfurt am Main.[12] In this festive setting, the new discipline critically examined its limits. The keynote address was given by Dr. Alfred Ploetz, the leading expert in race and hygiene, or *Rassenbiologie*, as this field was known in Germany, and editor of the field's flagship journal, *Archiv für Rassen- und Gesellschaftbiologie*. Ploetz's lecture, titled "Concepts of Race and Society and a Number of Ancillary Problems," aroused criticism among some of his audience, but there was one listener who lost all patience with the argument. In a sarcastic attack, Max Weber chose to take issue with Ploetz's claim that, in order for a society to thrive and prosper, there must be a similar flourishing in the racial sphere.[13] The acrimonious altercation between Ploetz and Weber about the relationship between environment and heredity formed part of a fundamental debate within the developing social sciences and took place in the context of the attempt by the up-and-coming German generation of researchers to put the social sciences on an ideologically neutral footing.[14] In countering Ploetz's biologistic understanding, Weber foregrounded the historical, social, and economic processes which, to his way of thinking, shaped human development.[15]

Two years later, at the German Sociological Association's second conference, held in Berlin in 1912, Franz Oppenheimer joined in the discussion. At the time Oppenheimer was a *Privatdozent* in Berlin. This was a middle-ranking academic grade held by numerous Jews, who, despite their ability, were denied admission to the groves of German academe.[16] Oppenheimer's talk was titled "Theoretical Aspects of Race in Historical Philosophy." He completely rejected Ploetz's scientific hypotheses, declaring them to be "pseudo-science," a "group ideology" intended to provide legitimacy for the ruling upper echelons.[17] Oppenheimer's lecture was not merely a reaction to Ploetz, but also a reaction to another colleague—to Werner Sombart, whose book *Die Juden und das Wirtschaftsleben* (The Jews and economic life) had appeared the previous year.[18] In his book, Sombart had argued that Jews shared special economic characteristics—for example, that they had a "commercial sense"—characteristics which he interpreted as "racial traits." These he linked to a biological Jewish existence which has been isolated from external influences in the course of history by discouragement of mixed marriages and conversion to Judaism. Oppenheimer profoundly disagreed with Sombart's attempt to ascribe features to race that Oppenheimer interpreted as deriving from "cultural capital."[19] As a proponent of a distinctly materialist scientific approach, Oppenheimer was utterly immune to the romantic approach concealed both in Sombart's book and in the marked biologism of Ploetz's outlook.

However, these kinds of debates went beyond the boundaries of Germany and its national professional associations. Opinions identical to those which Oppenheimer adopted in opposition to Ploetz were published by a senior colleague—a Jew—two years later: the American anthropologist Franz Boas. Born in Minden, Germany, in 1858, Boas emigrated to New York from Germany in the 1880s, in an indirect reaction to the obstacles facing Jewish intellectuals in German academe.[20] At the time, emigration constituted a personal solution for Boas, but as far as his academic career was concerned he perceived it to be a step backward, since research in the United States lagged distinctly behind that in Germany. Now, some thirty years after he had left the country, Boas joined in the German discussion from his New York home. Speaking from a senior academic position and as an established scholar, the American anthropologist decided to set the record straight. In 1914, when his book *The Mind of Primitive Man* appeared in German, Boas chose in the translated version not to publish the original concluding chapter, which discussed the United States. Instead, he wrote a different concluding chapter for the German edition, which briefly discussed the problems of race in social-political experience.[21] Boas's didactic approach for his German readership was to deliberately poke fun at the accepted views of the anthropology of the time, with its assertion that race and culture were one and the same. In order to leave no doubt whatsoever concerning his views about the relationship between racial purity and a cultural position, Boas wrote in an unmistakably ironic tone, "Were this to be true, one would expect to find [a high cultural level] in every out-of-the-way village."[22]

In order to provide a solid footing for his controversial views on the mutability and volatility of national identities and their debatable, questionable nature, Boas referred to American realities. And, indeed, from the perspective of a country of immigration it was possible to argue things that were just not visible in a nation-state. It is no accident that Boas focused on the German immigrant in America. As far as that immigrant was concerned, Boas argued, "the ease with which he is contaminated by another patriotism" is a byword.[23] What was true of Germans outside Germany, Boas argued, held equally true of individuals from other nations whose paths brought them to America. In America, he claimed, by the second generation it was impossible to differentiate between native-born Americans and European immigrants. "It would never even cross anyone's mind," he concluded, "to talk about racial qualities in this context."

Boas's comments in this chapter specifically, as well as in his book *The Mind of Primitive Man* in general, represented the conclusion to a comprehensive research project instigated and conducted by him on behalf of the American immigration authorities in the years 1908–10. A comparative study of the skull structures of two generations of New York immigrants, covering a total of eighteen thousand subjects, proved beyond any doubt that, taking into account the absolute changes in skull structure among members of these families, there was no basis for ascribing any genetic, let alone racial, significance to this data. Indirectly it was Boas who in 1908 single-handedly—or so at least it seemed—began to wean anthropological research off the misleading paradigm of anthropometry, from which Boas would definitively dissociate himself in the 1920s.[24]

In the long term, the conclusions of Boas's study would have far-reaching implications, but even in the short term its importance cannot be underestimated. His research shifted a considerable proportion of the weight ascribed to ethnic qualities and features from heredity to environment. His findings offered scientific legitimation for migration rather than—as the racially based studies did—making the case for strict controls.[25] However, whereas many later scholars have seen Boas's 1908 study as an exception, as an enlightened anthropological approach far ahead of that of his contemporaries, a thorough examination shows Boas to be very much a man of his time. Boas did not reject the concepts of race, but rather subordinated them to environmental influences.

Boas's writing, his research questions, his methods, and to some extent his conclusions were firmly rooted in contemporary assumptions. Rather than imposing a binary framework on Boas's work, and insisting on seeing him either as a representative of progress and enlightenment or as an exponent of racist ideologies, historian Christian Geulen offers a reading which grounds Boas firmly in the concepts of his day and refrains from projecting later developments onto him. Boas initially by no means rejected the racist paradigm, but the failure of racial anthropological models to explain his results in the end led him to generate different hypotheses. It was because Boas adhered to scientific positivism that the challenge posed by his results to basic approaches in the science of physical anthropology eventually led him to the cultural paradigm.

The discrepancy between Boas's acceptance of the scientific assumptions of his time, on the one hand, and the long-term anti-racist conclusions of his scientific work, on the other, is also evident when we examine his attitude to the status and position of African Americans. In this area, too, Boas's initial positions were fairly ambivalent, or, as George Stocking has argued,

> Given the atmospheric pervasiveness of the idea of European racial superiority, it is hardly surprising that Boas wrote as a skeptic of received belief rather than a staunch advocate of racial equipotentiality. Despite his basic liberal humanitarian outlook, he was a white-skinned European writing for other white-skinned Europeans at the turn of the century, and he was a physical anthropologist to boot.[26]

Boas's research up to 1911 moves uneasily between the rejection of cultural determinism and a commitment to physical anthropology. It intimated that, even though African Americans in the aggregate were not in his view inferior to the aggregate of whites, only a relatively very small number of the former had the potential to contribute to changing the world.[27] But as the years wore on, and in particular after the publication of *The Mind of Primitive Man*, the scales tipped in Boas's writings in favor of the power of the environment rather than that of heredity, and broad sectors of the African American intelligentsia came to look on his approach sympathetically. For example, W. E. B. Du Bois viewed it as strengthening his own work, using it to provide a grounding for his belief that black inferiority lay in class structure, i.e., society, rather than in hereditary factors.[28] This emphasis on issues of class or status rather than on the biologistic-heredity argument, as it developed in Du Bois's work, is to some extent identical with the materialist argument that Franz Oppenheimer presented in opposing Alfred Ploetz in 1910 and 1912 at the German Sociological Association's meetings.

Let us now return to Mosse's statement that "there is no warrant for the claim to see in the German and English doctrine of 'racial biology and hygiene' the immediate forerunner of the Nazi policy against the Jews." Should the anthropological and sociological debate about the relationship between environment and heredity be seen as ominously foreshadowing the relationships between the Jews and their environment? I would contend that, in a process which was not predetermined in any shape or form, but which occurred under certain historical circumstances, scientific interpretations which, for decades, had suffered from varying degrees of marginal status became crucial, not to say critical.

A process can be identified that extended over many years and comprised shifts in all subjects, but primarily in the liberal atmosphere characteristic of German anthropological studies.[29] The equating of race and culture, as presented by Ploetz, initially symbolized an essentialist biologistic understanding of culture. Other debates at the same time suggest that this was a general rather than an isolated understanding.[30] A culture, according to this way of thinking, could not be acquired: rather, according to Ploetz's theory, one had to be born into it. Views of the kind expressed by Ploetz attached very little weight to the influence of the environment.

Jewish integration in the German cultural sphere was not discussed directly in these contexts, but there was no disputing the fact that the biologistic paradigm of culture undermined the very notion of acculturation. True, as Mosse notes, the authors who appeared in Ploetz's journal were "friendly toward French, English, and Jews" and their hostility was directed at blacks only. Not until 1935, according to Mosse, were the signs and symbols of inferiority previously attributed to blacks transferred to the Jews.[31] But the views expressed by Ploetz held far-reaching negative implications for the Jewish context as early as the beginning of the century: positing a direct tie between culture and race, or more correctly, situating culture squarely within race, meant cutting off the very lifeblood of Jewish existence in Germany.

Scholars of Jewish history should integrate this chapter of the history of science into the study of antisemitism. Minorities possess a special ability to sense lurking dissonances in public debates to the extent that such dissonances affect their own existences. Precisely because this mainstream debate about heredity and environment only implicitly addressed Jewish existence in the society in which it was taking place, the way Jewish scholars positioned themselves in it can help us detect its inherent element of exclusion. In other words, because these scientific discussions of racialism lacked overtly antisemitic characteristics, the degree of sensitivity demonstrated by Jewish participants in these discussions can help us interpret the extent to which these debates were truly innocent, thus allowing a non-teleological interpretation of Jews and racialism.

IV

However, the Jews were simultaneously both subject and object of these views. Hence we must not ignore the enormous gravitational force that these scientific theories exerted on Jews—just like the gravitational pull that essentialist views generally have on ethnic minorities—and certainly there can be no talk of Jews not being susceptible to essentialist views on identity. In Germany, and more precisely in the framework of the German cultural sphere, it was above all the Zionists who made great use of essentialist views in order to bolster their argument.[32] An essentialist interpretation of identity is not limited to biologism alone: it also embraces a broad range of cultural phenomena. Essentialism hypothesizes the existence of defined characteristics applicable exclusively to all members of the group or class, applying in this context to Jews as a whole. Essentialist views were cited on two fronts: on the external front, in opposition to the antisemitic environment, and on the internal front, in countering the rapid processes of assimilation which, when combined with a declining birth rate and an increase in the number of mixed marriages, were portrayed by some Zionists as "race suicide."[33] Interestingly, such views were found among the proponents of a variety of trends in the central European academic debate, i.e., also among those who espoused scientific positivism, as well as among their opponents, the proponents of romantic and sometimes also mystic views.

A striking example of the latter are the lectures that Martin Buber gave in 1909–11 to members of the Zionist Bar Kochba association in Prague, and which constitute a basic text in the crystallization of spiritual Zionism.[34] In keeping with the spirit of the age, Buber compared the nation with a child who goes exploring. One of the significant discoveries is that of the family tree or dynasty: "the line of fathers and of mothers that had led up to him." The child, as Buber put it, "senses in this immortality of the generations a community of blood, which he feels to be the antecedents of his I, its perseverance in the infinite past." This feeling is accompanied by the discovery "that blood is a deep-rooted nurturing force within the individual man; that the deepest layers of our being are determined by blood; that our innermost thinking and our will are colored by it." This insight, once engendered, makes the Jew feel alienated from his surroundings, or, as Buber put it, "And he therefore senses that he belongs no longer to the community of those whose constant elements of experience he shares, but to the deeper-reaching community of those whose substance he shares."

Buber went on to contend that "this insertion in the great chain [of generations] is individual man's natural position." However, the Jew could not enjoy this natural state of affairs, since

Neither the land he lives in, whose nature encompasses him and moulds his senses, nor the language he speaks, which colors his thinking, nor the way of life in which he participates and which, in turn, shapes his actions, belongs to the community of his blood; they belong instead to another community. The world of constant elements and the world of substance are, for him, rent apart. He does not see his substance unfold before him in his environment; it has been banished into deep loneliness, and is embodied for him in only one aspect: his origin.

Buber acknowledged the pointlessness of trying to discard the external cultural foundations that the Jews had interiorized, or, as he put it,

> It would be senseless, for instance, to try to shed the culture of the world about us, a culture that, in the final analysis, has been assimilated by the innermost forces of our blood, and has become an integral part of ourselves. We need to be conscious of the fact that we are a cultural admixture, in a more poignant sense than any other people. We do not, however, want to be the slaves of this admixture, but its masters. Choice means deciding what should have supremacy, what should be the dominant in us and what the dominated.[35]

In the 1920s, and particularly as the Nazi Party gained ground in Germany, Buber found himself under attack for his *völkisch* views, and was challenged to explain his statements. In the Hebrew translation he therefore declared explicitly that "a few years after these lines were penned, evil persons distorted the concept of 'blood' which I had to use here. I therefore hereby serve notice that everywhere that I have used the term 'blood,' I in no way meant the race issue, which I consider to be utterly baseless, but a people's sequence of generations and births, the backbone vital to maintaining its quiddity."[36] A retrospective examination does indeed reveal an embarrassing similarity between Buber's blood metaphor and its German-racist counterparts.[37]

By scrutinizing the intellectual inspiration of Buber's remarks to the Bar-Kochba members in 1909, however, it becomes possible to identify the unreasonable nature of the *völkisch* interpretation.[38] Buber's observations were written in a spirit and language similar—indeed, almost identical—to what had been published six years earlier by his friend Gustav Landauer, the Jewish Socialist and revolutionary. From 1895 onward, Landauer expressed rather mystic and spiritual views. The culmination of this period in his life is expressed in his book *Skepsis und Mystik,* published in 1903. The imprint of Landauer's communitarian outlook is present in Buber's writing, which used identical imagery. It was Landauer, for example, who presented lineage—descent down through the generations—as something that imprints a manifest stamp on the individual. "What is heredity if not the almost uncanny, and yet in turn so familiar and instinctively recognizable power which the world of my forefathers exercises over my body as well as my mind, an inescapable influence? . . . We are the moments of the ever-living community of our ancestors."[39] Landauer used the metaphor of blood in order to depict the generational sequence and partnership, being-part-of: in other words, the power of a person's community (*Gemeinschaft*), whose influence, as he put it, was stronger than the superficial influence of state or society. "Blood," Landauer stressed, "is thicker than water."[40]

However, Landauer's use of blood as a metaphor must not be confused with then current racist views.[41] "At a time when reactionary *völkisch* thinkers were developing a pseudoscientific biological orientation for their view of the individual's rootedness in the community or the race . . . Landauer's communitarianism was focused upon a mystic growth of consciousness which was accessible to all men, regardless of their allegedly fixed, physical characteristics," as Landauer's biographer, Eugene Lunn, notes.[42] The individual, in both Landauer's conception and in *völkisch* outlooks, was rooted in the community, but in Landauer's approach, the community's existence was utterly dependent on the communitarian consciousness which was engendered in every individual separately.

Unlike Landauer, Buber fell into the trap that is always present for minorities that are suffering from discrimination. Paul Gilroy, who in recent years has highlighted the structural ties between antisemitism and racism, and between Jewish identity and black identity, warns in his book *Between Camps* against emphasizing cultural affiliation as the ownership of property and not as a lived experience. Thus he criticizes the tendency of minorities to accept racist views of them, but at the same time to give them a positive "spin" or interpretation by turning them into cultural qualities.[43] There is no doubt that Buber's three articles on Judaism, and, perhaps even more than Buber himself, his fervent Zionist listeners in Prague provide a convincing illustration of this process.

V

The neo-romantic, essentialist, cultural approach which characterized Buber's lectures in Prague, captivating those who heard him and becoming one of the cornerstones of the process of evolving a cultural alternative to political Zionism, can also be found in other, entirely non-Jewish, contexts. Jews were not exceptional in this context, as an examination of the parallel debate in the United States—through which I will discuss cultural essentialism as a position of minorities—will show.

This leads back to Du Bois's writings. In the context of Franz Boas's discoveries about the relationship between environment and heredity we have highlighted Du Bois's sympathetic stance on materialist environmental explanations. However, at the turn of the century the latter's writing was not devoid of a pronounced African American cultural essentialist tendency. Indeed, Du Bois was accused of inconsistency because of the way in which he swung from structural explanations to romantic essentialist views.[44] Like Buber, Du Bois was greatly influenced by German idealism, especially in his views on the relationship between race, nation, and culture. Paul Gilroy argues that

Germany was the locale which shaped Du Bois's African exceptionalism. In support of this claim he cites the following passage from Du Bois's memoirs:

> I can never forget that morning in the class of the great Heinrich von Treitschke in Berlin . . . his words rushed out in the floods; "Mulattoes," he thundered, "are inferior." I almost felt his eyes boring into me, although probably he had not noticed me. "Sie fühlen sich niedriger!" "their actions show it," he asserted. What contradiction could there be to that authoritative dictum?[45]

After pursuing his doctoral studies in Berlin from 1892 to 1894 and returning to the United States, Du Bois focused his energies on delving into questions of race and the status of African Americans. At the turn of the century, influenced by Franz Boas, Du Bois embarked on African studies,[46] in which field Du Bois would work out his essentialist views. The way that Du Bois the American expresses his attitude to Africa is very similar to Buber's conception of the continuity of generations:

> As I face Africa, I ask myself: what is it between us that constitutes a tie that I can feel better than I can explain? Africa is of course my fatherland. Yet neither my father nor my father's father ever saw Africa or knew its meaning or cared overmuch for it. . . . [S]till my tie to Africa is strong. . . . [O]ne thing is sure and that is the fact that since the fifteenth century these ancestors of mine have had a common history, have suffered a common disaster, and have one long memory. . . . [T]he badge of color [is] relatively unimportant save as a badge; the real essence of this kinship is its social heritage of slavery; the discrimination and insult; and this heritage binds together not simply the children of Africa, but extends through yellow Asia and into the South Seas. It is this unity that draws me to Africa.[47]

Du Bois himself would end his life in Africa, after emigrating to Ghana at the age of 93. But at a far earlier time, in 1919, he lent his voice to those African American activists demanding that the colonies that Germany had lost in the World War be placed at the disposal of educated African Americans. In the spirit of Zionism, he espoused a state for black repatriates from the West.[48] Du Bois's stance reveals strains and internal contradictions, which in part were identical to those facing Zionists in Europe.

Du Bois considered the idea of African return to be directly related to the Zionist idea of return, commenting that as a result, while maintaining the duality of settling in Africa together with "present-day work" in the United States,

> The African movement means to us what the Zionist movement must mean to the Jews, the centralization of race effort and the recognition of

racial fount. To help bear the burden of Africa does not mean any lessening of effort in our own problem at home.[49]

Du Bois's work on the idea of return therefore moved along the axis between a neo-romantic idealistic metaphor and an operational plan, shifting from "spiritual Zionism"—longing for Eretz Israel as a spiritual center and a reference for cultural renaissance—to "practical Zionism"—in the frame of a project for colonization as a political solution for the Jewish plight. Differentiating these two areas is, however, extremely difficult. In the African sphere, too, "return" was an operational plan, but neo-romantic images certainly had their place in its framework. Return was intended to establish a bridge over the complex and fraught experience by creating harmony, or more precisely by bringing about equilibrium between their inner essence and outer reality. In this sense, return deviates from the materialistic experience when it becomes a key—abstract—component in the self-definition of "diasporas."[50]

VI

At the turn of the twentieth century, Jewish scholars studying race were required to offer solutions to what, in their day, was considered the "Jewish Question." John Efron writes of "Jewish scholars of race" that they should be seen in the postemancipatory context:

> Educated Jews, as "good" acculturated Europeans, could not but believe in the concept of race. This was especially so for Jewish scientists, most of whom were trained as doctors in Europe's finest medical schools, where they had been exposed to curricula that were inherently racist.[51]

The issue raised by Efron is a fundamental one, since it touches a raw nerve: the way in which discriminated minorities make use of science which is driven by racist outlooks to define themselves. On this point, too, there is no need whatsoever to go looking for Jewish exceptionalism. Anthony Appiah identifies an identical internal tension in his analysis of Du Bois's position on perceptions of race.[52] After pointing out that Du Bois believed that the black race had a fundamental "mission" for mankind—a mission and contribution to humanity that the black race had not yet implemented—Appiah returns to a discussion of the paradox concealed in this contention. As in feminism, Appiah argues, a dialectic is revealed here between the thesis, embodied in the attempt to curtail the importance of differences—in this context, racial differences—and even to deny their existence, and the antithesis, embodied in the recognition of the existence of differences. Appiah identifies the attempt at synthesis in the declaration of a universal mission. In order to prove his argument, he quotes Du Bois's assertion:

> What, then, is a race? It is a vast family of human beings, generally of common blood and language, always of common history, traditions and

impulses, who are both voluntarily and involuntarily striving together for the accomplishment of certain more or less vividly conceived ideals of life.[53]

Appiah uses Du Bois's reference to blood relationship as a race marker to strengthen his argument.[54] "If he has fully transcended the scientific notion, what is the role of this talk about 'blood'?" asks Appiah.[55] He offers his interpretation of this ambiguity:

We need to make clear that what Du Bois attempts, despite his own claims to the contrary, is not the transcendence of the nineteenth-century scientific conception of race . . . but rather, as a dialectic requires, a revaluation of the Negro race in the face of the sciences of racial inferiority.[56]

Efron's discussion of Jewish race scientists, like Appiah's discussion of the significance of the conception of race in Du Bois's theory, raises the fundamental question about the ability to distinguish between racism and the way minorities use race markers. This question relates to "blood relationship" as a marker of affiliation, i.e., to the tension between genealogy and racism. And indeed, as Appiah demonstrated, a minority has absolutely no other way of defining itself than by means of a genealogical marker. Here Jonathan Boyarin and Daniel Boyarin argue "that when a shared family tree is used to strengthen identity, it is not necessarily destined to function politically as a basis for racism, even though such an outlook will always be suspect of being closely related to racism and there is always the danger that indeed it will become such."[57] The two authors argue that the family tree is the sole referential marker available to the Jews as a cultural essence and it is utterly different when it marks the minority, not the majority. Or, as they put it,

Each essence, whether it is claimed or it is ascribed to the Other, has two conflicting meanings which quite simply depend on the political conditions in a given situation. For people who are part of the ruling group, any assertion of essence is in any case the product of the system in control and a factor in its replication. But for the groups which are ruled, whose members are perceived as "Others" (subaltern groups), an essentialist position is opposition, insisting on the group's very "right" to exist.[58]

The claim of the Boyarins is a moral one; however, that does not make it correct. Their search for a synthesis that will make it possible "to hold on to ethnic and cultural uniqueness, but only in the context of a deep and real human solidarity," leads them to the concept of Diaspora. "Diaspora," they argue, "supplies the model for this synthesis, and only under conditions of Diaspora is it possible at all to try such a solution."[59] However, this hoped-for synthesis is itself trapped in internal contradictions, not unlike Du Bois's understanding of ethnicity.

Neither Du Bois nor the Boyarins manage to rise beyond biological concepts in their theoretical endeavors; on the contrary, they internalize and strengthen them. Jonathan Boyarin and Daniel Boyarin argue, "For the Jews, the family tree is tantamount to the female womb. It is this which creates some sort of feeling of relationship to a concrete thing in the world, of concrete grounding in difference,"[60] it is difficult not to be amazed and astonished, to wonder at this "concrete thing." True, they make the point that, indeed, "that structure of difference which is anchored in a family tree, . . . is not 'biological-genetic difference,' but precisely that meaning of 'biological' which provides the family tie."[61] But is it not, in this form, identical to Du Bois's confusions and agonizing when he was trying to determine his genealogical bond with Africa?

> On this vast continent were born and lived a large portion of my direct ancestors going back a thousand years or more. The mark of their heritage is upon me in color and hair. These are obvious things, but of little meaning in themselves; only important as they stand for real and more subtle differences from other men. Whether they do or not, I do not know nor does science know today.[62]

To conclude, let us return to Kafka's criticism, which can therefore be interpreted in diverse directions. Apish or simian essence, the essentialist reader will be able to argue, cannot be eliminated or dismissed: it surfaces in the small hours of the morning when the ape goes back to all fours and to his simian instincts. A constructivist, on the other hand, will rightly identify the absolute irony in Kafka's description of apishness, and will focus on the charged sentence

> your life as apes, gentlemen, insofar as something of that kind lies behind you, cannot be farther removed from you than mine is from me. Yet everyone on earth feels a tickling at the heels; the small chimpanzee and the great Achilles alike.

Kafka does not dismiss the essence, but when he broadens it to apply to the whole of mankind he neutralizes the particularist barb. What remains is an empty shell, a mere husk.[63]

Notes

1. Franz Kafka, "A Report to an Academy," in *The Penal Colony: Stories and Short Pieces*, trans. Willa Muir and Edwin Muir (New York: Schocken, 1976), 173–74.
2. Patrick Bridgwater, "Reporters Ahnherren, oder: Der gelehrte Affe in der

deutschen Dichtung." *Deutsche Vierteljahresschrift für Literaturwissenschaft und Geschichte* 56, no. 3 (1982): 460.

3. Bill Ashcroft, Gareth Griffiths, and Helen Tiffin, *Key Concepts in Post-colonial Studies* (London: Routledge, 1998), 139.

4. Homi K. Bhabha, *The Location of Culture* (London: Routledge, 1994), 86.

5. Mitchell B. Hart, *Social Science and the Politics of Modern Jewish Identity* (Stanford, Calif.: Stanford University Press, 2000), 10–11. Jay Geller makes the following observations on the direct meaning of this phenomenon in Kafka's story: "The story itself, a report delivered to a scientific academy, is the ultimate mimetic act: although he is the object of the report, Red Peter is also its subject. He is reading in the guise of a race scientist." Jay Geller, "Of Mice and Mensa: Anti-Semitism and the Jewish Genius." *Centennial Review* 38, no. 2 (1994): 374.

6. Franz Kafka, "Investigations of a Dog," in *Metamorphosis and Other Stories,* trans. Willa Muir and Edwin Muir (London: Vintage, 1999), 83–126.

7. Kafka, "A Report to an Academy," 183.

8. Ibid., 176.

9. Mitchell B. Hart, "Racial Science, Social Science, and the Politics of Jewish Assimilation," *Isis* 90, no. 2 (1999): 274.

10. George L. Mosse, *Toward the Final Solution: A History of European Racism* (London: J. M. Dent and Sons, 1978), 81.

11. Robert Proctor insists that the development of eugenics as a discipline in the United States and Europe predated the establishment of the social sciences: Robert N. Proctor, "Eugenics among the Social Sciences: Hereditarian Thought in Germany and the United States," in *The Estate of Social Knowledge,* ed. JoAnne Brown and David K. van Keuren (Baltimore: John Hopkins University Press, 1991), 181.

12. *Verhandlungen des ersten deutschen Soziologentages vom 19.–22. Oktober 1910 in Frankfurt a. M.* (Tübingen: J. C. B. Mohr, 1911).

13. Ibid., 152–53. Excerpts from the altercation between Alfred Ploetz and Max Weber have been published in B. Nelson and J. Gitteman, "Max Weber, Dr. Alfred Ploetz, and W. E. B. Du Bois (Max Weber on Race and Society)," *Sociological Analysis* 34 (1973): 308–12.

14. Robert N. Proctor, *Value-Free Science? Purity and Power in Modern Knowledge* (Cambridge, Mass.: Harvard University Press, 1991), 90–92, 108–11.

15. Max Weber, "Ethnic Groups," in *New Tribalisms: The Resurgence of Race and Ethnicity,* ed. Michael W. Hughey (New York: New York University Press, 1998), 17–30.

16. Helmuth Schuster, "Theorien, Utopien und rassistische Abgründe sozialwissenschaftlicher Bevölkerungsforschung zwischen wilhelminischem Mitteleuropa-Modell und SS-Generalplan Ost," in *Rassenmythos und Sozialwissenschaften in Deutschland: Ein verdrängtes Kapitel sozialwissenschaftlicher Wirkungsgeschichte,* ed. Carsten Klingemann (Opladen: Westdeutscher Verlag, 1987), 320–25.

17. *Verhandlungen des zweiten deutschen Soziologentages vom 20.–22. Oktober 1912 in Berlin* (Tübingen: J. C. B. Mohr, 1913), 135.

18. Werner Sombart, *Die Juden und das Wirtschaftsleben* (Leipzig: Duncker und Humblot, 1911).

19. Sombart had no qualms in the same context about ascribing Oppenheimer's materialistic outlook to his Jewish origins: *Verhandlungen des zweiten deutschen Soziologentages,* 185.

20. Julia E. Liss, "German Culture and German Science in the *Bildung* of Franz Boas," in *Volksgeist as Method and Ethic: Essays on Boasian Ethnography and the German Anthropological Tradition,* ed. George W. Stocking (Madison: University of Wisconsin Press, 1996), 155–84.

21. Franz Boas, *Kultur und Rasse* (Berlin: Du Gruyter, 1914), 223–37.

22. Ibid., 230–31.

23. Ibid., 233–34.

24. Christian Geulen, "Blonde bevorzugt: Virchow und Boas; Eine Fallstudie zur Verschränkung von 'Rasse' und 'Kultur' im ideologischen Feld der Ethnizität um 1900," *Archiv für Sozialgeschichte* 40 (2000): 163ff.

25. Hart, "Racial Science," 287–88.

26. Quoted in Vernon J. Williams, Jr., "Franz Boas's Paradox and the African American Intelligentsia," in *African Americans and Jews in the Twentieth Century: Studies in Convergence and Conflict,* ed. V. P. Franklin, N. L. Grant, H. M. Kletnick, and G. R. McNeil (Columbia: University of Missouri Press, 1998), 59.

27. Ibid., 62.

28. Ibid., 74–78.

29. Benoit Massin, "From Virchow to Fischer: Physical Anthropology and 'Modern Race Theories' in Wilhelmine Germany," in Stocking, *Volksgeist as Method and Ethic,* 79–154.

30. Jehuda Reinharz, *Fatherland or Promised Land: The Dilemma of the German Jew, 1893–1914* (Ann Arbor: University of Michigan Press, 1975), 188–206.

31. Mosse, *Toward the Final Solution,* 81–82.

32. Joachim Doron, "Rassenbewusstsein und naturwissenschaftliches Denken im deutschen Zionismus während der wilhelminischen Ära," *Jahrbuch des Instituts für deutsche Geschichte* 9 (1980): 400–27.

33. Ibid., 416–19; F. A. Theilhaber, *Die Schädigung der Rasse durch soziales und wirtschaftliches Aufsteigen bewiesen an den Berliner Juden* (Berlin: Louis Lamm, 1914); A. Ruppin, *Die Juden der Gegenwart: Eine sozialwissenschaftliche Studie* (Berlin: Jüdischer Verlag, 1920); Hart, *Social Science,* 74–95; and K. Hödl, *Die Pathologisierung des jüdischen Körpers: Antisemitismus, Geschlecht und Medizin im Fin de Siècle* (Vienna: Picus Verlag, 1997), 306.

34. Martin Buber, "Judaism and the Jews," in *On Judaism,* ed. Nahum N. Glatzer (New York: Schocken, 1967), 11–21.

35. Ibid., 19.

36. Martin Buber, "Judaism and the Jews," in *Teuda ve-yi'ud,* vol. 1 (Jerusalem: Ha-sifriya Ha-tzionit, 1963), 29 (Hebrew).

37. Hans Kohn, *Living in a World Revolution: My Encounters with History* (New York: Trident, 1964), 65–68.

38. Doron, "Rassenbewusstsein," 425–26.

39. "Was ist denn die Vererbung anders als eine fast unheimliche, dann aber wieder so vertraute und innig bekannte Macht, die die Ahnenwelt auf meine Leiblichkeit wie meinen Geist ausübt, eine unentrinnbare Herrschaft? . . . Wir sind die Augenblicke der ewig lebendigen Ahnengemeinde." Gustav Landauer, *Skepsis und Mystik: Versuche im Anschluss an Mathners Sprachkritik* (Berlin: Ego Fleischel, 1903), 31–33.

40. Ibid., 38.

41. On the development of blood into a metaphor for family and nation, see Walker Connor, "Beyond Reason: The Nature of the Ethnonational Bond," in Hughey, *New Tribalisms*, 41–57. On blood as a metaphor in European nationalism, see Uli Linke, *Blood and Nation: The European Aesthetics of Race* (Philadelphia: University of Pennsylvania Press, 1999).

42. Eugene Lunn, *Prophet of Community. The Romantic Socialism of Gustav Landauer* (Berkeley: University of California Press, 1973), 166–68.

43. Paul Gilroy, *Between Camps: Nations, Cultures, and the Allure of Race* (London: Allen Lane, Penguin, 2000), 24. See also "strategic essentialism": Stuart Hall, "Cultural Identity and Diaspora," in *Colonial Discourse and Post-Colonial Theory*, ed. Patrick Williams and Laura Chrisman (London: Harvester Wheatsheaf, 1993), 392–403, 397.

44. Thomas C. Holt, "The Political Uses of Alienation: W. E. B. Du Bois on Politics, Race, and Culture, 1903–1940." *American Quarterly* 42, no. 2 (1990): 301–23.

45. Paul Gilroy, *The Black Atlantic: Modernity and Double Consciousness* (Cambridge, Mass.: Harvard University Press, 1993), 134.

46. Ibid., 113.

47. Ibid., 126.

48. Robert A. Hill, "Black Zionism: Marcus Garvey and the Jewish Question," in Franklin et al., *African Americans and Jews*, 49.

49. W. E. B. Du Bois, "Africa, Colonialism, and Zionism," in *The Oxford W. E. B. Du Bois Reader*, ed. E. J. Sundquist (New York: Oxford University Press, 1996), 639.

50. William Safran, "Diasporas in Modern Societies: Myths of Homeland and Return," *Diaspora* 1 (1991): 83–99.

51. John M. Efron, *Defenders of the Race: Jewish Doctors and Race Science in Fin-de-Siècle Europe* (New Haven, Conn.: Yale University Press, 1994), 176.

52. Anthony Appiah, "The Uncompleted Argument: Du Bois and the Illusion of Race," in *"Race," Writing, and Difference*, ed. Henry Louis Gates, Jr. (Chicago: University of Chicago Press, 1986), 23–29.

53. Ibid., 23.

54. Wilson proposes a slightly different interpretation, arguing that in Du Bois's work, "blood" is not to be understood in its materialist sense but as a transcendental outlook concerning biology, and as such as an initial attempt at a discursive theory: Kirt H. Wilson, "Toward a Discursive Theory of Racial Identity: *The Souls of Black Folk* as a Response to Nineteenth-Century Biological Determinism," *Western Journal of Communication* 63, no. 2 (1999): 194, 206.

55. Appiah, "The Uncompleted Argument," 25.

56. Ibid.

57. Daniel Boyarin and Jonathan Boyarin, "The People of Israel Has No Motherland." *Theory and Criticism* 5 (autumn 1994): 79–104, here 88 (Hebrew). For an earlier version of this paper, see: Daniel Boyarin and Jonathan Boyarin, "Diaspora: Generation and the Ground of Jewish Identity." *Critical Inquiry* 19 (summer 1993): 693–725.

58. Boyarin and Boyarin, "The People of Israel," 91.

59. Ibid., 100.

60. Ibid., 93.

61. Ibid., 85.

62. Appiah, "The Uncompleted Argument," 33.

63. Ralf R. Nicolai, "Nietzschean Thought in Kafka's 'A Report to an Academy,'" *Literary Review* 26 (1983): 551–53.

Three

Prussia at the Margins, or The World That Nationalism Lost

Helmut Walser Smith

But if I see before me
the nervature of past life
in one image, I always think
that this has something to do
with truth. . . .

—W. G. Sebald, "After Nature"

Hospitality is culture itself and not simply one ethic
amongst others.
—Jacques Derrida, "Cosmopolitanism and Forgiveness"

I

It is no secret that the eastern margins of Prussia constituted a zone of contact for diverse religious and ethnic groups. Indeed, the linguistic term "contact zone," which has reentered mainstream historical parlance in the English-speaking world through the work of Mary Pratt, had long been used by conservative historians, like Walter Hubatsch, to describe the variegated landscape of the east.[1] These two scholars used the terms differently, however. Pratt defined "contact zones" as "social spaces where disparate cultures meet, clash, and grapple with each other, often in highly asymmetrical relations of domination and subordination."[2] For Pratt, whose approach is drawn from the linguistic analysis of localized languages of communication, the hardening of borders and the tempering of identities, the root assumption of nationalist historiography, is by no means given. It is instead conceivable that what remains is what lies between.[3] For Hubatsch, however, it was evident that out of the clash of cultures nations were made, and that the point of studying the east was to analyze their formation while privileging the civilizational work of the Prusso-German nation-state. In this sense, the assumptions of the conservative German historian Walter Hubatsch ran parallel to those of the legions of Polish historians who debated his conclusions about the numbers of

German and Polish citizens, their respective allegiances, and the qualities of their objective and subjective consciousness.[4]

Both historiographies, however, left life as it really was unexamined. With the ethnic and religious visage of the people changing like the crystals of a kaleidoscope, life on the northeastern margins of Prussia was mixed. Not unity but diversity defined the margins. Yet an immense amount of scholarship focuses on groups as if they existed in isolation. One tradition considers the history of German Protestants, who are often taken, *pars pro toto*, to represent Prussians as such. Within this historiography, Polish-speaking subjects are also considered, but separately.[5] Another tradition addresses the rise of nations and nationalism—whether German, Polish, Cassubian, or Lithuanian. But because the dynamics of group solidarity are considered paramount, the possibilities of everyday interaction between peoples are underplayed, even dismissed as reflections of "dormant" national identity.[6] Still another tradition emphasizes Prussian policy and its impact on minority groups. While immensely important, such studies inevitably see the hinge of history as turning in Berlin, and the local as mainly reacting to decisions taken at the center.[7]

Consider, however, the following description of the Masures—an ethnic group of Protestant, Polish-speaking, Prussian loyalists who inhabit the lake districts of southern East Prussia. The description comes from a dissertation, submitted in 1921, in the field of economics at the University of Königsberg:

> The Masurian is characterized in the main by his Polish heritage, his German schooling, his Slavic manners and customs, his German tradition, his Polish last name and his German first name, his Polish language and his German religious writings, the German song, Slavic religiosity, and Protestant confession.[8]

Historians attempting to understand collective identity will ask if this fictional person, a vessel of outside influences, is at bottom a German, a Pole, or something unique unto itself: a Masure. If the latter, the question of the status of this appellation remains, whether Masures constituted a nationality of their own or merely a regional identity.

A small world of scholarship sees the Masures as belonging to a nation that has largely become extinct.[9] There were other such nations in the Prussian East: the Cassubians, an ethnic group stemming from the Pomeranians who spoke a Polish dialect (some argued a distinct Slavic language) but who, because of their special history and customs, resisted assimilation into the Polish nation until the late nineteenth century. The Cassubians were themselves divided into two groups, those who lived within the borders of the state of Pomerania and were Protestant, and those who lived in West Prussia west of Danzig and north of Konitz and were Catholic. In the far reaches of East Prussia, there was still another nation—the Prussian Lithuanians. Unlike their co-nationals across the Russian border, the Prussian Lithuanians were Protestant and, like the Masurians, evinced intense loyalty to the Hohenzollerns. If we step down from ethnic groups who attempted to create a nation, we also soon encounter religious groups with complicated ethnic and national understandings. In the Ermland, many Polish-speaking Catholics readily gave their allegiances to Prussia instead of to the Polish national movement. And until deep into the history of the *Kaiserreich*, in both the Ermland and the mixed areas of West Prussia, many German-speaking Catholics cast their support for Polish candidates and shared sacral space with coreligionists across the ethnic line.

These groups, I want to argue, developed a kind of cosmopolitanism. It was not the cosmopolitanism of Kant, a disembodied love of humanity based on the maxims of universal reason, but rather a more modest, limited, rooted cosmopolitanism. Particularistic and plural, this cosmopolitanism, if we may call it that, was less an arch to humanity than a series of necessary bridges to the other.[10]

It is possible to train our analysis on these bridges, and to see the stuff of history as happening in the friction-filled margins of cultural groups and at the crossings between them. As Paul Rabinow already acknowledged in the mid-eighties, we also "live in-between" and engage in activities—contesting, accommodating, translating, hosting, sharing—that establish solidarities and mark differences outside our immediate identities.[11] To approach the "in-between," the liminal, the selvage in the pattern of culture means to search not for essences, or even for invented or constructed selves, but for the commonalities and ties, however frayed, that bind.[12]

To start, nationalist teleologies must be reversed. Where we formerly assessed the social groups that contributed to the formation of nationalism, we ask, instead, who bridged emerging divisions.[13] Where we analyzed lexicographers who put together historical dictionaries establishing the rootedness of a vernacular, we also consider those who compiled bilingual dictionaries in order to translate languages, thus making communication, in the sense intended by Karl Deutsch, beyond the nation possible. And where we focused on pastors and priests who provided now German, now Polish nationalism with a sacral aura, we take into our view those members of the clergy who—for a significant stretch of the long nineteenth century—attempted to straddle two languages, and to minister to their parishes now in German, now in Polish. Sites of ethnic exclusivity—nationalist associations and governmental pressure groups—might then be seen in relation to sites of ethnic mixing: the marketplace, the tavern (often run by trilingual Jewish innkeepers), and, if less often, the wedding altar. In short, to balance a historiography that scrutinized the seam for where and how the threads have come undone, we would look more closely at those that still hold.

This way of seeing things is deeply indebted to the recent work of a remarkable group of scholars associated with the German Historical Institute in Warsaw. These scholars—especially Jörg Hackmann, Andreas Kossert, Mathias Niendorf, and Robert Traba—have put new life into what had become tired debates between Polish and German historians about the "objective" national consciousness of ethnic groups in the borderlands.[14] Drawing on this new generation of research, and on German-language primary sources, I focus on three groups on the Prussian margins whose national status remained in flux through the latter half of the nineteenth century—the Prussian Lithuanians, the Masures, and the Cassubians. For each of these groups, everyday religious piety structured relations and opened surprising possibilities for what James Clifford has called "cosmopolitan competencies—the arts of crossing, translation and hybridity."[15]

II

In standard histories of the growth of nations, the relation of religion to ethnicity is often easily reckoned. Considered in terms of the Prussian margins, it is at the outset important to note the religious affinity between Lithuanian Protestants and German Protestants, Protestant Masures and Protestant Germans, and Catholic Cassubians and Catholic Poles. Indeed, for the first two groups, religious affinities sufficed to overcome ties of language and ethnicity that ordinarily would have bound Prussian Lithuanians to their co-nationals across the Russian border, and the Masures to ethnic Poles. With respect to the Cassubians, the story is more complicated because religion and ethnicity fell together. Nevertheless, each ethnic group developed national or even regional movements very late; each was highly agrarian, economically backward, and disproportionately illiterate. In each, the clergy carried a great deal of influence.

Religious belief erected barriers between people; it is the main reason why Protestant Lithuanians did not side with their Catholic co-nationals, or Masures with Poles, or Cassubians with Germans. Yet religion also provided the bricks and mortar for surprising bridges, which we can approach when we consider piety more closely. If Prussian Lithuanians and the Masures of the lake districts were Protestant, their Protestantism was of a kind that opened each group to surprising affinities, even to Catholicism. Like the Lithuanians, the Masures demonstrated impressive outward piety. "All the benches and aisles were full up to the altar and into the last corner," a church official reported of the Masurian churches he had observed in his visitation in Ortelsburg in 1884.[16] Nevertheless, sites of Marian piety in Protestant churches and statues of saints in Masurian homes gave church officials pause.[17] So too did the propensity of Protestant Masures to visit Catholic churches, and to offer sacrifices, often in the form of presents, to the holy altar.[18] Protestant Masurians also celebrated Catholic holidays and participated in pilgrimages to holy sites. To combat the former problem, Protestant organizations arranged meetings on the same days as Catholic holidays; to put a stop to the latter, they pleaded.[19] It seems that the pleas were in vain. Protestant Masures in the 1870s and 1880s made the journey to Heiligenlinde, to Wuttrienen, and, especially unsettling, to Dietrichswalde.[20]

Dietrichswalde, in the Ermland, west of Masuria, was the Marpingen of the eastern provinces. In 1877, the Virgin Mary allegedly appeared in an acorn shell outside the local church, which had been the site of a pilgrimage associated with the crowning of the Virgin of Czestochowa in the eighteenth century. In 1877, the Virgin supposedly spoke to two young girls, ages twelve and thirteen, and the local priest vouched for their credibility. Official investigations were not so generous, however, and the apparition never received church sanction. Yet for decades after, tens of thousands of the faithful, mainly from Poland, Posen, West Prussia, and Silesia, pilgrimaged there.[21] It also became an important site of Polish nationalism. "The Virgin Mary spoke to the two school girls . . . in excellent and beautiful Polish," ran one slogan. "She is the Polish queen, who has come to her oppressed people," ran another.[22] That Protestant Masures were among the Polish pilgrims was unsettling, for religious as well as national reasons.

The bridge of Masurian Protestantism to Polish Catholicism suggests one kind of connection unthinkable in the later years of nationalized publics. Equally remarkable was the permeability of the borders, with Masures traveling into Congress Poland in the Russian Empire to visit annual fairs and weekly markets, and to trade horses and cattle, especially with the far more numerous Jews across the line.[23] As we know from Siegfried Lenz, the border was also home to a flourishing black market in smuggled goods. Finally, Masurians crossed for religious reasons, just as Protestant Poles crossed into Masuria. Close to the border itself, in areas where pastoral care was thin, Protestant churches, like the one in Narzym in the deaconry of Soldau, held pews open for parishioners who hiked in from the other direction, from Mlawka across the border, a distance of roughly six miles.[24]

From the standpoint of the leadership of the Protestant church, ethnically German even in this region, the crossings did not pose the most serious problem, however. As with the Masurians, so also with the Lithuanians, the haunting specter was that of ecstatic piety and confessional sectarianism. In Prussian Lithuania, the community movement, the *Gemeinschaftsbewegung*, took hold of a significant portion of the faithful in the 1870s and 1880s. Pietist in orientation, close to everyday life, insistent that the word of God be spoken in the local dialect, the charismatic preachers of the community movement propagated an enthusiastic, all-embracing Christianity that spilled out from the church and into the home. Prayer leaders (*Stundenhalter*) held special sessions in the homes of the pious, a devotional form not easily controlled by the church. The most famous of the reformers was Christoph Kukat, a converted nobleman quick to denounce clergymen as "pastors of Baal" and to brand them for their "antipathy to the purity of God's teaching."[25] In 1885, he founded the East Prussian Evangelical Prayer Society, which church officials feared would turn into a secessionist movement. They had good reason to worry. These pietist movements proved especially attractive to poor, under-educated Lithuanians from the countryside.

The movements also crossed into Masuria, suggesting the power of reli-gious forms to overcome boundaries of language and nationality. The bridge was trilingual, predominantly Protestant, Goldap County, where Germans, Lithuanians, and Masures lived. A Polish-speaking proselytizer simultane-ously translated Kukat's sermons, and the movement, known in Masuria as the *Gromadki* (small herd) movement, gathered force. Peasants turned lay preachers led prayer hours and revival meetings throughout the countryside, and, as one anxious clergyman put it in 1884, "cast a net with an intricately tied mesh ensnaring the whole of Masuria."[26] The preachers called for repen-tance and abstinence from alcohol, gambling, and dancing, but they also "censured in flaming, angry words the seeming or actual worldliness of the Church, its servants and members, and thus strew a rich seed of mistrust in the soul."[27] Historians estimate that more than a quarter of the Masurian population was intimately tied to the revival. Among the Masurian miners in the Ruhr, especially in and around Gelsenkirchen, these movements were more powerful still; through ritual and devotional form they bound Masurians to their East Prussian *Heimat*.[28]

Religious revival possessed this force because of its Reformation insis-tence on the importance of the vernacular, whether Lithuanian or Polish, in the communication of scripture and the experience of faith. This insistence placed the revival movements on a collision course with the Prussian ordi-nance of July 24, 1873, which required the immediate introduction of Ger-man as the language of instruction in all elementary school classes except for religious instruction at the lowest level. As many commentators have re-marked, this language decree involved a fundamental transition from a com-paratively tolerant language policy toward more aggressive Germanization.[29] In conjunction with the battery of *Kulturkampf* laws handed down in the same year, this decree also shifted the terrain of nationality conflicts from the secular to the religious. This change was most evident in the case of Polish resistance, which henceforth centered on the nationalist activity of the Catho-lic clergy. Likewise in the countryside and in enclosed language areas of Prus-sian Lithuania and Masuria, potentially sectarian revival movements insisted on the importance of communicating the word of God in the mother tongue.

The Protestant Church understood this well enough. "The religious sphere," an official wrote of his visitation to Heydekrug in 1885, "is the last bit of ethnicity, to which the Lithuanians cling with almost desperate af-fection."[30] It is true that the Lithuanians never resisted with the political decisiveness of the Catholic Poles. In 1881, the deaconries of Memel and Heydekrug submitted petitions to the *Kultusministerium* complaining that "the children did not sufficiently understand German in order to follow religious instruction and that Germanization should not be carried out at the expense of the education of morals."[31] No action followed, and instead the mistrust of pastors perceived as Germanizing became increasingly palpable. As late as 1911, visitation reports from the Memel complained that Germanization occurred more in form than in substance, and that "in religious activity they [the Lithuanians] held on to their mother tongue and ethnic customs."[32] Meanwhile, however, the Protestant church of East Prussia had itself undergone a transformation from an initial position of toleration, even cultivation, of Lithuanian as the language for imparting scripture, to a middle position that saw slow Germanization as an inevitability for cultural progress in Prussian Lithuania. Starting in the 1890s, the church adopted a more aggressive stance: German whenever possible, Lithuanian when absolutely necessary. Christian Braun, the East Prussia superintendent from 1894 to 1912, embodied this transformation. Unlike his predecessors, he felt only the faintest sympathy for Lithuanian piety.

> They go to church diligently; they kneel to pray; they like to sing often and loud; they regularly approach the table of the Lord two to four times; but with few commendable exceptions that is all. After they have happily heard unbearably long sermons, preferably for the whole day, wailed and moaned as they repented, it is often the case that they intoxicate themselves [and] everywhere lie, steal, carry on, and the young engage in promiscuous behavior.

A model of German Protestant piety this was not, and Braun, whose disdain for the community movement was especially pronounced, urged Germanization.[33]

The process was very similar in Masuria, where the *Gromadki* movement became the center of a concerted effort to resist the encroachment of *Kulturkampf* language decrees, and the wellspring for the cultivation of a specifically Masurian identity—defined in religious terms. In some cases the protests led to threats to leave the state church. But if the *Gromadki* movement resisted the Germanizing impulse of East Prussian Protestantism, it was not a profession of allegiance to Poland.[34] Rather, it was a plea for a space in between.

This is the space that was, eventually, lost, though the loss did not become irreversible until after World War I, when plebiscites forced Prussian Lithuanians and Masures to decide between national cultures. As is well known, they opted for Prussia and Germany. But a space had existed, for a very long time, in which religion and language were sites of complex allegiances. In the course of the nineteenth century, this space, like fields before the bulldozers of suburban developers, certainly diminished.[35] Yet there was "a there there." It consisted of a place where churches were consecrated in two languages, where Sunday services were held now in German, now in Polish or Lithuanian, and where local languages were highly syncretic. Understanding thus became a matter of contact and of negotiation between languages.

Intellectuals not yet swept up in the new of the national shaped this space. They compiled Prussian dictionaries to capture the language "in between" and devoted themselves to understanding those across cultural borders. In 1870, Max Toeppen, a German historian of Prussia and a Gymnasium rector, penned a sympathetic account of the peculiarities of Masurian life. Caught between Germans and Poles, Masuria represented for Toeppen a place of "contradiction and reconciliation between the two nationalities."[36] Among the greatest collectors of Lithuanian folklore and defenders of the special language of Prussian Lithuanian was a German Gymnasium teacher from Tilsit named Eduard Gisevius. There were also less bright lights among the intellectuals, distant descendents of Herder, who bridged cultures; some translated religious writings, others wrote in local newspapers.[37]

The ability to build bridges and cross them was not unique to intellectuals, however. Prussian Lithuania in the second half of the nineteenth century was a bilingual zone, to a modest extent for the Germans, in still greater measure for Lithuanians, especially those in the villages. They had the ability to "change codes," as the historian Manfred Klein has put it, and "they made copious use of this ability."[38] Nowhere was this more evident than in the Masurian districts of the Ruhr, where by the turn of the century more than a third of all Masurians lived. Here, despite the active Germanization efforts of the Protestant church of Westphalia, Masures held fast to their mother tongue, kept their distance from Polish nationalists when they could, and insisted over and against their Westphalian detractors that they, the Masures, "were actually the older Prussians."[39]

III

The trajectory of the Cassubians reveals remarkable parallels with the Prussian Lithuanians and the Masures, and an important difference, namely confession, that proved decisive. Like the Lithuanians and the Masures, the Cassubians were loyal subjects of the Hohenzollern dynasty until deep into the nineteenth century and, as such, impervious to Polish national aspirations. They also constituted an extremely rural population, distinguished by their relative isolation and ill-starred for their superstitious ways. As late as 1787 and again in 1837, local witch hunts aroused the concern of Prussian officials, especially when, in the latter case, the woman accused was killed in a so-called *Hexenschwemmung*, a trial to see if the alleged witch could swim when tied up and weighted with stones.[40] Cassubians' proximity to their natural environment constituted one part of an identity strongly based on local manners and customs. But Cassubian was also a language, very close to Polish, which had become a religious language with the potential to be a literary language as well. By the time the first attempts were made to elevate Cassubian to a language of the pen, however, most Protestant Masures in eastern Pomerania had already been Germanized, with only a few parishes still holding services in the local language. For a significant period, stretching from the late eighteenth century to the mid-nineteenth century, Protestant Cassubia had been a bilingual space. In the early 1860s, the Russian Slavophile Alexander Hilferding portrayed this world and its disappearance. On a Sunday morning in the parish of Glowitz, near the banks of the Lebasee, he observed,

> The minister at first read the liturgy, then he gave a sermon in Polish. There seemed to be many churchgoers gathered but they were mainly older people, who had mostly come from nearby fishing villages. I hardly saw any children and young people. These carried on in their Sunday best in front of the church and waited until the end of the "Wendisch" service. If a woman in a traditional Cassubian costume walked by, they looked at her with disdainful curiosity. When they heard the last song of the Slavic service, a large number of polished young womenfolk, girls and boys pushed into the church and hurried to occupy the pews, which were slowly being vacated by the Cassubians, the remnants of a dying lineage.[41]

This world ended—to quote the quickly spoken final lines of Eliot's "Hollow Men"—with a whimper. In 1832, small riots occurred in Schmolsin in eastern Pomerania following the abolishment of Cassubian services.[42] In Stolp County, a German pastor had learned the Polish dialect in order to minister to his elderly parishioners. In 1886, he delivered the last Protestant service in Cassubian.[43]

In the Catholic parts of Cassubia, nationalization occurred in the opposite direction, as Cassubians identified more and more with their Polish coreligionists. In its outlines, though not its social historical details, this story is well known. In the 1860s, Cassubia was a bilingual region in which Germans, Cassubians, Poles, and Jews could make themselves understood across linguistic borders. According to an 1863 "statistical portrait" of Berent County, which was located in the heart of Cassubia, "in many families German and Polish is spoken at the same time." This was true for all groups, though the Cassubian population "was already drifting . . . completely into Polish."[44] The similarity of language between Cassubian and Polish naturally proved a powerful magnet. Yet, as we know from the Masures, an affinity did not necessarily entail identification. In Cassubia, which belonged to the bishopric of Culm, specific religious developments also played an important role. Under

Bishop von der Marwitz, who held the episcopal office for nearly three decades from 1856 to 1884, the Catholic clergy became almost exclusively Polish in origin and nationalist in sentiment, even though roughly one-third of the parishioners were German.[45] The local priest, moreover, held a position of special authority because, like the Lithuanians and Masures, the Cassubians remained rural, disproportionately illiterate, and pious. "The people are deeply religious, or, to put it better, pious [*kirchlich*]," the folklorist Ernst Seefried-Gulgowski wrote at the opening of the twentieth century. "Especially those from the most remote villages attend church most diligently."[46] This piety existed in a settlement context significantly different from that in Prussian Lithuania, where Lithuanians shared churches with German Protestants, or in Masuria, which was an ethnically enclosed area. In Cassubia, a proverb held that "what is Catholic is Cassubian, what is Protestant is German." Rural villages were not mixed, and Germans (and Jews) were associated with town and city.[47] Religious difference thus reinforced tensions between town and country. Finally, social and economic differences supported, like flying buttresses, the thick walls that already separated Cassubians from their German neighbors. These differences were considerable. In the 1890s in West Prussia, which was ethnically divided in roughly equal measure between Germans and Poles, more than ten times as many Germans as Poles could be counted in an income tax bracket of over 3000 marks per annum, and Poles were economically better off than Cassubians.[48]

This is the context in which *Kulturkampf* legislation occurred—it was designed to undermine the power of the clergy, essential to village life, and religious language, the lifeline of local culture. For Cassubians, it struck at the heart of what mattered. For all the obstacles stacked against common ties with Germans, Cassubians had yet to fully cast their identity in one direction, not the least because of Cassubian loyalty to a Prussian state whose legacy was, if not a land of bounty, at least not one of grinding poverty. Historians generally agree that the *Kulturkampf* marked the turning point in the story of Cassubian identification with the lot of the Polish nation.[49] Internal memoranda echoed what seemed like a permanent break. In 1896, the governor of West Prussia no longer felt sanguine about the possibility of rolling back the identification of Cassubians with Polish aspirations; rather, he worried about keeping German Catholics, another important bridge group, from becoming Polonized.[50]

Cassubian nationality evaporated like standing water in the sun—though not completely. Just as the Romantics valorized the primitive forest as it disappeared, intellectuals, non-Cassubians and Cassubians alike, now attempted to distill a Cassubian identity on the basis not of religion, but of language and custom. Friedrich Lorentz, a linguist and ethnologist from Mecklenburg and a member of the Russian Academy of Sciences, penned a number of works on Cassubian language, history, and civilization, and helped found, in 1907, an

Association for Cassubian Folklore that published its proceedings in German. He also wrote a Pomeranian and a Slovinzian dictionary as well as a history of Cassubia.[51] He declared Cassubian civilization a culture Slavic at its core, and his researches, still today the starting point for understanding this lost world, reminded Bronislaw Malinowski, the celebrated Polish anthropologist who wrote a preface to the English edition of Lorentz's work, "of the objective spirit of German science as we knew it of old."[52] On the Polish side, Stefan Ramult also compiled a Cassubian dictionary and worked out statistics on the development of Cassubian ethnicity. These works, in turn, inspired "the young Cassubian movement," whose members dedicated themselves to the cultivation of Cassubian literature and culture.[53] In their political aspirations, however, the Cassubians had squarely sided with the Polish nation.

IV

In a brilliant work on the small peoples of the Siberian taiga and tundra entitled *Arctic Mirrors*, Yuri Slezkine has shown how the Russian perception of the small nations on the extreme periphery reflected the aspirations and anxieties of the dominant nationality at the center.[54] This seems evident for our case as well. Anguished reports on border crossings, religious syncretism, and ecstatic religiosity similarly suggest a dominant nationality that drew the lines of ethnic community with increasing exactitude, and worried whether its Protestant center could hold. Yet Slezkine also underscores the hard materiality of the peoples of the north, and one should follow him on this point as well. For there was something genuinely surprising about life on the periphery of Prussia, where cultural systems were not mutually reinforcing in the way that German historians are used to, and the Mondrian lines of milieu theory seem out of place.[55] Instead, mutual penetration and bric-a-brac worldviews made up the everyday material of history, as necessity forced people to create common languages, shareable imaginative worlds, however particular and provisional.

Of course, it cannot be gainsaid that at the turn of the century, nationalism proved the more powerful force. The Prussian East was a historical landscape caught between what must have seemed like inexorable glaciers, powerful cultural-national pressures—German, Polish, to some extent Russian—pressing down and smoothing whatever lay in their path. These glaciers also determined the subsequent history of the region, shaped like few other areas in Europe by cataclysmic events of the twentieth century, including two world wars and massive population redistribution. In this sense, discerning the peculiar ties of small, largely extinct peoples must surely seem as quixotic as E. P. Thompson's rescuing "the deluded follower of Joanna Southcott ... from the enormous condescension of posterity" now, perhaps, appears to us.[56] Historians are poor social reformers, and considering history's alternatives does not necessarily halt its forward march. Yet if, as Greg Dening reminds us, considering such ties is little more than "a sentence in a conversation about ourselves," it surely sharpens our sense for the world that the nationalism of modern states covered over.[57] It also allows us to consider, as the counter-narrative to the rise of modern nation-states (a story still unfolding), the decline in human diversity.

Notes

For critical comments on this paper I am indebted to Geoff Eley (Michigan), Atina Grossmann (New York), Oded Heilbronner (Jerusalem), Andreas Kossert (Warsaw), Nicholas Stargardt (Oxford), Till van Rahden (Cologne) and Yfaat Weiss (Haifa).

1. Walter Hubatsch, *Masuren und Preußisch-Litthauen in der Nationalitätenpolitik Preußens, 1870–1920* (Marburg: Elwert, 1966), 8. See also, in this context, Werner Conze, *Hirschenhof: Die Geschichte einer deutschen Sprachinsel in Livland,* 2nd ed. (Hanover: Hirschheydt, 1963).

2. Mary Louise Pratt, *Imperial Eyes: Travel Writing and Transculturation* (London: Routledge, 1992), 4.

3. For a fuller account of this way of looking at regional history, with further notes, see Helmut Walser Smith, "Lokalgeschichte: Überlegungen zu Möglichkeiten und Grenzen eines Genre," in *Sachsen in Deutschland,* ed. James Retallack (Bielefeld: Verlag für Regionalgeschichte, 2000), 239–52.

4. On this problem, see the comprehensive and excellent work of Jörg Hackmann, *Ostpreussen und Westpreussen in deutscher und polnischer Sicht* (Wiesbaden: Harrassowitz, 1996).

5. For a good place to start, see Ernst Opgenoorth, ed., *Handbuch der Geschichte Ost-und Westpreußens, Teil III: Von der Reformzeit bis zum Vertrag von Versailles, 1807–1918* (Lüneberg: Institut Nordostdt, Kulturwerk, 1998).

6. See, for example, Lech Trzeciakowski, *The Kulturkampf in Prussian Poland,* trans. Katarzyna Kretkowska (New York: Columbia University Press, 1990).

7. An important work in this genre, though it is mainly about Posen, is William W. Hagen, *Germans, Poles, and Jews: The Nationality Conflict in the Prussian East, 1772–1914* (Chicago: University of Chicago Press, 1980). For a dated but still helpful review, see Geoff Eley, "German Politics and Polish Nationality: The Dialectics of Nation Forming in the East of Prussia," in *From Unification to Nazism: Reinterpreting the German Past* (Boston: G. Allen and Unwin, 1986), 200–28.

8. Quoted in Andreas Kossert, *Masuren: Ostpreußens vergessener Süden* (Berlin: Siedler, 2001), 202. See also his illuminating dissertation: Andreas Kossert, *Preußen, Deutsche oder Polen? Die Masuren im Spannungsfeld des ethnischen Nationalismus, 1870–1956* (Wiesbaden: Harrassowitz, 2001). Both of these works place research on the Masures onto an altogether higher analytical plane. See also Richard Blanke, *Polish-Speaking Germans? Language and National Identity among the Masurians since 1871* (Cologne: Böhlau, 2001), which emphasizes the political dimension of the story and the largely successful assimilation of the Masures into a German identity.

9. Kossert, *Masuren.*

10. Pheng Cheah and Bruce Robbins, eds., *Cosmopolitics: Thinking and Feeling be-*

yond the Nation (Minneapolis: University of Minnesota Press, 1998), especially the introduction by Bruce Robbins, 1–19. See also the conclusion to Lutz Niethammer, *Kollektive Identität: Heimliche Quellen einer unheimliche Konjunktur* (Reinbek bei Hamburg: Rowohlt, 2000).

11. Paul Rabinow, "Representations Are Social Facts: Modernity and Post-modernity in Anthropology," in *Writing Culture: The Poetics and Politics of Ethnography*, ed. James Clifford and George E. Marcus (Berkeley: University of California Press, 1986), 258; James Clifford, "Mixed Feelings," in Cheah and Robbins, *Cosmopolitics*, 362–69; and Sherry B. Ortner, ed. *The Fate of "Culture": Geertz and Beyond* (Berkeley: University of California Press, 1999).

12. We might think of this as a "trans-cultural" *Beziehungsgeschichte* in miniature. For an important programmatic statement, see Jürgen Osterhammel, *Geschichtswissenschaft jenseits des Nationalstaates* (Göttingen: Vandenhoeck und Ruprecht, 2001), 1–72, specifically 69–70. See, further, Sebastian Conrad, "Doppelte Marginalisierung: Plädoyer für eine transnationale Perspektive auf die deutsche Geschichte," *Geschichte und Gesellschaft* 28, no. 1 (2002): 145–69; and Christoph Conrad, ed., "Mental Maps," thematic issue of *Geschichte und Gesellschaft* 28, no. 3 (2002).

13. As even Miroslav Hroch, the nestor of a socially grounded approach to the study of nationalism, has recently admitted, "So far little work has been done on those intellectuals who, by reason of their education and ethnicity, could have participated in the national movement, but did not do so." Miroslav Hroch, "From National Movement to the Fully Formed Nation: The Nation-Building Process in Europe," in *Becoming National: A Reader*, ed. Geoff Eley and Ronald Grigor Suny (New York: Oxford University Press, 1996), 69.

14. See, in addition to the works of Kossert and Hackmann cited above: Mathias Niendorf, *Minderheiten an der Grenze: Deutsche und Polen in den Kreisen Flatow (Zlotów) und Zempelburg (Süepólno Krajenskie), 1900–1939* (Wiesbaden: Harrassowitz, 1997); and Robert Traba, ed., *Selbstbewußtsein und Modernisierung: Sozialkultureller Wandel in Preußisch-Litauen vor und nach dem Ersten Weltkrieg* (Osnabrück: Fibre, 2000).

15. Clifford, "Mixed Feelings," 368.

16. *Die evangelischen General-Kirchen- und Schulenvisitationen in Ost- und Westpreußen, 1853 bis 1944*, ed. Walther Hubatsch and Iselin Gundermann (Göttingen: Vandenhoeck und Ruprecht, 1970), 92.

17. Kossert, *Preußen, Deutsche oder Polen*, 31.

18. *Die evangelischen General-Kirchen- und Schulenvisitationen*, 52 (visitation to Ortelsburg, 1855). See also Walter Hubatsch, *Geschichte der Evangelischen Kirche Ostpreussens*, vol. 1 (Göttingen: Vandenhoeck und Ruprecht, 1968), 412.

19. Hubatsch, *Geschichte der evangelischen Kirche Ostpreussens*, 413.

20. Kossert, *Preußen, Deutsche oder Polen?*, 31. On Marpingen, see David Blackbourn, *Marpingen: Apparitions of the Virgin Mary in a Nineteenth-Century German Village* (New York: Vintage, 1994).

21. PAAA Bonn, R4083 Reg. Assessor Eilsberg, Oberpräsidium Königsberg, May 1902, "Die polnische Frage in der Provinz Ostpreußen."

22. Ibid.

23. Ibid.

24. Kossert, *Masuren*, 113, 127.

25. Christoph Ribbat, *Religiöse Erregung: Protestantische Schwärmer im Kaiserreich*

82

(Frankfurt am Main: Campus, 1996), 85, 89. See also Arthur Hermann, "Preußisch-Litauer und die Evangelische Kirche ostpreußens, 1871–1933," in Traba, *Selbstbewusstsein und Modernisierung,* 103.

26. *Die evangelischen General-Kirchen- und Schulvisitationen,* 93.

27. Ibid.

28. Kossert, *Masuren,* 214–20.

29. Trzeciakowski, *The Kulturkampf,* 125–27; Marjorie Lamberti, *State, Society, and the Elementary School in Imperial Germany* (New York: Oxford University Press, 1989); and Hermann, "Preußisch-Litauer und die Evangelische Kirche Ostpreußens," 90.

30. *Die evangelischen General-Kirchen- und Schulvisitationen,* 140–41.

31. Quoted in Hermann, "Preußisch-Litauer und die Evangelische Kirche Ostpreußens," 92.

32. *Die evangelischen General-Kirchen- und Schulvisitationen,* 787.

33. Hermann, "Preußisch-Litauer und die Evangelische Kirche Ostpreußens," 97–98, whose argument I follow very closely.

34. Kossert, *Preußen, Deutsche oder Polen?,* 82–83.

35. Robert Traba, "Einführung in die Problematik: Vereinsleben und Modernisierung als identitätsstiftende Faktoren in den ethnisch gemischten Gebieten von Preußisch-Litauen," in *Selbstbewußtsein und Modernisierung,* 12.

36. Quoted in Hackmann, *Ostpreußen und Westpreußen in deutscher und polnischer Sicht,* 113. See also Kossert, *Preußen, Deutsche oder Polen?,* 107.

37. Hubatsch, *Geschichte der evangelischen Kirche Ostpreussens,* 413.

38. Manfred Klein, "'Laß uns mal deutsch kalbecken, Margellchen!' Wirkungen des Sprachkontaktes in Preußisch-Litauen," in *Nationale Minderheiten und staatliche Minderheitenpolitik in Deutschland im 19. Jahrhundert,* ed. Hans Henning Hahn and Peter Kunze (Berlin: Akademie-Verlag, 1999), 199.

39. LHAK 403, 7048, 55–72. Bericht über die von dem [Oberkonsistorialrat Pelka] unterzeichneten nach Westfalen behufs einer Visitation der dortigen Masuren und der an denselben arbeitenden Vikare ausgeführte Dienstreise, November 30, 1898.

40. F. W. F. Schmitt, "Land und Leute von/in Westpreußen," *Zeitschrift für Preußische Geschichte und Landeskunde* 7 (1870): 22b.

41. Alexander Hilferding, "Die Ueberreste der Slaven auf der Südküste des baltischen Meeres," *Zeitschrift für slavische Literatur, Kunst und Wissenschaft* 1 (1862): 81–97, 230–239; and 2 (1864): 81–111.

42. Kazimierez Slaski, "Volkstumwandel in Pommern vom 12. bis zum 20. Jahrhundert," in *Beiträge zur Geschichte Pommerns und Pommerellens,* ed. Hans Georg Kirchhoff (Dortmund: Forschungsstelle Ostmitteleuropa, 1987), 107.

43. Ibid.

44. *Statistische Darstellung des Berenter Kreises im Regierungsbezirk Danzig . . .* (Berent, 1863).

45. *Akten zur preussichen Kirchenpolitik in den Bistümern Gnesen-Posen, Kulm und Ermland, 1885–1914,* ed. Erwin Gatz, vol. 75.

46. Ernst Seefried-Gulgowski, *Von einem unbekannten Volke in Deutschland* (Berlin: Deutsche Landbuchhandlung, 1911), 208–209.

47. Schmitt, "Land und Leute von/in Westpreußen," 22b.

48. PAAA Bonn R4063 Ober-Präsident der provinz Westpreußen, September 15, 1896.

49. Leszek Belzyt, *Sprachliche Minderheiten im preußischen Staat, 1815–1914* (Marburg: Herder-Institut, 1998), 22. For a fairly recent account of the literature on Cassubians, see Friedemann Kluge, "Ein Vielfach verändertes Kaschubenbild: Neuere polnische Forschungen zur Kaschubei und ihren Bewohnern," *Zeitschrift für Ostforschung* 43 (1994): 71–81.

50. On German Catholics in the eastern borderlands, see Helmut Walser Smith, *German Nationalism and Religious Conflict: Culture, Ideology, Politics, 1870–1914* (Princeton, N.J.: Princeton University Press, 1995), 185–90.

51. Friedrich Lorentz, *Slovinzisches Wörterbuch* (St. Petersburg, 1908–12); Friedrich Lorentz, *Gramatyka pomorska*, 4 vols. (Poznan, 1927–34); Friedrich Lorentz, *Geschichte der Kaschuben* (Berlin, 1926).

52. Bronislaw Malinowski, preface to *The Cassubian Civilization*, by Friedrich Lorentz, Adam Fischer, and Tadeusz Lehr-Splawinski (London: Faber, 1934), xii.

53. Josef Borzyszkowski, "Die Kaschuben," in Hahn and Kunze, *Nationale Minderheiten*, 97.

54. Yuri Slezkine, *Arctic Mirrors: Russia and the Small Peoples of the North* (Ithaca, N.Y.: Cornell University Press, 1994).

55. On the limited utility of milieu theory in religiously and ethnically complex areas of Germany, see Helmut Walser Smith and Chris Clark, "The Fate of Nathan," in *Protestants, Catholics, and Jews in Germany, 1800–1914*, ed. Helmut Walser Smith (Oxford: Berg, 2001), 3–32.

56. E. P. Thompson, *The Making of the English Working Class* (New York: Vintage, 1963), 12.

57. Greg Dening, *Islands and Beaches: Discourse on a Silent Land; Marquesas, 1774–1880* (Chicago: Dorsey, 1980), 6.

Four

Völkisch-Nationalism and Universalism on the Margins of the Reich

A Comparison of Majority and Minority Liberalism in Germany, 1898–1933

Eric Kurlander

I

The failure of liberalism in Germany is one of the central questions in Modern European history, and rightfully so, since the rise of Hitler and National Socialism is both a cause and a consequence of German liberal decline. Nevertheless, while most historians have touched on liberal disintegration as a primary leitmotif in modern German history, much of this work has been devoted to assessing the relative strengths and weaknesses of the German bourgeoisie. Were the German middle classes "feudalized" by a Junker-dominated administration, or did the German bourgeoisie choose to exercise its growing influence through more subtle forms of commercial and associational life (*Vereinswesen*)? Did the German *Bürgertum* slavishly emulate the social and cultural practices of a "social imperialist" aristocracy, or had middle-class morals displaced and subordinated those of the nobility by the end of the Victorian Age? In short, did Germany follow a "special path" from the Holy Roman Empire to the Third Reich because of the unusual timidity of its middle classes? Or would bourgeois liberalism have succeeded in Germany, if only the Versailles Treaty, hyperinflation, and the Great Depression had not impeded its progress?

In recent years, however, this *Sonderweg* debate has lost its luster. At the dawn of a new century, few historians would condemn the German middle classes for endorsing gradualist reform over a wearying succession of Gallic revolutions. Nor do most scholars deem German liberals peculiar for failing to construct a stable, parliamentary democracy along British lines. Before the First World War, after all, Great Britain was more the exception than the rule.[1] To the contrary, in order to explain the failure of German liberal democracy historians now cite the momentous political and cultural transformations produced by modern capitalism, what Detlev Peukert has called "the crisis of classical modernity."[2] After a quarter century of social and economic dislocation, amplified by a lost war, a devastating peace treaty, and the Great Depression, is it any wonder that Germany's liberal middle classes turned to National Socialism?

While more compelling than the *Sonderweg* in many respects, however, this revisionist narrative leaves one vital question unanswered. If the German bourgeoisie were just as dynamic as the French and as modern as the British—and there is plenty of evidence to support both assertions—then why did the vast majority of progressive, middle-class Germans defect to Adolf Hitler's NSDAP, a party which not only rejected the liberal tenets of free trade, individual rights, and parliamentary democracy, but likewise endorsed a *völkisch* utopia that excluded hundreds of thousands of German citizens on decidedly racist grounds? Was this rapid, wholesale abandonment of universalist liberalism the result of war and social crisis alone? Or, to put it another way, were British Liberals and French Radical Socialists only a Versailles Treaty away from embracing *völkisch* authoritarianism themselves?

Probably not, as I endeavor to argue in this paper. Whatever the historical success or failure of German liberals before the First World War, the vast majority were ethnic (*völkisch*) nationalists. Many were openly hostile to universalist conceptions of German national identity as well. Only the two marginal political cultures under investigation, the Danish and the Alsatian, nurtured a devoutly universalist worldview. By illustrating the discrepancies between universalist minority and *völkisch* majority liberalism, we might better understand not only the fate of political liberalism in Germany, but also the complexity and contingency of liberal values across Modern Europe.

II

Ethnically German but dynastically Danish, the duchies of Schleswig and Holstein first sought their independence in the unsuccessful German revolution of 1848.[3] Prussia's subsequent victories over Denmark (1864), Austria (1866), and France (1870) in the wars of unification, however, made Schleswig-Holstein's incorporation into the Second German Empire a fait accompli. While native Danish speakers constituted a small minority of fewer than one hundred thousand in a massive German Reich of fifty million, their very presence initiated a half century of political prodding and cultural persecution by Reich authorities, hypersensitive to the persistence of any "alien" presence in the new Empire. The First World War changed the stakes entirely. Articles 119–24 of the Versailles Peace Treaty guaranteed the Danish inhabitants of North Schleswig two plebiscites, one for each zone of North Schleswig. While 80 percent of the southern zone opted for Germany, in 1920 more than 75 percent of the northern zone voted to join Denmark. With nearly forty thousand Germans and hundreds of square miles of territory now ceded to Denmark, liberal efforts to preserve the German character (*Volkstum*) of Schleswig-Holstein became even more intense.[4]

III

Before the First World War, however, preserving German ethnicity in North Schleswig was perfectly compatible with permitting Danish cultural autonomy, provided that one accepted the *völkisch* liberal creed.[5] Schleswig-Holstein's premier liberal party, for example, the Progressive People's Party (*Fortschrittliche Volkspartei* or FVP), achieved extensive popularity in the region before 1914 by promising both free-market reforms *and* the preservation of a racially superior North German ethnicity (*Volkstum*); that is, in contrast to conservative, protectionist, "half-Slavicized" Prussia.[6] By emphasizing their mutual ties to Nordic blood and soil, German liberals found ample moral justification for preserving the rights of their Danish cousins. "East Germanic" Prussian nationalists, regional liberals argued, simply did not understand that Danes *should* determine their own cultural and linguistic policies precisely because they were an indispensable, kindred element of the North Germanic *Volksgemeinschaft* (racial community).[7] While this liberal endorsement of Danish cultural autonomy was compatible with universalist tenets, important political and cultural contradictions persisted within the *völkisch* rhetoric of tolerance. Racialist (*völkisch*) liberals registered altogether different attitudes regarding non-Germanic minorities, namely Poles. In nationality conflicts, wrote one left liberal (*Freisinnige Vereinigung*, Radical Union), there existed a "justification, indeed the duty . . . to remedy sickly limbs, or even to permit amputations of abnormal growths." Poles and Jews were just such "abnormal growths," ethnic tumors that required "amputation" from the racial body politic.[8] According to another Schleswig-Holstein liberal, the Danes were "Germans, like us, a well bred and capable nation . . . even if they overtake us, it is our own blood." As an "honorable nationality" the Danes could "choose their own way" until such time as they joined their German brethren, out of respect for the "overwhelming greatness" of Germany's "nation" and "culture." The Poles, however, were "depraved, intellectually and bodily inferior," warranting for many liberals the government's increasingly paternalistic and repressive "assimilation" policy.[9]

Some Progressives, to be sure, criticized those liberals who were willing to "sacrifice all liberal principles . . . in disdain of the universal applicability of the idea of nationality, viewing any oppression of other nationalities within or without the state borders as a patriotic deed and thereby expressing a fundamentally erroneous conception of patriotism."[10] But many liberals invoked liberal principles in defense of Germanization policy, arguing that Germanization would promote "egalitarian tendencies peculiar not only to liberalism, but to the essence of our entire state."[11] Those liberals who did support Danish cultural autonomy were motivated largely by *völkisch* precepts.[12] Tolerant of the racially superior Danes, but antagonistic toward Poles and Jews, this racist version of "multiculturalism" clearly lacked the universal applicability of classical liberalism. In this regard, *völkisch* liberalism contrasts starkly with the universalist position of Danish liberals in the *Nordmark*.

IV

The cultural and linguistic gulf between Danish and German Schleswig-Holsteiners was not terribly vast. A great number of ethnic Germans spoke or understood Danish, and many Danes spoke German fluently. Even staunch *völkisch* liberals like Otto Scheel were descended from Danish stock, while the surnames of Danish leaders often indicated multiple German ancestors. As one *völkisch* liberal explained, given the ethnic similarities between Schleswig-Holsteiners and Danes, a Danish speaker who "thought German" was better than a German speaker who "thought Danish."[13] But close ethnic brotherhood did not breed political fraternity, if for no other reason than the Danish liberals' profound political antipathy to *völkisch* ideologies. Though a small minority did promote outright Danish separatism—and often with good reason—virtually all Danish liberals, by far the strongest party in North Schleswig, challenged the racial assumptions of their German counterparts. Led by the left liberal H. P. Hanssen, the Danish Party (DP) believed that Danes and Germans could coexist only so long as Danish rights were respected alongside those of *all* Reich minorities. Thus inclined toward a "universalist" solution to the North Schleswig question, the Danish Party allied with Socialist, Polish, and Alsatian factions in the Reichstag in the interest of creating a liberal-democratic state with a well-defined bill of rights. Indeed, Hanssen always protested that the Danes were loyal citizens. He even sometimes called himself a German, depending on the audience. But he likewise explained that Danes could never abide a German government that fostered ethnic homogeneity over universalist principles.[14]

The North Schleswig Danes were consequently appalled by the *völkisch* tenor of German liberal politics after the outbreak of the First World War and the subsequent rise in annexationist demands on Belgium, Holland, Poland, and the Baltic states. Having once supported the colonial designs of the German liberal majority in order to secure Reichstag support for Danish rights, Hanssen drew the line at territorial aggrandizement. Sensitive to the increase in racial and religious intolerance in the wake of war, Hanssen noted how profoundly German liberals had imbibed the *völkisch*-nationalist sentiments of this period, recounting his dismay when the putative left liberal Kopsch (FVP) shouted antisemitic remarks to discredit a Socialist opponent.[15] In response to this burgeoning xenophobia and annexationist euphoria, Hanssen backed away from his prewar assimilationism, declaring that "We are Danes; we want to remain Danes and we demand to be treated as Danes."[16] While still asserting his support for the German troops, the lone Danish representative continued voting with the pacifist Socialists, Poles, Czechs, and Alsatians on most issues.[17]

Not surprisingly, Hanssen's universalist intransigence did little to improve the prospects of Danish cultural autonomy in the Nordmark. Even those *völkisch* liberals who once acknowledged the Danish right to self-determination insisted that all Germanic races, regardless of nationality, must fight side by side against the "Slavic and Roman peoples." When the Danes defied this covenant of race in the Reichstag they were threatened with figurative banishment from "Odin's tribe" and literal expulsion from North Schleswig. Having taken different positions on the "Danish Question" before the war, both the National Liberal Karl Strackerjan and the left liberal Johannes Tiedje now excoriated Hanssen and the Danish Party for committing "racial miscegenation" (*Rassenschande*) in allying with the "Slavic races."[18] Invoking the Danes' own Nordic mythology, Strackerjan compared German liberals who supported the Danes to Hödur, the blind gatekeeper of Asgard's rainbow bridge, and the Danes themselves to Loki, the traitorous stepson of Odin who secretly sought Asgard's ruin.[19] Unwilling to capitulate to an increasingly *völkisch* liberal majority, the Danes were increasingly persecuted and arrested.[20]

V

Völkisch ideologies found an even greater reception among Schleswig-Holstein liberals in the wake of the First World War. Weimar's two primary liberal parties, the German Democrats (DDP) and the German People's Party (DVP), were by no means immune. Although nominally a Democrat, Christian Tränckner demanded a "rebirth of German *Volkstum*" and a "quickening of Schleswig-Holstein's racial character [*Stammestum*]."[21] Like Tiedje, an erstwhile supporter of Danish-German reconciliation, Tränckner acknowledged the Danes' "Nordic character" and "roots of soil and race fixed deep in the earth." But, chastened by the war experience, he questioned Danish loyalty to a Greater Germanic Reich.[22] For many years a leader of the local DVP, Johannes Tonneson likewise admonished the Danes to recognize that German "*Volkstum* and the powers slumbering within it . . . must . . . be surrounded by a shimmer of mystical reverence, in which we witness with respect the life forces which will lead us into our new future."[23]

The so-called Regional Liberals (*Liberale Landespartei* or LLP) expressed openly racist and antisemitic sentiments. Indeed, in contrast to the DDP and DVP, the LLP allied with other particularist groups in the Weimar National

Assembly in order to sponsor a federalist constitution, which permitted extensive self-administration and ethnic autonomy, for Danes as well as Germans.[24] But the *Landespartei* also campaigned for the creation of a "racial democracy" based on the mutual constitutional affirmation and protection of all Germanic *Stämme,* whether Bavarian or Saxon, Danish or Frisian. Having drunk deep of these quasi-scientific theories of natural selection, the *Landespartei* insisted in its campaign literature upon the superiority of North Germans (Scandinavians and Nordic Germans) over all others and of Germanic peoples in general over any other race. These "liberal" principles of racial democracy, promoted tirelessly by the party's chairman, Hinrich Lohse, would later be applied by Lohse with great vigor in his capacity as Nazi *Gauleiter* for the Baltic provinces.[25]

The point here is not to argue that all German liberals were racist or even anti-Danish, but that a great many *völkisch*-nationalists were members of the liberal parties, particularly in Schleswig-Holstein. Devastated by the potential loss of blood (ethnic Germans) and soil (North Schleswig, Upper Silesia, Alsace-Lorraine, etc.) which the Versailles Treaty entailed, the *völkisch* liberal mainstream invoked the Wilsonian ideals of self-determination, but not to justify minority independence. Rather, the goal was to obtain official Weimar support for "languishing" German minorities in Denmark, Poland, France, Czechoslovakia, Belgium, and Italy.[26] Motivated by these common goals, Hjalmar Schacht, a member of the left liberal Democrats (DDP), welcomed Anton Schifferer, the former chairman of the right liberal People's Party (DVP), to a 1925 *Bierabend* celebrating two thousand years of German racial purity in Schleswig-Holstein. Schifferer delivered the keynote address, titled "German Cultural Work in Schleswig-Holstein." To rousing applause, Schifferer argued that the Nordmark was different from the Rheinland and Ostmark because there persisted in the latter two areas a conflict between the Germans on the one hand and the Latin and Slavic races on the other. In the Nordmark, however, there prevailed a "thousand-year exchange between West Germanic and North Germanic culture," which was made untenable only by the "political consequences" attendant to this dispute. Schifferer hoped to reconcile the renegade Danes to the German *völkisch* element on the basis of Schleswig-Holstein's "geographic position, history, and nationality in the framework of great German culture."[27]

Until the advent of the Third Reich a wide-ranging coalition of Schleswig-Holstein liberals demanded the return of "lost territories" and the preservation of Germans abroad, from the Memel and the Tyrol to Alsace and North Schleswig.[28] Indeed, the liberals often put forth progressive-seeming policies seeking "stronger self-administration for all German tribes." Yet self-determination could be employed by a multiplicity of actors, from Hanssen to Hitler, in very different ways.[29] This conceptual malleability made it difficult to discern what sort of liberal politics lay behind the invocation of self-determination in the Nordmark.[30] *Völkisch* liberals may have agreed with Hanssen that the Danes had a right to preserve their culture and language without being persecuted by the state. But the respective justifications for this "liberal" policy could not have been more disparate. Danish liberals made their case on universalist grounds. German liberals based theirs on *völkisch* principles that were inherently exclusionary toward Poles and Jews. Those universalist German liberals who did exist, largely Jewish in background, were always in the minority of their party. It was only on the political, cultural, and geographic margin of the Reich, in Danish North Schleswig, that one perceives a consistently universalist critique of illiberalism and intolerance.[31] But when given a choice between Hanssen's universalism and Hitler's *völkisch*-nationalism, the vast majority of Schleswig-Holstein liberals opted for the latter.

VI

During the Wilhelmine epoch (1888–1918) Alsatians were never a minority in the conventional sense. In terms of language, citizenship, and history, Alsace was a German state, having joined the German Reich in 1871, the same year as Baden and Bavaria, and only seven years after Prussia annexed Schleswig-Holstein from Denmark. At least 96 percent of Alsatians spoke German as a first language, constituting a larger percentage of native speakers than existed in East and West Prussia, Silesia, and Schleswig-Holstein.[32] Yet Alsace had been a part of France for almost two hundred years before 1871. Despite the region's ethnic German background, at least three generations of Alsatians had experienced life in the French Republic.[33] As one Alsatian particularist put it with only slight hyperbole, by 1871 Alsatians did not feel any more German "national feeling" than Bretons did for Britain, "at least not from a political perspective."[34] The "concept 'Alsatian' existed only in a geographical sense," argued another observer, and was based on an "extraordinarily high estimation of Frenchness" hardly glimpsed in the other German states.[35] Given their latent francophilia and democratic traditions, it is only logical that a conscious antipathy to the Reich might arise after Prussia wrenched Alsace from its proper political home and thrust it into the German Empire. I call this antipathy "republican particularism."

Republican particularism or "autonomism," the political campaign for Alsatian constitutional and cultural rights, was closely linked to liberal-democratic reform in the Reich. Since most Alsatians agreed on the importance of preserving French political and cultural values within a seemingly reactionary German Reich, republican particularism was as powerful among the clericals and socialists as it was in the liberal ranks. In a facetious lead article titled "Protecting and Nurturing Germanness" the province's leading Catholic paper, *Der Elsässer,* railed against the "injustices carried out by the

Prussian regime in its newest Polish policy." How could the Reich punish a Pole simply for preserving his native culture, even banning Polish-speaking individuals from working in the most rudimentary state jobs? No matter how favorably Germans might compare themselves to England, the paper added, the Reich's own "Irish policy" was far worse than Britain's.[36] Although a Catholic, German-language paper, the *Elsässer* praised French republican traditions, echoing Guizot's famous assertion that "'Afin qu'on aime la patrie, il faut que la patrie soit elle-même aimable.'"[37] Or as the more Germanophile but equally liberal Protestant Heinrich Ruland admitted, Alsatian Catholics "felt French" not because of their ethnic or confessional affinities for France, but out of a desire for the republican political values they associated with the French Revolution.[38]

This is not to say that particularist notions of Alsatian identity excluded all grammars of ethnic difference. The clerical autonomist Emil Wetterlé once remarked that a son of Polish Jewish immigrants—referring to his rival and intermittent party colleague, Daniel Blumenthal—was ill equipped to represent the "national" interests of native Alsatians. In turn Blumenthal made similar accusations against Wetterlé, labeling the acerbic priest a *Schwob* carpetbagger (his family originally hailed from Baden).[39] But all politics is local, and this kind of particularist posturing was less ethnic than it was geographic. Neither Wetterlé nor Blumenthal allowed such claims to metastasize into *völkisch* doctrines. For their constituencies did not react to racial "necessities" either. The "Polish Jewish" liberal Blumenthal, in fact, enjoyed the support of clerical autonomists across Upper Alsace. He was even elected mayor of Colmar, the province's most "clerical" city, in 1908. That Wetterlé's familial roots lay in Baden, meanwhile, did little to hinder the cleric's reputation as one of the undisputed leaders of regional autonomism.

VII

The drive for regional autonomy was therefore a decisive element in Alsatian republican circles. Unlike *völkisch* particularism in Schleswig-Holstein, however, republican particularism in Alsace was constructed not to preserve but to combat the ethnic nationalist typologies that pervaded contemporary German political culture. Respectively Polish Jewish, German Protestant, and German Catholic in origin, the leaders of the Alsatian People's Party (ElVp)—Blumenthal, Jacques Preiß, and Wetterlé—never missed an opportunity to deride the Pan-German ideals which prevailed in liberal circles across the Rhine.[40] Wetterlé enjoyed openly haranguing German nationalists in the Reichstag, remarking on how positively "brilliant" was their most recent scheme to send "a large number of big, strong girls from Brandenburg . . . to the Cameroons and East Africa for German farmers" so that that "lordly race [would] not prostitute itself by cross-breeding."[41] Just as Wetterlé alienated many mainstream German Catholics, Preiß and Blumenthal quickly built a *reichsfeindlich* reputation among their liberal benchmates as well.

Nevertheless, before the First World War it remained inconceivable that even the most ardent Alsatian "autonomists" might repudiate their rich and indelibly German heritage. What offended Alsatian liberals was not the hegemony of German language or culture per se, but the imposition of a monolithic, race-based conception of Germanness (*Deutschtum*), which precluded the "multicultural" Alsatian identity that republican particularism meant to preserve. "We do not oppose Germanism in itself," Wetterlé explained, "but Germanism as it is manifested with us—that meddlesome, pettifogging Germanism which is constantly fighting against our customs and traditions and which would deprive us of all our liberties."[42] Wetterlé's colleague, the "clerical autonomist" Anselme Laugel, also acknowledged that Alsace was German, "that is understood; but a German must have the right of being so in his own way, without being obliged in his Germanism to conform to a model proposed to him by an administration too much inclined to want to annihilate it."[43] Without dispensing with "the roughness of their too narrow patriotism," Laugel added, the "free exchange of ideas . . . the communal treasure from which all the world may draw" would die. Alsatians were "democrat[s] by temperament," Laugel concluded. They were dedicated not to the apotheosis of one race or nation, but to "liberty, holy and fecund liberty."[44] Thus even for so-called "clerical autonomists" like Laugel and Wetterlé, universalist liberalism was an integral and indispensable part of Alsatian identity. Without it Alsace would be left only with German liberalism's bland party doctrine of minimal state interference in the economy buttressed increasingly by *völkisch*-nationalism. This was the exact antithesis of those communal republican values which held together an otherwise disparate array of liberals, clericals, and socialists.

The First World War exacerbated this growing discrepancy between republican particularism and German *völkisch* liberalism. Forced to choose between a more virulently racist German nationalism than ever and a liberating French republicanism, Alsatian liberals found themselves drifting closer to their erstwhile countrymen west of the Meuse. During the war even Germanophile Alsatians formally committed themselves to preserving Alsatian "particularism"—a cultural code for French political and cultural tendencies—while publicly criticizing German annexations in Belgium and Russia.[45] Equally repelled by mounting *völkisch* sentiments, the Germanophile liberals Georg and Alfred Wolf implored the German public to lay aside their "German national glasses [*deutschnationale Brille*]" and accept the fact that Alsace was half-German, half-autonomist; that is, ethnically German, but politically French.[46] German nationalists, Wetterlé added, were too blind to understand that their wartime policy of "Germanization" in Alsace and elsewhere had nothing to do with enlightenment or progress, as many liberal apologists claimed. Germanization was a sign of political insecurity, a barbaric response to political and cultural difference that only compounded centuries of ethnic strife and cultural mixing across Germany. The Poles were "undoubtedly incorrect in belonging to the Slavic race," Wetterlé declared sarcastically. But "this indiscretion [wa]s shared by the Brandenburgers and Silesians who, for the most part, [we]re Germanized Slavs." Was it not absurd that Germans of Slavic background, namely Prussians, were now committing the same crimes of cultural imperialism which Teutonic knights had long ago inflicted upon them?[47]

Wetterlé, Laugel, Blumenthal were not autonomists by nature. All three would later participate happily and productively in a significantly more centralized and culturally homogenous Third Republic; indeed, so would Germanophile liberals like Georg Wolf and Charles Frey. Alsatian particularism did not emerge from some latent "anti-Germanism" on the part of an inherently Francophile populace. Alsatian liberals were not trying to become "French." Rather they emphasized French political and cultural traditions in order to define themselves against the *völkisch* illiberalism that German national identity seemed to entail. In this way, they seized upon a republican counterpoise ethno-national identity, neither French nor German, but assimilating the best elements of both cultures in the interest of liberal individualism and democracy.[48]

VIII

On November 22, 1918, when French troops "liberated" Alsace-Lorraine from German rule, they were greeted warmly. For the first time in fifty years, proclaimed the liberal pastor Charles Scheer, the Alsatian *Heimat* was truly free, rescued from the twin fires of German nationalism and militarism.[49] Having admired the Third Republic from afar for five decades, Alsatians like Scheer believed that French victory presaged the triumph of liberalism and democracy in Alsace. But the road to freedom would prove complicated. Alsace remained ethnically German and culturally particularist. Moreover, by creating two exceptional administrative bodies in 1919, the Paris *Service générale* and the Strasbourg *Commisariat supérieur* (later the *Commisariat générale* or CG), the French government helped reproduce the same problems of exceptional government that had existed under the German Empire.[50] Control of Alsatian affairs in the cultural and religious sphere was again lost to Chauvinist bureaucrats, only this time nestled in Paris instead of Berlin. Soon French assimilation policies created a new "Alsatian Question" nearly as divisive as the old, putting Alsace's tradition of republican particularism to a greater test than ever before.

Indeed, historians of the French right have claimed that that the "return of Alsace to French rule" produced "a crisis of the right caused by the mobilisation of rank and file conservatives. In Alsace . . . authoritarianism emerged from the crisis."[51] Many likewise argue that Alsace was a seedbed of nationalist and authoritarian politics, particularly susceptible to Nazism.[52] But these scholars, operating from a teleology of eventual Nazi triumph and French republican collapse, miss the most compelling point. Universalist liberalism was able to endure, even thrive, in Alsace despite many of the same political and economic crises that brought down the Weimar Republic. Although Alsace did succumb to fascism, it did so only after the Nazi occupation in 1940. If Alsatian political culture contained certain *völkisch* and authoritarian proclivities alongside its republican particularist traditions, these tendencies never gained a firm hold on the regional psyche.[53]

Though he was an ethnic German and devout Lutheran, the liberal pastor Charles Scheer took the occasion of Bastille Day 1919 to express his satisfaction at Alsace's reintegration into France. Under the Empire, he reminded the German-speaking audience, Alsatians "did not have a country." Germany had deprived Alsatians, not "only of the democratic institutions in which we rejoice," but of an "entire way of thinking, a special direction of thought, a particular equilibrium of spiritual forces; that is, a *great human ideal [un grand idéal humain]*." Alsatian patriotism was something more than a typically German "idolatry of natural egoism . . . This patriotism we repudiate with all our soul." In "celebrating this patriotic holiday," Scheer continued, "one must have a true international spirit . . . because humanity is one organism . . . different individuals and nations are not able to thrive unless the entire organism may thrive . . . the League of Nations must be praised . . . [because it] defends against all attacks of false patriotism; here is international heroism in a time of peace."[54] Bastille Day was a time not to extol the French race, but to celebrate the universal values of the French Republic. Thus a German-speaking Alsatian might still become a proud citizen of the French Republic.

This sermon is all the more remarkable because Scheer was a member of the putatively "right-wing" Democrats (*Parti Démocrate et Républicaine* or PRD), a party which perennially allied with the clericals (*Union Populaire et Républicaine* or UPR) against the left liberal Radicals (PRS) and Socialists (SPF).[55] Yet Scheer's views were eminently universalist, eschewing the essentialist qualities of blood, race, and religion, of innate *Kultur* and *Volksgemeinschaft* that we find expressed even within left liberal circles in Schleswig-Holstein. Certainly a great many of Scheer's Democratic colleagues were bourgeois Protestants who opposed state intervention in the economy, and therefore constituted a "right wing" in the vulgar Marxist sense. But this was a matter of France and Germany's having distinct political cultural traditions. In Wilhelmine Germany Scheer and the PRD chairman, Charles Frey, were prominent leaders of the left liberal Alsatian Progressives (FVP), while Frey acted as the Alsatian correspondent to the *Frankfurter Zeitung*, arguably the most radical non-socialist daily in Germany. Like the Alsatian FVP of 1914, the PRD endorsed a political creed based on constitutional freedoms, democratic pluralism, international law, and ethno-cultural tolerance, much in contrast to their FVP colleagues to the north, in Schleswig-Holstein. Scheer, Frey, and company earned their "conservative" moniker because they supported free-market liberalism, wished to see the Versailles Treaty strictly enforced, and maintained an alliance with the clericals (UPR) in order to defend Alsatian particularity in religion, language, and confessional education.

It would be historically disingenuous to deny the problems of cultural assimilation and political accommodation faced by Alsace's German-speaking, federalist-leaning, only moderately secular population, when thrown into a vehemently anti-clerical, heavily centralized, French republican state. Religious Catholics and Protestants refused to give up their right to state-supported confessional education.[56] And virtually all Alsatians wanted to preserve German as an official language alongside French, a quite reasonable request to which Parisian bureaucrats nonetheless took great offense.[57] Alsatians were also accustomed to federalist constitutional arrangements, which tolerated the preservation of their language, culture, and religion. Under previous regimes, from Napoleon I to Wilhelm I, there had been some accommodation of regional difference provided that Alsatians embraced the state and fulfilled their duties as citizens. It was not only Alsatian "francophilia" which frustrated Wilhelmine conservatives, but their refusal to barter away their republican inheritance. As a part of the German Reich, Alsace missed the Third Republic's revolution in administration and the extreme secularization and centralization which ensued. Naively, perhaps, liberals and clericals alike expected France to grant the same "autonomy" in culture and education that they had experienced under the German Empire. Instead the French leadership dishonored its wartime promise to respect Alsatian "traditions, values, liberties, and beliefs" by demanding assimilation with increasing vigor.[58] The "republican" autonomy that Alsatians fought so hard to win between 1870 and 1911 was now being abrogated on the basis of these "republican" principles, and whatever their initial enthusiasm *pour se retrouver,* Alsace and the interior were at loggerheads.

Despite these deepening resentments, however, a racialist majority never developed as it did in Schleswig-Holstein.[59] "Indigenous Jews" attended autonomist rallies, a fact that truly confounded and troubled local French officials who wrongly equated Alsatian particularism with Nazism. Meanwhile, Germanophile liberals like Georg Wolf and Camille Dahlet always employed the language of republicanism in criticizing French assimilation policies.[60] Although Paris labeled Wolf and Dahlet "right-wing autonomists," both would prove to be considerably more devoted to the Third Republic than the German Democrats were to Weimar. A member of the French Radical Socialists before defecting to the autonomist *Landespartei* in the mid-1920s, Camille Dahlet still commemorated the French Revolution as "that which proclaimed the equality not only of classes, but also of races, that offered to the inhabitants of its colonies the benefits that human dignity commands, that first raised the Jews into the rank of citizens; in the end, this is the France to whom General Pershing cried, in setting foot on European soil: Lafayette, we are here!"[61] Four weeks after Hitler's accession as chancellor of the German Reich, the ostensibly right-wing clerical Charles Haenggi warned all Alsatians against that "specific *völkisch* note" sounding a "regression into barbarism," namely "Hitlerian autonomism," which falsely asserts that "a *Volksgemeinschaft* arises from the community of blood [*Blutsgemeinschaft*]."[62]

As Dahlet, Haenggi, and others demanded independence from Paris in administrative and cultural affairs, the autonomist Charles Beckenhaupt wrote a booklet titled *Race, Langue ou Patrie?* Though intended as a defense of Alsatian language and culture against French incursions, the tract is much more decisive in attacking Pan-Germanism. There was a theoretical opposition, Beckenhaupt wrote, between "Pan-German and democratic conceptions of popular sovereignty." Describing the narrow-mindedness of otherwise gifted German scholars, Beckenhaupt found it striking that "the [German] historian invokes only race and language. He appears to have no awareness that it is the sentiment of the country that makes a people. He admonishes Germans to remain loyal to the blood, to the language, to heritage" without respecting "other peoples."[63] Whereas in most civilized nations only the most reactionary conservatives espoused such racist views, Beckenhaupt laments that it was the "German elite, that is, the university world, the clergy, the upper bourgeoisie . . . men who have consecrated their lives to scrutinizing history," that did so:

> What is dangerous is that these great minds, deformed by absurd German traditions, only know how to discern the superiority of the German race but not the notion that people are bound by a human solidarity assigning to each an indispensable and different task . . . two currents oppose one another: the democratic and Christian ideal of human solidarity, and the fatalist German conception of eternal struggle . . . The difficulty of reconciliation between France and Germany does not reside in different interpretations of the Treaty of Versailles, but in the divergent conceptions regarding the foundation of national aspirations . . . men of state only remain nationalist because they are convinced, not only that oppositions of race and interest remain predominant, but also that the struggles are necessary for conserving the virtues and vigor of peoples.[64]

Since the republican creed was "democratic, pacifist, and humanistic," Beckenhaupt believed the province could become "French," even while Alsatians preserved their "convictions, ethnic rights, and maternal language."[65]

In much the same way that the classic *Sonderweg* argument has underemphasized the social and political similarities between Germany and her western neighbors, revisionist historiography of the last decade has probably overestimated France's own fascist and nationalist proclivities.[66] Certainly many Alsatians became disenchanted with the mainstream republican parties over the course of the 1920s. Some, to be sure, would abandon these same republican parties for "right-wing" autonomists. Alsatian autonomism never succumbed, however, to the *völkisch* forces that consumed even the left liberal parties in Schleswig-Holstein. That does not mean that Alsace was necessarily more "liberal" than Schleswig-Holstein in economic terms; Alsace was never a commercially oriented, free-trading region on a par with Kiel, Flensburg, or Altona. But Alsatian liberals were less preoccupied with ethnic difference and purity than liberals elsewhere in the Reich. Witness, for example, Daniel Blumenthal's tri-confessional Alsatian Party, later known as the National Association, in which a gay Catholic priest (Wetterlé), a Protestant German liberal (Preiß), and a Polish Jewish Democrat (Blumenthal) joined forces in the name of republican particularism. Or consider, on the other hand, the leadership of the radically *völkisch Vaterlandspartei*, whose leadership would include a great many German liberals.[67] Unlike their Reich counterparts, Alsatian particularists sought a republican constitution and international peace *instead* of German racial hegemony and territorial aggrandizement. As the most compelling exception to the otherwise ubiquitous *völkisch* traditions within German liberalism, Alsatian political and cultural history deserves considerable attention.

IX

Bourgeois German Protestants, the majority of whom voted liberal throughout the late nineteenth and early twentieth centuries, were no less modern or dynamic than their French or British counterparts. In this respect, the *Sonderweg* argument has lost its salience. But being modern and liberal in Wilhelmine and Weimar Germany did not preclude an explicitly racialist conception of German national identity. Although later embraced by conservatives as an antidote to progress, ethnic nationalism was very much the product of nineteenth-century liberalism. It should come as no surprise that even more virulently *völkisch* ideologies might find a home in the national and social liberalism of the postwar era. Conversely, universalist values were strongest on the margins of German society, in those regions or among those minority populations where traditional German liberalism was weakest. In Schleswig-Holstein, Germany's most liberal region in electoral terms, only the small Danish minority defended universalist values with any consistency. In Alsace, where Germany's traditional liberal parties were weaker electorally than anywhere else in the Reich, universalist values found their widest general appeal.

Given their exceptional ethnic status within the Pan-German hierarchy, the Danes had ample reason to accept a *völkisch* rendering of the contemporary political situation. As we have seen, the *völkisch* liberal idea of racial community (*Volksgemeinschaft*) was much more tolerant of Danish language and culture than any model presented to the Poles. It required only that the Danes, in their preservation of their Danish ethnicity (*Dänentum*), remain politically loyal to the greater *Volksgemeinschaft* of all Germanic *Stämme*. Yet Hanssen rejected this "multiculturalist" solution on universalist grounds, incurring charges of "miscegenation" and acts of government repression. During the First World War and for three decades thereafter Hanssen's Danish Party spurned the *völkisch* liberals for the Socialist opposition, providing a universalist bulwark against Nazi oppression until the end of the Second World War.[68]

For German liberals republicanism was a heavy cross to bear. Alsatian liberals had little chance of success without it. The Radical Socialists, Democrats, clericals, and Socialists may have differed on a number of socio-economic and constitutional issues, but they all saw the merits in liberal democracy, civil rights, and a mutual understanding among peoples. Thus despite the Pan-German tendencies wafting in across the Rhine, Alsatian particularism remained altogether different from German *völkisch*-nationalism.[69] Alsatians truly believed that their land was a source of that "liberty . . . given to the world in the course of the Great Revolution." "In choosing France," Frédéric Hoffet writes, the Alsatians "did not seek to adopt the manners and the morals of a society that appeared superior. Their French patriotism was not only cultural, but also political. It rested on their attachment to the ideologies which made the Republic a champion for the world."[70] This ideology, universalist at heart and republican in principle, was the perfect antidote to German *völkisch*-nationalism and authoritarianism.

Yet for most Protestant middle-class Germans, an ardent nationalism, increasingly *völkisch* in tone, prevented the spread of universalist values. The vast majority of liberal voters in Schleswig-Holstein eventually shifted their support to the profoundly conservative German Nationalists and later the Nazis because for two generations they had imbibed a burgeoning "majority" culture of *völkisch*-nationalism. Strengthened by war, social crisis, and territorial dislocation, ethnic preoccupations inevitably displaced the universalist creed of nineteenth-century liberalism. There *were* regions of Germany, notably in the democratic, francophile southwest (Alsace, Baden, Württemberg, and parts of the Rhineland), some Catholic regions (Bavaria and Upper Silesia), and the cosmopolitan metropoles of Berlin and Frankfurt, where *völkisch* ideologies never made much headway.[71] Nor were all Schleswig-Holstein liberals unreconstructed *völkisch* ideologues. It is important to remember that liberal political economy and liberal universalism were never inextricable nor even necessarily compatible in Wilhelmine and Weimar Germany. The majority of German middle-class voters *did* support progressive social and political goals. That is why "majority" liberalism was so strong in Schleswig-Holstein before the First World War, at a time when Germany was both militarily prodigious and democratically deficient. Because they embraced *völkisch* sentiments as well, however, it is not difficult to understand why the liberal parties disintegrated after 1918. Indeed, except for the Socialists and a handful of bourgeois intellectuals, liberal democracy's greatest supporters—the Danes, Jews, and Alsatians—existed on the margins of German society. In this sort of political culture it is little wonder that National Socialism emerged victorious.

Notes

1. "Social imperialism" is a favorite term of the *Sonderweg* school, but its explanatory potential has been convincingly undermined by Geoff Eley and David Blackbourn, among others. On "social imperialism" see Hans-Ulrich Wehler, *The German Empire* (Dover, N.H.: Berg, 1985). For counterarguments see, most prominently, David Blackbourn and Geoff Eley, *The Peculiarities of German History* (London: Oxford University Press, 1984).

2. See Detlev J. K. Peukert, *The Weimar Republic: The Crisis of Classical Modernity* (New York: Hill and Wang, 1991).

3. In modified form, some portions of the material in this section appear in Eric Kurlander, "Multicultural and Assimilationist Models of Ethnopolitical Integration in the Context of the German Nordmark, 1890-1933," *Global Review of Ethnopolitics* 1 (March 2002): 39-52.

4. For more detail on the plebiscites of 1920 see Rudolf Rietzler, *Kampf in der Nordmark* (Neumünster: Wachholtz, 1982), 116-24. Also see Hans Dietrich Lehmann, *Der 'Deutsche Ausschuß' und die Abstimmungen in Schleswig, 1920* (Neumünster: Wachholtz, 1969).

5. See, for example, Ernst von Reventlow, *Wertung: Die völkische Eigenart und der Internationalismus*, Heft 5 (Leipzig: Fritz Eckardt, 1910); Oswald Hauser, *Gustav Frenssen als niederdeutscher Dichter: Untersuchungen zu Landschaft und Volkstum seiner Heimat* (Leipzig: Eichblatt, 1936); Julius Langbehn, *Rembrandt als Erzieher* (Weimar: Duncker, 1922); and Adolf Bartels, *Rasse: Sechzehn Aufsätze zur nationale Weltanschauung* (Hamburg: Hanseatische Druck- und Verlagsanstalt, 1909).

6. Peter Wulf, *Die politische Haltung des schleswig-holsteinischen Handwerks, 1928-1932* (Cologne: Westdeutscher Verlag, 1969). Also see Hans Jörg Zimmermann, *Der Kreis Herzogtum Lauenburg, 1918 bis 1933, unter besonderer Berücksichtigung von Wirtschafts- und Sozialstruktur und Wählerverhalten* (Neumünster: Karl Wachholtz, 1978). The seminal works on *Heimat* as a political, social, and cultural artifact are Mack Walker, *German Home Towns* (Ithaca, N.Y.: Cornell University Press, 1998); and Celia Applegate, *A Nation of Provincials: The German Idea of Heimat* (Berkeley: University of California Press, 1990).

7. See Langbehn, *Rembrandt als Erzieher*.

8. Johannes Leonhart, ed., *Fortschritt: Halbmonatschrift für Politik Volkswirtschaft und Marinefragen* (Kiel, 1908), 321–25.

9. "Do they want to institute German schools and the dispersion of the German language where it is not desired, no matter what? Nothing could be more unpleasant." *Schleswiger Nachrichten*, 9 January 1907; and *Itzehoer Nachrichten*, 19 August 1908.

10. Leonhart, *Fortschritt*, 321–25. Also see William W. Hagen, *Germans, Poles, and Jews: The Nationality Conflict in the Prussian East, 1772–1914* (Chicago: University of Chicago Press, 1980); François Igersheim, *L'Alsace des notables, 1870–1914: La bourgeoisie et le peuple alsacien* (Strasbourg: Presses du Nouvel Alsacien, 1981); and Hermann Hiery, *Reichstagswahlen im Reichsland: Ein Beitrag zur Landesgeschichte von Elsaß-Lothringen und zur Wahlgeschichte des Deutschen Reiches, 1871–1918* (Düsseldorf: Droste, 1986).

11. *Schleswiger Nachrichten*, 9 January 1907.

12. See Ulrich Lange, *Geschichte Schleswig-Holsteins* (Neumünster: Wachholtz, 1996), 478–79; *Schleswiger Grenzpost*, 26 January 1912; and *Sonderburger Zeitung*, 24 December 1912.

13. *Die Nordmark*, 15 November 1902.

14. See Johannes Leonhart in *Fortschritt: Halbmonatschrift für Politik Volkswirtschaft und Marinefragen* (Kiel, 1907), 71–74, 216. Also see *Sonderburger Zeitung*, 8 July 1908; and *Schleswig-Holsteinische Volkszeitung*, 8 August 1912.

15. Hans Peter Hanssen, *Diary of a Dying Empire* (Bloomington: Indiana University Press, 1955), 134.

16. Police Literary Bureau 10 September 1906, Landesarchiv Schleswig (hereafter LAS): Abt. 301, #59; also see Hanssen, *Diary of a Dying Empire*.

17. Hans-Peter Hanssen to Friedrich Naumann, 9 August 1914; Naumann to Hanssen, 14 August, 19 August, 12 September, 4 November 1914; Ernst Christiansen to Naumann, 7 September 1914; Naumann to Rade, 19 May 1915; all in NL Naumann, Bundesarchiv Berlin (hereafter BAB): N 3001, #229.

18. See Karl Strackerjan, *Nordmärkische Dänentreue: Eine während des Weltkrieges vertrauliche Denkschrift* (Hadersleden: Published by the author, 1916), i, 40, 59–60, 78–89, 102–107.

19. Karl Strackerjan, *Dänen an der deutschen Front: Nordmark und Weltkrieg; Eine Denkschrift* (Hadersleben: Published by the author, 1915), 89, 102–103.

20. Naumann in NL Naumann, BAB: N 3001, #229; *Kieler Zeitung*, 31 October 1918, 2 November 1913, 3 November 1913; *Itzehoer Nachrichten*, 6 November 1918.

21. Bröder Schwensen, *Der Schleswig-Holsteiner-Bund, 1919–1933* (Frankfurt am Main: Lang, 1993), 186–88.

22. Rietzler, *Kampf in der Nordmark*, 307–308.

23. Schwensen, *Der Schleswig-Holsteiner-Bund*, 191–92. Though "congruent with National Socialist ideas," they represented the *Weltanschauung* of many of Schleswig-Holstein's liberal elite. Rietzler, *Kampf in der Nordmark*, 308.

24. "Hand in hand with the popularization of race and 'border'-ideology came a reactivation of those irrational images of *völkisch* cultural pessimism" which influenced "public consciousness" widely before the War, and which now "found a political organizational framework in the *Landespartei*." Rietzler, *Kampf in der Nordmark*, 94.

25. Rudolf Heberle, *From Democracy to Nazism: A Regional Case Study on Political*

Parties in Germany (New York: H. Fertig, 1970), 46–47, 53, 58; and Rietzler, *Kampf in der Nordmark*, 306.

26. Johannes Schmidt-Wodder, *Der deutsche Weg zur Verständigung mit dem Norden* (Flensburg: Westfalen, 1919), 3–6; Schwensen, *Der Schleswig-Holsteiner-Bund*, 16–17, 46–72, 331–32; Lehmann, *Der 'Deutsche Ausschuß,'* 26–28; Rietzler, *Kampf in der Nordmark*, 93, 300–308; and Wilhelm Heile in *Die Hilfe*, 13 November 1919.

27. Anton Schifferer, *Deutsche Kulturarbeit in Schleswig-Holstein: Vortrag gehalten am 22. Juni 1925 auf dem Bierabend bei dem Herrn Reichsbankpräsidenten Dr. Schacht von dem Bevollmächtigten zum Reichsrat Dr. Schifferer, Charlottenhof* (Berlin: Schleswig-Holsteinische Universitätsgesellschaft/Ortsgruppe Berlin, 1925), 3–16; and Anton Schifferer, *Eingemeindung oder nicht?* (Marseburg: Published by the author, 1928), 18–21.

28. A majority of Nazi members "swore" themselves to the liberal Wilhelm Iversen (DVP) because he possessed impeccable *völkisch* credentials, *Führer* qualities, and "Nordic-Germanic" views. Schwensen, *Der Schleswig-Holsteiner-Bund*, 370–73, 403–404. Also see the article by Johannes Schmidt-Wodder in *Jahrbuch*, 1929, in LAS: Abt. 309, #35298.

29. As the historian Bruce Frye notes, liberal support for German self-determination was, at the very least, "ironic, given the indifference of [even] left liberals to such questions before 1919." Bruce Frye, *Liberal Democrats in the Weimar Republic: The History of the German Democratic Party and the German State Party* (Carbondale: Southern Illinois University Press, 1985), 129–31.

30. *Deutsch-Demokratische Beiträge*, 4 February 1921.

31. See, for example, *Der Fall Schücking in der Presse*, published by Naumann's *Die Hilfe*, 1908.

32. See Leonhart, *Fortschritt* (1908), 619–23; *Handbuch über den Preußischen Staat* (Berlin: Decker, 1930), 50–52; Dan P. Silverman, *Reluctant Union: Alsace-Lorraine and Imperial Germany, 1871–1918* (University Park: Pennsylvania State University Press, 1972), 76; and Hiery, *Reichstagswahlen im Reichsland*, 24–30, 40–41. Also see James J. Sheehan, "What Is German History? Reflections on the Role of the Nation in German History and Historiography," *Journal of Modern History* 53, no. 1 (1981): 1–23.

33. Abbé [Emil] Wetterlé, *Behind the Scenes in the Reichstag: Sixteen Years of Parliamentary Life in Germany* (London: Hodder and Stoughton, 1918), 51–52.

34. *Briefe eines Elsässers: Sonder-Abdruck aus der Täglichen Rundschau (Unparteiische Zeitung für nationale Politik)* (Berlin, 1898), 7. "It is certain that Germany can achieve her task of Germanizing Alsace, if she will only change her methods." Ibid., 5–14, 21–24.

35. *Briefe eines Elsässers*, 11, 21–24.

36. *Der Elsässer*, 3 September 1898.

37. "In order for one to love one's country, the country itself must be loveable." *Der Elsässer*, 3 September 1898.

38. Heinrich Ruland, *Deutschtum und Franzosentum in Elsass-Lothringen: Eine Kulturfrage* (Strasbourg: Straßburger Druck- und Verlagsanstalt, 1908).

39. Hiery, *Reichstagswahlen im Reichsland*, 99.

40. Wetterlé, *Behind the Scenes*, 75–78.

41. Ibid., 94–96, 138.

42. Ibid., 92–96, 138, 155–59.

43. Anselme Laugel, *L'avenir intellectuel de l'Alsace* (Paris: Bureaux de la Revue Politique et Parlementaire, 1908), 5–15; also see Eugen Weber, *Peasants into Frenchmen: The Modernization of Rural France, 1870–1914* (London: Chatto and Windus, 1979).

44. Laugel, *L'avenir intellectuel*, 19–31.

45. *L'express*, 24 July 1912.

46. See Alfred Wolf in *Der Tag*, 15 August 1912; Archives departmentales du Bas-Rhin (Strasbourg) (hereafter AStr) 132 AL, #2.

47. See AStr 132 AL, #21; *Nouvelliste*, 10 March, 23 October 1913 in AStr 132 AL, #2.

48. See police report, 25 July 1913, and *Straßburger Zeitung*, 20 July 1913, both in AStr 30 AL, #83; and H. G. Erdmansdorfer, *Fortschrittliche Volkspartei im Reichstag, 1907–1911* (Berlin, 1911), 21–24, 88.

49. See Charles Scheer, *"Wie ein Brand, der aus dem Feuer gerissen wird!"* (*predigt über Amos 4,11 gehalten in der reformierten Stephanskirche zu Mülhausen am 17. November 1918 wenige Stunden vor dem Einzug der französischen Truppen unter Führung des Generals Hirschauer*) (Mulhausen: Vosgienne, 1918); and Philippe Dollinger, *L'Alsace de 1900 à nos jours* (Toulouse: Edouard Privat, 1979), 99–100.

50. Dollinger, *L'Alsace*, 101.

51. Kevin Passmore, *From Liberalism to Fascism: The Right in a French Province, 1928–1939* (Cambridge: Cambridge University Press, 1997), 303–304. Also see Christian Baechler, *Le parti catholique alsacien, 1890–1939: Du Reichsland a la république Jacobine* (Paris: Ophrys, 1982); and Lothar Kettenacker, *Nationalsozialistische Volkstumpolitik im Elsaß* (Stuttgart: Deutsche Verlagsanstalt, 1973).

52. See Passmore, *From Liberalism to Fascism;* and Samuel Goodfellow, *Between the Swastika and the Cross of Lorraine: Fascisms in Interwar Alsace* (DeKalb: Northern Illinois University Press, 1999).

53. See a report on the German press by the chargé d'affaires, 20 June 1935, AStr AL 98, #691.

54. Charles Scheer, *Sermon de la première fête nationale à Mulhouse*, 13 July 1919 (Mülhausen, 1919).

55. To his "left" stood France's two most powerful parties, the left liberal Radical Socialists (PRS) and the Socialists (SFIO), and soon the Communist Party (CPF) as well.

56. See François G. Dreyfus, *La vie politique en Alsace, 1919–1936* (Paris: Armand Colin, 1969), 38–39, 81–89.

57. For more on the linguistic struggles, see Eugènie Phillips, *Les luttes linguistiques en Alsace jusqu'en 1945* (Strasbourg: Culture alsacienne, 1975), 160–212.

58. Phillips, *Les luttes linguistiques*, 210–11.

59. Dollinger, *L'Alsace*, 130–33. Also see examples from CG reports, 23 October 1935, and *Freie Presse*, 22 May 1938, AStr AL 98, #698.

60. CG reports, *Elsässische Landes-Zeitung*, 8 April 1933, Schall flier, 9 July 1933, AStr AL 98, #1087.

61. See police review of Dahlet's article in *République*, 14 July 1920, AStr AL 121, #163.

62. "Betray[ing] the racist, *völkisch* character in a Hitlerian spirit," Haenggi con-

cluded, all Alsatians, whatever their politics, needed to oppose any "new autonomism which openly acknowledges Hitler's way of thinking [*neuen Autonomismus, jenem, der sich offen zu Hitlerschen Gedankengängen bekennt*]." See CG report on the article "Hitlernder Autonomismus," by M. Haenggi, in *Elsässer Bote*, 23 February 1933, AStr AL 98, #1087.

63. Charles Beckenhaupt, *Race, Langue ou Patrie?* (Strasbourg: Istra, 1930), 4–14, 35–52.

64. Ibid., 53–57.

65. Ibid., 67–71.

66. Passmore, *From Liberalism to Fascism*, 303–304.

67. Hiery, *Reichstagswahlen im Reichsland*, 24–30; also see Igersheim, *L'Alsace des notables.*

68. Timothy Alan Tilton, *Nazism, Neo-Nazism, and the Peasantry* (Bloomington: Indiana University Press, 1975), 46–50.

69. See François G. Dreyfus, "L'Allemagne de Weimar et le problème alsacien," *Revue d'histoire moderne et contemporaine* 17, no. 2 (1970), 1–11.

70. Frédéric Hoffet, *Psychoanalyse de l'Alsace* (Paris: Flammarion, 1951), 145, 155.

71. For more on the universalist traditions of the German southwest, see James Hunt, *The People's Party in Wurttemberg and Southern Germany, 1890–1914: The Possibilities of Democratic Politics* (Stuttgart: Klett, 1975); and Walter F. Peterson, *The Berlin Liberal Press in Exile: A History of the Pariser Tageblatt—Pariser Tageszeitung, 1933–1940* (Tübingen: Max Niemeyer, 1987).

Five

"Volksgemeinschaften unter sich"
German Minorities and Regionalism in Poland, 1918–39

Winson Chu

I

In the wake of World War I, the Polish state was cobbled together from the remains of the Russian, Austro-Hungarian, and German empires. This feat was a test of political, cultural, and social integration not only for the Poles, since fully a third of the country's population was not considered "Polish." Ethnic Germans, while not the largest minority, were significant because the German Reich remained a formidable power and maintained a revanchist stance toward Poland. Yet these Polish citizens, considered "Germans" by both the Polish and German governments, were inherited from all three empires and were themselves very diverse. This chapter addresses how hierarchical concepts of Germanness influenced national cohesion within the German minority in interwar Poland. In particular, it examines how the creation of marginal and peripheral groups within the minority led to a growing sense of distinction that manifested itself in increasingly regionalist forms. Indeed, contrary to the German proclamations of unity and the sanctity of blood ties, there was not an onward march toward one German national community in Poland in the political sphere, but rather toward multiple, regionalized *Volksgemeinschaften*.

As Peter Sahlins's study of the French-Spanish borderlands shows, looking at the territorial margins allows new insight into the process of region-building and national identity.[1] In traditional nation-state narratives, regional distinctions are often considered backward anomalies that have managed to resist the national idea.[2] Recent work indicates, however, that national and regional imaginings are not necessarily competitive, but are both modern creations that complement one another.[3] Moreover, border studies also demonstrate that the dissolution of a political border can lead to the discovery of new differences and the construction of a territorial-cultural identity.[4] This chapter goes one step further and looks at the territorial margins of an already peripheral but significant group. Virtually all portrayals of the German minority in Poland reproduce the *Volksgruppe* narrative, in which the Germans in Poland slowly overcame the legacies of the partitions to become one national community. Most specialists on the German minority in Poland have acknowledged regional differences within the minority, but as the American historian Richard Blanke has noted, they have largely overlooked or even downplayed their impact.[5] By focusing on majority-minority conflict (*Volkstumskampf*), the scholarly literature has tended to attribute the same experience to *all* Germans living in the Polish state, thus underplaying the depth of political conflict within the minority. Even in recent works by German and Polish historians, the dominant narrative reaffirms the nationalist project of how Polish repression and National Socialist ideology transformed the Germans in Poland from a ragtag minority into a homogenous *Volksgruppe*.[6] This chapter refutes the *Volksgruppe* paradigm and reveals that, far from overcoming the fallen political borders and growing together, these German groupings became more regionally distinct with time.

This examination pays special attention to the some seventy thousand German-speakers in the city of Łódź, one of Central Europe's great industrial metropolises. In the nineteenth century, Łódź's textile mills attracted a large number of immigrants, making it the Russian Empire's third largest industrial center after Moscow and St. Petersburg. It was not only the second largest city in partitioned Poland, but also a major urban center for three different nationalities: Jews and Poles as well as Germans. In the interwar period, however, this polyethnic matrix ensured that the diaspora Germans—despite their numerical strength—would form only the margins of the minority.[7] The "Lodzer Mensch," a term deriving from Yiddish, reflected this purported "cosmopolitanism" and lack of national affinity. Chad Bryant's insightful work on the Sudetenland is valuable here, for the "Lodzer Mensch" also represented what Nazi scholars referred to as "amphibians"—those persons who were able to switch their public nationality or who could not be easily nationally identified.[8] As Bryant notes, "amphibians threatened the myth that the nation was eternal, unified, and homogenous; they threatened to bring the project of making nations to a halt."[9] As "not-quite-Germans," the "Lodzer Menschen" likewise posed a danger to unitary Germanness and thus challenged the concept of *Volksgemeinschaft*.

By examining the margins of the German minority, this chapter explores the fluidity of Germanness and seeks especially to break down the concept of *Volksdeutsche*.[10] Because the Germans in Poland were so heterogeneous, the Polish case can help clarify the murkiness of ideas like revisionism and irredentism, assumed to be widespread in interwar German society. As a threat to the project of building the German *Volksgruppe* in Poland, the Łódź Germans could be "racialized" as inferior to the Germans in western Poland, who were initially seen as being somehow more German. Yet the tenuousness of this discourse of inferiority became clear after 1933, when political and ideological changes redefined the borders of the *Volksgemeinschaft* and likewise reshuffled its hierarchy of Germanness. The increasing racialization of categories such as *Volksdeutsche*, "Slavs," and "Jews"[11] left less room for in-between entities such as the "Lodzer Mensch" whilst allowing for the racial upgrading of the Germans in Łódź. Moreover, an analysis of the shifting power relations in the German community in Poland also returns subjectivity to minority leaders by revealing how ideology and opportunism shaped one another.[12] As Helmut Walser Smith has demonstrated, the political right may dominate notions of what Germanness is and thus marginalize other social, political, and confessional groups, but these peripheries also attempt to re-define their own sense of Germanness vis-à-vis the center.[13] In doing so, ethnic margins do not just challenge the national center, but change it as well.[14] Thus, an examination of center-periphery competition within the German minority gives new insight into how radicalized ideology, including antisemitism, originated and spilled into practice. Only by understanding the process of stigmatization within an ethnic group can we understand the strategies of closure and exclusion vis-à-vis "foreign" groups.

II

A booming textile industry spurred the dramatic growth of Łódź in the nineteenth and early twentieth centuries, giving it the nicknames "Manchester of the East" and "the Polish Manchester."[15] In 1820, as part of an economic plan in the newly created Congress Kingdom of Poland, Łódź was one of seventeen cities slated to become industrial centers.[16] Entrepreneurs and workers from various German states played a major role in the initial phase of settlement and in the growth of the mills and factories.[17] Subsequent immigration of Poles and Jews, however, meant that the German proportion declined rapidly. By 1914, Łódź had 500,000 inhabitants. Of these, 50.9 percent were Poles and 32.5 percent were Jews. The 75,000 Germans made up only 15 percent of the population.[18] Despite their decreasing proportion in the city, the Germans in Łódź remained the largest concentration of Germans in the Congress Kingdom. Likewise, the city played an important role in the cultural, political, and economic life of Polish Jews: Łódź had Poland's second-largest Jewish community after Warsaw.[19] As the center of industry in the Congress Kingdom, Łódź was a flashpoint in the revolution of 1905–1907 and was central to Polish nationalist aspirations.

By the late 1800s, this multiethnic urban setting had given birth to the myth of the "Lodzer Mensch," which blended putative characteristics of all three ethnic groups.[20] Władysław Reymont, awarded the Nobel Prize in literature in 1924, wrote the classic depiction of the "Lodzer Mensch" in *The Promised Land* (1899). In this novel, speculation and greed, fortune and ruin dominate the lives of the three protagonists: a German, a Jew, and a Pole. Reymont's "lodzermensch" felt equally at home using Polish or German; his characters even spoke a pidgin form that combined elements from both these languages. The historian Bianka Pietrow-Ennker sums up the stereotype: "In the urban microcosm of Łódź, the 'Lodzer Mensch' type stood for the businessman of German, Jewish, or Polish heritage. He was characterized by a rational and individual way of life, and his work was dictated by the principles of the market economy. He remained loyal under any given political circumstances in order not to endanger his business dealings."[21] Thus, the "Lodzer Mensch" represented a form of interethnic accommodation that was commonplace in East Central Europe. This hybridity appeared not just in nationally undefined spaces like Upper Silesia;[22] as Chad Bryant has shown, "amphibianism" also existed in the Sudetenland, where ethnic boundaries are often considered to have been clearer and harder.[23]

Although the "Lodzer Mensch" had positive characteristics such as diligence, punctuality, and initiative, the term became increasingly synonymous with the social nightmares of the time. To contemporary observers, Łódź embodied the horrors of an onrushing capitalist modernity, including increasing individualism and the loss of one's cultural and national roots. One Polish observer of Łódź in 1904 wrote that the German settlers had lost their "Germanic patriotism" and had instead become "patriotic Lodzer Menschen." This assimilation, however, had not brought them any closer to becoming Polish.[24] Thus, the "Lodzer Mensch" was ethnicized as something essentially German and/or Jewish, which maintained the idea of a pure Polish nation, but the fear that many Poles were also becoming "Lodzer Menschen" reflected the cultural pessimism in the *intelligencja*.

Nor was the "Lodzer Mensch" a *Feindbild* for Polish nationalists alone; German observers often drew the conclusion that the Łódź Germans were somehow not German enough. This perception was widespread during the First World War, when Reich Germans who came to occupied Łódź were forced to rely on the traditional elites to govern the city and the region; while the Poles tended to belong to nationalist groupings, it was believed that the Jewish and the German members of the industrial bourgeoisie continued to support Russian-imperial ties.[25] Disturbed by the lack of national affiliation among the German population, the occupiers condescendingly called the Łódź Germans "ruble patriots."[26] While the "reality" behind the "Lodzer Mensch" is hard to pinpoint, it is important that its discursive foundations existed. As with all stereotypes, elements of it could be reactivated at a later date and mobilized in different contexts. As later examples will show, the concept was so engrained that even when the "Lodzer Mensch" was not explicitly mentioned by name, it became commonplace to ascribe to the Germans in Łódź signifying characteristics that were both informed by and referred back to the "Lodzer Mensch."

III

With about one million Germans (3.5 percent of the total population), Poland did not have the largest German minority in interwar East Central Europe. It was greatly affected by the problem of irredentist politics, however, because of not only the size of the German minority, but also its nature. A large proportion of the minority in Poland was composed of former Reich citizens, and their loss was particularly tangible and painful for Germany. When this was combined with the loss of Prussian territories, which made up 11.8 percent of Poland's total size in 1922,[27] a broad segment of German society was embittered by the "dictation" of Versailles. Throughout the interwar period, minority leaders and their caretakers in the Reich sought to build a German "we-group" that would function as a parallel society in Poland and that would better serve German interests.[28] Above all, the hundreds of thousands of Germans in the ceded Prussian territories who could not come to terms with their fall from *Staatsvolk* status played a vital role in maintaining claims for a return of these regions to Germany. Moreover, the "moral obligation" felt by many in Germany toward their former co-citizens meant that the Germans in western Poland received lavish subsidies and political support, thus complicating and fueling their resentments against Poland. As former *Reichsdeutsche,* the German minority in western Poland continued to enjoy a kind of informal, residual citizenship in the Reich. In the eyes of many Poles and Germans, the Germans in western Poland were generally considered to be more advanced economically, culturally, and nationally than the Germans in the formerly Russian and Austrian regions. Indeed, with their material and political support from Germany, their higher standard of living, and a livelier organizational and cultural life, these Germans became very much the "center" of the German minority.

Official revisionism during the Weimar period largely limited itself to Germany's 1914 borders and thus paid less attention to the Germans in the formerly Russian and Austrian regions, including the Łódź Germans.[29] This partiality was reflected in the distribution of Reich subsidies, which were supposed to maintain a high number of Germans in Poznania, Pomerelia, and Upper Silesia, thus improving the chances for a future border revision. The Germans in the formerly Russian and Austrian territories received but a tiny fraction of the subsidies, although they made up half of the minority. Not surprisingly, the material privileges enjoyed by the western Polish Germans led to considerable resentments *within* the minority and complicated long-term political cooperation between regional leaders. Germans from the Austrian and Russian territories accused these former Reich citizens of being arrogant "aristocrats" who treated the other Germans as if they were "pariahs."[30]

Reinforcing this second-class status was the position these Germans held in the discursive hierarchy of Germanness. Excluded from any experience of life in the German nation-state, the diaspora Germans in central and eastern Poland were considered culturally inferior and less supportive of the German (i.e., Germany's) cause. With little to no expectation of one day being annexed to Germany, the Germans in central and eastern Poland came to a quicker accommodation with their new situation. Yet this acceptance of the new Polish state did not square with the revisionist aims of the German leaders in western Poland and in Germany, and the more *völkisch*-minded nationalists were alarmed by the apparent ease with which the Germans further east seemed to suppress their national consciousness. Left on the discursive margins and constantly underfunded, the Germans in the eastern regions of Poland formed what could be termed the minority's "underclass."

In other words, precisely this marginality also made these Germans dangerous to the idea of German unity, and the widespread fear that the Germans in central and eastern Poland were somehow not national enough was reflected in their stigmatization. As is common with perceptions of the "underclass," a form of racialization evolved to "naturalize" their lower status. While this was not racism in the conventional sense, there was a sense of differentiation that drew upon its concepts, such as hierarchy and the immutability of differences. As Eric Weitz argues with regard to Soviet nationality policy, racial categories can exist without the concept of "race" itself.[31] In regard to the "Lodzer Mensch," the differentiation was also "racial" in the sense that this inferiority was seen as "genetic" and passed on from generation to generation. The determinants may not have been biological, but the harsh conditions in the poorer regions as well as the urban milieu of Łódź were seen as reproducing this problem by acting as incubators for the underclass. The fears of cross-cultural contamination and racial mixing with Poles and Jews led many German nationalists to see Łódź as a nest of "renegade Germandom."

In the early interwar period, this stereotype could readily build upon preexisting ideas of the "Lodzer Mensch." Reich officials, minority leaders, and *Ostforscher* regurgitated and applied this formula throughout the 1920s. The German consul in Łódź, Kurt von Luckwald, commented upon this apparent lack of national consciousness:

The heading ["Łódź Germandom"] encompasses a term that has not been honorable up to now. The "Łódź German" has held and still holds today the sound of hard cash, the value of one's assets, in the highest regard. The goal of material wealth is to be achieved at all cost; and because the changing political situation has not always made it "advantageous," but rather dangerous to show one's allegiance to the German homeland, one has avoided any positive *völkisch* views. The richer circles of the Łódź industrialists like to use the term "cosmopolitanism" to cover up their meager interest in the homeland and to shake off any expectations of giving active help.[32]

Even the *Ostforscher*, who generally held all things German in great esteem, contributed to this pattern of "racialization." Indeed, they were among the most vehement critics of the "Lodzer Mensch" condition. Most *Ostforscher* were at home in rightist milieus, and they tended to see the conservative, patriarchal, and agrarian structures of the various German minorities as making up an idealized community which could be juxtaposed to the much despised Weimar Republic.[33] Yet it was precisely this outlook that led them to despise the urban Germans in Łódź even more. *Ostforscher*-observers of the Germans in Poland largely repeated the trope of the denationalized, "cosmopolitan" Germandom in Łódź, thereby underlining the cultural contamination of the local Germans and their threat to Germany's revisionist goals. Given the ethnic makeup of the city, it is no coincidence that references to intellectual sterility, business orientation, and "cosmopolitanism" appeared to be informed by commonplace antisemitic stereotypes. Using insinuations of cultural proximity to Jews, this brand of antisemitism could be used to peripheralize and discipline the German minority in Łódź.

In an article in the journal *Deutsche Blätter in Polen*, Dr. Johann Reiners, a German economist from western Poland, bemoaned the stunted intellectual level of all national groups in Łódź. He compared Łódź with America in order to describe the shallowness of the city's inhabitants, who were purportedly interested only in business and engaged in nothing of deeper intellectual or cultural value. He noted that the "Lodzer German" could speak two or three languages, but for business reasons remained nationally cautious: he considered himself a Lodzer first and a German second, and he certainly did not want to be identified as a Prussian German. Reiners did not deny that there were signs that the "sleeping ethnic group" (*schlummerndes Volkstum*) was indeed waking up, but it was to be a slow selection process, a separation of the "chaff from the wheat."[34] The overall tone of his article was pessimistic and was dominated by his criticism of the signs of cultural hybridity and national contamination.

The trope of the "Lodzer Mensch" persisted into the early 1930s.[35] Even those interested in unifying the minority in Poland took a patronizing attitude toward the Łódź Germans. Hermann Rauschning, who before moving to Danzig was editor of *Deutsche Blätter in Polen*, introduced a special volume of the *Blätter* devoted to Germans in central Poland with a call for more unity through mutual understanding. He emphasized that the Germans in western

Poland were still new to their situation as *Auslandsdeutsche*, while the Germans in the East had preserved their elemental Germanness over a century. Yet his programmatic appeal to the western Polish Germans to lose their haughty attitude toward the Łódź Germans only underlined the persistence of such views, and his praise for the endurance of the Germans in Łódź was also undercut by his own apparent doubts about whether all German-speakers in the city could be considered Germans. Rauschning's essay seemed designed to enlighten western Polish Germans about their exotic eastern cousins and to ask them to understand their sometimes strange behavior: one should understand that their long exposure to foreign elements may have caused them to take on forms that appear "alienating and dishonest" (*befremdlich und unaufrichtig*). While he suggested that some "fruitful" results could be gleaned from their experience, this was far from having the Łódź Germans become a viable model for the western Polish Germans.[36] Rather, such statements merely confirmed the primacy of the West and legitimated its further management of the East.

Of course there were many Germans from Łódź who played an active role in nationalist minority politics, but they were the exceptions who proved the rule of stigmatization. Indeed, even central Polish German nationalists had largely internalized the idea of the "Lodzer Mensch," and they did not hesitate to apply the stereotype when they found it expedient to do so. Adolf Eichler, often considered one of the fathers of central Polish German nationalism, noted that the Łódź Germans still had to "excrete" the "creeping poison" of their "renegade disposition" (*Überläufergesinnung*).[37] In an issue of *Deutsche Blätter in Polen* from 1925, one commentator (apparently from central Poland) complained about the "cultural immaturity," the "political ignorance," and the lack of a "conscious *Volksgemeinschaft*" among the German inhabitants of Łódź.[38] While this central Polish criticism was to a large part informed by rural-urban antagonisms, the "Lodzer Mensch" could also strike beyond Łódź. Just as the stereotype had been carried over from the industrial elites to the whole of Łódź's (German) population, it was readily transferable from the city to the entirety of central Poland, of which Łódź was the undisputed center. In 1931, Albert Breyer, another German from central Poland (but not Łódź) who contributed often to *Ostforschung* publications, complained of the low evolutionary development of the German settlements and stated that the central Polish Germans there were driven by primitive instincts and thought only in practical terms. He came to the conclusion that one could not possibly have any lower expectations for the cultural-intellectual production of these Germans.[39] The emphasis on the local Germans' purported lack of national vigor was likely a result of the central Polish German nationalists' own lack of success in winning the Germans for their cause, thereby confirming the hegemonic discourse of the superiority of the Germans in western Poland.

Political developments in Łódź only reinforced these fears of the "Lodzer Mensch." While conservative-nationalist groupings dominated German political life in western Poland, they were considerably weaker in Łódź. The very existence of the nationalist *Deutscher Volksverband* (German People's Union, or DVV) in the 1920s and early 1930s seemed to confirm the national laziness of the Łódź Germans. The DVV did not overly impress even Polish authorities, with one report in 1932 calling its activities "more than modest."[40] Instead, the German socialists dominated minority politics in Łódź in the 1920s.[41] Although the German socialists were in most ways just as interested as the conservative-nationalists in maintaining a strong Germandom in Poland, the German Foreign Ministry and other authorities continued to see them as less capable in the nationality struggle.[42] Rightist ideologues especially found it difficult to fit these socialist Germans into their conceptions of what Germandom abroad should be.

What seemed even more menacing to the German national activists was the rise of an explicitly pro-Polish party in the early 1930s, the *Deutscher Kultur- und Wirtschaftsbund* (German Cultural and Economic Association, DKWB).[43] The DKWB renounced all political ties to Germany and claimed that the other German parties, including the socialists, were in the pay of the revisionist Weimar government.[44] The leaders of the DKWB even claimed that support for these parties would serve only the interests of the Germans in western Poland. In turn, the DVV and the German socialists were unified in their bitter criticism of the DKWB, denouncing it as a puppet of the Polish government. The anxiety the DKWB created among the Germans in Poland and officials in the Reich was out of proportion to its actual influence and size. The organization appeared to be the political embodiment of the "Lodzer Mensch," and its mere existence confirmed fears of the increasing Polonization of the Germans and the decreasing potency of the German nationalists in Łódź. It reinforced the purported dangers of Łódź for the rest of the German minority.[45]

Throughout the 1920s and 1930s, the "Lodzer Mensch" thus played a double role in the project of building a German *Volksgruppe* in Poland. On the one hand, the "Lodzer Mensch" represented the antithesis of what a good German should be. German nationalists believed that the local Germans had a tendency to become slackers in the nationality struggle (*Volkstumskampf*) who readily collaborated and mixed with Jews and Poles. Although it was claimed that the root of the problem lay in the lack of an adequate nationally conscious elite, the problem was perceived as a general affliction among the Łódź Germans. For the *Ostforscher*, especially, Germanness was a privilege that had to be protected, and the rootless, self-loathing Łódź German thus seemed to call into question the nature of this privilege and the durability of the German *Volk*. As a transgressor who had failed in the implicit duty to uphold his nationality, the Łódź German also appeared to lack principles or morals. While it was not doubted that a good many of the inhabitants of Łódź were somehow German, they were still "not-quite-Germans," and their dedication to Germandom remained under scrutiny. German nationalists considered the *Neue Lodzer Zeitung,* a liberal German daily newspaper that took a moderate stance on the nationality issue, to be too Polish-friendly.[46] During the Second World War, one German minority leader, the pastor Eduard Kneifel, called it the organ of the "Lodzer Menschen."[47]

Although he was a source of aggravation, the renegade Łódź German also fulfilled an important disciplining function in the nationalist attempt to build a German community in Poland. The projection of the "Lodzer Mensch" upon the Łódź Germans helped to delineate the limits of being German in Poland and reveals prevailing notions of Germanness. As Claus Leggewie suggests, the analysis of the "other" *within* the "in-group" is ultimately more fruitful than the simple "we-they" dichotomy present in most studies of national collective identity.[48] Being a member of a national minority inevitably led to compromises, and German nationalists routinely cooperated with the Jews and other minorities, as the rather fruitful elections with the Minorities Bloc in the 1920s show. Confining treason to the imagined renegade Łódź German allowed the nationalist Germans, even those in Łódź, to differentiate their own cooperation with Polish society and government from traitorous activity. In other words, dealing with the Poles was acceptable behavior as long as it did not go to the extreme of the "Lodzer Mensch." The "Lodzer Mensch" was considered an in-between entity, but he was not conceptualized as a bridge of reconciliation between Poles, Jews, and Germans. Rather, the "Lodzer Mensch" was proof of the need to redouble efforts to mobilize Germandom in Poland and to dissimilate the Germans from the other nationalities. Using the dangers of the "Lodzer Mensch" as a warning, German nationalists kept cultural issues at the forefront and exhorted Germans to hold onto Germandom while reprimanding those who betrayed it. Thus, the idea of the renegade Łódź German was not just an expression of cultural despair, but fostered this pessimism for political gain. Rather than breaking down social, cultural, and racial boundaries, the idea of the "Lodzer Mensch" served very much to maintain them.

Because this putatively unhealthy Łódź Germandom could be regionally isolated from the rest of the national body, the "Lodzer Mensch" fulfilled another important function. As a part of a racialized discourse, it supported the politics of domination and subordination within the minority by keeping the regional hierarchy in place. The externalization and construction of a negative milieu in the East confirmed the prerogative of German minority leaders in western Poland to lead the other regions. Various attempts by Germans in western Poland to remedy the purported ills of the eastern Germans reveal a form of colonialism within the minority. For example, a common activity among German minority organizations in western Poland was the collection of money for destitute Germans in Poland (known as the *Winterhilfe*, or winter relief). While the conservative-nationalist parties raised money and touted their solidarity, their calls for compassion also drew upon the stereotype of the needy Germans in the East. The title of one winter relief campaign asked in a shaming manner, "Do you know your brother in the East?" (*Kennst du deinen Bruder im Osten?*).[49] While Łódź Germans themselves were not necessarily the direct target of such charity, they were collectively part of the eastern Germans and were thus in need of guidance, be it moral, political, or financial, from their brethren in western Poland. Despite the constant invocation of *Volksgemeinschaft* and the calls for unity, regional distinctions continued to exist and indeed widened throughout the 1920s: Germans continued to be treated differently and to see themselves as different according to where they lived. The Germans in Łódź were not just on the margins of the *Volksgemeinschaft*, but the "other" within.

IV

This situation started to change after 1933, when political as well as ideological factors contributed to a new appreciation for the Germans in the eastern regions. Above all, National Socialist ideology and politics redefined the importance of the minority to Germany, allowing the diaspora Germans in Łódź to renegotiate their role within the minority and to turn the tables on the Germans in western Poland. Germany's foreign political priorities had also changed. Hitler was no longer interested in a mere revision of the borders, but in a sweeping new European order. Hitler's far-reaching strategic goals required long-term (if by no means equal) cooperation with the Polish state, resulting in a tactical reconciliation with Poland and a friendship pact in 1934. Shrill support for a border revision was no longer seen as an asset, but as a foreign political liability. Especially the reprioritizing of *völkisch* affairs over *étatist* matters after 1933 shifted attention away from questions of border revision and hence away from the borderland Germans in western Poland. Under the Nazis, the amount of subsidies to the German minority actually decreased,[50] a development that hurt the Germans in the western regions more substantially than in central and eastern Poland.

The seemingly reduced possibility of a border revision in the short term, due to the Hitler–Piłsudski pact, turned attention to the long-term prospects of survival for the German minority in Poland, and the Germans in Łódź were increasingly considered to be a solution to this problem. Demographic developments within the German minority encouraged a new appraisal of the Germans in the eastern regions. Throughout the interwar period, the number of Germans in the non-Prussian regions continued to grow, both absolutely and as a proportion of the minority, ensuring that the dominance of the German leaders in western Poland would steadily diminish. By 1939 the majority of Polish Germans lived in regions that had never belonged to the German Empire.[51] General economic developments in Poland also encouraged Germany to look to the East. According to Theodor Oberländer, an *Ostforscher* specialist in agriculture and later minister for expellees in the Federal Republic of Germany, economic and cultural life in western Poland was deteriorating rapidly, not least because of the region's separation from Germany.[52] On the other hand, in 1934 Łódź began a rapid recovery from a serious slump in the textile industry.[53] The steady demographic "easternization" was complemented by the mix of racist-*völkisch* ideologies espoused in the Third Reich, which opened up new room for reranking Germanness and now allowed the Łódź Germans to become more "German" than their western Polish counterparts. In this context, a growing recognition of the Germans in Łódź and central Poland came slowly but surely, although this acknowledgment still had to contend with some old stereotypes. In 1934, Franz Anton Doubek spoke of the borderland Germans as being nationally "stable," while the *Sprachinsel* Germans were weak (*labil*).[54] The same year, Walter Kuhn, a German in Poland from Austrian Silesia and a prodigious writer on the German minority in Poland, applauded the "healthy" aspects of the German farmers in central Poland but lamented the lack of a true German leadership for the Germans in Łódź. Still, he ended on the optimistic note that things were changing.[55]

By the mid-1930s, the collusion of demography with ideology and scholarship with opportunism had led to a recognizable shift in the perception of the Germans in Poland. The increased interest in central Polish German issues could be seen in the journal *Deutsche Monatshefte in Polen,* in which central Polish German themes made up a good quarter of all articles in the later 1930s. Scholars devoted to the study of Germans abroad imbued the eastern *Volksdeutsche* with positive characteristics derived from their long experience with nationality conflict. In such imaginations, the diasporic "language islands" were pockets of racially pure Germandom, while their soft and worldly Reich German cousins—including those incorporated into western Poland after World War I—had been pampered by the state and never had to struggle for their Germanness. The self-sufficiency and higher birthrates of the "East Germans"—and especially of the Volhynian Germans in formerly Russian Poland—proved their "racial value" and fitted well into *völkisch* conceptions of a rough and hardy Germandom.[56] Many saw the Germans in Poland's central and eastern territories as the very model of how an embattled Germandom should fend off foreign influences—and, importantly, they had done so with little or no financial assistance from Germany.

Self-help became the new buzzword, and one could speak of a "reverse racism" forming within the minority. Over a decade of heavy subsidies to the German minority in western Poland had failed miserably to stem the demographic slide there. Rather than holding on to their lands and businesses, they continued to flee Poland for Germany. In many ways, the Germans in western Poland had become the new discursive "underclass": they now appeared overly dependent on handouts from Germany, plagued by corruption, and tied into the old "system." There were increasing calls in Reich circles for these borderland Germans to learn from the diaspora Germans, and especially to copy the self-help activities of the Germans in Łódź. Indeed, one *völkisch*-oriented pamphlet enthusiastically invoked the long experience of self-help of Germans abroad as a model for Germans in Germany as well.[57] Viktor Kauder, editor of *Deutsche Monatshefte in Polen* and a member of the German minority in Polish Upper Silesia, wrote an article titled "Grundlagen volksdeutscher Politik in Polen," in which he called for a radical intellectual reorientation of the Germans in western Poland. Kauder recalled many of the older complaints concerning the Germans in the Prussian East, including their purported blind dependence on the state. What is now notable is that this problem of the western Polish Germans was configured in a pan-minority context. Western Polish Germans should not just understand their eastern cousins, but should now take their self-initiative and self-sufficiency as examples for themselves.[58] The German Foreign Ministry also saw the need for the Germans in western Poland to come to terms with being "Germans abroad" and to rid themselves of their "acute irredentist mentality."[59] Not surprisingly, diaspora Germans themselves imbibed these ideas and contributed to the fetishization of the eastern Polish Germans.[60]

What happened to the "Lodzer Mensch"? German nationalists still talked about the problem of renegade Germandom, but its application to the Germans in Łódź as a whole diminished noticeably. Rather, lack of national feeling was now attributed just to the dwindling members of the pro-Polish DKWB or seen as a past affliction from which the Germans in Łódź had since recovered. Clearly, central Polish Germans remained a versatile screen on which to project manifold ideological precepts: Dr. Hans Joachim Beyer, the leader of the *Arbeitsstelle für auslandsdeutsche Forschung* and later an influential racial expert in the SS, found them useful for demonstrating his *volksbiologische* theses on ethnic and racial assimilation. For Beyer, even those who had been denationalized could and should be regained for Germandom, but the process would not succeed without first removing all Jewish influence.[61] In an article that appeared around the German invasion of Poland, Beyer affirmed that even the earliest German settlers in central Poland had been deeply antisemitic. It was precisely their aversion to the Jews, he claimed, that drove many Łódź Germans facing Jewish economic competition into the arms of Polish nationalists. Beyer also described how pastors of Jewish descent had steadily undermined the German leadership of the Augsburg Lutheran Church in the nineteenth century, turning it into a potential instrument of Polonization. In a rather perplexing synthesis of *staatsdeutsch* and *volksdeutsch* projections upon events in the 1800s, he explained the resistance of most German peasants in central Poland by invoking the still lively

"Prussian-German state consciousness" as a basis for their "powers of instinct." Despite these allegedly Polonizing pastors and the "materialistic indifferentism" of the "Lodzer Mensch," Beyer also acknowledged the beginnings of an ethnic German renewal after 1905. Returning to the current situation in interwar Poland, he believed that the deeply rooted "community of fate" among Germans in Poland would triumph over all "appearances of foreign infiltration" (*Überfremdungserscheinungen*).[62]

The steady subversion of the old stereotype of the "Lodzer Mensch" undermined the regional hierarchy of the German minority in Poland. There were those in western Poland, of course, who readily recognized that the *Volksgruppe* was now supposed to rely on itself (and not on aid from Germany), and that the Germans in the formerly Prussian regions should look east and not west for inspiration.[63] Still, many western Polish German leaders were reluctant to acknowledge the sea change within the minority in the 1930s. A speech by Erich Spitzer, the "Gauleiter" of the Young German Party in Pomerelia (western Poland), in Łódź in 1935 exemplified this ambivalence:

> Despite a long period of foreign rule during which you have suffered some losses, we recognize that you have still kept the core of your Germandom intact. You have thus had experience as *Auslandsdeutsche*, which we do not yet have in the western regions. On the other hand, we have been quicker to discern the goal and the road to renewal because we have had greater opportunity to draw strength from the motherland.[64]

As the speaker reveals, this reversal of fortune was not always easy for the Germans in western Poland to swallow, and it is not surprising that they did not want to completely give up their role as the schoolmaster for their eastern cousins. Yet with their *Staatsvolk* heritage depreciating rapidly, the Germans in western Poland were increasingly forced to concede that they were not better than the Łódź Germans after all. The time had long since passed when western Polish Germans could give an occasional patronizing compliment to the Łódź Germans without undermining their own self-worth. While the growing assertiveness of the East caused much concern among German minority leaders in western Poland and among more traditional authorities in Germany, the growing "easternization" of the minority could not be denied.

National Socialist rhetoric played a vital role in empowering the minority's periphery. Discursive categories such as *Volk, Volksdeutsche,* and *Volksgemeinschaft* became increasingly important in this reshuffling of the hierarchy, precisely because they were unclear and opened up competing interpretations of Germanness. For those on the margins seeking entry into the club, this lack of clarity could also lead to a radicalization. Writing about the situation of ethnic Germans under German occupation in the Second World War, Doris Bergen notes that "the tenuousness of the concept of *Volksdeutsche* encouraged anti-Semitism as a way of establishing German credentials."[65] Having previously cooperated with Polish Jews in political institutions such as the city council, nationalist Łódź Germans were now eager to prove their national spirit and rapidly terminated contacts with Łódź's Jewish groups.[66] Moreover, the German nationalists quickly blamed the Jews for instigating an attack on German stores and presses in April 1933. While it is unclear who started the rioting, the infamous "Black Palm Sunday" became a useful tool to dissimilate Germans from their Jewish and Polish surroundings.[67]

A burst of nationalist political activity in the eastern Polish regions reinforced the improved image of the Łódź Germans in the 1930s. The rising popularity of National Socialism among Germans in Poland as well as the Polish government's suppression of German socialists in Poland proved especially beneficial to the nationalist DVV, which organized rallies and membership drives throughout central Poland. Leadership changes were crucial to this new activism. In February 1935, Ludwig Wolff became the deputy leader of the DVV, thus slowly edging out the founder, August Utta, who was widely seen as lacking the necessary dynamism. With much of the leadership now passing into Wolff's hands, the DVV in central Poland enjoyed a new burst of activity and growth in the later 1930s, organizing rallies and membership drives throughout central Poland and in neighboring Volhynia. With over twenty-five thousand members in 1937, the Łódź-based DVV had become a major player in minority politics. This dynamic display of nationalism impressed both Polish and German officials.[68] The socialists and the DKWB, on the other hand, declined steadily and were insignificant by 1935. Also, the Germans in central Poland were remarkably immune to the incursion of the *Jungdeutsche Partei* (Young German Party, JDP), an avidly pro-Nazi German party from formerly Austrian Silesia that had made considerable inroads in western Poland and was seen by many as being too radical. The internecine conflict there between the "Old German" *Deutsche Vereinigung* and the "Young German" JDP further undermined the dominance of the Germans in western Poland. Whereas the Germans in western Poland appeared increasingly tired and impotent, Łódź became the center of an "awakening Germandom."[69] Even the JDP saw central Poland as the most promising region for the expansion of the National Socialist idea and considered moving the party headquarters from Bielsko/Bielitz to Łódź.[70]

The recognition of the Germans in central Poland failed to bridge the differences in interests between the former German citizens in western Poland and the diaspora Germans in central Poland; indeed, if anything it increased them. Tensions between the groups were amply manifest in the question of finding a single leader for the whole minority. Previous unification attempts had been hindered by a combination of Polish regulations, Reich inhibitions, and minority regionalisms. The flux in power relations, which strengthened the periphery vis-à-vis the center, only made it more difficult for unification to take place. The egalitarian rhetoric of *Volksgemeinschaft* exacerbated tensions among German nationalists precisely because it created unrealistically high expectations of solidarity that conflicted with the political interests of regional leaders. In light of the threat from the *Jungdeutsche Partei*, the main German political organizations in western Poland and central Poland tried to conceal their differences with loud proclamations of solidarity and even with plans for unification. Yet the growing conflict of interests between the different regions was often expressed "from below" in the lower party echelons—a fact that makes Polish intelligence reports a valuable source. During a meeting of the western Polish *Deutsche Vereinigung* in January 1936, the plan to expand the DV to all of Poland was considered. Yet Polish sources reported rumors not only that the Łódź Germans opposed the plan, but that local leaders in Poznania-Pomerelia were themselves convinced that a fusion of all regional parties would lead only to their loss of influence vis-à-vis the Germans in Upper Silesia.[71] Indeed, the calculus of region and power was so divisive that the JDP quipped that the *Rat der Deutschen in Polen*, an anti-JDP coalition representing the main regional parties, was simply an arrangement of several national communities among themselves, or *"Volksgemeinschaften unter sich."*[72]

The successful amalgamation of Sudeten Germans under Konrad Henlein led to increasing calls to attempt the same in Poland. By 1938, the *Volksdeutsche Mittelstelle*, a Nazi Party bureau that was strongly linked to the SS, had come to dominate ethnic German affairs. Its head, Werner Lorenz, tried to unify the various regional German groups in an organization that eventually received the name *Bund der Deutschen in Polen* (Union of Germans in Poland, BDP). In his proposal, Lorenz emphasized that conditions in Poland made a unification of the minority both politically and administratively feasible. He stressed that the new organization would create "an effective unity of Germandom enabling the fulfillment of the duties belonging to a *Volksgruppe.*"[73] The plan had two components, a cultural organization and a political party, although the leadership of the two groups would later be fused in a personal union. Significantly, this plan recognized the importance of the eastern margins of the minority by naming Ludwig Wolff, who replaced August Utta as the leader of the DVV in May 1938, to lead the organization's political wing. In an initial draft of the proposal, Lorenz based his decision on the grounds that Wolff had turned the DVV into an authoritative (*maßgebende*) organization. Moreover, the draft suggested that the party be an expansion of Wolff's DVV, which already possessed the necessary statutes.[74]

The failure of this plan is usually attributed to the anxiety of the German Foreign Ministry and the objections of the *Jungdeutsche Partei*, whose own leader, Rudolf Wiesner, was "visibly disappointed" (*sichtlich betroffen*) by a proposal that had not offered to place him in any leadership position beyond his role as a senator in Poland.[75] Above all, however, the Young Germans opposed Ludwig Wolff as the leader of a unified party.[76] But it is likely that the "Old German" leaders in western Poland were also wary of Wolff, who had long been playing a double game with them. Although the DVV belonged to the *Rat der Deutschen in Polen* (Council of Germans in Poland, RDP), which was an "Old German" alliance, Wolff tried to increase the party's clout by flirting with the Young Germans, thus allowing the central Polish Germans to play a strategic middle position in the ongoing struggle between the DV and the JDP.[77] Events soon confirmed this distrust: Wolff, who was likely stung by the resistance to his candidature and probably wanted to emphasize his own indispensability, plotted throughout the summer against the "Old Germans" and the still nascent plans for creating a *Bund der Deutschen in Polen*. The "Old German" leaders sent a delegation to Łódź to bring Wolff back into the fold, but their hopes for a conversion were in vain.[78] Only in November 1938 could the *Volksdeutsche Mittelstelle* force him to stop conspiring against his erstwhile allies.[79] Even after these events, Wolff remained confident of his own role and that of the Germans in central Poland. In January 1939, he boldly asserted that Łódź would soon become the "metropolis" not only for the German minority in Poland, but for all German minorities in the world.[80]

Although the *Bund der Deutschen in Polen* was never realized and although Wolff never became the political leader of all the Germans in Poland, these events show just how influential the Germans in central Poland had become within the minority. The DVV in central Poland was not just the little sister of the *Deutsche Vereinigung* in western Poland, as it is often simplistically portrayed in the historiography. As the leader of the DVV, Ludwig Wolff had his own agenda and did not belong to any camp but his own. He could make or break deals not just between minority leaders, but between the minority and the Reich. The common acceptance of Nazism, it appears, did little to undermine the latent regional divisions within the German minority in Poland. These parties did less adapting to National Socialism and more adopting of National Socialist tenets. Minority leaders were able to synthesize prevailing ideological considerations with these concrete interests, often in ways quite frustrating to their Reich caregivers. Even the most Nazi-oriented of minority politicians, after all, still had considerations of power and authority at stake in maintaining regional parties. Hardly dependent vassals of the German state, these minority leaders enjoyed a mutual relationship of give and take with various state and party organizations within Germany. Meanwhile, the rise of a central Polish region created a counterweight to the Germans in western Poland and resulted in a leadership dilemma that lasted until the end of the interwar period. The continuing struggle between the western *Grenzlanddeutschtum* and the eastern German diaspora deepened old regional cleavages and hindered any attempt at unification. The radical ideological change in Germany after 1933, while subverting the previous hierarchy, did not stop this disintegrative process within the minority, but merely accelerated it further.

Notes

1. Peter Sahlins, *Boundaries: The Making of France and Spain in the Pyrenees* (Berkeley: University of California Press, 1989).

2. Celia Applegate, "A Europe of Regions: Reflections on the Historiography of Sub-national Places in Modern Times," in "Bringing Regionalism back to History," forum, *American Historical Review* 104, no. 4 (1999): 1161–65; and Eric Storm, "Regionalism in History, 1890–1945: The Cultural Approach," *European History Quarterly* 33, no. 2 (2003): 251–65, especially 252–55, 261.

3. Celia Applegate, *A Nation of Provincials: The German Idea of Heimat* (Berkeley: University of California Press, 1990); Alon Confino, *The Nation as a Local Metaphor: Württemberg, Imperial Germany, and National Memory, 1871–1918* (Chapel Hill: University of North Carolina Press, 1997); Abigail Green, *Fatherlands: State-Building and Nationhood in Nineteenth-Century Germany* (New York: Cambridge University Press, 2001); Nancy R. Reagin, "Recent Work on German National Identity: Regional? Imperial? Gendered? Imaginary?" *Central European History* 37, no. 2 (2004): 273–89; and Charlotte Tacke, *Denkmal im sozialen Raum: Nationale Symbole in Deutschland und Frankreich im 19. Jahrhundert* (Göttingen: Vandenhoeck und Ruprecht, 1995).

4. Daphne Berdahl, *Where the World Ended: Re-unification and Identity in the German Borderland* (Berkeley: University of California Press, 1999).

5. Richard Blanke, *Orphans of Versailles: The Germans in Western Poland, 1918–1939* (Lexington: University Press of Kentucky, 1993), 3–4.

6. Marian Wojciechowski, "Die deutsche Minderheit in Polen (1920–1939)," in *Deutsche und Polen zwischen den Kriegen: Minderheitenstatus und "Volkstumskampf" im Grenzgebiet; Amtliche Berichterstattung aus beiden Ländern, 1920–1939*, ed. Rudolf Jaworski and Marian Wojciechowski (Munich: K. G. Sauer, 1997), 4; and Jörg K. Hoensch, *Geschichte Polens* (Stuttgart: Eugen Ulmer, 1998), 274–75. One of the most notable proponents of the thesis that the German minority had transformed into a *Volksgruppe* was Richard Breyer, who grew up in central Poland and became director of the Herder-Institut in Marburg. See Richard Breyer, *Das Deutsche Reich und Polen, 1932–1937: Außenpolitik und Volksgruppenfragen* (Würzburg: Holzner, 1955), especially 49–51, 227–36, 255–56.

7. This peripherality is still discernible in the historiography, even though many of the postwar German historians came from central Poland. See Krzysztof Woźniak, "Forschungsstand und Forschungsdesiderata zur Geschichte der Deutschen in Mittelpolen," *Nordost-Archiv* 9, no. 2 (2000): 413–27.

8. Chad Bryant, "Either German or Czech: Fixing Nationality in Bohemia and

Moravia, 1939–1946," *Slavic Review* 61, no. 4 (winter 2002): 683–706, especially 684–85.

9. Ibid., 701.

10. See especially Jerzy Kochanowski, "Kto ty jesteś? Niemiec mały! Volksdeutsche: sprawa jest bardziej skomplikowana niż myślimy!" *Polityka,* no. 2417 (7 September 2003); and Jerzy Kochanowski, ed., *Die "Volksdeutschen" in Polen, Frankreich, Ungarn und der Tschechoslowakei* (Osnabrück: Fibre, forthcoming).

11. Doris L. Bergen, "The Nazi Concept of 'Volksdeutsche' and the Exacerbation of Anti-Semitism in Eastern Europe, 1939–45," *Journal of Contemporary History* 29, no. 4 (1994): 572.

12. The instrumental functions of invoking the national community are explored in John Connelly, "The Uses of *Volksgemeinschaft:* Letters to the NSDAP Kreisleitung Eisenach, 1939–1940," *Journal of Modern History* 68, no. 4 (December 1996): 899–930; and Vandana Joshi, *Gender and Power in the Third Reich: Female Denouncers and the Gestapo, 1933–45* (Basingstoke: Palgrave Macmillan, 2003).

13. Helmut Walser Smith, *German Nationalism and Religious Conflict: Culture, Ideology, Politics, 1870–1914* (Princeton, N.J.: Princeton University Press, 1995); Helmut Walser Smith, ed., *Protestants, Catholics, and Jews in Germany, 1880–1914* (Oxford: Berg, 2001).

14. One of the most influential theorists of center-periphery relations was the Norwegian political scientist Stein Rokkan. See Peter Flora, ed., *State Formation, Nation-Building, and Mass Politics in Europe: The Theory of Stein Rokkan; Based on His Collected Works* (Oxford: Oxford University Press, 1999).

15. Paweł Samuś, "Lodz: Heimatstadt von Polen, Deutschen und Juden," in *Polen, Deutsche und Juden in Lodz, 1820–1939: Eine schwierige Nachbarschaft,* ed. Jürgen Hensel (Osnabrück: Fibre, 1999), 13.

16. Bianka Pietrow-Ennker, "Ein Klischee lernt das Zwinkern: Der 'Lodzermensch' verkörpert eine Lebensweise, die in Lodz wieder modern wird," *Frankfurter Allgemeine Zeitung,* 3 January 2002, Feuilleton, 48.

17. The question of which ethnic group played the dominant role in building Łódź is contested. See Krzysztof Woźniak, "Spóry o genezę Łodzi przemysłowej w pracach historycznych autorów polskich, niemieckich i żydowskich," in *Polacy-Niemcy-żydzi w Łodzi w XIX–XX w. Sąsiedzi dalecy i bliscy,* ed. Paweł Samuś (Łódź: Ibidem, 1997), 9–26. For a listing of the different German groups contributing to the migration to Łódź, see Kurt Klötzner, "Die Industrie als Basis des Lodzer Deutschtums," in *Das Lodzer Deutsche Gymnasium: Im Spannungsfeld zwischen Schicksal und Erbe, 1906–1981,* ed. Peter E. Nasarski (Berlin: Westkreuz, 1981), 156.

18. Wiesław Puś, "Die Berufs- und Sozialstruktur der wichtigsten ethnischen Gruppen in Lodz und ihre Entwicklung in den Jahren 1820–1914," in Hensel, *Polen, Deutsche und Juden in Lodz,* 35–37.

19. Samuś, "Lodz," 13.

20. Richard Breyer, "Der 'Lodzer Mensch'—Legende und Wirklichkeit," in *Lodz: Die Stadt der Völkerbegegnung im Wandel der Geschichte,* ed. Peter E. Nasarski (Köln-Rodenkirchen: Liebig, 1978), 74–75.

21. Pietrow-Ennker, "Ein Klischee lernt das Zwinkern," 48.

22. Two recent works on the *Schlonsaken* and other Upper Silesians are Kai Struve and Philipp Ther, eds., *Die Grenzen der Nationen: Identitätenwandel in Oberschlesien in*

der Neuzeit (Marburg: Herder-Institut, 2002); and Manfred Alexander, "Oberschlesien im 20. Jahrhundert: Eine mißverstandene Region," *Geschichte und Gesellschaft* 30, no. 3 (July–September 2004): 465–89. Also, Tomasz Fałęcki compares the German minorities in Upper Silesia and Łódź, but unfortunately he touches upon the "Lodzer Mensch" only briefly. See "Niemcy w Łodzi i Niemcy w województwie śląskim w okresie międzywojennym: Wzajemne powiązania oraz podobieństwa i różnice pod względem społeczno-ekonomicznym i świadomościowym," in *Niemcy w Łodzi do 1939 roku,* ed. Marian Wilk (Łódź: Uniwersytet Łódzki, 1996), 79.

23. Bryant, "Either German or Czech."

24. Stefan Górski, *Łódź Spółczesna: Obrazki i szkice publicystyczne* (Łódź: Księg. Narodowa, 1904), 21–22, quoted in Samuś, "Lodz," 23.

25. Andreas R. Hofman, "Die vergessene Okkupation: Lodz im Ersten Weltkrieg," in *Deutsche-Juden-Polen: Geschichte einer wechselvollen Beziehung im 20. Jahrhundert; Festschrift für Hubert Schneider,* eds. Andrea Löw, Kerstin Robusch, and Stefanie Walter (Frankfurt am Main: Campus, 2004), 63.

26. Stefan Pytlas, "Problemy asymilacji i polonizacji społeczności niemieckiej w Łodzi do 1914 r.," in Wilk, *Niemcy w Łodzi do 1939 roku,* 19; and Adolf Eichler, *Das Deutschtum in Kongreßpolen* (Stuttgart: Ausland und Heimat Verlags-Aktiengesellschaft, 1921), 119.

27. Hoensch, *Geschichte Polens,* 258.

28. Wilhelm Fielitz, *Das Stereotyp des wolhyniendeutschen Umsiedlers: Popularisierungen zwischen Sprachinselforschung und nationalsozialistischer Propaganda* (Marburg: N. G. Elwert, 2000), 96.

29. Norbert F. Krekeler, *Revisionsanspruch und geheime Ostpolitik der Weimarer Republik: Die Subventionierung der deutschen Minderheit in Polen, 1919–1933* (Stuttgart: Deutsche Verlags-Anstalt, 1973), 93.

30. Hans-Adolf Jacobsen, ed., *Hans Steinacher: Bundesleiter des VDA, 1933–1937; Erinnerungen und Dokumente* (Boppard am Rhein: Boldt, 1970), 528–29; and Hans-Adolf Jacobsen, *Nationalsozialistische Außenpolitik, 1933–1938* (Frankfurt am Main: A. Metzner, 1968), 585 note 48.

31. Eric Weitz, "Racial Politics without the Concept of Race: Reevaluating Soviet Ethnic and National Purges," *Slavic Review* 61, no. 1 (spring 2002): 3–8.

32. Report by the German consul in Łódź, Kurt von Luckwald, to the German Foreign Ministry, "Inhalt: Lodzer Deutschtum," dated 14 March 1928, copy for *Regierungsrat* Erich Krahmer-Möllenberg, in Bundesarchiv Berlin, R8043 (Deutsche Stiftung), microfilm no. 62660.

33. Rudolf Jaworski, "Der auslandsdeutsche Gedanke in der Weimarer Republik," *Annali dell'Istituto storico italo-germanico in Trento* 4 (1978): 379–80.

34. Dr. Johann Reiners, "Von der Struktur des Deutschtums in Polen," Sonderheft Ständischer Aufbau, *Deutsche Blätter in Polen* 2, no. 1 (January 1925): 27. Dr. Reiners's dissertation at the University of Breslau in 1923 was entitled "Die landwirtschaftliche Produktivgenossenschaft in Theorie und Praxis, hinsichtlich ihrer Bedeutung für die innere Kolonisation."

35. One writer complained that the biggest problem was "die Gleichgültigkeit gegenüber geistigen und völkischen Fragen der erwerbsgebenen Menschen der Industriestadt Lodz." D. Borse, "Der Deutsche Schul- und Bildungsverein zu Lodz," *Deutsche Blätter in Polen* 8, nos. 8–9 (August–September 1931): 470.

36. Hermann Rauschning, "Zur Einführung," *Deutsche Blätter in Polen* 1, no. 5 (November 1924): 191–92.

37. Adolf Eichler, "Die nationale Selbstbehauptung der Lodzer Deutschen," *Deutsche Blätter in Polen* 1, no. 5 (November 1924): 197.

38. T. R., "Innere Zerrissenheit," in "Vom Deutschtum in Kongreßpolen II," special issue, *Deutsche Blätter in Polen* 2, no. 3 (March 1925): 112.

39. Albert Breyer, "Neuerscheinungen im Deutschen Schrifttum Mittelpolens (1925–1930)," *Deutsche Blätter in Polen* 8, no. 4 (April 1931): 227.

40. *Sprawy Narodowościowe* 6 (1932): 683, quoted in Breyer, *Das Deutsche Reich und Polen*, 249.

41. Mirosław Cygański, *Mniejszość niemiecka w Polsce centralnej w latach 1919–1939* (Łódź: Wydawn. Łódzkie, 1962), 29; and Otto Heike, *Die deutsche Arbeiterbewegung in Polen, 1835–1945* (Dortmund: Ostdeutsche Forschungsstelle im Lande Nordrhein-Westfalen, 1969), 82–83.

42. Petra Blachetta-Madajczyk, *Klassenkampf oder Nation? Deutsche Sozialdemokratie in Polen, 1918–1939* (Düsseldorf: Droste, 1997), 113–27.

43. Przemysław Hauser, "The German Minority in Poland in the Years 1918–1939: Reflections on the State of Research and Interpretation, Proposals for Further Research," *Polish Western Affairs* 32, no. 2 (1991): 31.

44. Its newspaper, *Deutscher Volksbote*, claimed that German-Polish reconciliation could be achieved only by cutting off all political contacts with Germany: "Die deutsche Minderheit in Polen muß sich von sämtlichen politischen Einflüsterungen fernhalten und muß selbst den Schein wahren." *Deutscher Volksbote*, 31 January 1932, newspaper found in Archiwum Państwowe w Łodzi (State Archive in Łódź).

45. Memorandum by the Prussian minister for science, art, and public education, dated 1 July 1931, in Staatsarchiv Münster, StAM VII no. 35, microfiche 5952. My thanks to Brian McCook for bringing this document to my attention.

46. Maria Dehmer, "Die deutsche Minderheit in Lodz nach dem Ersten Weltkrieg bis zum Ende der Ära Pilsudski, 1920–1931" (master's thesis, University of Konstanz, 1999), 4–5, 21, 25. Ironically, the *Neue Lodzer Zeitung* also commonly reprinted nationalist articles from western Polish German newspapers. Ibid., 28.

47. Eduard Kneifel, "Adolf Eichler: Ein Leben im Dienste des Deutschtums," in *Deutschtum im Aufbruch: Vom Volkstumskampf der Deutschen im östlichen Wartheland*, ed. Adolf Kargel and Eduard Kneifel (Leipzig: S. Hirzel, 1942), 15–16.

48. Claus Leggewie, "Ethnizität, Nationalismus und multikulturelle Gesellschaft," in *Nationales Bewußtsein und kollektive Identität: Studien zur Entwicklung des kollektiven Bewußtseins in der Neuzeit*, ed. Helmut Berding (Frankfurt am Main: Suhrkamp, 1994), 49.

49. Breyer, *Das Deutsche Reich und Polen*, 256.

50. Blanke, *Orphans of Versailles*, 161–62, 203–204.

51. Ibid., 3.

52. Theodor Oberländer, "Die wirtschaftliche Notlage der früher preußischen Provinzen Posen und Westpreußen," *Jomsburg: Völker und Staaten im Osten und Norden Europas* 1 (1937): 143–54, especially 153–54.

53. Karl Weber, *Litzmannstadt: Geschichte und Probleme eines Wirtschaftszentrums im Deutschen Osten*, Kieler Vorträge 70 (Jena: Gustav Fischer, 1943), 8.

54. Ingo Haar, *Historiker im Nationalsozialismus: Deutsche Geschichtswissenschaft*

und der "Volkstumskampf" im Osten (Göttingen: Vandenhoeck und Ruprecht, 2000), 219–20.

55. Walter Kuhn, "Das Deutschtum in Kongreßpolen und Ungarn: Ein sprachinselkundlicher Vergleich," *Deutsche Monatshefte in Polen* 1, no. 1 (July 1934): 14.

56. Fielitz, *Das Stereotyp des wolhyniendeutschen Umsiedlers*, 94.

57. An example of this attempt at popular reeducation can be found in a pamphlet from the Nazi period: Horand Horsa Schacht, *Du mußt volksdeutsch sein!* (Dortmund: Crüwell, 1935), 13.

58. Viktor Kauder, "Grundlagen volksdeutscher Politik in Polen," *Deutsche Monatshefte in Polen* 1, no. 3 (September 1934): 76–77.

59. Memorandum by Fritz von Twardowski, "Aufzeichnung betreffend die Deutsche Volksgruppe in den an Polen abgetretenen Gebieten," dated 30 November 1936, in Politisches Archiv des Auswärtigen Amts, Inland II geheim 221 (Geheime Verschlußsachen des Referats Kult A, Bd. 2), microfiche nos. 2322–23, pp. 222–29.

60. Albert Breyer, "Das Deutschtum in Mittelpolen: Bemerkungen zu der anliegenden Karte," *Jomsburg: Völker und Staaten im Osten und Norden Europas* 2 (1938): 77.

61. Karl Heinz Roth, "Heydrichs Professor: Historiographie des 'Volkstums' und der Massenvernichtungen: Der Fall Hans Joachim Beyer," in *Geschichtsschreibung als Legitimationswissenschaft, 1918–1945*, ed. Peter Schöttler (Frankfurt am Main: Suhrkamp Taschenbuch, 1999), 273.

62. Hans Joachim Beyer, "Mittelpolen in der neueren deutschen Volksgeschichte," *Vergangenheit und Gegenwart* 29, nos. 9–10 (1939): 514, 518–24. Further works by Beyer on central Poland include "Judenchristliche Einflüsse in der Augsburgischen Kirche und ihre Bedeutung für die Geschichte der Volkstumsfrage in Mittelpolen," *Deutsche Monatshefte in Polen* 6, no. 1 (July 1939): 5–15; and "Hauptlinien einer Geschichte der ostdeutschen Volksgruppen im 19. Jahrhundert," *Historische Zeitschrift* 162 (1940): 509–39. As editor of an *Ostforschung* journal, Beyer also oversaw two essays on the "re-*volking*" of the Germans in central Poland: Hans Koch, "Zur Frage der Umvolkung der evangelischen Deutschen in Kongreßpolen," *Auslandsdeutsche Volksforschung* 1 (1937): 398–406; and Hans Hopf, "Zur Frage der Assimilation der Deutschen Mittelpolens (unter Berücksichtigung ihrer sozialen Struktur)," *Auslandsdeutsche Volksforschung* 2 (1938): 487–99.

63. "Unsere Revolution von 1918," *Deutsche Nachrichten in Polen*, 18 August 1935, in Geheimes Staatsarchiv Berlin, I Hauptabteilung, Rep. 77, Tit. 856, no. 753 (Auseinandersetzungen innerhalb der deutschen Minderheit in Polen—Zeitungsausschnitte 1.4.35 bis 31.10.35), 93.

64. "Erwachen des völkischen Lebens in Mittelpolen," *Deutsche Nachrichten in Polen*, 16 March 1935, in ibid., no. 752 (Auseinandersetzungen innerhalb der deutschen Minderheit in Polen—Zeitungsausschnitte 30.8.33 bis 31.3.35), 197.

65. Bergen, "The Nazi Concept of 'Volksdeutsche,'" 575.

66. Beate Kosmala, "Lodzer Juden und Deutsche im Jahr 1933: Die Rezeption der nationalsozialistischen Machtübernahme in Deutschland und ihre Wirkung auf das Verhältnis von jüdischer und deutscher Minderheit," in Hensel, *Polen, Deutsche und Juden in Lodz*, 237–45.

67. Beate Kosmala, *Juden und Deutsche im polnischen Haus: Tomaszów Mazowiecki, 1914–1939* (Berlin: Metropol, 2001), 290–92.

68. Weekly report of the Nationalities Department in the Polish Interior Ministry, 11 August 1938 (no. 32), in Archiwum Akt Nowych w Warszawie (Archive of Modern Records in Warsaw), Ministerstwo Spraw Zagranicznych (Foreign Ministry), sign. 2352, microfilm no. B 18557; and memorandum sent by Werner Lorenz to German minority leaders in Poland, dated 18 May 1938, with attachment: "Vorschlag für die Neubildung der deutschen Volksgruppe in Polen" (I. Projekt), in Politisches Archiv des Auswärtigen Amts, Inland II geheim 227 (Geheime Verschlußsachen des Referats Kult A, Band 8), microfiche no. 2347, p. 159.

69. Breyer, *Das Deutsche Reich und Polen*, 250.

70. A. Potocki (vice-voivode), "Sprawozdanie miesięczne wojewody z ruchu zawodowego, spółeczno-politycznego i narodowościowego" (monthly report of the Voivodeship in Łódź), no. 12 from December 1935, dated 9 January 1936, in Archiwum Państwowe w Łodzi, Urząd Wojewódzki Łódzki, sign. 2507 L (microfilm no. L-12757).

71. Voivode in Poznań to the Interior Ministry (Political Department) in Warsaw, memorandum entitled "Deutsche Vereinigung—zjazd delegatów w Bydgoszczy," dated 1 February 1936, in Archiwum Państwowe w Bydgoszczy (State Archive in Bydgoszcz), Urząd Wojewódzki Pomorski, sign. 2788 (Wydział Społeczno-Politiczny —Sprawy organizacji niemieckich w Polsce i na Pomorzu 1933-1936), 25-30.

72. Breyer, *Das Deutsche Reich und Polen*, 251.

73. Memorandum by Lorenz, "Vorschlag für die Neubildung der deutschen Volksgruppe in Polen," 156.

74. Ibid., 158-59.

75. Consul general in Katowice (Wilhelm Nöldeke) to the Foreign Ministry in Berlin, "Neuordnung der deutschen Volksgruppe in Polen," dated 3 June 1938, in Politisches Archiv des Auswärtigen Amts, Inland II geheim 228 (Geheime Verschlußsachen des Referats Kult A, Band 9), microfiche no. 2348, p. 26.

76. Ibid., dated 21 June 1938, 49.

77. In early May, the shocked members of the *Rat der Deutschen in Polen* had to call a special meeting upon hearing that Ludwig Wolff planned to cooperate with Wilhelm Schneider, the former deputy leader of the JDP. Report sent by police headquarters in Katowice to the Administration of the Silesian Voivodeship (Sociopolitical Department) in Katowice, dated 6 May 1938, in Archiwum Państwowe w Katowicach (State Archive in Katowice), Dyrekcja Policji—Katowice, sign. 312 (Deutscher Arbeitskreis), p. 5.

78. Memorandum sent by the Municipal and County Police Command of the Silesian Voivodeship (Department of Investigation) to police headquarters in Katowice, dated 27 July 1938, in ibid., 10-11; and report sent by police headquarters in Katowice to the Administration of the Silesian Voivodeship (Socio-political Department) in Katowice, dated 30 August 1938, in ibid., 12.

79. Report sent by police headquarters in Katowice to the Administration of the Silesian Voivodeship (Socio-political Department), dated 10 November 1938, in ibid., 15.

80. Daily report of the Nationalities Department of the Polish Interior Ministry, 11 February 1939 (no. 34), Archiwum Akt Nowych, Ministerstwo Spraw Wewnętrznych, sign. 971, pp. 51-52.

Six

A Margin at the Center

The Conservatives in Lower Saxony
between Kaiserreich *and*
Federal Republic

Frank Bösch

I

On the face of it, German conservatism would not appear to offer fruitful territory for an exploration of German history "from the margins." True, conservative parties rarely won a majority of electoral support, but the strong position in society of those groups conventionally referred to as "the Conservatives" seems obvious. Politically, they wielded power through their dominance of the bureaucracy, the judiciary, and the military; their economic power was manifested in their ownership of property and exercised very effectively through organized interest groups; their cultural power, meanwhile, was rooted in the widespread acceptance of Christian morality and in their influence over the educational system.[1] Their values were not only propagated by the mass media, by the churches, and via powerful associational networks, but also defended by a dominant historiographical tradition which articulated conservative positions over a long period of time.

And yet there are strong grounds for suggesting that the history of German conservativism might also be reconsidered as a "history from the margins." Traditional master narratives—both affirmative and critical—have overwhelmingly tended to focus on the history of Prussian conservatives in the north and east, or on the history of Catholic conservatism in the south and west of Germany. The same is true of studies of conservative intellectuals and mass organizations.[2] The regional and marginal groups in between these dominant elements, meanwhile, have mostly been neglected.

One prominent example of such a minority inside the majority is the conservatives of the former kingdom of Hanover—the so-called "Guelph Conservatives"—who, following a period of protracted conflict at the beginning of the imperial era, developed their own milieu in contradistinction to both Prussian conservatism and German liberalism. Not only did they create their own party, mass organizations, and festivities, they also invented their own historical narratives and a memorial culture defined specifically against Prussian history. This regional conservative counterculture survived for nearly a century, but has rarely been the subject of scholarly research. Indeed, while its parliamentary agitation during the imperial era and its party organization after 1945 have been examined, the social history of this culture has been almost completely neglected.[3] This chapter seeks to open new perspectives on a marginal group within German conservatism by examining the development of the Guelphic-conservative milieu under the changing conditions of imperial, Weimar, Nazi, and postwar West Germany, placing an analysis of the Guelph-conservative stronghold of Celle within a broader context.[4]

II

As the emergence of both the Catholic milieu during the *Kulturkampf* and the socialist milieu during the period of anti-Socialist legislation demonstrate, cultural milieus are formed through conflict. In both cases it was the suppression by the state of their elites, their organizations, and their values which led to the creation of powerful parties and clubs, to the emergence of a separate mass media, to the adoption of special symbols, festivities, and rituals, and to a distinctive way of writing history.[5] By contrast, conservatives and liberals, it is usually claimed, did not form such a close milieu because they constituted the dominant culture and were in control of the organs of state.

If one shifts one's focus away from Berlin and toward Hanover, however, one gets a different perspective. In 1866 the king of Hanover was deposed and the kingdom became a province of Prussia. The "Guelph" king was forced to leave and went to Austria; the famous *Welfenschatz*, his private property, was taken by Bismarck to appease the press. The annexation created a constellation in which even Hanover conservatives felt politically, economically, and culturally suppressed. First, the dethronement of the monarch offended the fundamental political beliefs of the conservatives.[6] The taking of the *Welfenschatz* was seen as an act of arbitrary rule, and the Prussian officials installed in Hanover were regarded as occupation troops. The rural population, especially, continued to show loyalty to the Guelphic king. Second, confessional issues provoked discord. For conservative clergymen and believers it was an affront that the Prussian king, a reformist, should become *Summepiskopus* of the Hanoverian Lutheran Church.[7] Third, the annexation increased economic fears. Craftsmen felt threatened by freedom of trade and their new rivals in more developed Prussia. Farmers were hit by the tax increases which followed. Government officials protested against changes to the bureaucracy as many functions of the court were centralized and transferred to Prussian officials. In sum, many conservatives believed that Prussia was systematically bringing about the decline of their region.

The Guelph kingdom's supporters' protests were forcefully suppressed. During the 1870s and 1880s several aristocrats were arrested and had to endure judicial inquiries.[8] Guelphic war memorials and commemorations of the Hanover army were forbidden, while new memorials were pulled down and their yellow-white flag was banned.[9] Trials of Guelph clubs and their publishers followed.

Down to the 1890s this protest was mainly supported by the local elites. Next to the aristocrats, the clergy were its most important leaders. Especially influential in the countryside were sermons against Prussia which questioned the latter's Christianity.[10] The Prussian bureaucracy reacted much as it did against Catholic clergymen, with pastors being accused in the 1870s of recommending pro-Guelph literature from the pulpit.[11] These pastors enjoyed strong support—in Celle, for example, the district officer (*Kreishauptmann*) failed to push through the installation of a pastor loyal to Prussia against a supporter of the Guelph movement.[12] In some parishes, as in the famous example of the Hermannsburger Mission in 1878, a radical conclusion was drawn. In order to escape Prussian supervision they left the *Landeskirche* and founded a separate, free church, the *Evangelisch-lutherische Freikirche in Hanover*.[13]

This protest against Prussia was also supported by Hanoverian war veterans. The battle of Langensalza, at which Hanover was defeated by Prussia in 1866, became the reference point for countless activities.[14] In public speeches and in regional historiography it was stressed that the Hanoverian soldiers had been braver, more loyal, and more powerful than those of Prussia: they had been defeated on the day simply because they had been poorly supplied during the battle. The battle was praised in patriotic plays performed in uniform,[15] in popular songs and poems,[16] and with memorial buildings adorned with enormous paintings.[17] The memorial festivities of 27 June were celebrated as if referring to a victory. Revanchist speeches against Prussia united the Guelph-conservative milieu. The soldiers of Langensalza were celebrated as heroes and enjoyed great local prestige. After 1867 they founded veterans' clubs which preserved the memory of the fallen soldiers, whose deaths were construed as creating obligation to the values of the Guelphic movement.[18]

The sense of suppression led to the founding of a separate conservative party, the *Deutsch-Hannoversche Partei* (DHP). During the early years of the *Kaiserreich* the party, whose main intention was to fight for an independent kingdom of Hanover, gained about half of all votes in the province.[19] From the 1890s onward it also organized itself in local districts, with branches often having some hundred members each.[20] Its program represented typical conservative values, but it was more open-minded in questions of political rights.

The DHP thus cooperated with other suppressed minorities in the *Reichstag*, working with the Catholic minority in Hanover, with whom they formed common electoral lists and whom they also supported against the suppression of churches during the *Kulturkampf*.[21] They even voted against the Anti-Socialist Law, arguing that this legislation showed the same abuse of power as that represented by the annexation of Hanover in 1866.[22]

From the 1890s onward, the Guelph conservatives also developed a strong associational network. Following the example of other new mass movements, a network of singing societies and gymnastic leagues with names such as *Langensalza, Sachsenroß*, and *Hannoverscher Club* spread the specifically Christian and monarchical values of the pro-Hanover conservatives and perpetuated the memory of the experience of the 1870s for further generations. These clubs were usually chaired by aristocrats and were often far from mass organizations, but their activities reached large sections of the community, including women.[23] Their regionalist ideology was also spread through the *Heimat* museums and *Heimat* clubs which emerged everywhere, and in which teachers played an especially active role. The *Heimat* movement's close connections to the Guelph conservatives made it even more influential than in other regions.[24]

These organizational efforts were also, however, a response to the electoral decline of the Guelph conservatives after 1890. Political suppression of the Guelphs had ceased—after 1900 their public activities were still monitored by the police, but they were seldom brought to court. Meanwhile, a specifically Guelph memorial culture seemed to be fading in the face of new integrative developments which engendered more cooperation between the conservatives of Hanover and those of other regions. The rise of nationalism and the emergence of mass movements such as the veterans' *Kyffhäuserbund* helped to form a common club life, while the emergence of social democracy offered a common enemy against which to unite.[25] It is true that as late as 1907 the remaining Guelph conservatives formed a new, separate veterans' club, the *Hannoversche Kriegerverein*, which pointedly paid homage to the emperor, but not to the Prussian king.[26] However, this club was unable to compete with the *Kyffhäuser*, having only three thousand members by 1911. Similarly, the pastors' protests declined as they too began to participate in the *Kyffhäuser* and patriotic festivals.[27]

In the cities, especially, generational change diminished the differences between the pro-Hanover and pro-Prussian conservatives. From the turn of the century onward, social contacts between the two groups increased. The sons of local upper-class families started to choose the traditional conservative career route of the Prussian civil service more often.[28] Local officials became reconciled to the Prussian conservatives. Meanwhile, the Guelphs' electoral support continued to decline.[29] Finally, the reconciliation of the Guelph and Hohenzollern dynasties was sealed by the marriage of the emperor's daughter

Viktoria Luise and the Guelph prince Ernst August in 1913. This, together with the upsurge in nationalist sentiment in 1914, seemed to signal the end of the conservative minority within the majority.

III

In fact, the Guelph conservatives experienced a sudden revival following the Great War, as the circumstances of defeat and revolution, the advent of democracy, and the new-found power of the Social Democrats mobilized them anew. In the first postwar elections, in 1919, their separatist party won four times as many votes as it had in the province of Hanover in 1912 and became the second-strongest party, behind the Social Democrats.[30] Indeed, the circumstances of the 1920s gave its anti-Prussianism renewed focus. In addition to its opposition to Prussian conservatism and liberalism, it also defined itself against the Social Democrats, who led the Prussian "Weimar coalition" down to 1932. Their slogan "Los von Berlin" ("Away from Berlin") now became a call to defeat the "red" metropolis. The "spirit of Berlin" was now seen as a force which destroyed "German faith, German custom, and German Christianity."[31] Paradoxically, it was the electoral rights granted to women by the Weimar constitution which helped to increase the Guelphs' power, as women tended more often to vote for those parties associated with the local church.

Its separatist agenda aside, the program of the DHP was similar to that of the *Deutschnationale Volkspartei* (DNVP). Its overtly Christian stance, its defense of private property, and its critique of "pure capitalism" were essentially the same. However, the pro-Hanover conservatives tended to adopt less nationalistic and racist positions; their antisemitism and anti-Catholicism were also much weaker. Instead, they tended to stress the alleged superiority of Hanover since the Middle Ages. Their experience of having been a suppressed minority also seemed to sensitize them to the needs of other groups with less influence within the state.

More explicitly than the DNVP, the DHP demanded the reinvention of the monarchy, because "popular monarchy is the best guarantee of the support of the well-being of all parts of society."[32] Monarchism mobilized its supporters, while the birthdays of Guelph noblemen were celebrated throughout the region.[33] When the Guelph prince, the duke of Brunswick, traveled through the country, associations such as the *Hannoversche Kriegerverein* (Hanoverian veterans association), the *Großdeutsche Orden Heinrich des Löwen*, and the *Bund der Treue* lined the streets when his car passed through their villages. Their singing associations sang songs such as "Den Herzog segne Gott" ("God bless the duke") and "Der Hannoversche Königsgruss" ("The Hanover salute to the king"). Local DHP chairmen, club chairmen, and pastors gave speeches praising the kingdom of Hanover, while photographers did good business selling pictures commemorating such visits.[34] Prominent Guelphs such as the duke of Brunswick and the duchess of Cumberland came to DHP centers such as the *Hermannsburger Mission* and gave them financial support. For the Guelph conservative movement these visits were of great significance, the district president noting in his diary that "These visits of the young duke and duchess are more powerful than all articles in the newspaper *Hannoversche Landeszeitung.*"[35] Government requests not to invite the duke to mass events, and attempts to forbid such tributes to Guelph noblemen, were simply ignored.[36]

While the DHP's membership remained small and its organization weak, Guelph conservatism remained active through its clubs and associations, which were organized along lines similar to those of the DNVP.[37] As an equivalent to the paramilitary *Stahlhelm* the Guelph conservatives founded the *Großdeutsche Orden Heinrich der Löwe* and the *Deutsche Legion*, which attracted members through their rifle exercises and paramilitary sports.[38] The Guelph women's association, the *Herzogin-Viktoria Luise-Bund*, had only a few members, but on the whole conservative women's associations also demonstrated more activity than before.[39] Women's religious associations, such as the *Evangelische Frauenbund*, and housewives' associations, such as the *Hausfrauenverein* and *Reichsverband landwirtschaftlicher Hausfrauen*, were particularly strong supporters of the conservatives' goals.[40] The *Heimat* movement was also gaining in popularity. Even small villages regularly held *Heimatfeste*, organized by local DHP activists, which attracted several thousand visitors. At these festivals different constituents of the milieu came together: clergymen blessed the meeting; the DHP chairman spoke against "Prussian colonization" and praised the people of the *Sachsenstamm;* poems celebrating the *Heimat* were read in front of the yellow-white flags of Hanover; the singing society *Langensalza* presented songs glorifying the *Heimat*, and horsemen in old Hanover uniforms rode past.[41] These festivities were similar to those of the conservative veterans' associations, the difference being that they were mainly in praise of their own region.

Another similarity to the Prussian DNVP lay in the social background of the party. The Guelph conservatives were supported by the associations of the old middle classes, with the farmers' and craftsmen's associations in particular, the *Landbund* and the *Handwerkerbund*, recommending them before elections. Aristocratic involvement in the party declined, as it did in the DNVP.[42] A clear distance was maintained from the Prussian administration, while local parish councils also remained a stronghold of the Guelph conservatives.[43] Pastors and landowning farmers continued to play the most important roles in the village and signed the first proclamations of the party—as a result, the DHP was able to keep the support of around 40 percent of the electorate in its rural strongholds.[44]

In 1924, however, the Guelph conservatives failed in their most important goal. The "Pre-plebiscite on separation from Prussia" failed. Only in the DHP's rural strongholds did enough voters give their signature. Social Democrats, in particular, stayed at home. From that point onward, aspirations to independence were unrealistic. Electoral results declined again—in 1928 Guelph conservatives won only 9 percent of the votes, in 1930 only 7 percent. Only in rural areas did their milieu successfully retain their values.

Moreover, while on a national level their parties and associations kept their distance, locally they cooperated in the formation of movements of bourgeois unity, the so-called *Bürgerblocks*, with the DNVP and DVP. They cooperated in these bourgeois leagues in elections, in local parliaments, and at the club and festival level.[45] Paramilitary groups such as the *Stahlhelm* began to integrate all manner of conservative groups. This new unity was rooted in the common sense within the Right of being part of a minority. The Treaty of Versailles, the revolution, and the creation of the Republic had had the same impact on them as the annexation of 1866 had had on Hanover. They felt suppressed—by "Marxism," the Republic, and the victors of the war. They thus had to look for a new rallying movement against Socialism which embraced the Guelph conservatives. Overthrowing "red" Berlin became a shared goal: although they retained separate organizations, they felt more and more like a united minority, on the local level at least.

Such close cooperation between the right-wing parties and associations often even included the NSDAP and its forerunner, the *Deutsch-Völkische Freiheitspartei* (DVFP). Indeed, this local alliance was one of the main preconditions for the rapid rise of the NSDAP. It was not the fragmentation of society which led to the emergence of the new mass party but its successful efforts to create unity against the left: it was the intensive campaigns of the NSDAP which gave the associations' alliance common political representation.[46]

The radical right's practice of adapting its campaigns to local and regional ways of thinking and organizing led it to fight locally for the goals of the Guelph conservatives. The only difference was that its demands were more radical. Even the DVFP had begun to adopt its positions and ways of articulating them: while the Guelph conservatives celebrated the *Heidefest*, the DVFP celebrated the *Heideblütenfest*.[47] The program was the same as at the festivities of the DHP. They met at symbolic locations such as the *Löns* memorial near Hermannsburg; they started with a religious service; they marched through town performing traditional folk dances and performed plays in the *Plattdeutsch* regional dialect. The radical right thus shared the Guelphs' embrace of regional culture but tried, at the same time, to be better than the original. They emphasized the superiority of the tribe of Lower Saxony with racist arguments and called for a battle against Socialists and Jews to defend the natural rights of Hanover. The NSDAP continued this rhetoric. The regional name of its paper, the *Niedersachsen-Stürmer*, pretended that the fight for a free Lower Saxony was the main goal of the NSDAP. The traditional positions of the Guelph conservatives were to be found in the paper: the fight against the injustice of 1866, the appeal to the spirit of "Henry the Lion," and the demand for a free Lower Saxony.[48] The National Socialists adapted to local ways of thinking and organizing and presented themselves as an apolitical group defending the rights of conservatives, of Protestants, of the *Mittelstand.*

Correspondingly, local clubs and associations often included the NSDAP when they made their recommendations prior to the election. The farmers' and artisans' associations, which, previously, had usually recommended the DHP in northern Hanover, now switched to the NSDAP. Even in the DHP stronghold of Celle the artisanal *Handwerkerbund* proposed, in October 1932, "giving the National Socialists a chance because the other parties had failed."[49] The local press, which had usually supported the Guelphs' position, also embraced the NSDAP. Meanwhile, generational change acted in favor of the radical right in the late 1920s as the new chairmen of various associations were less steeped in the traditions of the imperial era and correspondingly more open to radicalism.[50]

The DHP fought the rising NSDAP even harder than it fought other conservative parties in the province, with local party leaders attempting to evoke the traditional fears of the northern regions by accusing the NSDAP of being a socialist party and the enemy of private property.[51] Yet while the Guelph conservatives were still not as antisemitic as other parties of the right, they failed to defend Jews against the attacks of the NSDAP and DNVP. And in fighting the National Socialists they were now also willing to play upon prejudices against another minority group in the north, namely the Catholics. The chairman of the DHP in Celle called the NSDAP a Catholic party which wanted to destroy Protestantism: "The Catholic tendency of Hitler is obviously visible in the book *Dialogues with Adolf Hitler.* The hero of Hitler is Pope Gregory VII, the biggest enemy of the German emperor Henry IV. Hitler hopes that once more a monk like Hildebrand will come to the German nation to undo the fatal schism, which means to eliminate Protestantism."[52] Indeed, as other regional studies have shown, not only did antisemitism increase during periods of crisis, but anti-Catholicism did too.[53] Beyond traditional prejudices, one possible reason for this is to be found in the almost permanent participation of the Center Party in government coalitions alongside the Social Democrats during the Weimar era.

Meanwhile, although the NSDAP developed from the south, its explicitly Protestant appearance in the north was a key factor in helping it to gain electoral support there; it was also a further way of copying the regional presence of the Guelph conservatives. NSDAP festivals often started with a church service. Similarly, the Hitler Youth often sang songs such as "Praise the Lord," impressing local newspapers.[54] The election meetings which drew the largest audiences were those with pastors. Further, the NSDAP presented itself in Lower Saxony as a party which also fought for Christian schools, against the "spreading of trash and smut" and for a Christian *Volksgemeinschaft*.[55] The National Socialist pastors often compared Germany's position to the suffering of Christ on the cross, killed by the Jews; anti-Catholicism also figured strongly in their rhetoric.

The NSDAP thus seemed to represent the values of the Guelph conservatives better than the Guelphs themselves. From at least the failure of the plebiscite onward it was clear that their goals could not be reached through democratic means. The DHP went into almost complete decline. In 1932 and 1933 it could retain only around 15 percent of the votes in a few villages where the influence of the clergy or other elites prevented people from switching to the new populist movement. Finally, even the Guelph prince Ernst August and his wife, the daughter of the emperor—the two most important people for the Guelph milieu—switched to the NSDAP. This was the best advertisement for the National Socialists. In the summer of 1933, at the commemorations of the battle of Langensalza, a pastor proclaimed that "with the submission of the duke Ernst August to the leadership of Adolf Hitler, Lower Saxony has also taken its place in the new great *Volksgemeinschaft*. The goal of Hanover—a new Germany united among its tribes—is now coming close to its realization."[56] In the last free elections of 1933 the traditional party of the Guelph conservatives really had become a minority. However, the Guelph conservative voters had found new political representatives who were supposed to protect them within a strong majority.

IV

Following the Nazi seizure of power the DHP adopted the radical slogans of the NSDAP. It attacked "parliamentarism," which "ha[d] become useless," and demanded a ruthless fight against all "parasites among the people."[57] In April 1933 the DHP delegates in the Hanover city council joined the parliamentary group of the NSDAP.[58] Nevertheless, some Guelph conservatives in small towns persisted longer than the party elite. Without asking party leaders, the local Celle DHP traveled to Berlin in May 1933 to try to secure the future of their party and associations. They were told by the NSDAP, "The DHP is different from the other parties; it has an ideal, and therefore has nothing to fear from the new government. Moreover, the D.L. [*Deutsche Legion*] and the *Orden* [*Heinrich des Löwen*] are recognized and certified as military associations."[59]

However, the National Socialists, who had pretended to want to strengthen regional culture, soon began to suppress the organizations, festivals, and symbols of the Guelph conservatives. In the summer of 1933 the DHP was forbidden along with the other parties, but its local elite did not give up everywhere. Associations such as the *Heimatvereine* could serve as a niche for the forbidden DHP. The police reports noted, "These associations, which only former party members join, give themselves harmless names such as *Klub Sachsenroß, Heimatverein Treue,* etc., and say that they only want to do local history and cultural work."[60] Their membership actually appeared to increase.[61] Alongside the clubs, there existed fixed "Guelph meeting places" and reserved corners in public houses.[62] Down to the end of the dictatorship the *Heimat-* and museum clubs in Celle were meeting places for the conservative-leaning educated middle classes—especially teachers, but also several pastors, district court lawyers, pharmacists, and officials.[63] The local police and authorities tolerated them. The head of the district government answered inquiries from above with appeasing reports, writing that the associations were "perfectly" adjusted to the state and had no niche function.[64]

Most of the DHP's auxiliary organizations were deemed to be separatist and were forced to join centralized associations.[65] The *Hannoversche Kriegerverein* was forced to join the *Kyffhäuserbund.* Its local groups showed considerable resistance—when the *Hannoversche Landeskriegervereine Celle* still refused to join the *Kyffhäuserbund* in summer 1934 it was threatened with dissolution by the police. However, local associations remained, under the new name *Kriegerkameradschaft Niedersachsen,* down to March 1935. Following their transfer they formed quite independent subunits within the *Kyffhäuserbund.* Their new regional names still referred to Guelph conservative traditions: once more, it was the continuity of local networks within the administration which protected the Guelph conservative identity.[66]

National Socialism could thus not completely dissolve the regional conservative consciousness of the area. Firstly, it remained alive in everyday practices. While it was forbidden, for example, to display the yellow and white flag of the Guelphs at festivals, the National Socialists could not ban the popular white-and-yellow dessert which served to remind diners of the Guelph colors. And while the clubs were forbidden to reenact the battle of 1866, they could not stop people recording scores of sixty-six points in card games as sixty-five, in a gesture of anti-Prussian protest. Guelph conservatives were also banned from attacking Bismarck in speeches and books, but continued the pleasant pastime of naming stray dogs "Bismarck" and teasing them.[67]

Secondly, the Protestant church fostered ideological and organizational links among the conservatives. Its religious clubs, such as the women's *Evangelische Frauenbund,* were not transferred to the National Socialists' organizations.[68] National Socialist support for local church life soon stopped. From 1936, party activists were told to leave the church, SA or Hitler Youth meetings were held at the same time as church services, and services themselves were disrupted. These conflicts served to emphasize the differences between the conservatives and National Socialists, who in many other areas had become indistinguishable. The church won this struggle, although church attendance declined between 1936 and 1940.[69] Conservative local notables, who kept their positions on parish councils, protested against disruptions of church services. The same conservative teacher in Celle who was pursuing racist research in his *Heimatverein* criticized the unchristian National Socialists in his bible lectures.[70] While the Protestants rarely held mass popular rituals such as the Catholics' *Corpus Christi*, the churches of the former Guelph strongholds continued to celebrate mass festivals such as the *Hermannsburger Missionsfest*. In 1938 this event attracted around eighteen thousand visitors, and an attempt to prohibit it in 1939 failed. Even during the war twelve thousand people came to celebrate this festival at the symbolic Guelph place where the church had fought for its independence from Prussia sixty years previously.[71]

Finally, the regional elites were able to maintain their positions not only within the administration, but in the traditional bourgeois clubs. In small towns and villages many DHP mayors were able to keep their jobs, as were some district presidents. At club festivals such as the *Schützenfest*, the riflemen's meeting, conservative local notables were still able to speak in public.

The activities of these local notables were not, however, always easy to distinguish from those of the National Socialists. How limited the differences could be is shown by the example of the *Heimatvereine*. Although they could function as a niche for Guelph conservatives on the one hand, they also engendered active cooperation with the new system on the other. The *Heimatverein* of Celle, for example, was much more active than before. Its activists collected regional myths, pursued genealogical research (*Erbhof- und Sippenforschung*), and initiated a "Beautiful Village" campaign.[72] Above all, collections of pictures of farmers with "details of age, size, shape, hair and eye color, and length of residence of the families were sent to the Institute of Race Research, to museums, and to *Heimat* and farmers' associations."[73] Such conservative clubs thus retained their independence but integrated themselves into the new state at the same time.

The DHP's political activists seldom began careers in the organizations of the NSDAP. Rather, the noblemen withdrew from public life. The euphoria of the clergy changed to increasing distance, although they did not recognizably resist beyond protecting their clerical interests. While the restriction of Guelph club life was greeted with protests, conservatives met the crimes of the National Socialists with as much indifference as they did in other regions. Reports from local police and district presidents noted only discontent with the economic situation and issues of everyday life. The agricultural policies of the regime, especially, were regarded as a yardstick of popular satisfaction with the regime.

Overall, National Socialism had two distinct sets of consequences for the Guelph conservative movement. On the one hand, the differences between it and other conservative groups declined. In many respects they shared broader conservative elements of content and discontent with the regime. The dictatorship left little space for public representation of special regional interests and no hopes for a reconsolidation of the kingdom of Hanover. On the other hand, the National Socialists strengthened the Guelph conservatives. The new centralism, the forced dissolution of many clubs and symbols, and the restrictions of clerical activity were leading to a new regional consciousness. Once more, Guelph conservatives felt themselves to be a counterculture, seeing in Berlin a symbol of repression even as they celebrated the revival of the nation.

V

Few expected a substantial Guelph revival following the collapse of National Socialism. However, their party, whose name was changed first to *Niedersächsische Landespartei* (State Party of Lower Saxony) and then to *Deutsche Partei* (German Party), enjoyed great success. Through the 1950s it won more than 40 percent of the votes in its strongholds in the north of Lower Saxony. Between 1947 and 1959 it won about 430,000 votes in each election, giving it between 12.4 percent and 19.9 percent of the votes. Its leader was minister-president of Lower Saxony from 1955 to 1959. In Bonn it had two ministers in Adenauer's cabinets continuously down to 1960. As electoral results thus showed, regional consciousness remained of great importance to many conservatives in the postwar years. As a result, the Christian Democratic party (CDU) consistently struggled in this state.[74]

The experience of dictatorship and war had clearly neither leveled social differences nor permanently eroded differences between different forms of conservatism. To the contrary, four developments ensured that regional conservative consciousness gained new significance. Firstly, the discrediting of nationalism led to a renewed embrace of notions of *Heimat* and a new regionalism. *Heimat* served as a metaphor for different things: for the nation, for apoliticism, and for the discredited ideas of the *Volksgemeinschaft*. This was typical of all parts of Germany, but for an area with strong regional traditions it had greater consequences.[75] The Guelph conservatives could argue that their movement had been a victim of the centralist National Socialism and therefore needed to be rebuilt. While the Prussian conservatives, especially the DNVP, were blamed for the rise of National Socialism, the Guelph conservatives appeared innocent. This served to legitimate and to mobilize them, for following the loss of the East they wanted to rebuild conservatism from Lower Saxony. National traditions were integrated into the discourse of *Heimat*. In Celle, the traditional "patriotic speech" at the riflemen's festival was renamed the "speech on the *Heimat*."[76] *Heimat* festivals with local references replaced forbidden national celebrations. The "parade of the stallions," in which the troopers wore the uniforms of the kingdom of Hanover, drew thousands of visitors.[77]

The conservative *Heimat* movement was promoted by the same people and organizations as it had been before 1945. The chairman of the *Heimatverein* in Celle continued to give speeches on the character of the people of Lower Saxony at festivals and club meetings—only words such as "race" and *völkisch* had to be changed.[78] The *Heimatverein* was thus able to sustain its membership through the 1950s.[79] From 1947 onward, the Guelph conservatives also espoused an increasingly nationalistic set of values. The British occupiers tolerated much, and quickly allowed the revival of the party and its associations. The Guelph movement seemed acceptable because it was anti-Prussian, it favored a strongly federalist system, and its former monarchy had been connected to the British one prior to 1837.

Secondly, the flood of refugees from the East renewed the unity of the Guelph conservatives. In the Guelph strongholds around 40 percent of the population were refugees after 1945. The liberation of prisoners of war and concentration camp inmates also heightened conservatives' fears and sharpened the distinction between those who belonged to the *Heimat* and those who did not. Individual crimes such as the murder of a pastor from Hermannsburg increased prejudice against "Polish gangs" and their "Marxism." Clergymen complained that these "alien people" introduced an "unchristian world view."[80] Farmers complained that the refugees were destroying their traditional properties, while another pastor opined that it was "the plan of the Allies to mix all the *Volksstämme* in order to break resistance through *völkisch* dissolution."[81] In this way, refugees clearly acted as a catalyst for the revival of regional milieus.[82]

Thirdly, the Guelph conservatives enjoyed the best local networks after 1945. As the majority of the DHP's activists had not held important offices in the NSDAP, they could easily enter politics and the administration. The last DHP chairman of Celle, for example, Hodo von Hodenberg, became president of the Higher State Court. From this position he was able to distribute numerous jobs, guaranteeing loyalty in return.[83] The new party was supported by several associations, in particular by the regional agrarian organization, the *Landbund*. The leading position occupied by the churches after the war also enhanced the conservatives' position. When the British occupiers sought the opinion of the Protestant clergy, the latter often recommended these local conservatives for such positions. The Christian Democrats, by contrast, had a much harder time finding support in this region.

Fourthly, regional consciousness was strengthened by a renewed anti-Catholicism, which emerged against the dominance of the CDU. Following the dissolution of Prussia the Hanover conservatives had lost their old enemy. Instead of Berlin, they now looked at Bonn and felt oppressed once more, arguing that the CDU, as a mainly Catholic party, could not represent the interests of the Protestant north. They also protested that the CDU would only give important posts in politics and public life to Catholics, and that the foreign policy of the CDU was focused solely on cooperation with the Catholic countries of the south and west, neglecting the issue of unification with the (Protestant) GDR.[84] Their new party, the *Deutsche Partei*, appeared as the party of the conservatives of Lower Saxony rather than a party of all German conservatives.[85] Many members and observers argued that this strategy was responsible for the decline of the DP, which managed success only in Lower Saxony and in some parts of the north. Conversely, the CDU struggled here.

During the 1950s the CDU tried to integrate the DP in two ways. On the one hand, it pursued close cooperation with it. It arranged coalitions, generously distributed posts to DP members, accepted their federalist demands, and organized joint campaigns against Marxism. On the other hand, the CDU tried to present itself as a party also closely connected to the regional traditions of Protestant conservatism. In particular, Chancellor Adenauer sought close contact with the bishop of Hanover, Hanns Lilje, and with the leader of the farmers' organization, Edmund Rehwinkel, although both often protested against the policies of the Bonn government.

In the 1960s these strategies bore fruit. In order to save their positions, the members of the DP in the *Bundestag* and Adenauer's government switched to the CDU in 1960. Two years later the DP's deputies in the parliament of Lower Saxony also switched. These new CDU members claimed in the villages that the CDU would protect Guelph traditions and the special interests of conservatism in Lower Saxony, but met with much local resistance. There were riots at village meetings and speakers were branded "traitors" and "opportunists."[86] It was said that such politicians "should switch directly to the Catholic church if they go to the CDU."[87] It took long discussions to persuade local mayors. Generous concessions led to a complete change in the CDU in Lower Saxony: in the mid-1960s, almost all important positions in the party were in the hands of former Guelph conservatives or association activists. The CDU thus became the conservative party in the region which spoke for the special interests of Lower Saxony.

From this point onward, the cultural organizations of the Guelph conservatives lost their importance. Following their integration into the CDU, they no longer represented a genuine counterculture. With the triumph of the CDU in the 1960s, the special path of the Guelphs within German conservatism finally came to an end.

Notes

1. There is a huge literature on this master narrative; see, especially, Hans-Ulrich Wehler, *Deutsche Gesellschaftsgeschichte*, 4 vols. (Munich: C. H. Beck, 1987–2003).

2. An introduction to recent research is given in Axel Schildt, *Konservatismus in Deutschland: Von den Anfängen im 18. Jahrhundert bis zur Gegenwart* (Munich: C. H. Beck, 1998). For an excellent collection of newer approaches, see Larry Eugene Jones

and James Retallack, eds., *Between Reform, Reaction, and Resistance: Studies in the History of German Conservatism from 1789 to 1945* (Providence: Berg, 1993).

3. Hans-Georg Aschoff, *Welfische Bewegung und politischer Katholizismus, 1866–1918: Die Deutschhannoversche Partei und das Zentrum in der Provinz Hannover während des Kaiserreiches* (Düsseldorf: Droste, 1987); Hans Prilop, "Die Vorabstimmung in Hannover, 1924: Untersuchungen zur Vorgeschichte der Deutsch-hannoverschen Partei im preußisch-deutschen Kaiserreich und in der Weimarer Republik" (Ph.D. diss., University of Hamburg, 1954); Ingo Nathusius, *Am rechten Rande der Union: Der Weg der Deutschen Partei bis 1953* (Mainz: Piper, 1992); and Hermann Meyn, *Die Deutsche Partei: Entwicklung und Problematik einer national-konservativen Rechtspartei nach 1945* (Düsseldorf: Droste, 1965).

4. The chapter is connected to other research projects on political culture; see Frank Bösch, *Das konservative Milieu: Vereinskultur und lokale Sammlungspolitik in ost- und westdeutschen Regionen (1900–1960)* (Göttingen: Wallstein-Verlag, 2002); and Frank Bösch, *Die Adenauer-CDU: Gründung, Aufstieg und Krise einer Erfolgspartei (1945–1969)* (Munich: Deutsche Verlagsanstalt, 2001).

5. See Olaf Blaschke and Frank-Michael Kuhlemann, eds., *Religion im Kaiserreich: Milieus, Mentalitäten, Krisen* (Gütersloh: Gütersloher Verlagshaus, 1996); and Karl Rohe, *Wahlen und Wählertraditionen in Deutschland: Kulturelle Grundlagen deutscher Parteien und Parteiensysteme im 19. und 20. Jahrhundert* (Frankfurt am Main: Suhrkamp, 1992).

6. Central positions of conservative ideology are discussed in Martin Greiffenhagen, *Das Dilemma des Konservatismus in Deutschland* (Munich: Piper, 1971), 192–93.

7. See Dietmar von Reeken, *Kirchen im Umbruch zur Moderne: Milieubildungsprozesse im nordwestdeutschen Protestantismus, 1849–1914* (Gütersloh: Gütersloher Verlagshaus, 1999); and Wolfgang Rädisch, *Evangelisch-lutherische Landeskirche Hannovers und der preußische Staat, 1866–1885* (Hildesheim: Lax, 1972), 271.

8. Heide Barmeyer, "Bismarck, die Annexionen und das Welfenproblem, 1866–1890: Der unvollendete nationale Verfassungsstaat in Verteidigung und Angriff," *Niedersächsisches Jahrbuch zur Landesgeschichte* 48 (1976): 397–432.

9. Compare on the local level: Clemens Cassel, *Geschichte der Stadt Celle mit besonderer Berücksichtigung des Geistes- und Kulturlebens der Bewohner Celles* (Celle: Ströher, 1930), 403–404.

10. Landratsberichte in Kreisarchiv Celle (hereafter KAC) A 88, 17; Prilop, "Die Vorabstimmung," 129.

11. Peter Völker, "Wahlen und politische Parteien im Raum Celle von 1867–1972" (Ms. Diss., Hannover, 1977), 100–101.

12. Comp. Landratsbericht, 13 May 1875, in KAC A 88, 17.

13. Only parts of the conservative Guelphic parish separated themselves: Rädisch, *Evangelisch-lutherische Landeskirche,* 173–91; and Ernst Schering, "Missionsdirektor D. Georg Haccius und das Vermächtnis der Lüneburger Erweckung," *Niedersächsisches Jahrbuch zur Landesgeschichte* 65 (1993): 297–334.

14. Gerhard Schneider, "Langensalza: Ein hannoversches Trauma; Gefallenengedenken auf dem Schlachtfeld von 1866," *Niedersächsisches Jahrbuch zur Landesgeschichte* 61 (1989): 265–323.

15. *Cellesche Zeitung* (hereafter CZ), 21 September 1908.

16. *Comp. Welfenliederbuch für hannoversche Clubs und Vereine,* ed. "A Young Hanoverian" [Ludwig Alpers, F.B.] (Hannover 1892).

17. A good example is the memorial hall in Celle, which can be visited in the Bomann-Museum.

18. Cassel, *Geschichte der Stadt Celle,* 414.

19. These results were reached in cooperation with the Catholic minority in the south of the province, which received about 7 percent; Aschoff, *Welfische Bewegung,* 101, 190.

20. In Celle there were about 350 in 1903; report dated 21 March 1903, in KAC A 513.

21. Aschoff, *Welfische Bewegung,* 101–108, 131–32.

22. Ibid., 133.

23. For the Celle District see Landratsbericht, 27 October 1898, in KAC A 513, 7a.

24. The German *Heimatbewegung* in Imperial Germany is well researched in different areas; see Werner Hartung, *Konservative Zivilisationskritik und regionale Identität am Beispiel der niedersächsischen Heimatbewegung, 1895–1919* (Hannover: Hahn, 1991); Celia Applegate, *A Nation of Provincials: The German Idea of Heimat* (Berkeley: University of California Press, 1990); and Alon Confino, *The Nation as a Local Metaphor: Württemberg, Imperial Germany, and National Memory, 1871–1918* (Chapel Hill: University of North Carolina Press, 1997).

25. See, for other regions, Harm-Peer Zimmermann, *"Der feste Wall gegen die rote Flut": Kriegervereine in Schleswig-Holstein, 1864–1914* (Neumünster: Wachholtz, 1989); Jakob Vogel, *Nationen im Gleichschritt: Der Kult der Nation in Waffen in Deutschland und Frankreich, 1871–1914* (Göttingen: Vandenhoeck und Ruprecht, 1997); and Thomas Rohkrämer, *Der Militarismus der "kleinen Leute": Die Kriegervereine im Deutschen Kaiserreich, 1871–1914* (Munich: Oldenbourg, 1990).

26. Teachers were therefore not allowed to speak here: Königliche Regierung to Kreisschuldirektoren, 2 March 1914, in KAC N 34, Nr. 3.

27. Even in Hermannsburg: Schering, "Missionsdirektor D. Georg Haccius," 314. In Celle the pastor was the chairman of the veterans club: CZ 10 December 1912.

28. Landratsbericht, 27 October 1898, in KAC A 513, 7a.

29. Aschoff, *Welfische Bewegung,* 217.

30. Jürgen Falter, *Wahlen und Abstimmungen in der Weimarer Republik: Materialien zum Wahlverhalten, München, 1919–1933* (Munich: C. H. Beck, 1990).

31. CZ, 7 February 1921.

32. Program, DHP Celle, in KAC N 34, 5.

33. See also Prilop, "Die Vorabstimmung," 226.

34. See Landratsbericht, 4 March 1930, in KAC 32, Nr. 6; and CZ, 16 July 1932.

35. Landratsbericht, 13 October 1924, in KAC N 34, 5.

36. See Anschreiben des Oberpräsidenten, 23 October 1924, in KAC N 34, 5; Anschreiben des Oberpräsidenten, 22 October 1928, in Hauptstaatsarchiv Hannover (hereafter HStAH) Hann 180 Lün III, XXX 76; and Landwirtschaftsminister to Landstallmeister Korndorff, 22 October 1924, in KAC N 34, 5.

37. Prilop, "Die Vorabstimmung," 473–74.

38. A review is given in DHP to Palte, 29 January 1926, in HStAH Hann. 310 III, Nr. 70.

39. Report, Regierungspräsident in Lüneburg, 19 December 1924, in HStAH Hann 80 II, XXV.

40. A lot of research has been carried out on the activism of conservative women's associations recently: see Andrea Süchting-Hänger, *Das "Gewissen der Nation": Nationales Engagement und politisches Handeln konservativer Frauenorganisationen, 1900 bis 1937* (Düsseldorf: Droste, 2002); Nancy R. Reagin, *A German Women's Movement: Class and Gender in Hanover, 1880–1933* (Chapel Hill: University of North Carolina Press, 1995); Doris Kaufmann, *Frauen zwischen Aufbruch und Reaktion: Protestantische Frauenbewegung in der ersten Hälfte des 20. Jahrhunderts* (Munich: Piper 1988), 51–52; and Renate Bridenthal, "Organized Rural Women and the Conservative Mobilization of the German Countryside in the Weimar Republic," in Jones and Retallack, *Between Reform, Reaction, and Resistance*, 375–405.

41. Even in small villages like Beedenbostel and Lachendorf, three thousand people participated (CZ, 1 September 1919); in Groß Hehlen two thousand (CZ, 31 July 1919).

42. See Wolfram Pyta, *Dorfgemeinschaft und Parteipolitik, 1918–1933: Die Verschränkung von Milieu und Parteien in den protestantischen Landgebieten Deutschlands in der Weimarer Republik* (Düsseldorf: Droste, 1996), 171–78.

43. However, Celle had many lawyers working for the administration and the court of the province (the *Oberlandesgericht*). Both chairmen of the DHP, Freiherr von Hodenberg and Bienhold, worked in law offices.

44. See the proclamations of the DHP in CZ, 7 January and 10 June 1919.

45. For bourgeois festivities in Lower Saxony see the excellent study by Peter Fritzsche, *Rehearsals for Fascism: Populism and Political Mobilization in Weimar Germany* (Oxford: Oxford University Press, 1990), 75–83.

46. The fragmentation of society is also questioned by Fritzsche, *Rehearsals for Fascism*, 235; and Rudy Koshar, *Social Life, Local Politics, and Nazism: Marburg, 1880–1935* (Chapel Hill: University of North Carolina Press, 1986), 283.

47. See Landratsbericht, 22 August 1923, in KAC N 32, Nr. 4.

48. See Prilop, "Die Vorabstimmung," 358–59; and Dirk Stegmann, "Nationalsozialismus in der Provinz: Aufstiegsbedingungen am Beispiel des Gaus Ost-Hannover (1925–1932)," in *Gegen Barbarei: Essays Robert M. W. Kempner zu Ehren*, ed. Rainer Eisfeld and Ingo Müller (Frankfurt am Main: Athenäum-Verlag, 1989), 79–105. Dietmar Schirmer's analyses of newspapers also showed that the NSDAP did not offer a distinctive interpretation, but rather demanded "ein trotziges, 'Noch mehr'"; see Dietmar Schirmer, *Mythos, Heilshoffnung, Modernität: Politisch-kulturelle Deutungscodes in der Weimarer Republik* (Opladen: Westdeutsche Verlag, 1992), 253.

49. CZ, 29 October 1932. The *Nordwestdeutsche Handwerkerzeitung* also recommended voting DNVP *or* NSDAP; see Friedrich Lenger, *Sozialgeschichte der deutschen Handwerker seit 1800* (Frankfurt am Main: Suhrkamp, 1988), 194.

50. The radicalization caused by the generational change of the late 1920s is analyzed in Ulrich Herbert, *Best: Biographische Studien über Radikalismus, Weltanschauung und Vernunft, 1903–1989* (Bonn: Dietz, 1996).

51. Report of Celle DHP to Hanover DHP, 18 September 1930, in HStAH Hann. 310 III Nr. 18.

52. CZ, 5 April 1932.

53. Anti-Catholicism was still probably stronger in other Protestant regions; for

the case of Franconia see Manfred Kittel, *Provinz zwischen Reich und Republik: Politische Mentalitäten in Deutschland und Frankreich, 1918–1933/36* (Munich: Oldenbourg, 2000); and more generally Manfred Kittel, "Konfessioneller Konflikt und politische Kultur in der Weimarer Republik," in *Konfessionen im Konflikt: Deutschland zwischen 1800 und 1970; Ein zweites konfessionelles Zeitalter,* ed. Olaf Blaschke (Göttingen: Vandenhoeck und Ruprecht, 2002), 243–97.

54. *Boten des ehemaligen Amtes Bergen,* 28 October 1930.

55. See Landratsbericht, 7 March 1931 and May 1932, in KAC 32, Nr. 6; CZ, 27 July 1932; and similarly in Franconia Kittel, *Provinz zwischen Reich und Republik,* 621–32.

56. CZ, 28 June 1933.

57. Engelbrechten in CZ, 23 February 1933; and advertisement for the DHP in CZ, 6 March 1933.

58. Hans-Georg Aschoff, "Die Deutschhannoversche Partei zwischen Revolution und Machtergreifung (1918–1933)," *Stader Jahrbuch* 78 (1988): 86.

59. Rust referring to Kruse jun. of Hermannsburg, 16 May 1933, in HStAH Hann. 310 III, Nr. 18.

60. Rundschreiben Regierungspräsident, 29 January 1934, in HStAH Hann 180 Lün III, XXV 24.

61. See membership list, Lönsbund Celle, in Stadtarchiv Celle (hereafter StAC) L 7 158.

62. See the local interviews conducted by Hanna Fueß in the years 1947–48; e.g., Pastor Baden, 25 June 1947, printed in Rainer Schulze, ed., *Unruhige Zeiten: Erlebnisberichte aus dem Landkreis Celle* (Munich: Oldenbourg, 1990), 195.

63. Even in the year 1943; membership list in StAC L 7 158.

64. See the letters of the local *Hauptwachtmeister* to the Landrat in KAC N 34, Nr. 4. In Lüneburg, for instance, the local police reported a monthly meeting of such a new club, *Zur Hoffnung,* with 150 persons; Ortspolizei Lün, 5 July 1934, in HStAH Hann 180 Lün III, XXV 24.

65. Oberpräsident to Hanover Landeskriegerverband, 9 August 1933, in KAC N 34, Nr. 4.

66. Oberbürgermeister to Regierungspräsident, 13 September 1934; Landrat to Regierungspräsidenten, 5 March 1935 and 24 June 1936; Meldung Staatspolizeistelle Lüneburg, 5 February 1935; all in HStAH Hann 180 Lün III, XXV 24.

67. Such examples were given in several interviews I conducted with the former local notables in Celle in spring 1999; the quoted examples were given by Dr. Günther Volker and Pastor Waack.

68. The continuity of the *Evangelische Frauenbund* is shown in Süchting-Hänger, *Das "Gewissen der Nation,"* 378.

69. See the reports in Fragebögen Landeskirchliche Archiv Hannover H III 513; and interviews in HStAH ZGS 1 VI. Hanna Fueß-Sammlung. Those interviews often stress who visited the church and who did not.

70. Interview of Dorothee Heinichen by the author.

71. Prof. Schmidt of Hermannsburg, 2 October 1946, in HStAH ZGS 1 VI. Hanna Fueß-Sammlung 533c.

72. See CZ, 20 November 1934 and 20 January 1936. This growing activity was common in other regions; see Dietmar von Reeken, *Heimatbewegung, Kulturpolitik*

und Nationalsozialismus: Die Geschichte der "Ostfriesischen Landschaft," 1918–1949 (Aurich: Ostfriesische Landschaft, 1995); and Karl Ditt, *Raum und Volkstum: Die Kulturpolitik des Provinzialverbandes Westfalen, 1923–1945* (Münster: Aschendorff, 1988).

73. Alpers and Meyer to Gaustellenleiter Marquadt, 21 March 1942, in StAC 2 G 83/1.

74. Bösch, *Die Adenauer-CDU,* 35–53, 74–83.

75. For the Palatinate, see Applegate, *Nation of Provincials,* 4.

76. Reports and speeches in StAC 2 F 20.

77. See the report in CZ, 3 October 1949; eight thousand visitors came to this event.

78. See the collection of articles in StAC L 7–11. Such an ideological and personal connection is also shown for the *Heimatbewegung* in Ostfriesland: Reeken, *Heimatbewegung, Kulturpolitik und Nationalsozialismus,* 290–93.

79. Report to the town in StAC 2 G 83/2.

80. Pastor Heinrich Kretzmeyer of Müden, 12 February 1948, in HStAH ZGS 1 VI. Hanna Fueß-Sammlung 565e.

81. Pastor Bensch of Winsen, 26 June 1947, printed in Schulze, *Unruhige Zeiten,* 73.

82. This question has already been raised by Karl-Heinz Naßmacher, *Parteien im Abstieg: Wiederbegründung und Abstieg der Bauern- und Bürgerparteien* (Opladen: Westdeutscher Verlag, 1989), 259.

83. Hartmut Wick, "Die Entwicklung des Oberlandesgerichts Celle nach dem 2. Weltkrieg," *275 Jahre Oberappelationsgericht-Oberlandesgericht Celle,* 235–95, especially 242–43, 253, 265. See also Ulrich Vultejus, "Goldene Jugendjahre," in *Hinter den Fassaden: Geschichten aus einer deutschen Stadt,* ed. Werner Holtfort (Göttingen: Steidl, 1982), 75–96.

84. Bösch, *Die Adenauer-CDU,* 109–38.

85. This transformation is analyzed in Nathusius, *Am rechten Rande;* and Meyn, *Die Deutsche Partei.*

86. Hans Joachim von Merkatz to Adenauer, 30 November 1960, in Stiftung Bundeskanzler-Adenauer-Haus 13.03; reports in *Archiv für Christlich-Demokratische Politik* (hereafter ACDP) I-148-91/5.

87. See report, Arnold Fratzscher to Otto Fricke, 4 January 1961, in ACDP I-248-012; Krüger to Fratzscher, 8 November 1961, in ACDP I-248-0012/2.

Seven

"Black-Red-Gold Enemies"

Catholics, Socialists, and Jews in
Elementary Schoolbooks from
Kaiserreich *to Third Reich*

Katharine Kennedy

I

The organization of German schooling in the late nineteenth and early twentieth centuries largely mirrored the division of German society according to religion, region, and class. This makes the varied and changing content of elementary education a potentially useful source for thinking about continuities and ruptures over time and about the layering of voices from the margins and the center. Textbooks adopted for use in Germany's religious and regional communities showcase the different, and changing, language, stories, myths, and images involved in schools' mediation between the state and its citizens.

Analysis of Wilhelmine, Weimar, and Nazi schoolbook depictions of three very different minority populations, Catholics, Socialists, and Jews, not only highlights relevant texts, but draws attention to what is missing and refocuses notions of continuity. Although all three groups faced exclusion and marginalization in the *Kaiserreich,* until the late 1930s elementary schoolbooks rarely defined Germanness in terms of hostile "un-Germans" within. Rather, the more usual pattern was for textbooks published by and for majority populations to ignore those on the margins, promoting an imaginary vision of a homogenous, harmonious Germany, which could vary from book to book according to the regional and religious population for whom it was primarily intended. Those texts that predominate in required reading books for children in Wilhelmine and Weimar Germany emphasize building and strengthening attachments to family, locality, God, nature, and nation, rather than promoting hostility toward an internal other. Many of these stories, with their sentimentality and focus on death, sacrifice, and nature, made their way smoothly into Nazi reading books. Nonetheless, the appearance of simplistic attacks on Jews and communists in Nazi textbooks marked a significant change in the officially authorized and vetted texts assigned in public schools. The title of this chapter, "Black-Red-Gold Enemies," comes, rather obviously, from Nazi texts, which attempt to blame all of Germany's problems on a huge conspiracy, by Jesuits and the Center Party; by Marxists, Communists, and the SPD; and by Jews, who were allegedly behind it all.

That these Wilhelmine and Weimar schoolbooks do not directly anticipate their Nazi successors by including attacks on Catholics, Socialists, and Jews does not, of course, negate evidence that prejudices were widespread during these years, that elites attempted to rally opposition to internal enemies, or that these animosities found their way into many classrooms. These schoolbooks represent only one stream in the flow of cultural values and images, but their wide distribution, in a printed, officially authorized form, to an involuntary and presumably malleable audience assured that their contents received special scrutiny. This examination of the treatment of minorities in schoolbooks urges caution in presumptions about "authoritarian continuities"[1] in German history. While explicit antisemitic lessons were largely absent from the Wilhelmine and Weimar curricula and textbooks, it is nonetheless noteworthy, if unsurprising, that schools of the pre-Nazi decades offered young Germans neither knowledge nor awareness of the diverse populations in their midst. Schooling may well have played a role in spawning the indifference, passivity, ignorance, "moral insensibility," and "detachment and general lack of active interest" later evidenced by so many Germans during the persecution of Jews and other marginalized people.[2]

The decentralization of German schooling prior to the Nazi era meant that educational materials and policy originated in a variety of places. In addition to providing a window into the majority's changing vision of minority populations, some schoolbooks gave voice to populations rendered invisible in other texts. Most notably, the Catholics, the largest and best established of Germany's minorities, compiled their own textbooks to incorporate their own history and symbols into their children's education. Socialists and Jews had less opportunity to use textbooks to overcome marginalization. The Nazis eventually ended both this traditional variety that had given some minorities voice, and the earlier emphasis on some degree of tolerance.

Throughout the years from the 1890s through the Second World War, the overwhelming majority of German children aged six through fourteen attended a public elementary school or *Volksschule*. This study considers only books used in the *Volksschule*, and only books for the older children, in their fifth through eighth years of schooling. The most important and ubiquitous textbook in the *Volksschule*, the reading book, was an anthology of several hundred short texts, both prose and poetry, designed to support instruction in reading and writing, but also in history and geography, and to provide moral and national education. Typically, prior to the Nazi period, a committee of "experienced schoolmen" compiled each volume, and another committee, or an individual, within each state's education ministry approved each book for use in the schools.[3] Although relatively few publishers produced most of the readers, many different books, each usually designed for a specific regional or religious readership, were in use until the Nazis mandated a uniform book.[4] In addition to readers, I have also looked at several history books for each of the three periods. Since it was not unusual for schools, especially smaller ones, to have no dedicated textbooks for the limited history curriculum, there is less certainty about the extent of these books' actual use. Nonetheless, I have included representative history books because they often include more explicit references to minority groups than the readers.

II

Let us begin by looking at the Catholics. The defining and enduring chasm in German society, and in its educational system, was that between Protestants and Catholics, with the latter group persisting as a large, well-organized minority. Separate confessional elementary schools for Protestants and Catholics remained the norm in most parts of Germany from the *Kaiserreich* through the early years of the Third Reich, reflecting this deep divide between the cultural, political, and religious worlds of Catholics and Protestants.[5] Confessional schools enabled each confession to color its depiction of German society and history with its own religious material. These schools offered religious instruction in the confession of the school, employed teachers who were members of the confession, enrolled mostly or exclusively children of that confession, and often assigned confessional reading books. Although several states in the *Kaiserreich,* among them Baden and Hessen, had interconfessional schools, liberals had little success in introducing such schools elsewhere.

In the aftermath of the *Kulturkampf,* Prussian guidelines for reading books specified that while "religious warmth" should permeate the books, their contents should reflect "the demands of tolerance."[6] Prussian Catholic readers included references to Catholic religious practice, to incense and holy water, to stations of the cross, and to "ancient Catholic beliefs," but they also contained moralizing texts by Protestant authors about God, nature, family, and fatherland.[7] Selections on monastic life received special attention in the historical units, and the Reformation was largely ignored.[8] Similarly, the reader for Württemberg's Catholic schools included selections entitled "Ave Maria," "The Throne of St. Peter," and "On Corpus Christi," and texts by popular Catholic writers such as Alban Stolz, Christoph von Schmid, and Friedrich Wilhelm Weber. Martin Luther was missing.[9] Indeed, although many Protestant authors were represented in the Catholic readers, Protestants received little or no explicit mention anywhere in these textbooks. Lay school officials limited the quantity and regulated the tone of religious material in approved reading books. In Bavaria, where non-confessional readers were common in confessional schools, the Catholic Teacher's Association, a small organization allied with the powerful Center Party, published its own heavily confessional reader. The state textbook commission, arguing that the quality of the text was poor, refused to add it to the list of approved readers, effectively prohibiting its use in schools.[10]

The most notable exception to the practice of providing Catholic children with textbooks generally sympathetic to their religion was in Polish areas, where large numbers of Catholic children were forced to attend Protestant schools by Prussian authorities who, fully aware of the link between Catholicism and Polish nationalism, employed schooling to suppress the latter.[11] Many Polish Catholic pupils read the *Lesebuch für Westpreussen* (*Evangelische Ausgabe E*), which contained a long, enthusiastic treatment of Luther's career, followed by texts defending the Protestant position in the Thirty Years' War and discussion of Protestant charitable activities.[12]

Such texts were typical of Protestant readers, which made the Protestant Reformation a centerpiece of German history. Other than in these texts about the Reformation, however, Catholics were largely invisible in Protestant readers. The *Realienbücher,* the most common elementary history textbooks during the *Kaiserreich,* also existed in Protestant and Catholic as well as interdenominational editions, largely because of sensitivities about treatment of the Reformation.[13] The dominant Prussian strand of national identification employed Protestant hymns and images, largely ignoring Catholics, who used their own schools to develop their own culture.

Throughout the Weimar years, differences over confessional schooling and the role of religion in education were a major source of disagreement between the SPD and the Center Party and within the German population. With the Center insistent on confessional schools and the SPD opposed, the Weimar Constitution deferred a decision, requiring that the wishes of parents be honored and that existing regulations remain in place until the passage of a new Reich school law. The Reichstag was never able to pass the envisioned law. Although the influence of the churches on schooling diminished, religious instruction remained a legally mandated subject in public schools, and the separation of Protestant and Catholic children in confessional schools remained the norm in many areas, including most of Prussia and Bavaria and all of Württemberg and Oldenburg. By 1931, after years of parliamentary and public debate, over 80 percent of Germany's elementary schools were still confessional, and 85 percent of Catholic children attended Catholic schools.[14]

In light of the changed political situation and new stated goals for the schools, the need for new textbooks was obvious, but chronic economic and political problems and delays in issuing curricular guidelines resulted in postponement. When new books did appear, confessional readers remained common, especially in Catholic schools. Bavaria actually replaced older inter-confessional readers with confessional ones. Official guidelines continued to specify that readers should include only material consistent with "promoting tolerance."[15]

There was no reduction of religious content in the new Weimar-era Catholic readers, which continued to include specifically Catholic texts and exclude the Reformation.[16] One new text was a message from the German bishops to returning soldiers, welcoming them home from war on behalf of their "spiritual mother."[17] The vision of the new Germany found in these readers is both very Catholic and very traditional. Some Catholic history textbooks also continued to appear, treating Luther as a troublemaker.[18]

This contrasts with the warm, heroic, German Luther of the Protestant books used in some Weimar-era Protestant schools. At least one Protestant reader placed a picture of Jesus on the frontispiece, and another published a text on Bismarck's confirmation.[19] Catholics received little or no mention. Reading books that were not explicitly confessional became increasingly common in the Weimar years, both in heavily Protestant areas and in regions with interconfessional schools. Some of these books differed from the Protestant readers in little more than the more tempered content of their sections about Luther.[20] In others, including readers for Hamburg, Thuringia, and Dresden, the religious content noticeably diminished.[21] As hostile as many educators in these areas were to Catholic educational strategies, and especially Catholic insistence on the persistence of confessional schools, the reading books did not express these animosities.

The abandonment of confessional schooling in the Nazi era was not immediate. Article 23 of the 1933 Concordat between Germany and the Vatican guaranteed the "maintenance of the existing Catholic schools and the establishment of new ones," marking a seemingly successful end to the Catholics' long struggle over confessional schooling. Existing textbooks and curricula largely remained in place until at least 1935.[22] At that time, however, Nazi school authorities were persuading, and intimidating, parents into enrolling their children in interconfessional schools, in preparation for the elimination of confessional schools by 1941.[23] Although confessional religious instruction continued, ministerial orders specified that neither schoolbooks nor other parts of the curriculum could have confessional content. Popular resistance stymied efforts to eliminate morning devotions and crucifixes from classrooms, but the Church lost considerable influence over the education of Catholic children.[24]

New reading books for all *Volksschulen*, published under the auspices of the Reich minister of education, appeared between 1935 and 1939, in four volumes that covered grades 2 through 8. There were no confessional editions of these readers, although each volume appeared in twenty-two regional editions. Two-thirds to 80 percent of the content of each volume was the same everywhere, consisting of a group of core texts and illustrations, with the goal of providing shared readings for the entire *Volksgemeinschaft*. Regional committees chose the remaining texts in each volume. Supporters praised the *Reichslesebuch* as the canon of the school's *Bildungsgut* and the "backbone" of the entire curriculum.[25] The reading book was to promote "character, will, and knowledge" among German youth. Although many of the readers' goals resembled those of the past, guidelines specified that special emphasis be given to the study of race, population and heredity, eugenics, history of the *Volk*, geopolitics, and Germans in the diaspora. The reading books remained the only textbooks adopted for mandatory use in *Volksschulen* throughout the Reich.[26]

As for religion, guidelines specified that while textbooks were to reflect "Christian sympathies," they were to emphasize "unifying" aspects of Christianity, not confessional differences.[27] Indeed, although many texts from the older reading books reappear in the Nazi readers, those absent include not only confessional texts but also many other religious pieces. Missing are poems, such as Ludwig Uhland's "Shepherd's Sunday Song" and "The Chapel," that had appeared in virtually every Wilhelmine and Weimar reader. There are several Christmas stories in the Nazi readers, among them one about a pious Catholic altar boy, but, otherwise, references to Catholicism are rare.[28] Regional editions for heavily Catholic areas contain no more Christian material than books for other areas.[29]

Prayers in the Nazi readers have little Christian content. For example, one beseeches, "Lord . . . send me enemies, man by man / for struggle keeps one's powers active."[30] A farmer's prayer begins "I turned the unploughed earth / You made it rich in a few weeks."[31] And then there are numerous prayer-like poems addressed to the nation and to Hitler.[32]

Until the Nazis finally replaced confessional readers and forbade confessional schooling, the Catholic minority had enjoyed considerable control over the education of Catholic children, especially the majority who attended Catholic confessional schools. In addition to offering dedicated religious instruction, these schools incorporated Catholic material in texts used in reading and history classes. Anti-Catholic lessons had little place in the official texts and curricula of the Protestant schools. As the Nazis, for the first time, imposed central state control on public elementary schooling, the influence of both churches diminished.

III

In contrast with German Catholics, socialists did not, of course, have their own public schools. While there was a critical mass of teachers sympathetic toward the SPD in some cities in the *Kaiserreich*, criticism of the *Volksschule*, for its heavy religious and patriotic content and low academic level, was a persistent theme among party leaders.[33] With its extensive alternative institutions, the SPD did offer programs for children, and *Für unsere Kinder,* the children's supplement to the women's newspaper *Die Gleichheit,* even rewrote some children's stories from a socialist perspective.[34] Although reading books of the early twentieth century added some stories about working-class life to the usual pastoral fare, it is certainly not surprising that none of the adopted readers reflected the socialist subculture.[35]

In light of Kaiser Wilhelm II's Cabinet Order of 1889, which stated that schools should be "made useful" to combat "the spread of socialist and communist ideas," it is of interest to see how schoolbooks published subsequent to this order actually treated the SPD.[36] The contents of reading books certainly conformed with the kaiser's desire for moral instruction in a religious context, and Prussian readers fulfilled his request that the Prussian kings be depicted as devoted to their subjects.[37] Most Prussian readers also included a selection with a title like "What our kaisers have done for the workers." Beginning with the assertion that Wilhelm I was "a true friend and father of his people, especially the poorer classes," one such text then described the various social insurance programs as a generous sign of the kaiser's "Christian responsibility" and of his commitment to the "internal peace of the fatherland."[38] Most texts did not explicitly mention socialism, although one widely used Prussian book did condemn socialism as anathema to "monarchy, religion, love of fatherland," and "even marriage."[39] Texts using the insurance programs as evidence of the kaiser's devotion were much less common in readers used outside Prussia, where there was a competing *Landesvater.*[40]

The kaiser's Cabinet Order by no means transformed elementary textbooks. No more than, at most, two or three of the hundreds of selections in a reading book reflected a possible explicit response to the Cabinet Order, and in a number of readers there was no evidence of one at all. Elementary history texts similarly celebrated the concern for working people exhibited by the kaiser and other princes, usually without mentioning socialism.[41]

The German socialist tradition achieved only modest visibility in elementary schoolbooks of the Weimar years. Prussian guidelines for reading books specified that texts could not bear the "imprint of party politics." Texts were, however, to reflect "the lifestyle and occupation of the population where possible."[42] Some readers incorporated new stories about urban and industrial life, but the preponderance of texts in most readers depicted rural and village life, often in idyllic settings.[43] Among the newly included selections were tributes to captains of industry, like Alfred Krupp and August Thyssen, but also to coal miners, riveters, steelworkers, and lathe operators.[44] Critics from the left condemned both the delay in the introduction of new reading books and the continued appearance in the new books of texts that were too religious, overly sentimental, poorly written, and irrelevant or unconvincing to urban children. According to one such critic, the new books offered only "intellectual lemonade, which conjures up a world that does not exist."[45] Some reform pedagogues even sought to eliminate reading books entirely, replacing the anthologies with a series of longer texts.[46] Nonetheless, by the early 1930s, new, modestly revised reading books were widely used in most regions of Germany.

More change was evident in the new history books. The Hohenzollerns and other monarchs largely disappeared, replaced by accounts of industrialization and the emergence of socialism, including generally balanced discussion of Ferdinand Lassalle and Marx, of the founding of the SPD and its subsequent banning and growth, and of its role in founding the Republic.[47] The victors in the World War were blamed for the "frightful conditions" of the *"Diktat* of Versailles,"* and "party hatred" was blamed for the assassinations and uprisings of the early years of the Republic.[48] Although schoolbooks were slow to include the contested new national symbols of the Republic, including its flag, the phrase "black–red–gold" did appear in at least one Weimar history book, in a piece about the history of the new flag.[49] As the Social Democrats assumed a role in the government of the Republic, their history entered the history books of the fragile new state. Missing were the German communists.

Not only were communists among the first victims of Nazi political violence and the first concentration camp inmates, but they were also among the first to be labeled internal enemies in Nazi reading books. Among the new Nazi texts in the reading books published between 1935 and 1939 are stories of Nazi street battles which often resulted in martyrdom for young Nazis, who are presented as Germany's saviors from the communist threat. In one story, Werner Gerhardt, a dedicated *Jungvolk* leader, becomes a martyr, stabbed by a *Reichsbanner* man during a peaceful conversation. SA and SS men always appear reasonable and dignified in encounters with cold-hearted, lazy, violent, duplicitous, unattractive communist and socialist hooligans.[50] At the same time, newly added stories valorize labor and depict the Nazis as friends to workers. One such text describes a bridge construction site as "the battlefield of labor," where the workers are soldiers. The later wartime reader includes a text by Robert Ley entitled "We are all soldiers of labor."[51] The same volume contains a picture of a solemn working man, with a mallet over his shoulder and a smoke-belching smokestack behind him. The caption, a quotation from Hitler, reads, "In the future, there will be only one nobility, the nobility of labor."[52] The Nazi reader also includes Hitler's speech of 1 May 1933, announcing that the day would be a celebration of unity and labor, rather than an expression of class hatred. The national community depicted in the textbooks vilifies communists, but welcomes workers to the *Volksgemeinschaft.*[53]

IV

Jewish pupils faced difficult challenges in the thoroughly Christianized but confessionally bifurcated school systems of the German Empire. Jews comprised about 1 percent of the population but only about 0.5 percent of the pupils in the elementary schools. A disproportionately large number of Jewish children enrolled in secondary schools, which generally were not organized confessionally. Jewish elementary schools existed in some states, but they typically were small and underfunded. In turn-of-the-century Prussia, only 29 percent of Jewish *Volksschüler* attended Jewish schools, and 50 percent attended Protestant or Catholic confessional schools. Most of the others enrolled in interconfessional schools. In contrast with the detailed protections provided to Christian minorities in confessional schools, there was much less regard for Jewish children.[54]

Although the small Jewish schools often used textbooks published for Christian institutions, there were several Jewish reading books.[55] The Jewish reader for Hanover included many texts from other readers, on such themes as love of family and fatherland and the virtues of diligence, honesty, and cleanliness. Well represented were the works of Jewish writers, especially Berthold Auerbach and Heinrich Heine, although few of their characters are identifiably Jewish. Like most Protestant and Catholic readers, the Jewish book contained a unit of religious texts, including poems about Jewish holidays and religious observances and texts about Moses Mendelssohn and Maimonides. Immediately following this unit came a series of German history texts under the heading "Bind yourself to your dear fatherland."[56] These historical texts made no mention of Jews' role in German history. This book, although available to few Jewish pupils, attempted to offer a Jewish version of Germanness.

In readers for the dominant populations of the *Kaiserreich*, Jews were invisible. Most volumes included texts by Auerbach and Heine, without identifying them as Jews, and the occasional history text mentioned Jewish emancipation. Otherwise, Jews appeared neither as characters in stories, nor as actors in history, nor as religious figures. The absence of antisemitic material in these schoolbooks tells us little, of course, about the extent and nature of antisemitism in German culture, but it does suggest that the educators and officials responsible for schoolbooks did not consider this theme essential to the basic moral and political education of children. It is clear, however, that the strong Christian cast of German schooling and the fusion of Germanness with Christianity, in both its Protestant and Catholic forms, contained no framework for teaching children to recognize and respect non-Christian Germans.

The republican constitution of 1919 improved the legal status of Jewish education, and the modest expansion of interconfessional and even secular schools offered new options for Jewish pupils.[57] In the array of textbooks published for the majority Christian populations, Jews remained largely invisible. One history book contained a piece praising Walther Rathenau, and mourning his death, without mentioning that he was a Jew.[58] Again, the only mention of Jews in the history books was often a reference to their improved legal status.[59] Although mention of Judaism was rare in Weimar-era reading books, a reader published in 1927 for the fifth and sixth grades of the Prussian province of Saxony contained a selection called "The Eternal Jew," an antisemitic piece recounting the legend of Ahasver, the Jew who refused Jesus's request for a resting place and was condemned to wander.[60] Written by Ludwig Aurbacher (1784–1847), a Swabian Catholic, this text depicts the Jew as alien, mobile, and enduring. Apparently this book was published and adopted routinely. Although there is no pattern of antisemitic texts in Weimar reading books, the presence of this one suggests, perhaps, a growing acceptance of such messages in the Weimar years, as Jews became scapegoats in Germany's many crises.[61]

The Weimar Constitution stated that instruction in public schools should endeavor "not to hurt the feelings of those of differing opinion." While the content of instruction varied considerably according to the location and religious orientation of the school, these schoolbooks included few attacks on other German citizens. This contrasts with hostile treatment of the external "other," particularly the nations who had won the recent war.[62] Education suffered from the economic disruptions and political differences that plagued the republic. While schools clearly did not immunize young Germans against the appeal of National Socialism, and probably could not have done so, it is probably also mistaken to overstate the role of these schools in instilling the hateful racial attitudes characteristic of Nazi ideology.

The Nazi assumption of power adversely affected the education of Jewish children immediately. Quotas limited the number who could enroll in secondary schools, and Jewish pupils faced abuse from classmates and teachers. Enrollment in Jewish schools expanded rapidly, encompassing 60 percent of Jewish children by 1937. Shortly after *Kristallnacht*, the Nazis excluded Jewish children from all but Jewish schools, and on 30 June 1942 they terminated all Jewish schooling, "in view of the development of the resettlement."[63]

One of the early curricular changes instituted by the National Socialists was the addition of instruction about heredity and race, with emphasis on opposition between "the nordic racial mixture of today's German people" and "alien groups of other races, especially Jews."[64] The focus on race consciousness and purity of blood was to influence disciplines ranging from history and geography to natural science, German, and art. The first Nazi reader to be published, in 1935, the volume for grades 5 and 6, responds to this requirement by including several texts about genealogy and the importance of one's ancestors. While a number of texts seek to heighten children's racial identity as Germans, Jews are missing from this volume. Not only are the poems of Heine and Auerbach now absent, but there is no mention of Jews. At the time of the book's compilation, in 1934–35, prior to the Nuremberg Laws, the Nazis' effort to transform the content of education was not yet fully underway and they had not reached consensus about the pedagogical treatment of Jews.[65] If, indeed, many Germans were attracted to antisemitism because they found Nazism appealing, rather than "the other way around,"[66] the gradual, somewhat tentative introduction of antisemitic themes in textbooks is not surprising. A collection of lesson plans, based on the new reader and published in 1936, did not share this reticence, suggesting that teachers introduce antisemitic themes in conjunction with various reading selections. For example, the lesson suggested for a short text on the Beer Hall Putsch explains that "Jews and their friends ruled Germany at the time" but that the "Jewish character made Jews unfit to govern."[67]

In 1938, selection of the 155 texts for the core of the final volume of the reader, for the seventh and eighth grades, was complete, and antisemitic texts entered the canon of required readings. Among these texts is a passage from *Mein Kampf,* entitled "All Sacrifice in Vain?" in which Hitler describes how the Jewish-led revolution undermined Germans' wartime sacrifice.[68] In the same volume, another text by Hitler, about the Nazi flag, concludes that the swastika represents the "struggle for the victory of Aryan people."[69] Also around this time, a growing collection of antisemitic teaching materials, including numerous wall charts, were becoming available to teachers.[70] Better known today than the official Nazi reading book of the late 1930s, with its unmistakable but occasional antisemitic outbursts, are the rabidly and relentlessly antisemitic children's books published by Julius Streicher's publishing house *Der Stürmer.* Among these was *The Poison Mushroom,* by Ernst Hiemer.[71]

After several years of war, with attendant disruption of schooling, a new official reader, known as the "war reading book," appeared for the 1943–44 school year, this time with no regional editions. The effects of the war prevented its universal adoption. In 1940, on an order from Hitler, responsibility for schoolbooks had shifted from the Ministry of Education to the Nazi Party, in the person of Philipp Bouhler, who became director of the Office for School and Instructional Texts. This represented a further radicalization of education in the Third Reich and shaped the new readers.[72] These books include texts about the ongoing "war of liberation" and more stories of Nazi martyrdom. The antisemitic passages have become more virulent. A new selection about the swastika describes Jews as a "global pestilence" and "global contamination."[73] A story called "From the Ghetto to the Kurfürstendamm" tells of a Jewish boy from Bialystok who moved to Berlin, assimilated, succeeded in business, and raised two sons. After employing a series of crude, disparaging adjectives to describe the protagonist and his family, the text concludes that Jews would have been the "gravediggers of the German essence" if Hitler had not "put an end to the specter of Judaism with the Nuremberg Laws."[74] Here, as was common in Nazi antisemitism, Jews appear simultaneously to be inferior and all-powerful. Following this text is a string of antisemitic passages by Luther, Treitschke, Schiller, Hitler, Himmler, and Rosenberg, under the heading "The Jew, Our Archenemy."[75] In these final reading books of the Third Reich, full-blown Nazi antisemitism becomes part of the official schoolbook canon.

The growing willingness not only to vilify Jews but to blame them for all of Germany's problems is even more evident in Nazi history books. There was no officially approved history textbook for elementary schools, with school systems choosing among available options. In the early 1940s, Bouhler's office was still lamenting the lack of serviceable history books and busy eliminating unacceptable ones.[76] A text that shaped the interpretation in subsequently published Nazi history books was Bouhler's own *Kampf um Deutschland,* published in 1938 by the Nazi Central Press in Munich, with orders from Minister of Education Bernhard Rust that it be used in schools throughout Germany.[77] At that time, Bouhler was the head of Hitler's chancellery, and was soon to assume an even more notorious role as director of the "Euthanasia" project.[78] Bouhler dedicates his book to Hitler, and credits him with suggesting the need for a short history of the NSDAP for schoolchildren. The book begins by blaming "un-German influences," especially religious conflicts, liberalism, and Marxism, for the failure of Bismarck's Reich. But, according to Bouhler, Jews, thoroughly implicated in liberalism and Marxism, were the "deeper cause."[79] By preventing German victory in the World War, the SPD furthered the goal of world Jewry, and the resulting "black-red-gold" republic came to challenge the young National Socialist Party. Hitler came to power in 1933, just months before the Bolsheviks would have imposed terror on Germany, and the Nuremberg Laws prevented a "further bastardization of the German people through mixing with alien Jews."[80]

The themes in Bouhler's book recurred in later history books, including *So ward das Reich,* a popular volume published in 1943 for use in *Volksschulen* and edited by Dietrich Klagges, a prolific author of Nazi history textbooks. Here, Jews are implicated in everything from the exploitation of peasants, the French Revolution, the Frankfurt Parliament, and British imperialism to World War I, the Russian Revolution, the Treaty of Versailles, the Dawes Plan, and the Second World War. According to this account, some of the first Jesuits were of Jewish descent, and Jews beheaded blond, blue-eyed people during the French Revolution.[81] After German unification, the black, red, and gold enemies, namely the Center Party, the SPD, and the Jews, undermined the state, only to betray Germany in the World War. The same cabal, according to this book, took control of the government after the war and produced a constitution in which freedom and self-determination were a cover for rule by Jews and Freemasons.[82] The author praises the assassinations of "the communist leaders Liebknecht and Rosa Luxemburg, the communist Jew Eisner, the Jew Rathenau, and the Center Minister Erzberger." Given the treachery of the black-red-gold conspiracy, elimination of political parties was the first goal of the Nazis, followed by adoption of the Nuremberg Laws.[83] Jews, Marxists, and Freemasons then decided to destroy Germany, leading to the continuing war against Great Britain and other nations that were assisting the Jews. The book concludes with the claim that Jews, Freemasons, and Jesuits had been responsible for keeping Germany weak and divided for centuries.[84]

The Nazis had transformed elementary schoolbooks, and the schools that assigned them, to an extent that the previous generations had not. The entry of antisemitic texts was only one indication of the complete abandonment of the old (and to a considerable degree actually implemented) requirement that reading books avoid advocating intolerance and meddling in party politics. By the late 1930s, reading books, traditionally resistant to change, had become a vehicle for disseminating hatred and the cult of the leader and for blaming enemies, internal as well as external, for everything that went badly for Germany. For the first time, the German states lost control of textbooks to the national government, and eventually the ruling party. Also for the first time, religious and regional educators lost most of their voice in shaping education for their constituencies. Treatment of the three minorities was, of course, quite different, both in textbook lessons and in reality. There was no symmetry among the black, red, and gold enemies, even though the Nazis on occasion conflated them. In condemning and degrading the Center Party and Jesuits, the Nazi texts stop short of attacking all Catholics. While lambasting communism and socialism, the texts hold out the possibility that adherents of these movements can and will convert to National Socialism. The Nazis obviously could not afford to alienate the large populations of Catholics and the working class. Conversion was not an option, according to the texts, for Jews, who as a race embodied un-Germanness and lurked behind everything the Nazis opposed. The small, sometimes invisible, Jewish population became the metaphor for all enemies, internal and external.[85] The vehemence of these fabrications of a Jewish threat peaked as the Germans were murdering Europe's Jews.

Wilhelmine textbooks have been easy, and often deserving, targets, both for contemporary critics and for later historians. Weimar textbooks had short lives and plenty of contemporary critics, but their chaotic history has attracted less scholarly attention.[86] Sentimentality, pathos, a fixation on death and sacrifice, maudlin patriotism, and a preoccupation with the local and the familiar permeated most of the readers from both periods; and, although this has not been the focus of this chapter, many texts in these books made their way from one generation of readers to the next, and passed muster with Bouhler's textbook agency in the 1940s.[87] Nonetheless, this examination of textbooks' treatment of three major minority groups shows that, at least for Catholics, both the Wilhelmine and Weimar periods offered an opportunity to shape public schooling for their own communities. The small network of Jewish public schools provided similar possibilities, but many Jews sought assimilation in interconfessional schools. Socialists had little control over schooling until the end of World War I. While Wilhelmine and Weimar elementary reading books, and the schools that used them, certainly had political agendas, they generally refrained from publishing attacks on minority populations. The dominant cultures did, however, marginalize minority populations by making them invisible. The Nazis, in contrast, silenced all educational voices on the margins, attacked internal enemies, and established unprecedented organizations for political indoctrination of youth outside the classroom.

It is, of course, difficult to ignore the fact that most adults in the Third Reich had themselves attended Weimar or Wilhelmine schools. Knowing what they read in school does not tell us much about the young readers' reception of these texts, their teachers' instructional approaches, or the countless other experiences that shaped children's worldviews. Nonetheless, widely used, officially authorized schoolbooks do expose the themes that were present, and missing, in the texts chosen by representatives of the elites to transmit culture and values to the nation's children. Antisemitic themes were largely absent from Weimar and Wilhelmine reading books, but so were the Jewish people. The silence of the Wilhelmine and Weimar schoolbooks anticipates the silences of those who stood by and looked on during the Nazis' atrocities.

Notes

1. Geoff Eley, *From Unification to Nazism: Reinterpreting the German Past* (London: Routledge, 1986), 11.

2. David Bankier, *The Germans and the Final Solution: Public Opinion under Nazism* (Oxford: Oxford University Press, 1992), 156; and Ian Kershaw, *Popular Opinion and Political Dissent in the Third Reich: Bavaria, 1933–1945* (Oxford: Oxford University Press, 1983), 377.

3. See Walter Müller, *Schulbuchzulassung: Zur Geschichte und Problematik staatlicher Bevormundung von Unterricht und Erziehung* (Kastellaun: Henn, 1977); and Michael Sauer, "Zwischen Negativkontrolle und staatlichem Monopol: Zur Geschichte von Schulbuchzulassung und Einführung," *Geschichte in Wissenschaft und Unterricht* 49 (1998): 153–55.

4. See Ferdinand Bünger, *Entwicklungsgeschichte des Volksschullesebuches* (1898; reprint, Glashütten: Auvermann, 1972), 608–16. For this study, I have analyzed volumes for the middle and upper grades of sixteen Wilhelmine readers and thirteen Weimar readers adopted for use in different regions of Germany. For the Nazi era, I

have used the common core texts that constituted the majority of all regional editions of the Nazi reader.

5. See Helmut Walser Smith, *German Nationalism and Religious Conflict: Culture, Ideology, Politics, 1870–1914* (Princeton, N.J.: Princeton University Press, 1995), 233–39.

6. "Prüfung der Volksschullesebücher durch die Regierungen. Allgemeine Grundsätze," *Zentralblatt für die gesamte Unterrichts-Verwaltung in Preussen* (1902): 328.

7. *Lesebuch für die katholischen Volksschulen der Rheinprovinz*, Ausgabe für die Regierungsbezirke Aachen, Coblenz, Cöln und Trier, 3. Teil: Oberstufe (Dortmund: Crüwell, 1912), 8, 16–17.

8. *Lesebuch für die Rheinprovinz*, 476–77, 497–98.

9. *Lesebuch für die katholischen Volksschulen Württembergs*, Teil 2, (Stuttgart: Grüniger, 1910), 79–83, 93.

10. MK-22895, Lesebuch für die Oberklassen der katholischen Volksschulen in Bayern, 1896–1912, Bayerisches Hauptstaatsarchiv, Munich.

11. *Zentralblatt für die gesamte Unterrichts-Verwaltung in Preussen* (1880): 466; Marjorie Lamberti, *State, Society, and the Elementary School in Imperial Germany* (Oxford: Oxford University Press, 1989), 110–15; and John Kulczycki, *School Strikes in Prussian Poland, 1901–1907: The Struggle over Bilingual Education* (New York: Columbia University Press, 1981), 14–16.

12. *Lesebuch für Westpreussen für Schulen mit einfachen Verhältnissen*, 2. Teil (Breslau: Ferdinand Hirt, 1913), 531–56.

13. See, e.g., *Ferdinand Hirts Neues Realienbuch*, Nr. 1: Grosse Gesamt-Ausgabe für evangelische Schulen (Breslau: Ferdinand Hirt, 1916), 50–59.

14. René Brunet, *The New German Constitution* (New York: A. A. Knopf, 1922), 329–11, 337; Günther Grünthal, *Reichsschulgesetz und Zentrumspartei in der Weimarer Republik* (Düsseldorf: Droste, 1968), 294–95; Marjorie Lamberti, *The Politics of Education: Teachers and School Reform in Weimar Germany* (New York: Berghahn, 2002), 44–64; Geoffrey G. Field, "Religion in the German Volksschule," in *Leo Baeck Institute Year Book* 25 (1980): 53–64; and Ernst Helmreich, *Religious Education in German Schools: An Historical Approach* (Cambridge, Mass.: Harvard University Press, 1959), 110–23, 133–37.

15. C. L. A. Pretzel and E. Hylla, *Neuzeitliche Volksschularbeit: Winke zur Durchführung der preussischen Lehrplanrichtlinien* (Langensalza: Beltz, 1929), 154.

16. *Rheinisches Lesebuch*, fünftes bis achtes Schuljahr (Dortmund: W. Crüwell, [1924]), 39–46, 280–302; and *Lesebuch für den 6. und 7. Schülerjahrgang katholischer Volkshauptschulen Bayerns*, 5th ed., (Munich: Oldenbourg, 1930), 30–31, 71–72.

17. *Rheinisches Lesebuch*, 302–304.

18. *Teubners Sachkunde für Volksschulen*, Fachband 1: Geschichte, für katholische Schulen (Leipzig: Teubner, 1930), 42–47.

19. *Lesebuch für die evangelischen Schulen Westfalens: Ausgabe für das Gebiet der Lippe, Ruhr und Lenne*, III. Teil, 5. bis 8. Schuljahr (Bielefeld: Velhagen und Klasing, 1931), frontispiece; and *Lesebuch für den 6. u. 7. Schülerjahrgang evangelischer Volkshauptschulen Bayerns* (Munich: Oldenbourg, 1928), 13–16; 53–54.

20. *Ferdinand Hirts Deutsches Lesebuch für das 5. bis 8. Schuljahr*, Ausgabe B (Breslau: Ferdinand Hirt, 1925); and A. Schmidt and O. Zenker, eds., *Kind und Heimat: Volksschullesebuch für die Provinz Sachsen* (Langensalza: Beltz, [1928]).

21. *Muttersprache: Lesebuch für Volksschulen*, hrsg. vom Dresdner Lehrerverein, Ausgabe B, 3. Teil (Leipzig: Klinkhardt, 1932); *Deutsches Lesebuch*, hrsg. von der Gesellschaft der Freunde des vaterländischen Schul- und Erziehungs-Wesens, 6. Teil (Hamburg: Gesellschaft der Freunde des vaterländischen Schul- und Erziehungswesens, 1929); and *Thüringer Lesebuch*, 4. Teil. (Weimar: Thüringer Staatsverlag, 1927).

22. Guenter Lewy, *The Catholic Church and Nazi Germany* (New York: McGraw-Hill, 1964), 83; and Helmreich, *Religious Education*, 158–59, 173.

23. Lewy, *Catholic Church*, 156; Helmreich, *Religious Education*, 173–74; Gertraud Gruenzinger and Carsten Nicolaisen, *Dokumente zur Kirchenpolitik des Dritten Reiches*, vol. 3 (Gütersloh: Christian Kaiser Verlag, 1935–37), 273; *Deutsche Wissenschaft, Erziehung und Volksbildung: Amtsblatt des Ministeriums für Wissenschaft, Erziehung und Volksbildung und der Unterrichtsverwaltungen der Länder* 5 (1939): 226; Rolf Eilers, *Die nationalsozialistische Schulpolitik* (Cologne: Westdeutscher Verlag, 1963), 85–91; and Kershaw, *Popular Opinion*, 213–18.

24. Helmreich, *Religious Education*, 163; Gruenzinger and Nicolaisen, *Dokumente zur Kirchenpolitik*, 255–61; Kershaw, *Popular Opinion*, 340–53.

25. Richard Alschner, "Zum neuen Volksschullesebuch für das 5. und 6. Schuljahr," *Neue Bahnen* 47 (1936): 114–16; and Eilers, *Die nationalsozialistische Schulpolitik*, 29.

26. "Aus den Richtlinien zur Schaffung neuer Lesebücher," *Deutsche Volkserziehung* 4 (1937): 119–21; and Kurt-Ingo Flessau, *Schule der Diktatur: Lehrpläne und Schulbücher des Nationalsozialismus* (Munich: Fischer, 1977), 21.

27. "Aus den Richtlinien," 121; and Alfred Pudelko, "Das Reichslesebuch," *Weltanschauung und Schule* 2 (1938): 339. See also Richard Steigmann-Gall, *The Holy Reich: Nazi Conceptions of Christianity, 1919–1945* (Cambridge: Cambridge University Press, 2003), 84–85.

28. *Deutsches Lesebuch für Volksschulen: 5. und 6. Schuljahr*, 3. Band, vol. 8 (Westfalen) (Bielefeld und Leipzig, [1935]), 252–66.

29. See, e.g., *Deutsches Lesebuch für Volksschulen*, 4. Band, vol. 18, (Oberfranken u. Niederbayern) (Munich: Oldenbourg, 1942); and *Deutsches Lesebuch für Volksschulen*, 4. Band, vol. 17 (Oberbayern u. Schwaben), (Munich: Oldenbourg, [1939]).

30. *Deutsches Lesebuch für Volksschulen*, 4. Band, vol. 8 (Westfalen), (Bielefeld, [1939]), 295.

31. *Deutsches Lesebuch für Volksschulen*, 3. Band, vol. 8, 193.

32. See, e.g., Hans H. Seitz, "Mein Führer," and Will Vesper, "Dem Führer," in *Deutsches Lesebuch für Volksschulen*, 3. Band, vol. 8, 374–75.

33. Hildegard Milberg, *Schulpolitik in der pluralistischen Gesellschaft: Die politischen und sozialen Aspekte der Schulreform in Hamburg, 1890–1935* (Hamburg: Leibniz Verlag, 1970), 91–94. See Otto Rühle, *Die Volksschule, wie sie ist* (Berlin: Vorwärts, 1903).

34. See, e.g., Brand [pseud.], "Aus der Schule: Stadtmaus und Feldmaus," *Für unsere Kinder*, November 1908, 25–26; and Brand [pseud.], "Modernes Heldentum," *Für unsere Kinder*, October 1908, 9–12.

35. See, e.g., "Das rüstige Wupperthal" and "Solingen und Remscheid," in Heinrich Gabriel and Karl Supprian, eds., *Deutsches Lesebuch für Stadt- und Landschulen: Ausgabe für den Regierungsbezirk Düsseldorf*, 2. Teil, Oberstufe (Bielefeld: Velhagen und Klasing, 1900), 476–80.

36. Egon von Bremen, ed., *Die preussische Volksschule: Gesetze und Verordnungen* (Stuttgart: Cotta, 1905), 230.

37. Ibid., 231.

38. W. Nohl and M. Ullmann, eds., *Lesebuch für Brandenburg*, 3. Teil (Breslau: Ferdinand Hirt, 1906), 531; *Lesebuch für Westpreussen*, 392–93; Heinrich Flügge, *Zweites Lesebuch für Volksschulen*, neue Bearbeitung von Karl Dageförde, Mittel- und Oberstufe (Hannover: Carl Meyer, 1912), 483–84; and *Lesebuch für die Rheinprovinz*, 603. See also *Ferdinand Hirts Realienbuch*, 134.

39. *Ferdinand Hirts Deutsches Lesebuch*, Ausgabe A, 2. Teil (Breslau: Ferdinand Hirt, 1898), 270.

40. *Lesebuch für die evangelischen Volksschulen Württembergs*, 3. Teil (Stuttgart: Union, 1910); F. W. Putzger and K. E. Rasche, eds., *Deutsches Lesebuch für einfache Volksschulen*, Ausgabe A (Leipzig: Dürr, 1903); *Lesebuch für das sechste und siebente Schuljahr der niederbayerischen Volksschulen* (Munich: Oldenbourg, 1910); and *Lesebuch für die Oberklassen der Volksschulen: Ausgabe für den Regierungsbezirk Unterfranken und Aschaffenburg* (Munich: Oldenbourg, [1905]).

41. See *Ferdinand Hirts Realienbuch*, 134; *Ferdinand Hirts Neues Realienbuch*, Nr. 16: Gekürzte Gesamt-Ausgabe für konfessionell gemischte Schulen (Breslau: Ferdinand Hirt, 1911), 82–84, 86; and Lamberti, *State, Society*, 7–9. Compare Gabriele Jaroschka, *Lernziel: Untertan; Ideologische Denkmuster in Lesebüchern des deutschen Kaiserreichs* (Munich: Waxmann, 1992), 95–98.

42. Pretzel and Hylla, *Neuzeitliche Volksschularbeit*, 154–55.

43. See, e.g., *Ferdinand Hirts Deutsches Lesebuch für das 5. bis 8. Schuljahr*.

44. *Rheinisches Lesebuch*, 262–75; and Schmidt and Zenker, *Kind und Heimat*, Ausgabe B, 2. Band, 108–11.

45. Leo Weismantel, "Grundsätzliches zur Schullesebuchfrage," in *Bayerisches Bildungswesen* 2 (1928): 301; and Oskar Huebner, *Das Lesebuch der Republik* (Berlin-Leipzig: Vereinigung Internat, Verlagsanstalt [Frankes-Verlag], 1922).

46. Wilhelm Fronemann, *Der Unterricht ohne Lesebuch: Entwurf eines schulliterarischen Programms auf Grund von Schaffsteins blauen und grünen Bänden* (Cologne: Schaffstein, 1921).

47. *Geschichtsbuch für die deutsche Jugend*, Kurzausgabe, 3. Teil, (Leipzig: Quelle und Meyer, [1930]), 20–22, 27, 44; *Ferdinand Hirts Tatsachen und Arbeitshefte*, 1. Gruppe: Geschichte, Ausgabe A (Breslau: Ferdinand Hirt, 1929), 26–27, 44; *Teubners Sachkunde*, 18–19, 23–24, 36; *Geschichtsbilder: Zum Gebrauch für den Geschichtsunterricht in den Volksschulen des Freistaates Braunschweig* (Braunschweig: Rieke, 1929), 118–22; and Max Reiniger and Hermann Nickol, *Neues Geschichtliches Lesebuch*, 2. Teil, 27. Aufl., (Langensalza: Beltz, 1927), 118–24.

48. *Geschichtsbuch für die deutsche Jugend*, 44–45; *Ferdinand Hirts Tatsachen und Arbeitshefte*, 45; and *Teubners Sachkunde*, 36–39, 41.

49. *Teubners Sachkunde*, 5–6, 8, 40.

50. *Deutsches Lesebuch für Volksschulen*, 3. Band, vol. 8, 311–14; *Deutsches Lesebuch für Volksschulen*, 4. Band, vol. 8, 205–207; and *Deutsches Lesebuch für Volksschulen*, 4. Band (Berlin: Deutscher Schulverlag, 1944), 417–22. See Jay Baird, *To Die for Germany: Heroes in the Nazi Pantheon* (Bloomington: Indiana University Press, 1990), 108–29.

51. *Deutsches Lesebuch für Volksschulen*, 4. Band, vol. 8, 106; *Deutsches Lesebuch für Volksschulen*, 4. Band, 1944, 198.

52. *Deutsches Lesebuch für Volksschulen*, 4. Band, 1944, 261; see Alf Lüdtke, "The 'Honor of Labor': Industrial Workers and the Power of Symbols under National Socialism," in *Nazism and German Society, 1933–1945*, ed. David F. Crew (London: Routledge, 1994), 74–89, 97–98.

53. *Deutsches Lesebuch für Volksschulen*, 4. Band, vol. 8, 204–207, 217–18.

54. P. v. Gizycki, *Das Volksschulwesen und das Lehrerbildungswesen im deutschen Reich*, vol. 3 of *Das Unterrichtswesen im Deutschen Reich* (Berlin: Ascher, 1904), 62; Marjorie Lamberti, *Jewish Activism in Imperial Germany* (New Haven, Conn.: Yale University Press, 1978), 124–28, 134–56; Till van Rahden, "Weder Milieu noch Konfession: Die situative Ethnizität der deutschen Juden im Kaiserreich in vergleichender Perspektive," in *Religion im Kaiserreich: Milieus, Mentalitäten, Krisen*, ed. Olaf Blaschke and Frank-Michael Kuhlemann (Gütersloh: Gütersloher Verlagshaus, 1996), 428–29; Helmreich, *Religious Education*, 66; and *Zentralblatt für die gesamte Unterrichts-Verwaltung in Preussen* (1906): 639.

55. Claudia Prestel, *Jüdisches Schul- und Erziehungswesen in Bayern, 1804–1933: Tradition und Modernisierung im Zeitalter der Emanzipation* (Göttingen: Vandenhoeck und Ruprecht, 1989), 190–91.

56. *Lesebuch für Bürgerschulen*, für jüdische Schulen umgearbeitet von Levy, Reuss, Spanier, 2. Teil—Oberstufe (Hannover: Hahn, 1901), 96–112.

57. Helmreich, *Religious Education*, 136–37, 146–49; Prestel, *Jüdisches Schul- und Erziehungswesen*, 217–28.

58. *Geschichtsbilder*, 146–47.

59. *Ferdinand Hirts Tatsachen und Arbeitshefte*, 27.

60. A. Schmidt and O. Zenker, eds., *Kind und Heimat: Volksschullesebuch für die Provinz Sachsen*, Ausgabe B, 1. Band (Langensalza: Beltz [1927]), 369–71.

61. Robert Gellately, *Backing Hitler: Consent and Coercion in Nazi Germany* (Oxford: Oxford University Press, 2001), 6; and Omer Bartov, "Defining Enemies, Making Victims: Germans, Jews, and the Holocaust," *American Historical Review* 103, no. 3 (1998): 777–816.

62. See Joachim S. Hohmann, ed., *Erster Weltkrieg und nationalsozialistische "Bewegung" im Deutschen Lesebuch, 1933–1945* (Frankfurt am Main: Lang, 1988), 12.

63. *Deutsche Wissenschaft, Erziehung und Volksbildung* (1938): 520–52; Marion Kaplan, *Between Dignity and Despair: Jewish Life in Nazi Germany* (Oxford: Oxford University Press, 1998), 94–96, 103; Helmreich, *Religious Education*, 205–208; and Eilers, *Die nationalsozialistische Schulpolitik*, 98–102.

64. *Deutsche Wissenschaft, Erziehung und Volksbildung* (1935): 44–45. See Gregory Paul Wegner, *Anti-Semitism and Schooling under the Third Reich* (New York: Falmer, 2002), 67–70, 103–16.

65. H. Scholtz, *Erziehung und Unterricht unterm Hakenkreuz* (Göttingen: Vandenhoeck und Ruprecht, 1985), 45–48; and Wegner, *Anti-Semitism and Schooling*, 112–13.

66. William Sheridan Allen, *The Nazi Seizure of Power: The Experience of a Single German Town, 1930–1935* (Chicago: Quadrangle, 1965), 77; and Michael R. Marrus, *The Holocaust in History* (New York: Brandeis University Press by University Press of New England, 1987), 12.

67. P. Roessing, K. Zaum, W. Huels, L. Irie, Ch. Herfurth, and W. Schaefer, *Wege zum Deutschen Lesebuch*, 5. und 6. Schuljahr (Bochum: Verlags- und Lehrmittel-Anstalt Ferdinand Kamp, [1936]), 200–201.

68. *Deutsches Lesebuch für Volksschulen*, 4. Band, vol. 8, 195–97.

69. Ibid., 213.

70. Wegner, *Anti-Semitism and Schooling*, 74–84.

71. Ernst Hiemer, *Der Giftpilz* (Nuremberg: Verlag Der Stürmer, 1938); Wegner, *Anti-Semitism and Schooling*, 158–71; for photographs of pages from *Der Giftpilz*, see http://www.ushmm.org/uia-cgi/uia_query/photos?query=dc4o5526.

72. *Deutsche Wissenschaft, Erziehung und Volksbildung* 10 (1944): 138; Hansulrich Horn, "Die Neuordnung des Schulbuchwesens und Schulbuchfragen im Kriege," *Deutsche Schulerziehung* 2 (1943): 77–78, 84–85; and Eilers, *Die nationalsozialistische Schulpolitik*, 30.

73. *Deutsches Lesebuch für Volksschulen*, 3. Band (Berlin: Deutscher Schulverlag, 1943), 337.

74. *Deutsches Lesebuch für Volksschulen*, 4. Band, 1944, 402–404.

75. Ibid., 404–405.

76. Horn, "Die Neuordnung," 79, 82; and Eilers, *Die nationalsozialistische Schulpolitik*, 30.

77. *Deutsche Wissenschaft, Erziehung und Volksbildung* 4 (1938): 309.

78. Michael Burleigh, *The Third Reich: A New History* (New York: Hill and Wang, 2000), 383–86.

79. Philipp Bouhler, *Kampf um Deutschland: Ein Lesebuch für die deutsche Jugend* (Berlin: Eher, 1938), 11, 12, 15.

80. Ibid., 23, 28, 48, 96–98.

81. Heinrich Blume, *So ward das Reich, Volk und Führer: Deutsche Geschichte für Schulen*, Ausgabe für Volksschulen, Klasse 6, 7 und 8, ed. Dietrich Klagges (Frankfurt am Main: Diesterweg, 1943), 71, 103, 122.

82. Ibid., 140–43, 165–67. See Gilmer W. Blackburn, *Education in the Third Reich: Race and History in Nazi Textbooks* (Albany: State University of New York Press, 1985), 150.

83. Blume, *So ward das Reich*, 183, 193, 197.

84. Ibid., 204, 208–12, 254–55.

85. See Omer Bartov, "Defining Enemies, Making Victims," 779.

86. Horst Schallenberger, *Untersuchungen zum Geschichtsbild der wilhelminischen Ära und der Weimarer Zeit* (Ratingen: Henn, 1964); Peter Lundgreen, "Analyse preussischen Schulbücher als Zugang zum Thema, Schulbildung und Industrialisierung," *International Review of Social History* 15 (1970): 85–121; James M. Olson, "Nationalistic Values in Prussian Schoolbooks prior to World War I," *Canadian Review of Studies in Nationalism* 1 (1973): 47–59; and Jaroschka, *Lernziel*.

87. See, e.g., Katharine Kennedy, "African Heimat: German Colonies in Wilhelmine and Weimar Reading Books," *Internationale Schulbuchforschung/International Textbook Research* 24 (2002): 7–26; Katharine D. Kennedy, "A Nation's Readers: Cultural Integration and the Schoolbook Canon in Wilhelmine Germany," *Paedagogica Historica* 33, no. 2 (1997): 459–80; and Katharine D. Kennedy, "Visual Representation and National Identity in the Elementary Schoolbooks of Imperial Germany," *Paedagogica Historica* 36, no. 1 (2000): 225–45.

Eight

"Productivist" and "Consumerist" Narratives of Jews in German History

Gideon Reuveni

I

It is a truism that historians need sources for their research. A good historian, it is generally agreed even by those who emphasize the importance of models and theory, is one who allows her- or himself to be guided by the records. Thus the history of nineteenth-century German antisemitism, for example, has usually been written citing the published utterances of antisemites or contemporary reports on their behavior. But, important as it is to allow such testimonies to speak about the past, how should historians respond when the material they consult in anticipation of finding relevant information does *not* provide the picture we expect? How eloquent can we allow silence to be, and what rules govern our analysis of such silence? Currently, what historians imagine the past "to be" is to a great extent based on representations in historical sources rather than on what is absent from these sources. It appears to me that historians too often shun the question of the omissions and absences. To confront what is *not* recorded, indeed, challenges basic methodological and theoretical notions of historical writing but might open new ways of reading the past. This, I would argue, is particularly true in the case of Jewish history, which usually relies on material that treats Jews as its main subject matter and as a result can misinterpret the role of Jews in history. A concrete example will hopefully illuminate my point.

Shulamit Volkov's influential essay on "antisemitism as a cultural code" is a powerful example of the problem I am referring to.[1] According to Volkov, toward the end of the nineteenth century Germany underwent a process of cultural polarization symbolized by two concepts: antisemitism and emancipation. Thus, professing antisemitism became a kind of "cultural code" de-

165

noting one's belonging to a specific cultural camp that, as Volkov observes, was characterized by a radical anti-modern mentality that included the rejection of liberalism, capitalism, socialism, and democracy as well as a call for the reestablishment of a "national community" (*Volksgemeinschaft*). Volkov's argument is based solely on utterances of antisemites and pleas in favor of Jewish emancipation. By portraying German society's relationship to Jews exclusively through documents that treat Jews as their main subject, Volkov generates a picture of straightforward binary opposition that in many ways reproduces the images of the sources she used. The question arises: was the "Jewish theme" of such centrality? Can the Jews indeed be regarded as the touchstone of German society? If this is the case, we would expect to find the "Jewish theme" or at least anti-Jewish sentiments in areas that could be regarded as part of the nationalistic, anti-modern, or anti-capitalist camp. Yet, as the following will show, this kind of nexus cannot always be established. Jews were not always either included or excluded and they were not always treated, as we might expect on the basis of earlier research, within the broad framework of so-called "reactionary modernism."[2]

II

The first example that I would like to examine here is the fight against so-called *Schund- und Schmutzschriften* (literally translatable as "dirt and trash writings"). An amazing number of works which fall under the heading of "the struggle against *Schund- und Schmutzschriften*" emanated from Germany between 1870 and 1933. Articles in the press, pamphlets, books, lectures, exhibitions, and special journals designed to combat this form of literature, as well as calls to boycott the shops where it was sold and the burning of the books in question, were just some of the ways that works considered to be "trash" and "pulp" were attacked. The list of institutions and organizations which participated in this struggle is impressively long. The government and local authorities, the churches, the educational system, the political parties, the different kinds of libraries, a variety of cultural and moral associations, organizations set up in more than thirty-three cities specifically to wage war on pulp literature, and the Book Dealers' Association were the main bodies which set themselves the goal of combating pulp fiction and promoting good literature.[3] Practically all of Germany's state and local archives have holdings documenting this struggle.

Today's observer may wonder about the intense preoccupation at the time with the phenomenon of *Schund und Schmutz*, especially since there was never a commonly accepted definition of these two concepts. *Schund und Schmutz* was not used to describe a particular sort of literary genre, but instead used as a label to mark writings of reputedly low aesthetic and ethical value in order to exclude them.[4] Basically any publication could have been branded

Schund und Schmutz. Before the First World War the novels of Karl May, for example, were labeled *Schund* and their distribution attacked. Writings with socialistic touches and radical nationalistic literature were also often treated in the same way. This circumstance seems to explain the great variety of publications about the topic as well as the various types of *Schund und Schmutz* that they referred to.

Contemporaries viewed pulp literature as a social problem of the first order.[5] The vast amount of material available to today's researcher is perhaps the best proof of fears about the destructive influence of these works, which were called "pulp" (*Schmutz*), "trash" (*Schund*), "smut" (*Unzucht*), "inferior" (*untergeistige*) writings, and kitsch. *Schund und Schmutz* writings became the scapegoat for all of society's social ills. Those who actively engaged in combating trash (*Schundkämpfer*), most of them educated men, saw these writings as a manifestation of a rival culture which was threatening to undermine the social order at whose head the educated male bourgeoisie had established itself. In particular, pornography, homosexuality, internationalism, and capitalism were viewed as diseases of society and blamed for the popularity of *Schund und Schmutz* writings. At the same time, these phenomena were generally associated with Judaism and the Jews.[6] However, despite the prominence of Jews in the publishing world, an examination of the history of the war on *Schund und Schmutz* writings shows that it was not particularly marked by antisemitism. Even *Hochwacht*, a magazine designed to wage war on trash and with manifestly nationalist leanings, did not voice antisemitic positions in its struggle against pulp literature.[7] On the contrary, during the period prior to the First World War, we find articles in the context of the anti-trash struggle praising the cultural virtues of the Jews and their superior taste in reading. Moreover, both before and after the War Jewish individuals and organizations played an active role in the struggle against *Schund und Schmutz* in the name of high culture and *Bildung*.[8] After 1918 the first official lists of pulp publications contained a number of works with a manifestly nationalistic and antisemitic character. These works, which fell into the category of "patriotic trash literature" (*patriotische Schundliteratur*), were banned from distribution by the 1926 Law for the Protection of Young People against Trash and Filth (referred to below as "the Law").[9]

Despite the positive image enjoyed by the Jews in the context of the struggle against pulp writings, as well as efforts to repress works with a manifestly antisemitic character, it would be going too far to conclude that the struggle against pulp literature was used as a tool for combating antisemitism. At the end of 1928, for example, the Rhine-Westphalian Youth Welfare Department in Düsseldorf tried to ban an issue of the Nazi Party newspaper *Westdeutscher Beobachter* because of an article entitled "Sex Crime in the House of Tietz." The article described in great detail indecent sexual acts which a Jew was alleged to have perpetrated against a "German girl" at the department store owned by Leonhard Tietz, a Jew, in Cologne. The Düsseldorf Youth Welfare Department considered this article to be pornographic and harmful to young people, and demanded that distribution of that issue of the newspaper be banned. After the application was rejected by the Berlin Examining Bureau for Trash and Filth on the grounds that banning the paper would constitute political censorship, the Chief Examining Bureau for Trash and Filth, based in the German Library (*Deutsche Bücherei*) in Leipzig, ruled that the need to protect young persons against corruption of their moral values outweighed freedom of political expression. However, since the article was published in a daily newspaper the Bureau ruled that the risk of corrupting youth had passed and it no longer saw fit to ban the newspaper.[10]

III

Antisemitism was therefore viewed as a political outlook, not a social problem. Why, in the light of this state of affairs, did antisemitism, as a political ideology which provided a response to the "social question," not play a key role in the framework of the struggle against pulp writings?[11] Undoubtedly an entire complex of factors was responsible for this situation. I would argue that a key element was the special nature of the struggle against pulp works: It was what may be called a "consumer discourse" rather than a "producer discourse." That is, it was a discourse dealing with consumption and the relationship between consumer and producer, rather than with production or with the character and the situation of the bourgeois classes. It should be emphasized that the two concepts of "consumer discourse" and "producer discourse" are not "two sides of the same coin" or "discourse" and "counter-discourse," as could be assumed from the opposition of the two terms "consumer" and "producer." Instead, they are two types of discourse with different sorts of references and functions.

The "consumer discourse" deals with the "masses," which, as the main audience for commercialized culture, are most exposed to its supposedly detrimental or harmful influences. In many ways this discourse reflects the fears of what contemporaries conceived as the dictatorship of the consumers: i.e., of a situation in which consumers' taste and demand would determine production and supply. One of the main features of this discourse is the presentation of a self-controlled bourgeois individual as opposed to the allegedly easy-to-manipulate masses. Those who belonged to these masses, mainly women, workers, and youth, were seen as "the other without" and were considered a danger to the dominance of bourgeois "enshrined values." In other words, "consumer discourse" was used as a means to strengthen bourgeois self-definition.[12]

The producers themselves, however, are at the center of the "producer discourse," which reflects the competition between different elements within these classes. This type of discourse deals more with the divisions and conflicts among the bourgeois classes, i.e., with what can be defined as "the other within." There is here a certain affinity between the so-called "other without" and the "other within." Both are assigned negative attributes, such as femininity, materialism, and mimicry. Yet, while the "consumer discourse" is defensive, because it is trying to defend bourgeois values, the "producer discourse" reflects schisms and frictions within the bourgeois classes.

Bearing this proposed division between producer and consumer discourses in mind, let us return to our example and try to explain why Jews did not play any topical role within certain types of discourses. The Jews, I would argue, were viewed not as one of the groups making up the masses which were the target audience of commercialization, but instead as part of that group of producers whose power was weakened in direct proportion to the growing power of the consumer masses.

The so-called capitalism debate, which took place at the beginning of the twentieth century, is a further striking illustration of this state of affairs. Although Jews played a central role in the discussions of the origins of capitalism, especially after the publication of Werner Sombart's book *Juden und das Wirtschaftsleben* (1911), they were marginalized in the discussions of the need to discipline consumers.[13] Even Sombart himself, when writing on the problem of consumption, did not mention Jews, but rather dealt in this context exclusively with women as initiators of consumer culture.[14]

The point that I am trying to raise here becomes even more evident in a comparison of parallel debates, for instance in the discussions of the situation of book reading after the Great War. As it did many other areas of life, a feeling of crisis pervaded the book trade after the First World War. The main reasons for the so-called "book crisis" (*Buchkrise*) were identified as the enduring economic instability and the political crises of the postwar period, but especially the great social changes in German society after the War.[15] As Hans Zehrer (writing as "Hans Thomas") who since 1929 had been the editor of the German new-right magazine *Die Tat* (The Deed), and the ideologist of the group which gathered around him, had put it in his characteristic style: "Your buying circles are changing. Readers' intellectual demands are dwindling. The scourge of proletarianization and vulgarization is spreading at the speed of light and supporting the tendency, already present, to a flattening and general leveling out."[16]

The core of this change was perceived as the "disintegration of the bourgeoisie" on the one hand and "the advent of mass society" on the other. Terms such as *Vermassung*—literally "massification"—"proletarianization," and "Americanization" were often used to describe the transition from a bourgeois society to a mass society. The growing popularity of new media such as film and radio and new leisure-time occupations and entertainments such as sports and dance were particularly seen as manifestations of the new mass society. In light of these developments, librarian Max Wieser even asked whether books still suited the modern mentality as a means of education, enlightenment, and artistic expression. He predicted that in the future, books would no longer play such a central role in society as they had for the past three hundred years, from the sixteenth century onward.[17] In other words, in the eyes of contemporaries, the popularity of the new media—film, the gramophone, and radio—meant the end of the monopoly of the written word as the repository of human knowledge and marked the transition from a reading and writing culture in which the book was the main means of mediation between humans and their surroundings to a seeing and hearing culture which perceived reality through the new media.

This sort of cultural pessimism was not unique to conservative right-wing discourse in the Weimar period, but rather characterized the general discourse about the situation of culture at the time. Right and left, men and women, Jews and Gentiles struggled together to preserve the German book culture, and in so doing they formed a joint culturally conservative front. "People practice sports, dance, spend their evening hours by the radio, in the cinema, and, outside working hours, everyone is so busy that nobody has time to read a book,"[18] the famous Jewish liberal publisher Samuel Fischer wrote in 1926. He claimed that the World War and the subsequent economic suffering had impoverished the bourgeoisie and destroyed the bourgeois social fabric, which had been the bedrock of German intellectual and cultural life.[19] Fischer identified the collapse of the bourgeois associations which had represented the interests of various groups within the middle classes, organized cultural and leisure activities, and generally acted as a central component in the process of society-building and social communication as one of the key processes which had changed the face of German society following the First World War. He thus interpreted the loss of interest in reading as a clear reflection of these changes. The literary associations, evenings of readings, libraries, and drama associations were more than mere means of disseminating culture and knowledge: in fact, according to Fischer, they were responsible for creating a feeling of shared German culture (*Gemeinschaftsgefühl deutscher Kultur*), and it was these associations which made reading a social event, and concomitantly books a means of forging bonds between people.

The "book crisis" was therefore a book-selling crisis and mirrored the fear of publishers, booksellers, and authors—the core of the male bourgeois educated classes—of the demise of "reading culture," which was regarded as a main component of bourgeois culture. With its decline the social position of the male educated bourgeois was also at stake. The fear of reader power, which decided the fate of a book, shows that the book crisis was discussed as a "consumer discourse." Hence it is not surprising that "Jews," despite their weight and apparent presence in the German publishing world, were not a topic within this discourse.

IV

A further example that contains a similar pattern is the war on alcohol. Toward the end of the nineteenth century alcohol came to be recognized as a social problem. Military officials, the churches, factory owners, and Social Democrats viewed alcoholism as a sign of moral failure and even as a disease in itself. Contemporaries established a connection between alcohol and productivity, as well as between alcohol and military service, and warned against the devastating influence of drinking both on the human body and on society. Studies of alcoholism confirmed these fears. They presented insobriety as responsible "for the degeneration of entire nations" and for "the deterioration of the race."[20] These studies reflect worries about the endurance of the German nation in an age of modernization and rapid industrial development. At the same time they also indicate the growing influence of science in the social process and demonstrate how scientific languages penetrated and shaped social discourse. An analogy was drawn between the human body and society; both became subjects of observation, potentially pathological. Not surprisingly, physicians played a central role in this development. As Abraham Baer noted in his extensive 1878 study entitled "Alcoholism: Its Divulgation and Effects on Individuals and the Social Organism": "The medical practitioner is probably in the best position to observe alcoholism in the physical degeneration of the population; as lunatic asylums show the devastation of intellectual life, the workhouses, jails, and prisons show in equally terrible dimensions the destruction inflicted by excess directly and indirectly on the moral fiber of human society."[21]

Here it is important to note that Abraham Baer, who worked as a medical adviser at the city jail of Plötzensee in Berlin, was a Jew from Posen.[22] His study of alcoholism rapidly came to be seen as the standard work and gave rise to the modern anti-alcoholism movement in Germany. One of the most important of the new organizations was the *Deutscher Verein gegen den Mißbrauch geistiger Getränke* E. V. (1883), which invited Baer to serve as its honorary chairman.

More interesting than the active involvement of actual Jews in the fight against alcohol is the role Jews played in the discourse on alcoholism. As in the fight against *Schund- und Schmutzschriften*, Jews played a marginal role in the fight against alcoholism. Even in the discussions of the so-called *Alkoholkapital*, Jews did not evoke special attention and were not treated separately. This can also be seen in visual representations of the so-called "alcohol capitalist," which are not necessarily recognizable as Jews. The only known exception in which Jews constituted a theme in the fight against alcoholism was the attempt within the Order of Good Templars in Austria to exclude Jews, as well as other "non-Aryan" elements, from the organization. The dispute between opponents and supporters of the "Aryan paragraph" hindered the work of the Order and almost led to its disintegration. At the end Stephan Schöck, the leader of the antisemitic fraction, was forced to leave the Order of Good Templars to found a new anti-alcoholism organization based on the principles of *völkisch* ideology in 1920.[23]

Yet this incident remains at the margins of the German anti-alcohol movement, which did not seem to reveal any special antisemitic tendencies, even though the concepts of race and class were central within this discourse. In fact, more frequently we encounter positive references to Jews, who were considered by some non-Jews and especially by Jews as a kind of a role model as a "sober race." This attitude offered an opportunity to promote a positive image of Jews in German society. Simon Katzenstein, for instance, a member of the German Social Democratic Party and one of the central figures in the party's campaign against alcoholism, warned in his widely circulated booklet *Wofür kämpfen wir?* (What are we fighting for?) of the damages caused by alcoholism to the working-class movement in Germany.[24] He claimed that the alcohol industry's promotion of workers' consumption of alcohol by all available means was to blame for alcoholism among the working classes. "It is not true," he declared, "that alcoholism is caused only by adversity. Wide strata of workers who experience deep hardship and scarcity, such as women workers who are working as domestics, workers in the confection and textile industry, or Jewish workers in Russia are much less affected by alcoholism than other social groups."[25] Katzenstein did not explain, unfortunately, why these specific groups were particularly immune to alcohol abuse.

In his famous study of alcoholism, Abraham Baer conveys a similar attitude toward the drinking habits of Jews. He lists a series of studies which displayed their special sobriety. He even presents the Jews as a kind of "universal representative of sobriety" who, although scattered in different climates and areas where all types of alcohol are available, continue their sober way of life. According to Baer, the reasons for this state of affairs lie in Jewish religious practices, such as the celebration of Shabbat as a day of rest, as well as in the particular social and cultural disposition of Jews, i.e., in their inclination to avoid exhausting physical professions and to cultivate strong family ties. The low rate of alcohol consumption among Jews explains, according to Baer, why Jews tend to live longer than non-Jews and why criminality and suicide rates among Jews are much lower than among their drinking neighbors.[26]

Some even considered drinking habits as a kind of criterion, or even a racial quality, that distinguished Jews from other people, especially those from northern and eastern Europe. The Zionist sociologist Arthur Ruppin, for example, observed that, while Christians prefer stimuli (*Reitzmittel*) like alcohol which degrade alertness, Jews prefer those which increase awareness. "The Christian," he concluded, "seems to like the gloom (*Dämmerung*), while the Jew [prefers] the brightness (*Helle*)."[27] It is no wonder that in light of such views alcohol consumption came to be regarded as one of the signs of assimilation and was even conceived as a threat to the endurance of the Jewish race.[28] Nonetheless, such discussions took place at the margins of the general discourse on alcoholism. Jews on the whole did not constitute a theme in this discourse. They were not considered as part of the alcohol-consuming public and thus did not pose a threat to the social order.

V

In contrast to the examples we examined thus far, where no special attention was paid to Jews although one could have expected it, other areas of social discourse reveal a different pattern. Here Jews played a central topical role, even if at first sight they did not have any special connections with the subject matter of these discourses. An example is the discussion of animal protection in Germany.[29]

The idea that animals should be protected is a product of the nineteenth century.[30] It reflects a change in the approach to nature that accrued with the advance of modernization. During this period many people moved from the countryside to the cities, leaving behind a centuries-old mode of living and working together with animals. The demand for nature, for living together with animals, was met in the cities in a rudimentary form through house pets. Domestic animals began to symbolize the lost connection to life in the countryside and even to nature as such. Yet whereas in the countryside the human-animal relationship was predominantly functional, in the industrial and technological world it was based on sentiment and emotion. Eating an animal resident of the modern cities became taboo; domestic animals were given names, and sometimes even received respectable burials. In short, animals were humanized. These developments constituted a central prerequisite for the growing feeling of sympathy toward animals and evoked a concept of animal rights and an urge to protect such creatures. Not surprisingly, animal rights activists applied mainly ethical and moral arguments in their campaign to protect animals.[31] They stated, for instance, that cruelty toward animals encourages human violence and even homicide. An upbringing that fostered love of animals (*Tierliebe*) was thus conceived as a prerequisite for a peaceful life among humans.[32]

Apparently these pacifistic ideals, which supposedly endorsed tolerance among all people, were not always realized in the work of the animal protection societies. From the mid-nineteenth century these societies gained public attention mainly through their vigorous struggle against the exploitation of animals for medical experiments and industrial use.[33] An enthusiastic supporter of the anti-vivisection movement was the composer Richard Wagner. In an open letter written in 1879 to Ernst von Weber, the founder of the Dresden animal protection society, Wagner declared his support, suggesting measures like breaking into laboratories where experiments on animals were conducted, as well as physical attacks on vivisectionists.[34] In Wagner's outrage against the use of animals in experiments he not only condemned vivisectionists as enemies, but explicitly identified them with Jews. The fact that Jews were indeed among this group of specialists who conducted experiments on animals undoubtedly helped to establish this identification. However, it was mainly the slaughter of animals by kosher butchers that reinforced the targeting of Jews as enemies of animals.

Jewish ritual slaughter, known as *shehitah*, was perceived as inhuman, cruel, and torturous. Already at their first conference, in Gotha in 1879, animal protection societies in Germany had decided that *shehitah* had to be stopped by legislative means. The charge that *shehitah* was cruel was based on the observation by opponents of Jewish animal slaughter that following the cutting of the throat, there is a torrential discharge of blood, and the animal gives several convulsive shudders. Animal protectionists saw this method of slaughter not only as cruel to the animal, but also as dangerous to the butcher. They dismissed all references to the ritual significance of this method of slaughter as "ridiculous and superstitious" and insisted that it should be forbidden.[35]

Switzerland was the first European country to adopt an anti-*shehitah* law, doing so as early as the mid-nineteenth century.[36] Inspired by this success and despite numerous reports written by specialists that maintained that Jewish animal slaughter was no more inhuman or cruel than other methods of slaughter, animal welfarists in Germany launched an energetic propaganda campaign, with strong antisemitic leanings, against *shehitah*, portraying the Jews as enemies of both animals and Germans alike.[37] Jews responded immediately to these attacks and sought to prevent anti-*shehitah* legislation in Germany. Their arguments accentuated the importance of animal rights in Judaism and displayed Jewish ritual slaughter in a positive light; Jews also lobbied German politicians. Ironically, as John Efron noted, all camps of German Jewry defended *shehitah*, though only a minority of them kept kosher.[38] According to Efron, this "united front" was a result of mounting antisemitism during the period. Indeed, it seems that the anti-*shehitah* campaign was not merely a movement to improve animal slaughter, but was part of a larger antisemitic movement that had accelerated in late nineteenth-century Germany.[39]

Paul Förster, one of the leading figures of the anti-*shehitah* campaign in Germany, exemplifies this connection. Förster was a devoted animal welfarist who edited the journal of the Dresden Animal Protection Society, *Thier- und Menschenfreund* (Friend to animals and humans). He was also a well-known antisemite and one of the founders of the antisemitic *Deutsch-Soziale Partei* (which became the *Deutsch-Soziale Reformpartei* in 1894), which he also represented in the Reichstag.[40] Although all attempts to pass anti-*shehitah* legislation in the Reichstag failed, Förster and his party successfully introduced the so-called *Schächtfrage* ("slaughter question") into the political agenda of their time. An anti-*shehitah* law in Germany came into force only after the National Socialist Party assumed power. The Nazis were indeed committed to animal rights. In August 1933, after passing the anti-*shehitah* legislation, Hermann Göring threatened to "commit to concentration camps those who still think they can continue to treat animals as inanimate property."[41]

The question arises: Why did antisemitism play such a central role within the framework of animal protection, whereas in the other examples we examined antisemitism was marginal? I would argue that a key reason for this difference is the special nature of the discourse of animal protection as what I called "producer discourse." As well as being concerned with animal rights, Paul Förster was also an adherent of naturopathy and a devoted vegetarian. Both enthusiasms were part of the *Lebensreformbewegung*, a movement dedicated to reforming bourgeois life in Germany.[42] Förster was no exception here, but was a bona fide representative of those who regarded themselves as *Freidenker* (free thinkers) and *Fortschrittskämpfer* (fighters for progress). His involvement in attempts to reform bourgeois life and his antisemitism thus embody no contradiction. On the contrary, antisemitism was widespread among different sections of this so-called reform movement. Indeed, the discourses of the *Lebensreformbewegungen* seem to fit well with Volkov's suggestion of an affinity between elements such as preindustrial romanticism, anti-modernism, anti-capitalism, and nationalism, all of which she sees as indicators of belonging to the antisemitic camp. Nevertheless, as I have argued throughout this paper, what made the *Lebensreformbewegungen*'s discourse antisemitic was not only the combination of these elements, but its nature as a "producer discourse." The societies for animal protection support this claim. In contrast to the cases we discussed thus far, animal protectionists were mainly concerned with the bourgeois classes and particularly with the need to reform their way of life as a result of the rapid advance of modernity. They were much less occupied with the "wide masses" and the threats that they posed to bourgeois society.

VI

An even more obvious example that confirms this pattern can be found in the fight against department stores. The department store was a new and highly innovative form of retail organization which developed rapidly during the last third of the nineteenth century to occupy a pivotal position within the German distribution system.[43] The significance of the department store was related not only to its revolutionary selling methods, but also to its active role as an agent in extending a modern consumer culture in which individuals and groups could find social definition through the act of buying. The key to the department store was display and mass. By laying out consumer items in profusion, in arrays deliberately designed to lure shoppers' eyes and stimulate their imagination, the department stores created what historian Rosalind Williams calls a "dream world" of material luxury.[44] The department store was thus not merely a huge sales hall for an array of goods, but a place that changed the act of buying to a "perceptual adventure," thereby turning consumption from an activity with a purpose to a purpose in and for itself.[45]

Given the rapid development of department stores toward the end of the nineteenth century, it is no wonder that the "cathedrals of consumption," as contemporaries already referred to them, were at the center of public debate. Social critics of the time condemned department stores as avatars of materialism, accusing them of promoting moral turpitude. Thus the department stores were held responsible for encouraging criminal behavior, particularly among women from well-off strata. It was argued that the department store operated as a retail version of a factory, displaying goods in a seductive way and hence taking advantage of—or indeed abusing—what was regarded as the easily influenced female psyche.[46]

Leading the attacks against the department stores were small shopkeepers, the group doubtless most affected by the emergence of this new form of business enterprise.[47] Many shopkeepers feared that the department stores would undermine their trade and established special organizations to fight them. At first just the institutionalized expression of shopkeepers' collective attempts to protect their economic position, these organizations were rapidly politicized, becoming an integral part of what contemporaries referred to as the *Mittelstandsbewegung* (the political movement of the petite bourgeoisie). As a political movement the shopkeepers were a strong pressure group, expecting a policy of "social protectionism" from the authorities. Indeed, their application to the state to protect their interests and to prohibit what they considered unfair competition was not ineffective. In the period before the First World War, they successfully enforced legislation that made department stores pay special taxes.[48] These limited successes, notes the historian Robert Gellately, "operated as a kind of safety-valve which helped to reduce or neutralize inner social tension of the Wilhelmian society."[49]

Their hostility toward the department stores revealed the difficulty shopkeepers and the *Mittelstand* in general had in grasping—let alone mastering—the upheavals and challenges of modernity. Fears for their economic well-being merged with anti-modernization, anti-socialism, and antisemitic sentiments, making up what historian Philip Nord calls "the politics of resentment."[50] Jews played a key role in this context. They became the major target of the attacks on department stores, so that antisemitism became a kind of integrative ideology of the *Mittelstandsbewegung*, culminating in a view that associated the "social problem" with the "Jewish problem." The slogan *Die sociale Frage ist wesentlich die Judenfrage* ("the social problem is essentially the Jewish problem") rapidly became popular among the lower middle classes, indicating the emergence of a new kind of antisemitism.[51] The fact that the owners of many department stores were indeed Jewish eased and even promoted the acceptance of this bigotry. Jews were viewed as *Grosskapitalisten* (big capitalists) who lived in a grand fashion at the expense of the nation as a whole.

This resentment of Jews as large-scale capitalists calls to mind Georg Simmel's analysis of the stranger.[52] In Simmel's terminology, the stranger is not the wanderer who comes today and leaves tomorrow, having no specific structural position within a group. On the contrary, he is an element of the group itself, although not fully part of it. According to this view, the stranger belongs to what Simmel classifies as the "inner enemy." Nevertheless, being a stranger is for Simmel a positive thing, as "it is a specific form of interaction." Moreover, in Simmel's view, not being "bound by commitments which could prejudice his perception, understanding, and evaluation of the given" make the stranger an ideal intermediary in the traffic of goods as well as in the traffic of ideas. According to Simmel, the prototype of the stranger is the merchant and the classical example is the Jews.[53] By treating the stranger as a sociological phenomenon, Simmel provides an analysis that goes beyond the old binary oppositions of colonizers and colonized, of oppressors and oppressed. In this respect he reveals the ambivalent ontological status of the Jew, at once included in and excluded from society. However, the extent to which Simmel's theory, which ascribes to the stranger a positive and even privileged position, can be applied to the post–First World War period is doubtful. With the foundation of the Weimar Republic, the national assembly abolished all laws against department stores, which, despite economic instability, entered into a period of growth and expansion. This success did not improve the public's opinion of them,[54] and hyperinflation and mass unemployment further intensified popular resentment of department stores. Attacks on them, like assaults on Jews in general, grew in number and intensity.[55] Contemporaries even described the reaction of the *Mittelstand* in this period as panic.[56] The Nazis were quick to utilize this situation. All kinds of Nazi organizations were mobilized for this cause, turning the field of consumption into a combat zone where (Jewish) department stores were battled. Thus, for example, the leader of the National Socialist Women's Organization declared to a mass meeting in Munich held in May 1929, "When a Jewish palace, one department store after the other, can be built, we women must bear the responsibility. It is through the hands of the woman that the earnings of the man flow back into the economy, and only she possesses the weapon against the Jew."[57]

The boycotts of department stores at the end of the 1920s do not seem to have achieved their objectives. The lower middle class did not appear eager to renounce the pleasures of going to department stores and they continued to visit them.[58] Nevertheless the calls to boycott department stores, within the struggle against the department stores as a whole, are a further indication of the centrality of the "Jew" in what I initially defined as a "producer discourse." That is, in an age in which bourgeois culture developed into something purchasable, as Michael Miller noted in his work on the Bon Marché, the department stores, as the principal medium of consumption, became the arbiter of bourgeois identity.[59] In this sense the fight against the department stores was also a struggle for bourgeois identity, and it revealed the schisms and frictions within these classes.

VII

As we have seen, the role and significance of antisemitism as a cultural code was not unequivocal. Jews were neither included nor excluded all of the time. In significant discourses they did not figure at all. This discovery comes as something of a surprise, indicating a discrepancy between the actual situation of Jews within German society and our assumptions about how they were treated and perceived. Indeed, one can trace areas of social discourse that did not display any special antisemitic leanings, despite the fact that they contained elements—such as preindustrial romanticism, anti-modernism, anti-capitalism, and nationalism—commonly associated with hostility toward Jews. In this sense the absence of the "Jew" from specific discourses is as striking as his presence in others. Analyzing the situational character of antisemitism thus challenges that prevailing historiographical approach that conceptualizes antisemitism mainly within the broad framework of so-called "reactionary modernism."

Why then do "Jews" figure in some discourses and not others? This essay has tentatively suggested that the answer to this question lies in different modes of discourse, referred to here as "consumer discourse" and "producer discourse." Examination of these discourses showed that while in "consumer discourse" (the struggle against pulp writings and alcohol, and the "book crisis") antisemitism played a subordinated role, in "producer discourse" (the fight for animal rights, and the struggle against department stores) antisemitism was far more central. This model of explanation recognizes not only the situational character of antisemitism but also the fact that very different forms of it can coexist simultaneously. It reveals the complexity of social reality and the difficulty, especially for contemporaries, of interpreting it. Jews found themselves in a social situation in which antisemitism, at least in the period before the Nazis assumed power, played an equivocal role. In a sense, this claim seems to reinforce Hannah Arendt's observation that German society did not force individual Jews to assume a specific "Jewish identity," but posited them in a kind of a twilight zone, rendering them with "an empty sense of being different."[60]

Historians of German-Jewish relations have often oversimplified the picture, ignoring ambiguities that call into question conventional notions about the place of Jews in German history.[61] Given what happened in Germany after

1933, it is understandable that historians have tended to concentrate more on what could be called the "producer" narrative, but they have thus neglected the "consumer" perspective of this history. An attempt to generate a "consumer" narrative of Jewish German history could deepen our understanding of the multifaceted interrelationships between Jews and other Germans and move research beyond rather sterile binary divisions that tend to oscillate between approaches stressing inclusion and those which highlight exclusion. At this stage, however, this statement should be seen as a tentative conclusion only, requiring a more extensive investigation which goes beyond the limits of the current essay.

Notes

1. Shulamit Volkov, "Anti-Semitism as a Cultural Code: Reflection on the History and Historiography of Anti-Semitism in Imperial Germany," *Leo Baeck Institute Year Book* 23 (1978): 25–46.

2. Jeffrey Herf, *Reactionary Modernism: Technology, Culture, and Politics in Weimar and the Third Reich* (Cambridge: Cambridge University Press, 1984).

3. "Organisationen, Vereine etc. zur Bekämpfung der Schund- und Schmutz-schriften," in Geheimes Staatsarchiv Preußischer Kulturbesitz, Berlin, Rep 77, Tit 2772 Nr. 12.

4. Wolfgang Kaschuba and Kaspar Maase, eds., *Schund und Schönheit: Populäre Kultur um 1900* (Cologne: Böhlau Verlag, 2001); and Mirjam Storim, *Ästhetik im Umbruch: Zur Funktion der "Rede über Kunst" um 1900 am Beispiel der Debatte um Schmutz und Schund* (Tübingen: Max Niemeyer Verlag, 2002).

5. Georg Jäger, "Der Kampf gegen Schmutz und Schund: Die Reaktion der Gebildeten auf die Unterhaltungsindustrie," *Archiv für Geschichte des Buchwesens* 31 (1988): 163–91; Detlev Peukert, "Der Schund- und Schmutzkampf als 'Sozialpolitik der Seele': Eine Vorgeschichte der Bücherverbrennung?" in *"Das war ein Vorspiel nur . . . ": Bücherverbrennung Deutschland 1933; Voraussetzungen und Folgen* (Berlin: Akademie Verlag der Künste, 1983); and Gideon Reuveni, "Der Aufstieg der Bürgerlichkeit und die bürgerliche Selbstauflösung: Die Bekämpfung der Schund- und Schmutzliteratur in Deutschland bis 1933 als Fallbeispiel," *Zeitschrift für Geschichtswissenschaft* 51 (2003): 131–44.

6. On these images of the Jew see, for example, Sander L. Gilman, *Smart Jews: The Construction of the Image of Jewish Superior Intelligence* (Lincoln: University of Nebraska Press, 1996); Michael Schmidt and Stefan Rohrbacher, *Judenbilder: Kulturgeschichte antijüdischer Mythen und antisemitischer Vorurteile* (Reinbek: Rowohlt, 1991); and Julius H. Schoeps and Joachim Schlör, eds., *Bilder der Judenfeindschaft* (Augsburg: Bechtermünz Verlag, 1999).

7. On this magazine and its publisher Karl Brunner, who became famous after the War as the Weimar Republic film censor, see Samuleit Paul, "Aus der Geschichte des Kampfes gegen den Schund," in Samuleit Paul and Brunckhorst Hans, *Geschichte und Wege der Schundbekämpfung* (Berlin: Carl Heymanns Verlag, 1922), 3–22.

8. Rudolf Schenda, *Die Lesestoffe der Kleinen Leute* (Munich: C. H. Beck, 1976), 172; and Gabriele von Glasenapp and Michael Nagel, *Das jüdische Jugendbuch: Von der Aufklärung bis zum Dritten Reich* (Stuttgart: Verlag Metzler, 1996), 103.

9. Margaret F. Stieg, "The 1926 German Law to Protect Youth against Trash and Filth: Moral Protectionism in a Democracy," *Central European History* 23 (1990): 22–56.

10. Archiv der Deutschen Bücherei Leipzig, 351/4/1, Protokolle der Oberprüfstelle für Schund- und Schmutzliteratur 1929, 13. See also Hans Wingender, *Erfahrungen im Kampf gegen Schund- und Schmutzschriften* (Düsseldorf: Published by the author, 1929), 50–54.

11. On the "social question" and antisemitism, see Moshe Zimmermann, "Die 'Judenfrage' als 'die soziale Frage': Zu Kontinuität und Stellenwert des Antisemitismus vor und nach dem Nationalsozialismus," in *Faschismus und Faschismen im Vergleich*, ed. Christoph Dipper, Rainer Hudemann, and Jens Petersen (Cologne: HS-Verlag, 1998), 149–63.

12. For more on this notion see, for example, Martin Jay, "In the Empire of the Gaze: Foucault and the Denigration of Vision in Twentieth-Century French Thought," in *Foucault: A Critical Reader,* ed. David Counzens Hoy (New York: Basil Blackwell, 1986), 175–204.

13. Werner Sombart, *Die Juden und das Wirtschaftsleben* (Leipzig: Duncker und Humblot, 1911). On the issue of disciplining consumption in Germany, see Warren G. Breckman, "Disciplining Consumption: The Debate about Luxury in Wilhelmine Germany, 1890–1914," *Journal of Social History* 24, no. 3 (1990–91): 485–505; and Hartmut Berghoff, ed., *Konsumpolitik: Die Regulierung des privaten Verbrauchs im 20. Jahrhundert* (Göttingen: Vandenhoeck und Ruprecht, 1999). On Sombart and the Jews: Alfred Philipp, *Die Juden und das Wirtschaftsleben: Eine antikritisch bibliographische Studie zu Werner Sombart, "Die Juden und das Wirtschaftsleben"* (Strasburg: Heitz, 1929); Arthur Mitzman, *Sociology and Estrangement: Three Sociologists of Imperial Germany* (New Brunswick, N.J.: Transaction, 1987); Toni Oelson, "The Place of the Jews in Economic History as Viewed by German Scholars," *Leo Baeck Institute Year Book* 7 (1962): 183–212; David S. Landes, "The Jewish Merchant: Typology and Stereotypology in Germany," *Leo Baeck Institute Year Book* 19 (1974): 11–30; Paul R. Mendes-Flohr, "Werner Sombart's 'The Jews and Modern Capitalism': An Analysis of Its Ideological Premises," *Leo Baeck Institute Year Book* 21 (1976): 87–107; Avraham Barkai, "Judentum, Juden und Kapitalismus: Ökonomische Vorstellungen von Max Weber und Werner Sombart," *Menora* 5 (1994): 25–38; and Jehuda Reinhartz, *Fatherland or Promised Land: The Dilemma of the German Jew, 1893–1914* (Ann Arbor: University of Michigan Press, 1975), 190–95.

14. Werner Sombart, *Liebe, Luxus und Kapitalismus: Über die Entstehung der modernen Welt aus dem Geist der Verschwendung* (Berlin: Wagenbach, 1983), first published 1913.

15. Gideon Reuveni, "The 'Crisis of the Book' and German Society after the First World War," *German History* 20, no. 4 (2002): 438–61.

16. Hans Thomas, "Das Chaos der Bücher," *Die Tat* 23 (1931): 647.

17. Max Wieser, "Die geistige Krisis des Buches und die Volksbibliotheken," *Preußische Jahrbücher* 191 (1923): 184. For similar views, see Johannes Molzahn,

"Nicht mehr Lesen! Sehen!" *Das Kunstblatt* 12 (1928): 78–82; Hans Siemsen, "Bücherbesprechung," *Die Weltbühne* 21 (1923): 857–59; and Siegfried Kracauer, "Die Photographie," in *Der verbotene Blick* (Leipzig: Reclam, 1992), 185–203.

18. Samuel Fischer, "Bemerkungen zur Bücherkrise," in *S. Fischer Verlag: Von der Gründung bis zur Rückkehr aus dem Exil*, ed. Friedrich Pfäffin and Ingrid Kussmaul (Marbach: Ausstellungskatalog, 1985), 357.

19. For late formulations of the thesis of the collapse of the bourgeoisie, which is really a form of the theory of Germany's "special path" in history, see, particularly, Hans Mommsen, "Die Auflösung des Bürgertums seit dem späten 19. Jahrhundert," in *Bürger und Bürgerlichkeit im 19. Jahrhundert*, ed. Jürgen Kocka (Göttingen: Vandenhoeck und Ruprecht, 1987), 288–315; Konrad H. Jarauch, "Die Krise des deutschen Bildungsbürgertums im ersten Drittel des 20. Jahrhunderts," in *Bildungsbürgertum im 19. Jahrhundert: Politischer Einfluß und gesellschaftliche Formation*, ed. Jürgen Kocka (Stuttgart: Klett Cotta, 1989), 180–206; and Horst Möller, "Bürgertum und bürgerlich-liberale Bewegung nach 1918," in *Bürgertum und bürgerlich-liberale Bewegung in Mitteleuropa seit dem 18. Jahrhundert*, ed. Lothar Gall (Munich: Oldenbourg, 1997), 243–342.

20. On these studies, see Alfred Hegge, *Alkohol und bürgerliche Gesellschaft im 19. Jahrhundert* (Berlin: Colloquium Verlag, 1988); and Hasso Spode, *Die Macht der Trunkenheit: Kultur- und Sozialgeschichte des Alkohols in Deutschland* (Opland: Leske und Budrich, 1993).

21. "Wohl am meistens ist der Arzt in der Lage, den Alkoholismus in der physischen Degeneration der Bevölkerung zu beobachten; und wie in den Irrenanstalten die Verwüstungen des geistigen Lebens, so zeigen sich ihm in den Arbeits-, Gefangen- und Zuchthäuser in gleich erschreckender Weise die Zerstörungen, welche die Unmässigkeit mittelbar und unmittelbar dem sittlichen Leben der menschlichen Gesellschaft zufügt." Abraham Baer, *Der Alkoholismus: Seine Verbreitung und seine Wirkung auf den individuellen und sozialen Organismus sowie die Mittel, ihn zu bekämpfen* (Berlin: Hirschwald, 1878), iii.

22. On Baer, see Salomon Wininger, *Große jüdische National-Bibliographie* (Cernăuti: Buch und Druckerei Orient, 1925).

23. Johan Bergman, *Geschichte der Nüchternheitsbestrebungen* (Hamburg: Neulandverlag, 1925), 468.

24. After World War I Katzenstein became a member of the Weimar national assembly for the SPD. See Joseph Walk, *Kurzbiographien zur Geschichte der Juden, 1918–1933* (Munich: K. G. Saur, 1988), 188.

25. Simon Katzenstein, *Wofür kämpfen wir?* (Berlin: Deutscher Arbeiter-Abstinenten-Bund, 1909), 6.

26. See John M. Efron, *Medicine and the German Jews: A History* (New Haven, Conn.: Yale University Press, 2001), 108–17.

27. Arthur Ruppin, *Soziologie der Juden*, vol. 2 (Berlin: Jüdische Verlag, 1931), 100.

28. For this kind of approach see, for example, the article "Abstinenz," written by the physician Aron Sandler in *Jüdisches Lexikon*, ed. Ismar Elbogen et al. (Berlin: Jüdischer Verlag, 1927), vol. 1, 55.

29. I would like to thank John Efron for drawing my attention to this case.

30. Miriam Zerbel, *Tierschutz im Kaiserreich: Eine Beitrag zur Geschichte des*

Vereinswesens (Frankfurt am Main: Peter Lang, 1993); and Ute Hahn, "Die Entwicklung des Tierschutzgedankens in Religion und Geistesgeschichte" (Ph.D. diss., Tierärztliche Hochschule Hannover, 1980).

31. Orvar Löfgren, "Natur, Tier und Moral: Zur Entwicklung der bürgerlichen Naturauffassung," in *Volkskultur in der Moderne: Probleme und Perspektiven empirischer Kulturforschung,* ed. Utz Jeggle et al. (Reinbeck: Rowohlt, 1986), 122–44.

32. For an example of these arguments, see the programmatic writings of Eduard Bilz, *Der Zukunftsstaat: Staatseinrichtung im Jahr 2000* (Leipzig: Bilz Verlag, 1904); and Ludwig Ankenbrand, *Tierschutz und moderne Weltanschauung* (Bamberg: Verlag und Druck der Handelsdruckerei, 1906).

33. Hermann Stenz, ed., *Die Vivisektion in ihrer wahren Gestalt: Unwiderlegliche Thatsachen aus der Fachlitteratur* (Berlin: Weltbund zur Bekämpfung d. Vivisektion, 1899); Hubert Brentschneider, *Der Streit um die Vivisektion im 19. Jahrhundert: Verlauf, Argumente und Ergebnisse* (Stuttgart: G. Fischer, 1962); and Nicolaas Rupke, ed., *Vivisection in Historical Perspective* (London: Croom Helm, 1987).

34. Richard Wagner, "Offenes Schreiben an Ernst von Weber," *Gesammelte Schriften und Dichtungen* (Leipzig: G. W. Fritsch, 1888), 195–210.

35. Quoted in Miriam Zerbel, "Tierschutz und Antivivisektion," in *Handbuch der deutschen Reformbewegungen, 1880–1933,* ed. Diethart Krebs and Jürgen Reulecke (Berlin: Peter Hammer Verlag, 1998), 41.

36. Pascal Krauthammer, "Das Schächtverbot in der Schweiz, 1854–2000: Die Schächtfrage zwischen Tierschutz, Politik und Fremdenfeindlichkeit" (Ph.D. diss., University of Zurich, 2000).

37. On this, see especially Dorothee Brantz, "Stunning Bodies: Animal Slaughter, Judaism, and the Meaning of Humanity in Imperial Germany," *Central European History* 35, no. 2 (2002): 167–94; and Robin Judd, "The Politics of Beef: Animal Advocacy and the Kosher Butchering Debates in Germany," *Jewish Social Studies* 10 (2003): 117–50.

38. Efron, *Medicine and the German Jews,* 206–22.

39. Ibid. On this see also Reinhard Rürup, *Emanzipation und Antisemitismus: Studien zur "Judenfrage" der bürgerlichen Gesellschaft* (Göttingen: Vandenhoeck und Ruprecht, 1975).

40. On this party, see Dieter Fricke, "Deutsch-Soziale Reformpartei," in *Lexikon zur Parteiengeschichte: Die bürgerlichen und kleinbürgerlichen Parteien und Verbände in Deutschland, 1789–1945,* ed. Dieter Fricke et al., vol. 2 (Cologne: Pahl Rugenstein Verlag, 1984), 540–49; and Stephan Ph. Wolf, *Für Deutschtum, Thron und Altar: Die Deutsch-Soziale Reformpartei in Baden (1890–1907)* (Karlsruhe: Heinz Wolf Fachverlag, 1995).

41. Quoted in Arnold Arluke and Boria Sax, "The Nazi Treatment of Animals and People," in *Reinventing Biology: Respect for Life and the Creation of Knowledge,* ed. Lynda Birke and Ruth Hubbard (Bloomington: Indiana University Press, 1995), 244; also useful in this context is the website of the anti-vivisection group "The Absurdity of Vivisection," at http://vivisection-absurd.org.uk, especially "Myths of the Pro-vivisectionist," http://vivisection-absurd.org.uk/myths.html.

42. On this movement, see Klaus Bergmann, *Agrarromantik und Großstadtfeindschaft* (Meisenheim am Glan: Hain, 1970); and Wolfgang R. Krabbe, *Gesellschaftsveränderung durch Lebensreform: Strukturmerkmale einer sozialreformerischen Bewegung*

in Deutschland der Industrialisierungsperiode (Göttingen: Vandenhoeck und Ruprecht, 1974).

43. The history of the department store in Germany has been an object of research for some time. For an overview, see Tim Coles, "Department Stores as Retail Innovation in Germany: A Historical-Geographical Perspective on the Period 1870–1914," in *Cathedrals of Consumption: The European Department Store, 1850–1939*, ed. Geoffrey Crossick and Serge Jaumain (Aldershot: Ashgate, 1999), 72–96; Klaus Strohmer, *Warenhäuser: Geschichte, Blüte und Untergang im Warenmeer* (Berlin: Klaus Wagenbach Verlag, 1980); and Siegfried Gerlach, *Das Warenhaus in Deutschland: Seine Entwicklung bis zum 1. Weltkrieg in historisch-geographischer Sicht* (Stuttgart: Steiner Verlag, 1988).

44. Rosalind H. Williams, *Dream Worlds: Mass Consumption in Late Nineteenth-Century France* (Berkeley: University of California Press, 1982); see also Anne Friedberg, *Window Shopping: Cinema and the Postmodern* (Berkeley: University of California Press, 2000); and Rachel Bowlby, *Just Looking: Consumer Culture in Dreiser, Gissing, and Zola* (New York: Methuen, 1985).

45. The term "perceptual adventure" was coined by Elizabeth Ewen and Stuart Ewen, *Channels of Desire: Mass Images and the Shaping of American Consciousness*, 2nd ed. (New York: McGraw-Hill, 1992), 45. On the special contribution of the department stores to the emergence of consumer culture, see also Susan Porter Benson, *Counter Cultures: Saleswoman, Managers, and Costumers in American Department Stores, 1890–1940* (Urbana: University of Illinois Press, 1986), especially chapter 3; and Rudi Learmans, "Learning to Consume: Early Department Stores and the Shaping of the Modern Consumer Culture (1860–1914)," *Theory, Culture, and Society* 10, no. 4 (1993): 79–102.

46. On the phenomenon of shoplifting, see Elaine S. Abelson, *When Ladies Go A-Thieving: Middle-Class Shoplifters in Victorian Department Stores* (New York: Oxford University Press, 1989); Patricia O'Brien, "The Kleptomania Diagnosis: Bourgeois Women and Theft in Late Nineteenth-Century France," *Journal of Social History* 17, no. 1 (1983): 65–77; and Uwe Spiekermann, "Theft and Thieves in German Department Stores, 1895–1930: A Discourse on Morality, Crime, and Gender," in Crossick and Jaumain, *Cathedrals of Consumption*, 135–60.

47. Robert Gellately, "An der Schwelle der Moderne: Warenhäuser und ihre Feinde in Deutschland," in *Im Banne der Metropolen: Berlin und London in den zwanziger Jahren*, ed. Peter Alter (Göttingen: Vandenhoeck und Ruprecht, 1993), 131–56.

48. Uwe Spiekermann, *Warenhaussteuer in Deutschland: Mittelstandsbewegung, Kapitalismus und Rechtsstaat im späten Kaiserreich* (Frankfurt am Main: Peter Lang, 1994).

49. Robert Gellately, *The Politics of Economic Despair: Shopkeepers and German Politics, 1890–1914* (London: Sega, 1974), 214.

50. Philip G. Nord, *Paris Shopkeepers and the Politics of Resentment* (Princeton, N.J.: Princeton University Press, 1986); see also Heinrich August Winkler, *Zwischen Marx und Monopol: Der deutsche Mittelstand vom Kaiserreich zur Bundesrepublik Deutschland* (Frankfurt am Main: Fischer, 1991).

51. On modern antisemitism see, for example, Rürup, *Emanzipation und Antisemitismus;* Jacob Katz, *From Prejudice to Destruction: Anti-Semitism, 1700–1933* (Cambridge, Mass.: Harvard University Press, 1980); Moshe Zimmermann, *Wilhelm Marr:*

184

The Patriarch of Antisemitism (New York: Oxford University Press, 1986); and Shulamit Volkov, "Zur sozialen und politischen Funktion des Antisemitismus: Handwerker im späten 19. Jahrhundert," in *Antisemitismus als kultureller Code: Zehn Essays* (Munich: C. H. Beck, 2000), 37–53.

52. All quotations are from Georg Simmel, *The Sociology of Georg Simmel*, trans. Kurt Wolff (New York: Free Press, 1950), 402–408.

53. On Simmel's attitude toward the Jews, see Amos Morris-Reich, "The Beautiful Jew Is a Moneylender: Money and Individuality in Simmel's Rehabilitation of the 'Jew,'" *Theory, Culture, and Society* 20, no. 4 (2004): 127–42.

54. Werner Rubens, "Der Kampf des Spezialgeschäftes gegen das Warenhaus (mit besonderer Berücksichtigung der Zeit von 1918 bis 1929)" (Ph.D. diss., University of Cologne, 1929).

55. On violence against Jewish department stores in this period, see Simone Ladwig-Winters, *Wertheim: Ein Warenhausunternehmen und seine Eigentümer; Ein Beispiel der Entwicklung der Berliner Warenhäuser bis zur "Arisierung"* (Münster: LIT, 1996). On antisemitism as a whole during the Weimar period, see Anthony Kauders, *German Politics and the Jews: Düsseldorf and Nuremberg, 1910–1933* (Oxford: Clarendon, 1996); Dirk Walter, *Antisemitische Kriminalität und Gewalt: Judenfeindschaft in der Weimarer Republik* (Bonn: Dietz, 1999); and Cornelia Hecht, *Deutsche Juden und Antisemitismus in der Weimarer Republik* (Bonn: Dietz, 2003).

56. Theodor Geiger, "Die Panik im Mittelstand," *Die Arbeit* 7 (1930): 637–54; and Winkler, *Zwischen Marx und Monopol*, 38–51.

57. Quoted in Heinrich Uhlig, *Die Warenhäuser im Dritten Reich* (Cologne: Westdeutscher Verlag, 1956), 36.

58. On this see Uhlig, *Die Warenhäuser*, as well as Robert Gellately, "German Shopkeepers and the Rise of National Socialism," *Wiener Library Bulletin* 28 (1975): 31–40.

59. Michael B. Miller, *The Bon Marché: Bourgeois Culture and the Department Store, 1869–1920* (Princeton, N.J.: Princeton University Press, 1981), 185.

60. Hannah Arendt, "Privileged Jews," *Jewish Social Studies* 8 (1946): 30.

61. On this, see also Moshe Zimmermann, "Jewish History and Jewish Historiography: A Challenge to Contemporary German Historiography," *Leo Baeck Institute Year Book* 35 (1990): 35–52; and Samuel Moyn, "German Jewry and the Question of Identity: Historiography and Theory," *Leo Baeck Institute Year Book* 41 (1996): 291–308.

Nine

How "Jewish" is German Sexuality?

Sex and Antisemitism in the Third Reich

Dagmar Herzog

I

Most scholars presume that the Third Reich was characterized by generalized sexual repression. Throughout the 1980s and 1990s and into the twenty-first century, the Third Reich has routinely been described, in an assertive sort of shorthand, as "sex-hostile," "unhappy, lifeless, pleasureless," distinguished by "strict physiological-sexual norms of behavior" or "official German prudery."[1] The "National Socialists' fear of sexuality" is taken to be self-evident; "sexual abstinence until an early marriage was the highest command"; under Nazism, "sexuality and its representation were . . . thoroughly tabooed"; "whatever progressivism Weimar had imagined and partially put into practice was radically denied or terminated"; "the total state left no room in German beds for self-determined sex."[2] Such assumptions continue to saturate the literature.

This turns out, however, to be quite a one-sided reading. It neglects not only the fact that Nazis were in conflict among themselves over sexual mores, but above all the pro-sex elements of Nazism, and the ways the regime deliberately and openly used sexual incitement to consolidate its appeal. Paying attention to the diverse ways Jewishness was mobilized in discussions of sex provides a much more differentiated picture. What emerges is a complex field in which Christians and conservative Nazis mobilized Jewishness in one way, while other Nazis, indeed the most influential ones, made references to Jews in a completely different way as they worked actively to detach emancipatory impulses from their association with "Marxism" and "Jewishness" and to redefine sexual liberation as a "Germanic," "Aryan" prerogative. The regime ultimately offered, to those broad sectors of the populace that it did not per-

185

secute, a great many inducements to pre- and extramarital heterosexuality. Although in countless instances, above all in its thorough racialization of sex and in its heightened homophobia, the Third Reich represented a brutal backlash against the progressivism possible in the Weimar Republic, for the majority of the populace Nazism brought with it a continuation and even a dramatic expansion of preexisting liberalizing trends. Partially, the liberalization would be the result of the massive disruptions caused by war and labor mobilization and population transfers. But we need to take just as seriously the fact that the liberalization of heterosexual mores was also, already before the war, actively advanced as part of NSDAP policy.

Under Nazism, this growing liberality was handled in a double way: it was *both* decried as Jewish *and* celebrated as an Aryan privilege. In order to understand how assumptions about the links between sexual liberality and Jewishness were manipulated under Nazism, it is crucial to revisit the discussions about sex and Jewishness that evolved during Weimar, and then trace the complex combination of continuities and discontinuities across the divide of 1933. It is also necessary to think in fresh ways about how Nazi tactics of ideological persuasion worked, and to consider the role of deliberate contradiction and disavowal within these. Finally, and even as we understand Nazi efforts to remake sexuality in the context of Nazis' broader contributions to the modernization of German consumer culture (from the marketing of Coca-Cola to the travel opportunities afforded by *Kraft durch Freude*) we need also to confront the disconcertingly proto-postmodern elements of Nazism.[3] Doing so permits new insight into how assumptions about the fluidity and instability of identity categories (Jewish versus German, homosexual versus heterosexual) were essential to Nazism's ideological effectiveness.

II

Sexual demonization of Jews was a pervasive feature of antisemitism already during the Weimar years. Building on older associations of Jews with carnality and Christians with spirituality, the twentieth-century version emphasized the threat posed by a rapacious, bestial Jewish male to innocent German femininity. Typical was an early Nazi election campaign poster from the 1920s which showed an unattractive Jewish man paired with a beautiful non-Jewish woman beside a coffin labeled *Deutschland*.[4] Also typical of this time was a cartoon of the Jewish male as a repulsive large octopus raping Germania, the female representative of Germany.[5] The racist novelist Artur Dinter, author of the best-selling *Die Sünde wider das Blut* (1921)—it was said to have been read by 1.5 million Germans—not only reinforced the antisemitic cliché of the Jewish pimp who violated young girls under his control, but also argued that one drop of Jewish sperm permanently contaminated a German woman. Even if she later partnered with a German man, the children they had together were nonetheless polluted by her earlier encounter with a Jew.[6] Adolf Hitler made Dinter's notion of "the sin against the blood" his own, and *Mein Kampf* (1925) famously included a passage in which Hitler fantasized how "for hours the black-haired Jew-boy, diabolic joy in his face, waits in ambush for the unsuspecting girl whom he defiles with his blood and thus robs from her people."[7] The antisemitic Nazi newspaper *Der Stürmer,* founded in 1923 and edited by Julius Streicher, elaborated on these themes in dozens of variations, ranting repetitively about male Jews' supposed compulsion toward sexual criminality (including rape, pedophilia, and systematic seduction of German girls into prostitution). It printed myriad images of the Jewish man as a vulgar, animalistic, or diabolical figure driving German womanhood into disaster.

Yet there was a countervailing association between sexuality and Jewishness in Weimar: the representation of Jewish Germans as leaders in various campaigns for sexual liberalization. This association contained more than a kernel of truth. Jewish medical doctors and political activists were indeed often at the forefront of campaigns to abolish Paragraph 218 (which criminalized abortion) and Paragraph 175 (which criminalized male homosexuality) as well as the broader efforts to make contraceptive information and products more widely available and to assist couples (through sex enlightenment films and sex and marriage counseling centers) not only with family planning but also with achieving greater sexual satisfaction. The prominent physician Max Marcuse, for instance, made the (at the time radical) claim that "*The purpose of sexual activity is the achievement of pleasure.* Nothing more and nothing less." His major work, *Der Präventivverkehr* (1931), not only explained in detail how condoms might be properly stored for repeated use (since most working-class couples could scarcely afford them), but also offered the advice that oral and anal sex were excellent strategies for preventing conception.[8] Another prominent activist, Magnus Hirschfeld, was the leader of the movement for homosexual rights in Weimar Germany (which had hundreds of thousands of supporters); he had also established the Institute for Sexual Science in Berlin in 1919, which included a sex counseling center as well as the major library in Germany for sexological research (subsequently burned by the Nazis). He stood not only for homosexual rights but—like Marcuse—for an accepting attitude toward premarital heterosexuality and toward contraceptive use both before and during marriage.[9] Max Hodann, another well-known physician, provided some of the earliest sex advice writings for proletarian youth.[10] And the abortion rights activist Friedrich Wolf was a leader in the fight against Paragraph 218 (which in the final years of Weimar had developed into a huge mass movement) and was the author of the widely seen play (and then movie) *Cyankali,* which dramatized poor women's desperation over unwanted pregnancies.[11]

However, and despite these and numerous other examples of Jewish sex rights activism, the idea of Jews as the main advocates of sexual liberalization was also a racist, right-wing construct. Taking shape already in the later years of Weimar, this construct became even more important after the Nazis came to power in 1933, and in fact became central to the Nazis' retrospective representation of the Weimar Republic as a whole. In this rendition, Weimar was reduced to sex. All the complexities and contrary political and social impulses of German life between 1919 and 1933 were obscured and displaced by an image of Weimar as a hothouse of decadence and promiscuity, a time of the "most vulgar stimulation of steamy, debauched eroticism."[12] In addition, since the Weimar Republic had been governed by Socialists, since many of the sex counseling centers in Weimar had been set up as services provided by the Socialist and Communist parties for their predominantly working-class members, and since many of the Jewish physicians active in various sexual rights campaigns were also leftists, it was simple for Christian conservatives and Nazis alike to assimilate the phenomenon of sexual rights activism to the larger phantasmagorical menace of "Judeo-Bolshevism." Even the founder of psychoanalysis, the Austrian Sigmund Freud, decidedly not a leftist, was portrayed as part of the same pernicious conspiracy. Freud's purported proclivity for seeing sex everywhere and at the root of all individual and social phenomena (an interpretation of his work that Freud categorically rejected) became a constant motif for Nazi authors. Freud was accused not only of having a "dirty fantasy" which projected sexuality onto children, but also of inventing the idea of an id—or "unconscious force"—solely to keep the consciences of "Nordic" people from bothering them when they engaged in masturbation or extramarital relations. Freud's teachings, it was claimed, robbed people of all ethical orientation as they struggled to master their own drives. Individuals were cast into the Jews' "Asiatic worldview: 'Enjoy, because tomorrow you'll be dead.'"[13] As one pediatrician complained, for the Freudian the human being "existed only as a sex organ, around which the body vegetates."[14] Sex education experts influenced by psychoanalysis were declared to be "Jewish sex criminals."[15] For years, Freud remained a favorite object for Nazi attack, even as Nazi psychotherapists and physicians routinely appropriated his ideas (while denying they were his); borrowing from Freud while simultaneously denigrating him was a common Nazi strategy.

Similarly, Magnus Hirschfeld and Max Marcuse became major objects of Nazi venom. As one Nazi-identified doctor put it, "the psychoanalysts are not yet the worst. Far more offensive is that which gathers around Magnus Hirschfeld, the director of the Institute for Sexual Science, and around Mr. Marcuse and Co. Here, one can be sure, there is a quite conscious effort to destroy the German soul."[16] Hirschfeld's contention that sexual orientation was biologically determined, and his widely reported success organizing Germans in favor of the abolition of Paragraph 175, were both labeled appalling. But Hirschfeld distressed conservatives also because he promoted an ethics of consent. Challenging the standard Christian view that premarital intercourse was by definition a sin, Hirschfeld emphasized that the key moral issue was that there be no coercion in sexual encounters. Marcuse too argued that non-marital love relationships, if based on mutual respect and affection, were also morally legitimate. Nazi commentators voiced their outrage at what they considered an insidious attempt to "obscure the simple concepts of right and wrong and relocate the boundaries between them" and—rejecting what they deemed a Jewish celebration of sexuality as a central force in human life—announced that they had rid Germany of this "abominable specter of the idol-worship of sex appeal."[17]

Nazis eager to advance a sexually conservative agenda drew on the ambivalent association of Jews with both sexual evil and sexual rights. Attempting to mobilize antisemitism for sexually conservative ends, they argued that "the Jew just has a different sexuality from that of the German."[18] Jews undervalued spirituality and love and overvalued sensuality and physical contact.[19] Far from advocating a natural sexuality, Jews exhibited a "disgusting lechery."[20] Jews were working "*to strike the Nordic race at its most vulnerable point: sexual life.*"[21] Jewish doctors' willingness to provide abortion services was portrayed as above all a calculated attempt to destroy the racially superior German *Volk*.[22]

Such constructions of Jews as the main celebrants of sexual pleasure or as the key proponents of sexual diversity and perversity belied the simple fact that what these activists had offered was what millions of non-Jewish Germans fervently wanted. Indicative of such longings was that the birthrate in Germany had been declining in all classes since at least the turn of the twentieth century. Significantly, moreover, and despite the monetary and other incentives proffered by the Nazis, nearly a third of all couples married in 1933 were still childless five years later, and a further quarter of them had only one child. Even church-going Christians reportedly considered the use of contraception commonsensical. Although the overall birthrate rose from 970,000 in 1933 to 1.4 million in 1939 (it sank again during the war to just over 1 million births annually), scholars have suggested that in many cases a woman's decision to have another child was less a response to regime propaganda than a strategy to avoid conscription into the labor force once the regime switched course and decided, against its earlier attempt to put women back into the home, that it needed women's labor power.[23]

It is important to register as well how much sexual misery existed in Germany in the early decades of the twentieth century—even if there was also considerable hope that this misery could be alleviated. For many women anxiety about pregnancy was not only orgasm-inhibiting but also libido-suppressing. Coitus interruptus could be unnerving and stressful for both partners; condoms, if even affordable, inhibited sensation. Disinfectant-soaked sponges placed in front of the cervix before coitus or postcoital douches often irritated and inflamed the vaginal area and made sex painful rather than pleasurable. And illegal abortions performed inexpertly and under less than aseptic conditions could cause infections and uterine damage. Lack of privacy in over-crowded proletarian housing could make relaxation difficult, and heavy alcohol use, especially among men, often made marital sexual encounters little more than violations for the women.

Without question, however, greater sexual satisfaction was also becoming an increasingly important ideal for broad sectors of the population, both men and women. Many felt a profound yearning for something better in their lives. Against this background, it was no wonder that the sex counseling clinics established by the Socialist and Communist parties had been unable to keep up with mass demand.

Indeed, as the Third Reich unfolded, the most striking aspect of sexual conservatives' writings was their dismay in the face of non-Jewish Germans' apparent lack of interest in conforming to more constrictive mores. References to Jews continued to function as a negative counterpoint to underscore the value of a sexually conservative perspective. But precisely some of the most conservative texts also included important evidence of just how unpopular sexual conservatism was. In a book published in 1938, for example, the Nazi-identified physician Ferdinand Hoffmann fumed that although Germans were appropriately antisemitic in most parts of their lives, they were apparently loath to let go of their emancipated sexual habits. "Approximately 72 million condoms are used in Germany each year," he announced, noting also that "in the surroundings of big cities, evening after evening, the roads into the woods are covered with automobiles in which, after the American pattern, so-called love is made." Premarital heterosexual intercourse was near-ubiquitous in Nazi Germany, Hoffmann said; the idea that anyone should stay chaste until marriage "possesses absolutely no more validity." And even after marriage Germans often did not remain faithful to their spouses. Trying to pin on Jews what he simultaneously admitted was a pandemic phenomenon, Hoffmann claimed that Jews had managed to transform Germans' "erotic deep structure [erotische Tiefenschicht]." He cautioned his readers that "there are not two sides to the Jewish question, and it is not admissible to damn the Jew in his political, economic, and human manifestations while secretly, for personal convenience, to maintain the customs he has suggested in the realm of love- and sex-life." Yet the majority of Germans were clearly not convinced. Sex remained the site—Hoffmann complained—at which it was "evidently the most difficult to be a good National Socialist."[24] While Hoffmann offered one of the more elaborate expositions of the theory that "Jewishness" was deeply rooted also within non-Jewish Germans, he was certainly not alone in advancing this view.

Paul Danzer, writing in 1936 in a Nazi journal concerned with population policy, argued that whether Jews "exploited our economy, whether they confused our legal life or encouraged social divisions, all that pales before the very most serious damage they have done to our *Volk*, the *poisoning of marital- and sex-morality* . . . Just remember the semitically saturated entertainment- and theater-literature, the filmmaking of the last decades, and the persistent effort that was made from that side in the ripping asunder of all moral barri- ers, the glorification of adultery and sexual uninhibitedness!" And yet Danzer, too, like Hoffmann, worried openly that the German masses could not care less about cleaning up their sexual act. Men continued to see it as an "indis- pensable proof of their masculinity, to run after every skirt and in so doing notch up as many successes as possible . . . And one cannot say that the fe- male sex is much more circumspect."[25] Similarly, another leading "race ex- pert" complained that "the notions about sex life, marriage, and family" pro- moted in Weimar had "eaten . . . more deeply [*tiefer . . . einfressen*]" into the German *Volk* than any "purely political teachings" from that era.[26] Along related lines, an NSDAP-affiliated physician vociferously lamented in 1937 that "we have experienced a revolution in ways of understanding the world and a *völkisch* awakening like never before. And yet we thoughtlessly repeat the Jewish or Jewish-influenced vulgarities concerning the relations of the two sexes . . . It is astonishing how little our great National Socialist revolu- tion has moved forward in this area!"[27] Yet another variation on these themes appeared in the work of a Berlin urologist who condemned what he saw as an unfortunate pressure on men to please women sexually. He blamed this pres- sure on Jewish physicians and psychoanalysts who put into women's heads the idea that women too were capable of orgasm. He recommended that men re- turn to "'automatic-egotistical' sexual intercourse," warning that solicitous concern for women only led to erectile dysfunction and prostate problems.[28] As late as 1940, the women's newspaper *Frauenwarte* was accusing other Nazi periodicals of displaying a spirit that was "Jewish—all too Jewish," as they— in millions of copies—printed titillating images of bikini-clad glamour girls rather than folk-dancing dirndl-wearers.[29] In sum, Germans were apparently not too keen to let go of this last "Jewish" vestige. And however paradoxically, this was not a form of antisemitism in which Jews were abjected. Sexually conservative Nazis—whether intentionally or not—reinforced the idea that what Jews supposedly represented also had undeniable appeal for vast num- bers of non-Jewish Germans.

III

In any case, the need for greater conservatism was not the sole message about sex promoted by Nazism. For there was also another strand of Nazi argumen- tation about sex, one which was far more deliberately inciting and one explic- itly aimed at encouraging playful, pleasurable heterosexuality among those ideologically and "racially" approved by the regime. Importantly, however, this second strand of argumentation too was thoroughly saturated with anti-semitism. For these pro-sex advocates, references to the supposed shameless-ness and impropriety of "Jewish" versions of sexuality functioned preemi-nently as a technique of disavowal—a strategy to distract attention away from Nazism's own inducements to premarital and extramarital sexual activity.

Nazis espoused their pro-sex vision especially in attacks on the Christian churches. The mid-1930s—a few years into the Third Reich, as the regime strove to consolidate its hold on the populace—saw a particular efflorescence of discussion of the acceptability of both premarital and extramarital coitus; Nazi-endorsed authors openly defended both. In one widely discussed 1936 essay, for instance, the physician Walter Gmelin reported on his work evalu-ating couples' "racial" and "hereditary" suitability for marriage, and also commented on the high incidence in Germany of premarital intercourse. Al-though Gmelin found that less than 5 percent of the women and men he in-terviewed were virgins—indeed, most had begun to have intercourse in their late teens and early twenties, approximately seven years before they married—Gmelin did not find this trend alarming. And although he pondered why the majority had more than one premarital partner (and some had several dozen), he nonetheless insisted that premarital sexual experience was a good thing, a phenomenon to be read above all as "a healthy reaction against the social in-hibitions and against morality-preachers," a sign that "also today—in spite of everything—people at the age of sexual maturity satisfy the drive given them by nature!" In fact, Gmelin interjected, those few who denied having had premarital experience "certainly did not display above-average hereditary re-sources [Erbgut]."[30] Also in 1936, the jurist Rudolf Bechert energetically de-fended extramarital affairs. In the context of explaining a proposed new law which would give illegitimate children the father's name and equal rights with legitimate children to financial support, Bechert ventured this:

> Non-marital bonds are superior to marriages in many ways. It is not just life experience that proves that non-marital connections rooted in sexual love are an unchangeable fact; rather, all of human culture teaches that they can represent the highest moral and aesthetic value. Without sexual love no poetry, no painting, indeed, no music! In all cultured na-tions concubinage is *not criminalized,* with churchy Italy ahead of all the rest . . . Never can non-marital sexual intercourse be prevented.

Indeed, Bechert concluded effusively, "Love is the only true religious experi-ence in the world."[31]

Such an emphatic rejection of Christian moralizing—coupled with a glori-fication of sex—was even more evident in a 1937 book by the physician Carl Csallner. Csallner argued that only "unnatural sanctimoniousness" and "priestly cant" had turned the sexual drive, which was "wanted by nature and spontaneously presses toward activity," into something "base and mean . . . a deadly sin." The sexual drive, in Csallner's view, was "great" and "holy."[32] The Nazi pedagogue Alfred Zeplin put the point even more succinctly as he unveiled his five-point plan for encouraging premarital heterosexual sex while discouraging masturbation and homosexuality. "*Sexual activity*," Zeplin announced, "*is not sinful, it is sacred.*"[33] Along related lines, in 1941, race theorist Hans Endres told an audience of high-ranking Nazis and their guests that "We have been raised in criminal bigotry, because the Oriental Christian mentality has suppressed our healthy Germanic instincts in sexual matters. Our younger generations . . . must become proud of their bodies and enjoy the natural pleasures of sex without being ashamed."[34]

These ideas about the reprehensibleness and unnaturalness of prudery and the transcendental, quasi-divine qualities of human sexual expression were made widely available, not least through the official SS journal, *Das schwarze Korps*, launched in 1935. This was one of the most popular weeklies of the Third Reich and one enthusiastically endorsed by the regime. In an entertaining and acerbic style, *Das schwarze Korps* advanced its recipe for sexual happiness and national health. The overall tone was conversational and informative, and—especially in the prewar years, and continuing into the early war years as the war still went well for Germany—also decidedly cheerful. Even in the more desperate later years of the war, as the paper championed the ever more crass and histrionic clamor of the regime for each and every individual's total self-sacrifice on behalf of the nation, it never lost its distinctively ironic tone. This tongue-in-cheek and sardonic approach did not disguise the paper's many ruthless attacks on Jews, the handicapped, homosexuals, "asocial" criminals, and political critics of the regime—including, for example, unabashed calls for the murder of the disabled—but certainly it contributed mightily to the paper's morally disorienting effect.

Christian efforts to draw the population away from Nazism, especially by documenting Nazi encouragement of naked self-display and of pre- and extramarital heterosexuality, provided a running joke for the journal from its inception. Repeatedly, the paper reprinted excerpts from Christian complaints about Nazi policies and injunctions, only to then repudiate these complaints in the most forceful terms, even as, simultaneously, the elaborating remarks actually confirmed aspects of the Christians' criticisms (although they reversed the Christians' assessments). At the same time, the paper delighted in detailing craven Christian accommodation to Nazism and shared acceptance of Nazi values.

Das schwarze Korps brazenly—and obsessively—mocked Christian efforts to defend the sanctity of marriage, and aligned itself with young people's impatience with traditional bourgeois mores. "Eager clerical 'moralists'" had "pathetic complexes"; "*original sin*" was a "foreign" and "oriental" idea; medieval Christianity's dogmatism was designed to bring down the "vibrant" and "life-affirming" Germanic and Nordic peoples.[35] When a female author remonstrated in another Nazi journal about how men treated women as objects, and argued that Germanic tradition demanded that men be more respectful of an unmarried woman's chastity, *Das schwarze Korps* rebuked her and rebutted her version of history. The paper declared that what she took to be Germanic tradition was nothing but another example of "the pathological tendency to Catholic virginalism."[36] In no uncertain terms, *Das schwarze Korps* attacked "the denominational morality . . . that sees in the body something to be despised, and wants to interpret what are natural processes as *sinful drives.*" The paper explicitly blamed Christians for condemning "healthy drive-forces" and thereby redirecting these drives into "unnatural" paths; it brashly defended sex with "frivolous, immoral" girls as much less dangerous than "youthful aberrations toward one's own sex."[37]

Thus, the radical rejection of homosexuality in *Das schwarze Korps* was combined not with a more generally conservative attitude toward sex, but rather with an intensified encouragement of premarital heterosexual activity. Many Nazi "experts" advanced a social constructionist view of sexuality which insisted that sexual identity was variable and vulnerable. (They presented this view not least as a vigorous refutation of Magnus Hirschfeld's belief that homosexuality was constitutionally determined.) In this context, social constructionist approaches did not ameliorate anti-homosexual sentiment but rather exacerbated it. The punitive intensification of homophobic persecution in the Third Reich—escalating especially from 1937 on—was fueled precisely by the idea that homosexuality was very much a possibility lurking within the majority of men, and that for many men it was in fact a phase they went through in their youth. *Das schwarze Korps*, for example, attacked homosexuals as dangers to the *Volk* and traitors to the state. But it also blamed "bourgeois moralists" for being so busy presenting the "natural aim" (i.e., sex with a woman) as a "shameful sin" that they permitted a youth's still completely "*unspecific*" "sexual yearning . . . to be given a false aim—same-sex love."[38] In *Das schwarze Korps*'s view, 98 percent of accused homosexuals were fully capable of heterosexuality; they were simply "seduced" "fellow travelers" whom the state could help therapeutically to become "healthy." But the remaining 2 percent (by the paper's count, forty thousand men) would be turned into "a crystallization point of repulsion"; *Das schwarze Korps* uncomplicatedly endorsed "brutality" against these men, and expressed nostalgic appreciation for the ancient Germanic and Friesian customs of castrating homosexuals or drowning them in swamps.[39]

Moreover, just as sexually conservative Nazi mores were expressed through antisemitism, so too were Nazis' particular versions of sexually emancipatory ideas. Yet *Das schwarze Korps* handled the purported "Jewishness" of sex differently than sexual conservatives did. As with homophobia, so also with antisemitism; *Das schwarze Korps*'s techniques were deliberately self-reflexive. Even as *Das schwarze Korps* castigated Christianity for its hostility to sex, the journal also continually worked to distance Nazism from any possible association with Weimar-era liberality; it did so by deliberately calling attention to the differences between Weimar and Nazism. Thus, for instance, the journal contrasted the kind of "propaganda for nudism" purportedly evident during the Weimar era (or, as *Das schwarze Korps* put it, during "the years of Jewish domination," when "the Semitic manipulators" were busy working to undermine "every natural order, such as marriage and family") with the aims of National Socialism, which were to resist "that prudery . . . which has contributed to destroying the instinct for bodily nobility and its beauty in our *Volk*," and "to represent the noble body in its natural shape" (for "the pure and the beautiful were for the uncorrupted German never a sin").[40]

Over and over, the paper denied that it advocated "free love" (this it associated with "Marxism"), and it insisted that Nazism was supporting and restoring marriage (in opposition to what it described as "Jewish" attacks on this institution).[41] It repeatedly described Nazism as a movement that above all demanded *"cleanliness"* in *"matters of love"* and the realm of *"sex [Sexus]."*[42] But simultaneously, often in the same articles, the paper unapologetically defended both illegitimacy and non-reproductive premarital and extramarital heterosexual intercourse. It also printed numerous pictures of nudes—paintings, statues, and photographs—and defended nudity as pure, natural, and life-enhancing.

Along these same lines, in 1938, in two full-page photo spreads, *Das schwarze Korps* showcased the "beautiful and pure" nudity advocated by Nazism (exemplified by pulchritudinous naked women luxuriating in sun, sand, and sea) and juxtaposed this with the "shameless money-making" of the previous "cultural epoch" (illustrated by photos of half-clothed and excessively made-up women from what look like Weimar dance halls). Once more, as it had so often done in its attacks on Christian sexual conservatives, *Das schwarze Korps* chastised those who "campaign against the supposed immorality of National Socialism." The paper accused the regime's critics of playing into the hands of Nazism's enemies, deeming them "vermin" whose invocation of "the cultural will of the state" for their own prudish agenda was an "insolence" and against whom only "the police" could bring relief.[43]

Not only the continual self-labeling as "pure" and "clean," then, but also the fiercely hyperbolic attacks on Jews, Marxists, and Weimar-era cultural arbiters for *their* purported advocacy of extramarital sex, pornography, and nakedness, served to distract attention from Nazi advocacy of those very things. *Das schwarze Korps*, in short, expressly disavowed exactly the activities in which it was engaged. Incitement and disavowal were inseparable.

Considering the strategies employed by *Das schwarze Korps* in this way also offers a fresh perspective on that other most popular and rabidly antisemitic Nazi journal, *Der Stürmer*. *Der Stürmer* could simply be interpreted as an example of Nazism's sexually repressive, conservative side. Indeed, in view of its relentless obsession with "documenting" Jewish sex criminality and the prevalence in Germany of "race defilement" (i.e., consensual sex between Jews and non-Jews), reading it one could easily get the impression that non-Jews seldom if ever had sex with one another. Yet, at the same time, it is readily apparent that in its narrative pacing, its luxuriantly detailed descriptions of sex crimes, and its many pictures of naked blondes defiled by big-nosed Jews, *Der Stürmer* served as pornography. While it is impossible to know with which characters in *Der Stürmer*'s scenarios readers identified (was it the sexually successful Jewish man? the violated or seduced non-Jewish woman? the outraged non-Jewish male or female voyeur?), the multiplicity of possibilities for libidinal identification may have been precisely the point, and could help to explain the paper's appeal, especially for teenage boys. What is clear is *both* that *Der Stürmer*'s recurrent detailed descriptions of sexual outrages gave readers crucial moral permission to hate without guilt (since Jews were continually described as aggressing on Germans) *and* that the ubiquitous declaration that Nazism was battling filth provided a ready excuse to display voluptuous naked women and keep people's attention fixed on sex.

Even into the war, the good cop–bad cop routine of permitting contradictory messages about sex to coexist persisted unmodified, and both the sexually conservative and the (hetero)sexually tolerant views were expressed through antisemitic invective—crucially, even as both sides continued to present Jewishness as something inferior to Germanness. Thus, for example, in 1942 the military officer Major Ellenbeck directed his men not only to choose "squeaky clean [*blitzsaubere*]" women as their wives but also to desist from "raunchy joking" and to hold themselves to a high standard of sexual cleanliness as well. Any German man, Ellenbeck announced, who thought men had trouble reining themselves in and who adhered to a double standard of sexual morality obviously needed to expel the "poisonous substances of the Jewish moral perspective . . . sitting in his bones. Out with them!"[44]

Yet the war years also saw a further deployment of the antisemitic strategy of disavowal: blaming Jews for non-Jewish Germans' sexual licentiousness even as in the same breath that licentiousness was defended as normal and natural. Military doctor Joachim Rost, for instance, in 1944 took direct jabs at Sigmund Freud and a certain "Viennese school" for their efforts to find the roots of all "drive-life" (*Triebleben*) in the sex drive. And he declared that in the aftermath of the First World War, "the demand for free love, nurtured by the parasites on our *Volk* . . . went hand in hand with a denigration of higher ethical feelings." But simultaneously, Rost defended the sex drive as a powerful and important force, wondered aloud whether "*one can ever demand of a grown human being the mastery of the strongest of all drives, the sex drive,*" and also announced that "male natures with strong drives" are "frequent among the good soldiers," and they "naturally find a limitation of sexual activity oppressive." Moreover, in an extended analysis of the ways military men spoke among themselves about the legitimacy of adultery, Rost noted that quite a few contended that sexual activity outside of marriage was acceptable so long as there was no emotional involvement with the sex partner. And he remarked on how frequently soldiers tried to convince their officers to permit them to circumvent the "racial" prohibitions on sex with women in occupied countries as they jestingly quipped "that the relations of the sexes are international law and therefore have nothing to do with the war." Yet although relaxed mores were pervasive among non-Jewish German men, it was still Jews who were at fault for non-Jews' interest in sex. Rost argued that despite the "gratifying progressive development" initiated in 1933 one could not, of course, expect such a habit-forming belief as that "everything that is pleasing is permitted" to be overcome overnight.[45]

IV

Only the military defeat of Nazi Germany brought an end to the powerful association between sexual liberality and Jewishness. Religious conservatives (who had been miffed during the Third Reich because Nazis had not kept their original promise to clean up sexual mores) were, within a few years of Nazism's collapse, politically ascendant. In a stunning inversion of prior meaning-making processes, these conservatives worked to link sexual liberality not with Jews but with the Judeocide.

While the immediate postwar years were a time of considerable sexual libertinism and avid and open public discussion of sexual issues, the founding of the Federal Republic in 1949 and especially the early to mid-1950s saw a dramatic shift toward far greater sexual conservatism. Most scholars, in keeping with their conviction that the Third Reich was sex-hostile, presume that the sexual conservatism of the 1950s was a watered-down inheritance from Nazism. When further explanations for the 1950s' "yearning for normalization" or "search for 'moral' restabilization" are sought at all, these are identified—by conservative and liberal historians alike—as primarily logical responses to the intensely disruptive experiences of war and its immediate chaotic aftermath.[46] Yet what remains unaddressed is how sexual conservatism served as a crucial strategy for managing the memory of Nazism and Holocaust.

Within the version of Christianity that became politically dominant in the early Federal Republic, the narrow emphasis on sexual morality to the exclusion of other moral concerns was not merely a matter of political expediency but also one of deeply held belief. Sexual morality had of course for centuries been one of Christianity's major concerns, and sex had been a main element in Christians' specific conflicts with Nazis. But restoring conservative sexual mores was important to Christians also because World War II, at the home and battle fronts, had been the concrete context in which many Germans had experienced infidelity and because Nazi incitement to sexual pleasure within

and outside of marriage had in many people's minds become closely associated with Nazi racism and hubris. Thus Catholic physician Anton Hofmann
in 1951 criticized the way "NS-schools and the like" had forced "premature
sexual contact" on young people under the guise of "'natural and free experiencing' of the erotic event." He also directly linked Nazi encouragement of
sexual activity with Nazism's other crimes, contending that the disrespect for
the spiritual dimension of life evident among people overly obsessed with
erotic pleasure was intimately connected with disrespect for the bodies of
others and therefore facilitated brutality and mass murder. Or, as he put it,
what needed to be understood was "the paradoxical matter that the same person who raises the body to dizzying heights, can in an instant sacrifice the
bodies of a hundred thousand others."[47] Under the circumstances, this was an
entirely plausible interpretation.

Precisely because incitement to sexual activity and pleasure had been a major feature of National Socialism, turning against sexual licentiousness in the
early 1950s, especially in the name of Christianity, could, quite legitimately
and fairly, be represented and understood as a turn against Nazism. But there
was a great deal of tactical maneuvering as well. Numerous Christian commentators presented sexual cleanliness as *the* cure for postwar Germany's
moral crisis, and thereby implied that sexual immorality, not mass murder,
was the source of that crisis. Catholics regularly railed against the Nazis' encouragement to "libertinage" and described disrespect for virginity as just so
much "hackneyed Goebbels claptrap."[48] Protestants argued that as significant as "the sin of yesterday" (defined as the "horrors and crimes" of the
Nazis) was "the sin of today": "the licentiousness . . . with which women
and girls today surrender themselves and men profane female honor."[49] Re-
Christianization was a logical countermove to the secularization so manifestly
furthered by Nazism, and it also provided an unexpectedly effective way of
adapting to the expectations of the American occupiers. Shifting moral debate
away from mass murder and onto sexual matters was one of the major strategies used by West Germans both in domestic politics and in international
relations.

Moreover, and by a turn just as paradoxical though no less important,
postwar Christians' emphasis on cleaning up sexual mores also provided a
convenient strategy for concealing the memory of the churches' very strong
complicity with Nazism—not only with its nationalism, militarism, and anti-
Bolshevism, but also expressly with its antisemitism. The need to cleanse
postwar Christianity of the taint of its own anti-Judaism and pro-Nazism,
and to present Christianity as the obverse of Nazism, made it especially imperative to suppress the former association between sexual liberality and Jewishness and instead connect sexual liberality with Nazism. Yet, and while in
the early years of the Federal Republic rhetorical linkages such as those be-

tween "uninhibited sexuality" and "Auschwitz" were common, in the subsequent course of the 1950s the sexually inciting aspects of Nazism would be increasingly downplayed.[50]

While emphasis on the sexually inciting aspects of Nazism was important in early efforts to secure postwar Christianity's moral stature, in short, Nazi encouragements to pre- and extramarital heterosexuality not only for the purpose of procreation but also for the pursuit of pleasure were precisely the aspect of Nazi policies that would be assiduously forgotten in the postwar era. That the regime that had been sexually inciting was also responsible for continent-wide carnage and the systematic torture and murder of its own citizens and millions of citizens of other nations made it especially desirable to erase the memory of popular receptivity to Nazism's pleasure-enjoining aspects. Excising certain elements from the retrospective portrait of Nazism while highlighting others was both psychologically and politically congenial. For admitting to their children or to the rest of the world that they had any particular pleasures during the Third Reich increasingly did not fit with one of postwar Germans' most successful strategies for dealing with guilt (whether internally felt or externally imposed) about the Third Reich: the tendency to present themselves as victims of Nazism rather than its supporters and beneficiaries. Stressing that sexual conservatism was a timeless German value that transcended political regime changes, or even declaring directly that Nazism had been, in sexual terms, especially conservative and repressive, offered a way of hiding from view and from subsequent memory one's own youthful departures from traditional norms, as these were facilitated by Nazism, and one's own enthusiasm for Nazism more generally. One of the great ironies of postwar West German history was that when the young New Left rebels of 1968 justified their struggles for sexual freedom on the grounds that fascism had been sexually repressive, their formerly Nazi- sympathizing elders had reasons all their own for not contradicting them.

Notes

1. Joachim Hohmann, *Sexualforschung und -aufklärung in der Weimarer Republik* (Berlin: Foerster, 1985), 9; Sabine Weissler, "Sexy Sixties," in *CheSchahShit: Die sechziger Jahre zwischen Cocktail und Molotow,* ed. Eckhard Siepmann (Berlin: Elefanten, 1984), 99; Christian de Nuys-Henkelmann, "Wenn die rote Sonne abends im Meer versinkt," in *Sexualmoral und Zeitgeist im 19. und 20. Jahrhundert,* ed. Anja Bagel-Bohlan and Michael Salewski (Opladen: Leske und Budrich, 1990), 109; and Scott Spector, "Was the Third Reich Movie-Made? Interdisciplinarity and the Reframing of 'Ideology,'" *American Historical Review* 106, no. 2 (April 2001): 472. See

also John Borneman, "*Gottvater, Landesvater, Familienvater:* Identification and Authority in Germany," in *Death of the Father,* ed. John Borneman (New York: Berghahn, 2004), 148.

2. Angela H. Mayer, "'Schwachsinn höheren Grades': Zur Verfolgung lesbischer Frauen in Österreich während der NS-Zeit," in *Nationalsozialistischer Terror gegen Homosexuelle: Verdrängt und ungesühnt,* ed. Burkhard Jellonek and Rüdiger Lautmann (Paderborn: Ferdinand Schöningh, 2002), 84; Friedrich Koch, *Sexuelle Denunziation: Die Sexualität in der politischen Auseinandersetzung* (Frankfurt am Main: Syndikat, 1986); Annette Miersch, *Schulmädchen-Report: Der deutsche Sexfilm der 70er Jahre* (Berlin: Bertz, 2003), 69; Udo Pini, *Leibeskult und Liebeskitsch: Erotik im Dritten Reich* (Munich: Klinkhardt und Biermann, 1992), 11; and Stefan Maiwald and Gerd Mischler, *Sexualität unterm Hakenkreuz: Manipulation und Vernichtung der Intimsphäre im NS-Staat* (Hamburg: Europa-Verlag, 1999), 57.

3. On Nazi contributions to modernization, see for example Hans Dieter Schäfer, *Das gespaltene Bewusstsein: Über deutsche Kultur und Lebenswirklichkeit, 1933–1945* (Munich: Carl Hanser, 1985); Norbert Frei, "Wie modern war der Nationalsozialismus?" *Geschichte und Gesellschaft* 19 (1993); and Peter Fritzsche, "Nazi Modern," *Modernism/Modernity* 3, no. 1 (1996): 1–21. On the proto-postmodernism of Nazism, see also Sophinette Becker, "Zur Funktion der Sexualität im Nationalsozialismus," *Zeitschrift für Sexualforschung* 14, no. 2 (June 2001): 142–44; and Dagmar Herzog, *Sex after Fascism: Memory and Morality in Twentieth-Century Germany* (Princeton, N.J.: Princeton University Press, 2005).

4. The poster is reprinted in Klaus Theweleit, *Male Fantasies,* vol. 2 (Minneapolis: University of Minnesota Press, 1989), 9.

5. The cartoon (from the *Deutschvölkische Monatshefte* in 1923) is reprinted in Christina von Braun, "Und der Feind ist Fleisch geworden: Der rassistische Antisemitismus," in *Der ewige Judenhass: Christlicher Antijudaismus, deutschnationale Judenfeindlichkeit, rassistischer Antisemitismus,* ed. Christina von Braun and Ludger Heid (Berlin: Philo, 2000), between pp. 192 and 193.

6. See Arthur Dinter, *Die Sünde wider das Blut: Ein Zeitroman* (Leipzig: Matthes und Thost, 1920); and the discussion of Dinter in Erich Goldhagen, "Nazi Sexual Demonology," *Midstream* (May 1981): 7–15, especially 11.

7. Adolf Hitler, *Mein Kampf* (Munich: Franz Eher / Zentralverlag der NSDAP, 1943), 357.

8. Max Marcuse, *Der Präventivverkehr in der medizinischen Lehre und ärztlichen Praxis* (Stuttgart: Enke, 1931), 4, 65–66, 91, 103–104.

9. See Manfred Herzer, *Magnus Hirschfeld: Leben und Werk eines jüdischen, schwulen und sozialistischen Sexologen* (Frankfurt am Main: Campus, 1992).

10. For example, see Max Hodann, *Bub und Mädel: Gespräche unter Kameraden über die Geschlechterfrage* (Rudolstadt: Greifenverlag, 1929). On Hodann's significance, see Kristine von Soden, *Die Sexualberatungsstellen der Weimarer Republik, 1919–1933* (Berlin: Hentrich, 1988), 72–74; and Atina Grossmann, *Reforming Sex: The German Movement for Birth Control and Abortion Reform, 1920–1950* (New York: Oxford University Press, 1995), 122–26. Grossmann provides an incisive critical assessment of the limitations of the Weimar-era sex reform movement, including among other things its imbrication with eugenicism, its tendency to normativity, and its inconsistent attention to women's perspectives on sex.

11. See Grossmann, *Reforming Sex*, 81–84; and Cornelie Usborne, "Representation of Abortion in Weimar Popular Culture," paper delivered at the German Historical Institute, Washington, D.C., 26 October 2002.

12. Georg Schliebe, "Die Reifezeit und ihre Erziehungsprobleme," in *Wege und Ziele der Kindererziehung in unserer Zeit*, ed. Martin Löpelman, 3rd ed. (Leipzig: Hesse und Becker, n.d.), 148.

13. "Die Rolle des Juden in der Medizin," *Deutsche Volksgesundheit aus Blut und Boden* (August–September 1933), reprinted in *"Hier geht das Leben auf eine sehr merkwürdige Weise weiter . . . ": Zur Geschichte der Psychoanalyse in Deutschland*, ed. Karen Brecht et al. (Hamburg: Verlag Michael Kellner, 1985), 87.

14. Chemnitz-based pediatrician Kurt Oxenius, quoted in M. Staemmler, "Das Judentum in der Medizin," *Sächsisches Ärzteblatt* 104 (1934), 208. See the similar complaint about "Jewish" psychoanalysis's overemphasis on "what lies below the navel" in Heinz Hunger, "Jüdische Psychoanalyse und deutsche Seelsorge," in *Germanentum, Judentum und Christentum*, vol. 2, ed. Walter Grundmann (Leipzig: G. Wigand, 1943), 323–40.

15. Quoted in Koch, *Sexuelle Denunziation*, 62.

16. Staemmler, "Das Judentum in der Medizin," 210.

17. See ibid., 208; and "Dreht sich alles um die Liebe?" *Das schwarze Korps* (hereafter *DSK*), (25 June 1936), 7.

18. Staemmler, "Das Judentum in der Medizin," 208.

19. See Alfred Zeplin, *Sexualpädagogik als Grundlage des Familienglücks und des Volkswohls* (Rostock: Carl Hinstorffs, 1938), 31.

20. Alfred Rosenberg, *Unmoral im Talmud* (Munich: Deutscher Volksverlag, 1933), 15, quoted in Koch, *Sexuelle Denunziation*, 72.

21. "Die Rolle des Juden," 87.

22. "Der Kastrierjude," *Der Stürmer* 10, no. 43 (October 1932), 2.

23. See Dörte Winkler, *Frauenarbeit im "Dritten Reich"* (Hamburg: Hoffmann und Campe, 1977), 193; Gisela Bock, "Racism and Sexism in Nazi Germany: Motherhood, Compulsory Sterilization, and the State," *Signs* 8 (spring 1983): 400–21; and Claudia Koonz, *Mothers in the Fatherland: Women, the Family, and Nazi Politics* (New York: St. Martin's, 1987), 185–87.

24. See Ferdinand Hoffmann, *Sittliche Entartung und Geburtenschwund*, 2nd ed. (Munich: J. F. Lehmanns, 1938), 13, 16, 21, 24–25, 30, 34, 49, 50, 55.

25. Paul Danzer, "Die Haltung zum anderen Geschlecht als unentbehrliche Grundlage völkischen Aufbaus," in *Streiflichter ins Völkische: Ausgewählte Lesestücke für deutsche Menschen aus dem "Völkischen Willen"* (Berlin: Rota-Druck, 1936), 5–6.

26. Hans F. K. Günther, *Führeradel durch Sippenpflege*, quoted in Walter Hermannsen and Karl Blome, *Warum hat man uns das nicht früher gesagt? Ein Bekenntnis deutscher Jugend zu geschlechtlicher Sauberkeit*, 4th rev. and exp. edition (Munich: J. F. Lehmanns, 1943), 120.

27. Dr. Knorr, "Eine noch nicht genügend beachtete weltanschauliche und bevölkerungspolitische Gefahr," *Ziel und Weg: Organ des Nationalsozialistischen Deutschen Ärztebundes* 7, no. 22 (November 1937), 570.

28. P. Orlowski, "Zur Frage der Pathogenese und der modernen Therapie der sexuellen Störungen beim Manne," *Zeitschrift für Urologie* 31, no. 6 (1937): 383.

29. "Sie meinen: Apart und lustig," *Frauenwarte* 8, no. 16 (February 1940).

30. Excerpts from Gmelin's essay "Bevölkerungspolitik und Frühehe" (published in the *Deutsche Ärztezeitung*) reprinted in "Mütterheim Steinhöring," *DSK*, 7 January 1937, 13–14.

31. Excerpt from Rudolf Bechert's essay (published in *Deutsches Recht*, nos. 23–24 [15 December 1936]), in "Mütterheim Steinhöring," 14.

32. Carl H. Csallner, *Das Geschlechtsleben, seine Bedeutung für Individuum und Gemeinschaft* (Munich: Otto Gmelin, 1937), 10.

33. Zeplin, *Sexualpädagogik*, 12, 24.

34. Endres quoted in George W. Herald, "Sex Is a Nazi Weapon," *American Mercury* 54, no. 22 (June 1944), 661.

35. "Anstössig?" *DSK*, 16 April 1936, 13.

36. Hans Lüdemann, "Neues Stadium der Frauenbewegung?" *DSK*, 19 June 1935, 10. Lüdemann is criticizing Marie Joachimi-Dege's essay in Will Vesper's journal *Neue Literatur*.

37. ". . . Unzucht in der Soldatenzeit," *DSK*, 5 March 1936, 6.

38. "Was sag ich meinem Kinde?" *DSK*, 15 April 1937, 6.

39. "Das sind Staatsfeinde!" *DSK*, 4 March 1937, 1–2; and "Ächtung der Entarteten," *DSK*, 1 April 1937, 11. Notably, *Das schwarze Korps* went out of its way to self-reflexively acknowledge the ubiquitous potential of homosexual feeling in men. Guessing what readers might be guiltily thinking, while also cleverly offering readers the out that their feelings might have been "unconscious," the paper made a point of saying that "above all we know, that every person in his development unconsciously goes through a phase, in which he is to a certain extent receptive to the poison." For "the drive-life [*Triebleben*] awakens in a stage of life, in which the other sex cannot yet appear as the conscious ideal." In earlier essays, *Das schwarze Korps* had already self-consciously thematized the way Nazi single-sex organizations provided an environment worryingly conducive to homosexual relations. See ". . . Unzucht in der Soldatenzeit," 6; and "Frauen sind keine Männer!" *DSK*, 12 March 1936, 1. On other Nazi-era commentators' beliefs in the fluidity of sexual orientation, see Herzog, *Sex after Fascism*.

40. "Ist das Nacktkultur? Herr Stapel entrüstet sich!" *DSK*, 24 April 1935, 12.

41. For example, see "Ehestifter Staat," *DSK*, 26 March 1936, 11; "Kinder—ausserhalb der Gemeinschaft?" *DSK*, 9 April 1936, 5; "Das uneheliche Kind," *DSK*, 9 April 1936, 6; and "Mütterheim Steinhöring," 13.

42. "Frauen sind keine Männer!" 1.

43. "Schön und Rein" and "Geschäft ohne Scham," *DSK*, 20 October 1938, 10, 12.

44. Major Dr. Ellenbeck, "Der deutsche Unteroffizier und das Thema 'Frauen und Mädchen,'" *Die Zivilversorgung*, 15 October 1942, 281–82.

45. Joachim Rost, "Sexuelle Probleme im Felde," *Medizinische Welt* 18 (1944): 218–20.

46. See Hans-Peter Schwarz, *Die Ära Adenauer: Gründerjahre der Republik, 1949–1957* (Stuttgart: Deutsche Verlags-Anstalt, 1981), 382; and Ulrich Herbert, "Legt die Plakate nieder, ihr Streiter für die Gerechtigkeit," *Frankfurter Allgemeine Zeitung* no. 24 (29 January 2001): 48.

47. Anton Christian Hofmann, *Die Natürlichkeit der christlichen Ehe* (Munich: J. Pfeiffer, 1951), 9–10, 38–39.

48. Maria Jochum, "Frauenfrage 1946," *Frankfurter Hefte,* no. 1 (June 1946): 25; and Johannes Leppich, "'Thema 1,'" in *Pater Leppich Spricht,* ed. Günther Mees and Günter Graf (Düsseldorf: Bastion, 1952), 46.

49. "Kundgebung der Landessynode der Evangelisch-Lutherischen Kirche in Bayern in Ansbach, 9.–13. Juli 1946," in *Kirchliches Jahrbuch für die evangelische Kirche in Deutschland, 1945–1948,* ed. Joachim Beckmann (Gütersloh: Gütersloher Verlagshaus, 1950), 45, 48.

50. CDU/CSU Bundestag representative Maria Probst, quoted in Angela Delille and Andrea Grohn, "Es ist verboten . . . Empfängnisverhütung und Abtreibung," in *Perlonzeit: Wie die Frauen ihr Wirtschaftswunder erlebten,* ed. Angela Delille and Andrea Grohn (Berlin: Elefanten, 1985), 124.

Ten

Defeated Germans and Surviving Jews

Gendered Encounters in Everyday Life in U.S.-Occupied Germany, 1945–49

Atina Grossmann

I

As we write the history of the post-1945 years, we are only now, it seems, rediscovering what was amply obvious to contemporaries: that occupied Germany in the immediate postwar period was the unlikely, unloved, and reluctant host to hundreds of thousands of its former victims, housed both in and outside of refugee camps mainly in the American zone and in the American sector of Berlin. A significant number of the millions of people uprooted by war and persecution who remained on western Allied territory as "unrepatriable" DPs (displaced persons) were Jewish survivors of Nazi genocide and involuntary migration, precisely the people both the Allies and the Germans had least expected to have to deal with in the aftermath of National Socialism's exterminatory war.

In 1933, at the beginning of the National Socialist regime, Germany counted some five hundred thousand Jews. In 1946–47, three years after Germany had been declared *judenrein*, over a quarter of a million—the numbers are rough and some recent estimates top three hundred thousand—Jews, survivors of the Final Solution, were living in Germany, albeit in occupied and defeated territory in the British and especially the American zones.[1] They included a small remnant of German Jews who had emerged from hiding, forced labor, death camps, or a precarious above-ground existence in "privileged" mixed marriages or as *Mischlinge*. Others were returned emigrés, many of them now in occupier uniform, freshly minted citizens serving as translators, interrogators, and civil affairs and cultural officers. Most were Eastern Europeans; Jews who had been liberated by the Allies on German soil (some ninety thousand were liberated alive; many died within three weeks, leaving about sixty or seventy thousand), and, as the months passed, tens of thousands of Jewish "infiltrees" who poured into the American zone from Eastern Europe. These predominantly Polish Jews comprised three distinct (but sometimes overlapping) groups: survivors of death marches and of concentration and labor camps who had been freed in Germany but initially returned to their hometowns hoping, generally in vain, to find lost family members or repossess property; Jews who had survived among the partisans or in hiding; and finally, beginning in 1946, a very important cohort—almost ⅔ of the total—of perhaps two hundred thousand Jews who had been repatriated to Poland from their difficult but life-saving refuge in the Soviet Union and then fled again, this time in a western direction, when postwar antisemitism convinced them, especially after the notorious pogrom in Kielce on 4 July 1946, that even after liberation there was no future for Jews in Communist-occupied Eastern Europe. The Jewish survivors who poured into the American zone became a key element in what Frank Stern called the "historic triangle" of Germans, Jews, and Americans that defined postwar western Germany.[2] Moreover, those categories themselves were ambiguous and fluid; a significant distinct group among the American occupiers were American Jews, chaplains, officers, and GIs and employees of Jewish relief agencies, notably the American Jewish Joint Distribution Committee (JDC or Joint). To further complicate the categories, some of these victors, in turn, were themselves European, mostly German and Austrian, Jewish refugees who had only recently emigrated and acquired U.S. citizenship through their army service.

In the liminal period 1945 to 1949, before the establishment of the two postwar German states, Germans and Jews lived, as is often remarked, in different worlds on the same terrain, divided by memory and experience. But, regulated and observed by their occupiers, they also continually interacted, as they negotiated daily life and contested issues of relative victimization, guilt, and responsibility, commemoration, reparations, and a possible future for Jews in post-Nazi Germany. In this article I am interested in examining these complicated and yet commonplace encounters, with a particular focus on gendered experiences of sexuality and reproduction. By 1946–47, Jewish survivors residing among Germans in the land, now defeated and occupied, which had launched the extermination of European Jewry were marrying and producing babies in record numbers; they had, at a "rough estimate," a birth rate "higher than that of any other population" in the world.[3] I will suggest that in the years immediately following the war, Jews perceived their always (in various and sometimes unexpected ways) hierarchical interactions and confrontations with Germans and Americans, including especially those related to sex, pregnancy, and childbirth, as a means of resignifying their lives after the catastrophe of the Holocaust, indeed as a certain kind of revenge as well as "life reborn."

The existence of displaced persons and the "DP problem" in postwar

Europe are certainly not new topics for historians. Yet it has been, I think, particularly difficult to chronicle or understand adequately the Jewish experience in occupied Germany during the "DP years" from 1945 to 1949. For both scholars and survivors, the transitional years as displaced persons have generally been bracketed and overshadowed by the preceding tragic drama of war and Holocaust and the subsequent establishment of the state of Israel and other new communities outside Europe. Moreover, the history of the Jewish DPs, like perhaps that of any community which had endured overwhelming losses and lived in transit, was not only their own but that of many other interested parties. It involved Allied occupation policy and its trajectory from unconditional surrender and denazification to Cold War anti-Communism and cooperative reconstruction in western Germany; British policy toward Palestine; U.S. policy on immigration in general and American Jewish pressures in particular; Zionist demands and actions to deliver Jews to Palestine for the establishment of a Jewish state; the politics of the Soviet Union and the newly Communist Eastern European nations from which many of the survivors came; the emerging mandates of the United Nations and the international relief organizations; and finally the varied experience of the by no means monolithic Jewish survivor population itself.

The problem is certainly not one of available sources. As with any "administered group," subject to large bureaucracies like armies and relief organizations, DP life was methodically and voluminously documented. But despite a recent proliferation of publications, conferences, films, and exhibitions, pushed in large part by the efforts of the baby-boom "second generation" born to the DPs, we are just beginning to think about their social (rather than political) history. There has been very little reflection—from either side—on the interactions, the encounters and confrontations between surviving Jews and defeated Germans, or for that matter on relations between German Jewish and DP survivors. Researchers have also not adequately addressed the crucial fact—and what it meant for Jewish DP perceptions of their German surroundings—that the majority of Jewish survivors in Germany had actually spent a good part of the war years as refugees in the Soviet Union and not under Nazi occupation. General postwar German history has mostly ignored the presence of living Jews; their story has been told as one of absence, tragic loss, and memorialization. Histories of Jewish survivors in Germany, and there are more and more, have generally treated them as a self-enclosed collective—*She'erit Hapletah*, the saved remnant—coexisting temporarily and separately from Germans, in a kind of extraterritorial enclave.[4] An extensive Israeli historiography has presented DPs and Jewish survivors as part of the contested history of Zionism and the state.[5]

Studies of American policies toward DPs have tended to focus on the negative aspects of American policy, initially laid out in former immigration commissioner Earl G. Harrison's August 1945 fiercely critical report on Military

Government policy toward survivors, which denounced their continued detention behind barbed wire and famously (and hyperbolically) concluded that "we appear to be treating the Jews as the Nazis treated them except that we do not exterminate them."[6] Harrison's report was reinforced by the horrified and furious reports American Jewish GIs sent home to their families and congregations. Often instigated by the passionate holiday sermons of army chaplains, their letters described the bedraggled survivors and their perceived neglect by the U.S. military and (at least initially) American Jewish aid organizations.[7] Understandably, historians have drawn attention both to American antisemitism and to U.S. Military Government tolerance for German hostility toward DPs, especially as it increased in the later years of the occupation.[8]

These are all important approaches, but contemporary accounts and records as well as memoirs and oral histories read "against the grain" can also present a rather different picture of complicated and close connections, and regular interactions, not only between Jews and Germans but also between surviving Jews and their American keepers and protectors. Ironically, it often seemed, both to Germans and to American Military Government, that Jews in post-Nazi Germany were more present than ever before, increasing in numbers and demands daily; populating the black-market bazaars, demonstrating loudly and sometimes violently for emigration permits, even outnumbering defeated Germans in small towns in Bavaria and Hesse. Survivors who had expected to be treated as allies, not troublesome refugees, by the occupiers vociferously protested the injustice of their plight, bitter that their German victimizers were free in what remained, even under occupation, their own country, while Jews were confined in DP camps waiting to leave "bloodied cursed" German soil.

As the memory of liberation, with its horrific images of Nazi atrocities, faded, and the Cold War and German reconstruction proceeded, both victors and Germans came to see the victims of Nazism, still displaced and unruly, as inconvenient and disreputable disturbers of the peace. Germans, meanwhile, with their "clean German homes and pretty, accommodating German girls," styled themselves, and were increasingly recognized as, victims—of war, bombings, expulsions, and denazification—and soon as industrious partners and anti-Communist allies.[9] But it was also true, at least after Harrison's intervention and despite rapidly improving relations with the former enemy, that Jewish DPs did have a privileged relationship with the Allies. They "were on exhibit to visitors," including journalists, congressional delegations, and American Jewish groups, "from the moment of their liberation," and their leadership knew very well how to manipulate and stage these calls for better treatment and entry to Palestine. It was not an accident that the only department of the Central Committee of Liberated Jews with an English, not Yiddish, name was "Public Relations."[10]

Sullen (hands down the term most frequently used by the American victors to describe their former enemies), resentful, and self-pitying in defeat, Germans viewed the DP communities that sprang up in and around former *Wehrmacht* barracks, Nazi schools, and confiscated German housing blocks as a kind of *Schlaraffenland* (magic kingdom) of "sugar and spam, margarine and jam, plus cigarettes and vitamized chocolate bars," centers of black-market activity fed by easy access to the cigarette and food rations of the occupiers and Jewish relief organizations, notably the Joint.[11] In numerous towns and villages, such as Feldafing, near Munich, the locals, suddenly confronted with the presence of tattered and emaciated *KZ-niks* and then with a further influx from Eastern Europe, approached their new neighbors with, to quote one survivor's memoir, "a mixture of fear, contempt, and bewilderment." German resentment was fed by the Americans' initial quick requisitioning of homes and official buildings to house the survivors. In his Feldafing camp memoir, DP Simon Schochet describes, with both "bitter remorse" and satisfaction, the dismantling of a "glorious Bechstein" grand piano that was sent plunging down the villa stairs to make room for beds and lockers, and to this day, Feldafingers remember General Eisenhower in 1945 strolling through their picturesque lakeside town, pointing out villas for confiscation.[12] General Eisenhower's visit to the Bismarck Strasse DP housing block in Stuttgart, on the same day in September 1945 that he, together with other American top brass (including General Patton), attended Yom Kippur services in Feldafing, signaled initial American support for these takeovers and solidarity with Jewish victims. Germans still recount their outrage at the DPs' less than gentle treatment of still elegant and well-stocked furnishings, gardens, and houses. Especially in the early period from summer through fall 1945 and in areas with many DPs, Germans were shocked that the conquerors (the invading Americans had no ambition to be welcomed as liberators), to whom they always insisted that they had never been Nazis, forced them to clear out their homes, sometimes within hours, to make room for scruffy refugees from Eastern Europe.[13]

Even later, as American occupation and denazification became steadily gentler, and Jews complained about both harsh treatment by U.S. troops and inadequate and patronizing relief efforts by the Joint, U.S. army rabbis, working with local Military Government officials, requisitioned German institutions and housing blocks to make room for the increasing flow of Jews from Eastern Europe. Relieved of their initial anxieties about violent revenge by their former victims, Germans now faced, as Jewish observers saw it, "another kind of fear, fear lest the few tens of thousands of Jews remain where they are. The Germans and Austrians are afraid that their countries, made *judenrein* by the Nazis, may again be 'flooded' by Jews from the East." In the reversals characteristic of the time, it was now the Jews who were seen as the villains. "The guilt of the Germans was forgotten. The Jewish DPs are looked upon as intruders, the Germans as the autochthonic population suffering from the plague of DPs."[14]

Fortified by their initial alliances with the American victors, survivors also made their presence known when they identified and brought to (usually temporary) official or lynch justice guards, *Kapos,* and other collaborators they recognized on the street or in other public places; sometimes they deliberately sought to hunt them down. Indeed, rather than producing awareness of Germany's crimes, the survivors' very obvious presence—their astonishingly rapid (at least superficial) physical recovery, and their entrepreneurship in black-market commerce—not only produced resentment and competition for Allied favors, but also served to reinforce doubt about the Allies' insistence in denazification programs that the Germans had murdered millions of Jews. Such sentiments could be summarized as "if there really were so many death camps, then why are there so many Jews around and why do they look so healthy and well-dressed and have so many children?" The fact that within a year of war's end, Jewish DP camps were crowded with "infiltrees" from newly Communist Poland, most of whom had survived the war years in the Soviet Union rather than under Nazi occupation and who could now be labeled as fleeing Communism rather than Nazism, only reinforced these perceptions. The survivors were indeed a disparate and traumatized group; many of them the last remaining members of their large prewar families, they spoke different languages, came from various nations, subscribed to different political beliefs and levels of religious observance, and had endured quite varied experiences during the war. Yet, to the surprise of both Americans and Germans, and in continual negotiation with, but also independent of, their fluctuating relationships with Germans, occupiers, and relief organizations (notably the Joint and UNRRA, the United Nations Relief and Rehabilitation Administration), Jewish DPs in occupied Germany, centered on the large camps near Munich and Frankfurt from 1945 to 1949, generated a unique transitory society; simultaneously a final efflorescence of a destroyed Eastern European Jewish culture, a preparation for an imagined future in *Eretz Israel,* and a "waiting room" in which new lives were indeed—against all odds—begun. From a ragged and exhausted group of displaced persons there emerged over several years a new Jewish collectivity, which named itself the *She'erit Hapletah* (surviving remnant, or, more literally, left-over remnant of a remnant), looked forward to the establishment of new homes and new families, and engaged with its unlikely and unloved German environment.

At the same time, the small but significant German Jewish presence, especially in Berlin, should not be overlooked.[15] German Jews, both those who had remained and those who returned (often only temporarily), were crucial to Allied administration and the divided former capital's aura of rapid revival. In contrast to the reluctant reception of Polish Jewish infiltrees for whom the city became an important entry point to the American zone, the return of

Berlin Jews, such as the "homecoming" of well-known stage and screen stars, the return of the only Jewish child from Berlin to survive Auschwitz, or the repatriation in 1947 of 295 Berliners from Shanghai, was celebrated with some fanfare by occupation and municipal authorities. The tentative but remarkably rapid restoration of peaceful civil society, first by the Soviet military administration and then by the other three victor powers, was marked by events with a specifically Jewish component. Surviving Jews were often deployed as instant public officials and the showcasing of a Jewish aspect was virtually de rigueur for early Allied licensed cultural activities. Among the first signs of Berlin's resurgence from the rubble were command performances of *Nathan the Wise* and what one somewhat cynical cultural officer called the "unavoidable" Mendelssohn compositions.[16]

This regime of German Jewish culture was certainly encouraged by an open secret of the occupation (and still a relatively untold story): that many if not most of the cultural officers in the four occupying armies were themselves former German Jews.[17] During the brief early postwar period, all these quite different groups of Jews staked out a public presence which not only would have been unimaginable before May 1945 but has been, until recently, largely forgotten. The intensity of the early debates about identity, memories of the very recent past, and relative guilt and victimization was fueled by their attachment to concrete questions of livelihood, money, property, privileges, and compensation, and by the engagement of provocatively present and alive Jews. Germans and Jews under Allied, especially American, occupation continually negotiated and contested issues of everyday life: from the most urgent needs for food, clothing, and housing to the reparation of bank accounts and property. *Wiedergutmachung* was immediately on the agenda and the determination to extract monetary compensation was inextricably linked to the memorialization of the dead and revenge for horrors suffered, and produced the inevitable resentments.

Clearly, also, attitudes changed over time, and Germans were certainly influenced by the shifting responses of their American occupiers: from the sympathetic shock of liberation to frantic irritation at the mass influx of 1946–47 combined with enthusiastic or reluctant admiration, especially for Zionist commitments (which not incidentally promised to relieve Americans of having to worry about large-scale Jewish immigration), and finally the well-known disdain for the "hard core" of about fifteen thousand DPs who had either integrated into German economic life (generally via the black market) or were simply too sick or exhausted to move, and therefore remained after 1948–49. But the basic themes of interaction—a difficult but ever-present connection mediated and regulated by Americans, both Jewish and gentile, who were themselves continually negotiating their relationships with both Germans and Jews—can be traced through the whole period 1945 to 1949, setting the stage also for later German-Jewish relations in the Federal Republic.

II

Most improbably, perhaps, the remarkable baby boom among the youthful survivors, along with a purported "hypersexuality" which both impressed and appalled observers, provided the occasion for multiple encounters and interactions with Germans and the point at which gender became most salient. It is crucial to keep in mind that this explosion in births and marriages, and in Jewish life in general, did not simply go on behind the—in any case porous—gates of the DP camps, unnoticed by Germans. Nor was Jewish interaction with Germans limited to the oft-cited arenas of black- (or grey-) marketeering or management of bars and cafes catering to GIs and their *Fräuleins* (and prostitutes), although all those arenas were certainly important.[18]

Jews gave birth in German hospitals, where they were attended by German physicians and nurses. Jews hired German women as housekeepers and nannies. In fact, DP camp medical records indicate that virtually all young Jewish mothers—exhausted, inexperienced, and bereft of the support traditionally provided by mothers, sisters, and other relatives—were assigned a German baby "nurse" from the surrounding camps and villages, paid and employed by UNRRA and the camp administration. Applications for such assistance invariably included a formal certificate of medical necessity from a (nearly always German) physician, and these certificates were notable for their peculiar combination of medicalized terminology, sympathy, and (if one reads between the lines) a touch of contempt for young mothers unable or apparently unwilling to care for their own children. Doctors sometimes hedged their diagnoses of severe postpartum complications with a dubious "she claims . . . " (*sie gibt an*). Or they seemed to deem poor housekeeping an indication of pathology, noting, for example, "an extreme state of nervous exhaustion that makes it impossible for the patient to do her housework in addition to caring for her child. She urgently requires a baby nurse."[19]

The applications from the Jewish DPs themselves, both women and men, express a quite different complicated jumble of need, anxiety—and entitlement. A typical request to the Feldafing camp administration health department on 6 May 1947 read (in German), "I ask for a permit for a nurse for the care of my five-month-old child. Since my wife is still sick, as can be seen from the enclosed affidavit, and cannot take care of the child, I ask most sincerely that my request be granted, especially since the infant is also very weak." A day later, another Feldafinger sought "permission to engage a German maid. My reason is that I have a child of eleven months and also work as custodian [in an interesting continuity of language, the term used was

Blockverwalter] of the Villa Andrea. I also intend to employ the German (*die Deutsche*) for clean-up duties in the kitchen of the villa."[20] The requests, by young mothers, or sometimes by husbands whose wives were either ill or themselves employed, were painfully honest about how unprepared for parenthood and painfully alone many men and women felt, even in the middle of a crowded camp: "As you surely know, I am busy all day as a building manager (*Hausverwalter*) so that my wife is totally alone and since she has not a clue (*keine Ahnung*) about childcare, I need . . . help."[21]

These applications document, therefore, not only Jewish claims on German labor and service, but also the very real exhaustion and ill health of the survivors, belying their generally healthy appearance. Jews, whose survival had so often depended on their work capacity, could now use their very lack of it as a lever for gaining the assistance of Germans in performing their daily chores. It also enabled them to meet demands by camp administrators for levels of hygiene and cleanliness that were unrealistically high for a refugee population housed in overcrowded and temporary quarters. In a complicated multivocal (and medicalized) transaction, Jews, legitimated and regulated by their own camp authorities and certified by mostly German physicians, constructed themselves as needy victims in order to gain the benefits of service from Germans (who in turn thought of themselves as victims!). A German *Pflegerin* or *Bedienerin* (servant) was one of the odd privileges of survivor status in postwar Germany.

German women, for their part, often themselves raising children alone, were pleased to secure a job with a salary and health benefits as well as access to black-market goods. At the same time they were acutely aware that Jews, now under the protection of the Americans and the Joint, "could now play the masters" (*haben schon die Herrschaften gespielt*). Jewish women were simultaneously pleased to be able to demonstrate (in the words of a German woman who registered those births in Feldafing near Munich) that they "could afford such services" (*konnten sich die leisten*),[22] and anxious for advice and help with their precarious "life reborn" (*Leben aufs Neu*). In the aftermath of a Nazi Final Solution that had specifically targeted pregnant women, mothers, and young children for immediate and automatic extermination, childbearing was desperately overdetermined and Jewish survivors had little compunction about hiring the most competent help or insisting that a sick baby be seen by the best *Herr Dr. Professor* at the University of Munich or Frankfurt, his record during the war notwithstanding.

On both sides, it seems, the immediate larger past was silenced (*völlig totgeschwiegen*, wrapped in deathly silence) in favor of an explicitly temporary but mutually advantageous interaction. These complicated but ubiquitous—and highly pragmatic—relationships which developed between German and Jewish women so quickly and apparently harmoniously after liberation and the defeat of Nazi Germany—about something as intimate as infant care—

require much further research and analysis and may only be accessible via oral history, with all of the difficulties (and pressures of passing time) inherent in that approach. Trying to make initial sense of these everyday experiences, I found myself frustrated by the absence of serious analysis by historians. The trauma analysis that has been so important in Holocaust studies has been characterized by an overemphasis on memory and literary narrative and a concomitant neglect of the seemingly mundane and quotidian (i.e., "non-traumatic"). To understand the everyday I turned therefore to anthropology (rather than, for example, the more obvious fields of psychology or psycho-analysis).[23] In his study "Reconciliation after Ethnic Cleansing," looking at contemporary conflicts, John Borneman posits that "two common attempts to recuperate" after traumatic violent loss involve "physical reproduction and revenge."[24]

Certainly, both elements are present and highly politicized in the story I am telling about Jewish-German interactions. Indeed, in glaring contrast to German figures, not only was the Jewish birth rate extremely high, the infant mortality rate of this traumatized refugee population was "phenomenal[ly] low."[25] With many German men of marriageable age lost in battle or still held in prisoner-of-war camps, these demographic differences—another aspect of the perceived privileged status of DPs—were certainly not lost on German officials. They bemoaned "the horrific bloodletting that the German *Volk* has suffered during the last war" (*Der furchtbare Aderlass, den das deutsche Volk durch den letzten Krieg erlitten hat*) and noted with concern and clear envy "the unusually great marriage- and birth-willingness of foreigners (*Ausländer*) living in Germany" (*die ungewöhnlich grosse Heirats- und Geburtenfreudigkeit*).[26]

In fact, this perceived flood of Jewish babies reflected not only a post-1945 boom in births, but also the influx of Jews who had survived in the Soviet Union, had returned to Eastern Europe after the war, and were now fleeing westward with their relatively intact families. In 1946 the Joint dramatically reported that "nearly one third of the Jewish women in the zone between 18 and 45 were either expectant mothers or had new-born babies." But it is impossible to know whether those infants had been conceived in the DP camps or conceived or born on the trek west from Poland, or even while still in the Soviet Union.[27] Nonetheless, Germans, Jews, and Americans observing DP life made repeated references to camps filled with pregnant women and new-borns. Taken in conjunction with the emphasis placed by the survivors themselves on showcasing their new offspring, it does seem that we are dealing with an extraordinary demographic phenomenon.

Indeed, demographic research on the impact of the Holocaust on European Jewry has confirmed that the "wave of Jewish births immediately after the second World War," while certainly part of a "baby boom in all the developed countries" (albeit delayed among Germans by war casualties and the slow return of prisoners of war), reflected a particularly conspicuous trend among Holocaust survivors "who sought to reconstitute truncated families and who comprised relatively high numbers of adults of reproductive age." They were compensating for the "drastic reduction of Jewish births" that would have otherwise been expected to occur by "natural increase" during the years that had been lost to war and genocide. Actually, the short-lived intense postwar baby boom represented a definite spike even in what had been "normal" pre-war rates, which had already began to drop rather precipitously even in prewar Poland. Nor would the high birth rates persist, relatively quickly yielding to the continued overall twentieth-century tendency toward fertility declines in the West.[28] In that sense, the DP baby boom was an exceptional development for European Jews, and can be understood as a specific conscious and direct response to the catastrophic losses of the Holocaust.

In Borneman's view, and indeed, that of many contemporary observers, this leap into "compulsive reproduction"—usually, as was the case with the Jewish DPs, in endogamous marriages born of deep distrust of outsiders—not only denied the time necessary for losses to be mourned but carried the danger that children born of despair would be burdened by the trauma of loss and possibly perpetuate the cycle of violence. But he also suggests that a "departure from violence" does not require common long-term visions but simply the sharing of "a present, a present that is nonrepetitive." Reflecting on daily life in Feldafing, Simon Schochet stressed the "transient aspect of our lives" and insisted that "when we do strike up an acquaintance with a German, we do so safe in the knowledge that he is but a temporary acquaintance who in time will be separated from us, much to the relief of both parties involved."[29] It is significant, for example—and an indication of the limits to the personal connections between German and Jewish women—that interactions in childcare did not extend to the intimate activity of breastfeeding. Jewish women sought out Jewish *Milchschwestern* (nursing sisters) if they did not have enough milk, a relatively easy task since so many women were pregnant or had infants at the same time.[30]

Borneman goes on to argue, however, that this transient present also requires "new relations of affinity marked not by cyclical violence but by trust and care." The Jewish baby boom in occupied Germany certainly fits in many ways his negative criteria for "compulsive reproduction" and the instrumentalization of women as mothers in the wake of ethnic catastrophe. Yet it also created precisely those relationships between Germans and Jews, notably between mothers and their nannies, which required a certain amount of the "trust and care" Borneman imagines as necessary, if not for reconciliation, at least for a "departure from violence" and active hatred, even or especially if they were time-limited.[31]

In this case, I would argue, reproduction served both as symbolic revenge and as occasion for contact. Every day, DP mothers crisscrossed the streets of

German towns with their baby carriages; they veritably "paraded their babies," Meyer Levin remarked.[32] The many Jewish marriages and births in the DP camps were registered in the German *Standesämter* (marriage bureaus). Sleepy Bavarian population registry offices (*Einwohnermeldeämter*) were staggered by the stream of Jewish DPs—as many as fifteen daily—who suddenly appeared, offering their rations of American cigarettes in exchange for official certificates registering marriages and births.

III

There were also numerous opportunities for other encounters and interactions, among women, among men, and between women and men: on the soccer field where DP and German teams faced off (sometimes an especially good Jewish player was recruited by a German *Verein*), in the village cafés, bars, and cheap *Varieté* dancehalls run by Jewish DPs, or when the local youth snuck into the DP camps to watch American movies not yet available to Germans. Local bands played at the many weddings celebrated in the DP camps. Even though the camps were officially off limits, Germans with permits (*Lagerausweise*)—which required medical, if not political, clearance—entered daily, not only as baby nurses, but as cleaning women, skilled workers, teachers, and doctors. DP camp functionaries employed German secretaries, virtually a necessity at a time when all official communiqués had to be in German (and often translated into English as well for the military government). One artifact, both poignant and bizarre, of the regular contact between Jewish camp residents and German employees was the formal but—it would seem—heartfelt greeting sent by the German staff in Feldafing for Rosh Hashonah 1947: "We as your more distant co-workers nonetheless know very well what sorrows and burdens rest on your shoulders. We partake of your fate and want to stress again our openness to further productive cooperation." More than five hundred young DPs attended German universities, especially in technical fields like medicine and engineering.[33] So-called "free livers" (maybe 20 percent) chose to live in German towns and cities outside the camps, freed of UNRRA controls but still supported by the Joint. Numerous DPs maintained outside apartments but also remained registered in the camps, not only to qualify for rations (and swell the camp allotments) but to provide a safe place to return to in case of trouble.

Of course, Germans, too, benefited from the black and grey markets operated by DPs, which could provide otherwise unavailable goods in the seemingly exotic bazaars of the *Möll Strasse* in Munich, or *Schlachtensee* and *Hermannplatz* in Berlin. In certain parts of Germany, Jewish DPs were an integral part of the social and commercial landscape. Trolley car no. 12, which traveled through Munich Bogenhausen to the Jewish agency offices in the *Siebert Strasse* or shops on *Möll Strasse,* was dubbed the Palestine Express. On

Fridays, in Feldafing and in other small towns in the American zone, Jewish women would take over the local bakery, exchanging their strange white flour rations (*Amerikanerbrot*) for the use of ovens to prepare challah for Shabbat. For any number of goods and services they traded the chic jackets that the skilled tailors in camp workshops produced, much more elegant than anything the German women had seen in years. Furthermore, Jewish men, who found themselves in surplus as a result of the approximately 60/40 sex ratio among Jewish survivors, dated, had sex with, and even (in a stigmatized minority of cases) married German women. By 1950, at least a thousand such marriages had been registered. Surely there were many more relationships, as we know from records of bitter debates within the camps and even prosecutions by DP tribunals.[34] Relations between Jewish men and German women remained a painfully contentious issue for survivors long after the Allied military had given up trying to enforce anti-fraternization regulations for their troops and the German *Fräuleins*. The problem had two distinct aspects. On the one hand, most of the remaining German Jews owed their survival to "Aryan" spouses. Reemergent Jewish congregations had to negotiate their policies in regard to the participation of non-Jewish spouses. On the other hand, there were the generally illicit relationships between DPs and German women. As a male survivor ruefully recalled, even though German women had "gained a reputation for easy virtue and are held in contempt by the group," they were "as a whole . . . more physically attractive than the refugee women, if only for the reason that they did not live under such bestial conditions." He acknowledged that while most such relationships were motivated by "a mixture of revenge and the desire to taste the forbidden fruit," there were also "singular cases" of "deep reciprocal feelings" in which "the answer would simply have to be that a man and woman met and fell in love."[35]

The much-photographed parades of baby carriages proudly steered by DP parents were intended as conscious displays of self-assertion, for themselves and also for others, and in other ways so were the liaisons between Jewish men and German women or the use of German labor. Such displays clearly communicated the politics of "we are here" not only to politicians debating Palestine and immigration policy and to relief organizers adjudicating rations and housing, but to German citizens confronted with their discomfiting former victims. Jewish survivors in Germany, it should be stressed, did not see their presence on that "cursed soil" only—as we tend to do today—as a perverse historical "irony" but also as a kind of justice and "payback," even "revenge."

The Germans, Jews contended, owed them their space, their former barracks and estates, their rations, and their services. There was a kind of "in your face" quality to Jewish mothers' brandishing of their babies, just as there was to the banners flying from former German official buildings and the posters carried in processions and parades through German towns. There was pleasure in rousing a village baker and insisting that he bake challah for Shabbat, or ordering a grocer to supply pounds of herring for a holiday feast. As another survivor bluntly recalled, "Revenge did not mean only killing Germans. We had revenge when we saw the Germans acting as hewers of wood and drawers of water . . . when we saw them cleaning Jewish houses, the Jewish school I attended, buying cigarettes and paying for them in gold—gold that had undoubtedly been taken from Jews. We sold them bread and coffee and they gave everything they had . . . Revenge also meant living with German women."[36]

One of the most striking features of the DPs' presence was the calculated appropriation of former Nazi "shrines" and German space for their own practical and symbolic purposes. Representatives from the first conference of liberated Jews, in July 1945, chose to announce their demand for open emigration to Palestine in the Munich Brau Keller, from which Adolf Hitler had launched his 1923 attempted putsch. When Lucy Dawidowicz arrived in Munich in fall 1946 as a Joint worker in U.S. uniform, she found that the Hofbräuhaus had been converted into a "Red Cross center where you could get hot dogs, ice cream sodas, and other American fare";[37] others praised the "excellent beer."[38] And when the Central Committee of Liberated Jews of Bavaria moved into a "bombed out floor" of the Deutsches Museum in Munich, U.S. Military Government lawyer Abraham Hyman pointed out with a certain amount of glee that "Hitler once prophesied that the time would come when a person would have to go to a museum to find a Jew."[39] In August 1945, a German Jewish private in the Jewish Brigade described arriving at Berchtesgaden, "the holiest [shrine] of German National Socialism," to be greeted by an American sentry with a hearty "*scholem Aleichem.*" Adolf Hitler, he concluded, must have "turned over in his grave or scratched his head somewhere in Argentina."[40] Examples of such resignifying abound; perhaps the most famous was the *Streicherhof,* a socialist Zionist kibbutz on the former estate of the notorious Bavarian *Gauleiter.* It "became a prime attraction for journalists and others," where "[a]ll the visitors were treated to the experience of seeing the dogs on the farm respond to Hebrew names that the trainees had taught them, as their salute to Streicher."[41]

While historians have had little problem recognizing such public actions as "symbolic revenge," they have generally not problematized interactions involving childbearing or sexuality in such terms, situating them rather as "personal" responses on an individual or familial level, naturally linked to the effort to restore a sort of normality to traumatized, disrupted lives.[42] Attention to the histories and memories of everyday life, however, clearly indicates that for Jews, these "personal" experiences, and the interactions with Germans they provoked, were also part of this fraught and defiant resignifying. Their everyday lives demonstrated that while they did insist on documenting and memorializing the catastrophe—establishing a historical commission, collecting eyewitness accounts—they did not dwell obsessively on the traumatic past. Survivors were keenly aware of their role as guardians of memory and eyewitness to the indescribable but also of the obligation, often repeated, to "find revenge in existence."[43]

Observers were often astonished by the "incredible self-restraint" Jews practiced toward Germans, impressed, relieved, and suspicious that they did not "tear them limb from limb."[44] Despite some dramatic incidents and plans, such as assassinations of SS men, the aborted well-poisoning scheme linked to Abba Kovner, and an only minimally successful plan to taint the bread supply of an American POW camp near Nuremberg in 1946 which resulted in the (non-lethal) sickening of some two hundred SS and Gestapo prisoners, there were few real efforts at large-scale revenge, a reflection of survivors' painful awareness that in the face of genocide there could be no adequate retribution.[45] The evidence is actually quite varied and contradictory. On the one hand, Jews, exhausted and bitter, insisted that they lived in a separate extraterritorial universe, not even wanting to engage with Germans enough to violate them. Indeed, philosopher Susan Brison has recently reflected, in her book on the aftermath of a brutal sexual assault, that survivors of trauma may not want to risk anger because to do so requires a certain level of engagement with and "proximity" to one's violator.[46] On the other hand, there were violent confrontations, and Military Government officials groused that "they love getting into fights with Germans"[47]—this was definitely a population with a chip on its shoulder. Finally (on the third, least examined hand), we have the countless everyday instances of matter-of-fact, even friendly, interaction, fixed in the present moment, apparently heedless of the recent past and denying that there would be any shared future.

Jews had contempt for the oblivious self-pity of defeated Germans but also had to confront the reality that, as one survivor told a German researcher, "on an individual basis it was very hard to hate them once you knew a person and faced them and you lived with them in the same apartment. . . . It was different when you knew someone."[48] Writing in both the Yiddish *Landsberger Lager Cajtung* and in the German-language *Die jüdische Rundschau*, DP leader Samuel Gringauz bitterly formulated his farewell to Western enlightenment culture:

We do not believe in progress . . . we do not believe in the two-thousand-year-old Christian culture of the West, the culture that, *for them,* created the Statue of Liberty in New York and Westminster Abbey on the Thames, the wonder gardens of Versailles and the Uffizi and Pitti palaces in Florence, the Strassbourg *Münster* and the Cologne cathedral; but *for us,* the slaughters of the Crusades, the Spanish Inquisition, the blood bath of Khmielniki, the pogroms of Russia, the gas chambers of Auschwitz and the massacres of entire Europe.[49]

The ideology of the *She'erit Hapletah* turned away from Germany and from Europe. But in fact, in the years right after the war, Germans and Jews did, indeed, know each other and come face to face in daily life. A British officer who was a German Jew reported back to friends in Palestine in 1946,

> "I hate the Germans" is a common expression. "I can't stand to look at them, I could kill them all in cold blood." But when the conversation continues, it becomes evident that one is speaking about "my friend Schmidt" and "our dear neighbors, the Müllers," because, after all, even the biggest hater cannot live in total loneliness if he is compelled to continue to live at the sites of his tortures (*Orte der Qual*).[50]

Revenge—and the word comes up a lot—meant proving that there was a future. This future was envisioned in terms of both the establishment of a Jewish state in Palestine ("a kind of magic word" which, as an American reporter astutely noted, "might be anywhere they could live freely," a "never-never utopia"[51] where they would be peaceful, safe, and above all amongst themselves) and the birth of babies and the formation of new families. In a sermon on 17 September 1945, the first Yom Kippur after liberation, Gringauz exhorted the survivors, especially the young, "the carriers of our revenge," "You must show the world that we live. You must create and build, dance and sing, be happy and live, live and work."[52] But on an immediate level, revenge as well as recovery also encompassed the careful calibration and negotiation of pragmatic contact with, and distance from, Germans, always, to be sure, in the context of a perhaps disapproving but nevertheless protective Allied presence.

The personal and the political of survival were linked: in the birthing of babies, the social glue of fervent Zionism which dominated the fractious political life in the DP camps, and the pursuit of everyday life. That this *Leben aufs Neu* should develop on German territory surrounded by, and in interaction with, defeated and occupied Germans was, I would argue, seen by the DP survivors not only as a great irony of history, but somehow also as just and appropriate. We might want to examine further how and why that brief but intense history—both joint and separate—has been so assiduously forgotten by both Germans and Jews.

Notes

Research for this article was supported by grants from the National Endowment for the Humanities, the American Council of Learned Societies, and the German Marshall Fund, as well as residencies at the American Academy in Berlin and the Remarque Institute at New York University. I am grateful for comments and criticism from the German Women's History Group, New York City; the conference "German

History from the Margins," University of Southampton, September 2002; and a host of other seminars and conferences.

1. Statistical data is inexact and bewildering, largely because of change over time, inconsistencies in categorizations among those collecting data, and the difficulties of counting a highly mobile and sometimes illegal population. In November 1946, the American Joint Distribution Committee reported 145,735 Jewish DPs officially registered in the American zone, 101,614 in DP camps, 35,950 "free-living" in German towns and cities, 4313 in children's homes, and 3858 in *Hachscharah* (agricultural kibbutzim). Current estimates are considerably higher. Most sources now agree that by spring 1947, the Jewish DP population in Germany was approximately two hundred thousand, but "some 300,000 Jewish DPs and refugees are believed to have passed through Austria and/or Germany for longer or shorter periods of time." For the latter figure and a succinct summary of the estimates, see Hagit Lavsky, *New Beginnings: Holocaust Survivors in Bergen-Belsen and the British Zone in Germany, 1945–1950* (Detroit, Mich.: Wayne State University Press, 2002), 34, 27–36. Yosef Grodzinsky, *In the Shadow of the Holocaust: The Struggle between Jews and Zionists in the Aftermath of World War Two* (Monroe, Maine: Common Coverage Press, 2004) (revised version of *Human Material of Good Quality* [in Hebrew] [Tel Aviv: Hed Artsi, 1988]), has figures in a similar range: an estimated 70,000 in late summer 1945, 220–260,000 Jewish DPs altogether at the height of Jewish flight west in late 1946, and 245,000 in summer 1947. However, by looking at migration patterns to target countries (rather than trying to establish figures in Europe) he comes to an even higher total of 330,000 Jewish DPs altogether between 1945 and 1951. The higher figures for 1946 and 1947 include the influx into the American zone of mostly Polish Jews who had been repatriated from the Soviet Union, and a later wave in 1947 from Czechoslovakia, Hungary, and Rumania. Given the conflicts with British authorities over immigration to Palestine and recognition of Jews as a special separate group, those "infiltrees" were steered to, or themselves migrated to, the U.S. zone.

2. Frank Stern, "The Historic Triangle: Occupiers, Germans, and Jews in Postwar Germany," *Tel Aviver Jahrbuch für deutsche Geschichte* 19 (1990): 47–76.

3. See, among numerous other sources, Kurt R. Grossmann, *The Jewish DP Problem: Its Origin, Scope, and Liquidation*, with an introduction by Abraham S. Hyman (New York: Institute of Jewish Affairs, World Jewish Congress, 1951), 18–20.

4. There is a relatively new and constantly growing historical literature on Jewish survivors in Germany. See, for example, Michael Brenner, *After the Holocaust: Rebuilding Jewish Lives in Postwar Germany* (Princeton, N.J.: Princeton University Press, 1997); Susanne Dietrich and Julia Schulze Wessel, *Zwischen Selbstorganisation und Stigmatisierung: Die Lebenswirklichkeit jüdischer Displaced Persons und die neue Gestalt des Antisemitismus in der deutschen Nachkriegsgesellschaft* (Stuttgart: Klett-Cotta, 1998); Angelika Eder, *Flüchtige Heimat: Jüdische Displaced Persons in Landsberg am Lech, 1945 bis 1950* (Munich: UNI-Druck, 1998); Angelika Königseder, *Flucht nach Berlin: Jüdische Displaced Persons, 1945–1948* (Berlin: Metropol, 1998); Juliane Wetzel, *Jüdisches Leben in München, 1945–1951: Durchgangsstation oder Wiederaufbau?* (Munich: UNI-Druck, 1987); Angelika Königseder and Juliane Wetzel, *Waiting for Hope: Jewish Displaced Persons in Post–World War II Germany* (Evanston, Ill.: Northwestern University Press, 2001); Ruth Gay, *Safe among the Germans: Liberated Jews after World War II* (New Haven, Conn.: Yale University Press, 2002); and Eva Kolin-

sky, *After the Holocaust: Jewish Survivors in Germany after 1945* (London: Pimlico, 2004). A fine and diverse collection of articles can be found in Julius H. Schoeps, ed., *Leben im Land der Täter: Juden im Nachkriegsdeutschland (1945–1952)* (Berlin: Jüdische Verlagsanstalt, 2001). See also discussion and references in Atina Grossmann, "Victims, Villains, and Survivors: Gendered Perceptions and Self-Perceptions of Jewish Survivors in Postwar Germany," *Journal of the History of Sexuality* 11, nos. 1–2 (January–April 2002): 291–318.

5. Indeed, the liveliest (and most controversial) discussions about Jewish DPs have been conducted in the context of Israeli debates about the treatment of Holocaust survivors in Palestine and Israel and the general revision of the Zionist historiographical narrative. Much of this material is only slowly being translated from Hebrew. See the review essay by Yfaat Weiss, "Die Wiederkehr des Verdrängten: Das jüdische Siedlungsgebiet in Palästina (Jischuw) und die Holocaustüberlebenden in der israelischen Historiographie," *Babylon: Beiträge zur jüdischen Gegenwart* 18 (1998): 139–47; also Anita Shapira, "Politics and Collective Memory: The Debate over the 'New Historians' in Israel," *History and Memory* 7, no. 11 (spring–summer 1995): 9–40. In Hebrew, see, for example, Grodzinsky, *Human Material of Good Quality;* Arieh Kochavi, *Displaced Persons and International Politics* (Tel Aviv: Am Oved, 1992); David Engel, *Between Liberation and Flight: Holocaust Survivors in Poland and the Struggle for Leadership, 1944–1946* (Tel Aviv: Am Oved, 1996); and Irit Keynan, *Holocaust Survivors and the Emissaries from Eretz-Israel: Germany, 1945–1948* (Tel Aviv: Am Oved, 1996). In English, see Tuvia Friling, *Arrows in the Dark: David Ben-Gurion, the Yishuv Leadership, and Rescue Attempts during the Holocaust* (Madison: University of Wisconsin Press, 2003); Yisrael Gutman and Avital Saf, eds., *She'erit Hapletah, 1944–1948: Rehabilitation and Political Struggle; Proceedings of the Sixth Yad Vashem International Historical Conference* (Jerusalem: Yad Vashem, 1990); Tom Segev, *The Seventh Million: The Israelis and the Holocaust* (New York: Hill and Wang, 1993); Shabtai Teveth, *Ben Gurion and the Holocaust* (New York: Harcourt Brace, 1996); Idit Zertal, *From Catastrophe to Power: Holocaust Survivors and the Emergence of Israel* (Berkeley: University of California Press, 1998); Aviva Halamish, *The Exodus Affair: Holocaust Survivors and the Struggle for Palestine* (Syracuse, N.Y.: Syracuse University Press, 1998); Arieh J. Kochavi, *Post-Holocaust Politics: Britain, the United States, and Jewish Refugees, 1945–1948* (Chapel Hill: University of North Carolina Press, 2001); Grodzinsky, *In the Shadow;* and Hanna Yablonka, *Survivors of the Holocaust: Israel after the War* (Basingstoke: Macmillan, 1999). See, most importantly, Zeev Mankowitz's study *Life between Memory and Hope: The Survivors of the Holocaust in Occupied Germany* (Cambridge: Cambridge University Press, 2002); and, for the British zone, Lavsky, *New Beginnings.*

6. The full text of Harrison's report and Truman's response can be found online at http://www.ushmm.org/dp/politic6.htm. The text is also in the appendix to Leonard Dinnerstein, *America and the Survivors of the Holocaust* (New York: Columbia University Press, 1982), 292–304.

7. See the extraordinary collection of letters to families, rabbis, and Jewish organizations sent in summer and fall 1945, especially those sent in response to Rabbi Abraham Klausner's call at military high holiday services in Munich, September 1945. American Jewish Joint Distribution Committee Archives, New York, folders 399 and 399A.

8. See Dinnerstein, *America and the Survivors;* Mark Wyman, *DPs: Europe's Displaced Persons, 1945–1951* (Ithaca, N.Y.: Cornell University Press, 1998); and for a very critical view, Joseph W. Bendersky, *The Jewish Threat: Anti-Semitic Politics of the U.S. Army* (New York: Basic Books, 2000). For the perspective of a non-American historian, see, for example, Frank Stern, *The Whitewashing of the Yellow Badge: Antisemitism and Philosemitism in Postwar Germany* (Oxford: Pergamon, 1992).

9. Samuel Gringauz, "Our New German Policy and the DPs: Why Immediate Resettlement Is Imperative," *Commentary* 5 (1948): 510. See the recent debates about German suffering during the war, incited by texts by W. G. Sebald, *On the Natural History of Destruction* (New York: Random House, 2003); Günter Grass, *Crabwalk* (Orlando: Harcourt, 2002); and Jörg Friedrich, *Der Brand: Deutschland im Bombenkrieg, 1940–1945* (Munich: Propyläen Verlag, 2002). See also the review articles by Robert G. Moeller, "Sinking Ships, the Lost *Heimat,* and Broken Taboos: Günter Grass and the Politics of Memory in Contemporary Germany," *Contemporary European History* 12 (2003): 147–81, and "What Has 'Coming to Terms with the Past' Meant in Post–World War II Germany? From History to Memory to the 'History of Memory,'" *Central European History* 35, no. 2 (2002): 223–56; and Eric Langenbacher, "The Return of Memory: New Discussions about German Suffering in World War II," *German Politics and Society* 21, no. 3 (fall 2003): 74–88.

10. See Abraham S. Hyman, *The Undefeated* (Jerusalem: Gefen, 1993), 251. See also file 175, *Abt[eilung]* Public Relations, YIVO Archives, New York, Record Group 294.2, Displaced Persons Camps and Centers in Germany, Records, 1945–1952.

11. Kathryn Hulme, *The Wild Place* (Boston: Beacon, 1953), 211–12.

12. Simon Schochet, *Feldafing* (Vancouver: November House, 1983), 131, 22–23. The statement about memories is based on my interview of Frau U. Jaschinski, former employee of *Gemeindeverwaltung,* Feldafing, 12 February 2002. I am grateful to Frau Jaschinski for her openness and willingness to share her memories of the immediate postwar period and the encounter with Jewish DPs in Feldafing. See also Angelika Heider, "Das Lager für jüdische 'Displaced Persons' Feldafing in der amerikanischen Besatzungszone, 1945–1951" (M.A. thesis, Technische Universität Berlin, 1994).

13. See, for example, Dietrich and Wessel, *Zwischen Selbstorganisation und Stigmatisierung,* 47, 59.

14. Zorach Wahrhaftig, 27 November 1945, on "Life in camps 6 months after liberation," in *American Jewish Archives, Cincinnati: The Papers of the World Jewish Congress, 1945–1950; Liberation and the Saving Remnant,* ed. Abraham J. Peck, vol. 9 of *Archives of the Holocaust* (New York: Garland, 1990), 133–34.

15. For fuller discussion, with citations and bibliographic references, see Atina Grossmann, "Home and Displacement in a City of Bordercrossers: Jews in Berlin, 1945–1949," in *The Changing German/Jewish Symbiosis,* ed. Jack Zipes and Leslie Morris (New York: St. Martin's, 2002), 63–99.

16. See the reports in Brewster S. Chamberlin, *Kultur auf Trümmern* (Stuttgart: Deutsche Verlagsanstalt, 1979); the quotation is from Davidson Taylor, "Report on Trip to Berlin," July 20, 1945, 68. Emigré British officer Julius Posener also noted, "It was already a bit embarrassing [*Es war schon leicht peinlich*] that in the early days one could not hear a single concert in which there was not at least one Mendelssohn." Julius Posener, with afterword by Alan Posener, *In Deutschland, 1945 bis 1946* (Berlin: Siedler, 2002), 53.

17. Frank Stern has noted the significance of Jewish actors, directors, and themes in early Allied licensed cinema. Frank Stern, "The Culture of Dissent: Jewish Writers and Filmmakers and the Re-casting of Germany," paper presented at the meeting of the German Studies Association, Atlanta, October 1999. See also Wolfgang Schivelbusch's wonderful evocation of postwar Berlin, *In a Cold Crater: Cultural and Intellectual Life in Berlin, 1945-1948* (Berkeley: University of California Press, 1998).

18. For a fascinating discussion of the relationships that emerged in West German towns and villages among Germans, American occupiers (especially also African American GIs), and Polish Jewish DP bar owners, see Maria Höhn, *GIs and Fräuleins: The German-American Encounter in 1950s West Germany* (Chapel Hill: University of North Carolina Press, 2002).

19. See the medical affidavits and applications from Feldafing in YIVO Record Group 294.2, Displaced Persons Camps and Centers in Germany, Records, 1945-1952, files of Central Committee Health Department, record group 294.2, folders 402, 403, 410, 413.

20. Ibid., folder 402. This folder contains about 150 such applications, for May, June, and July 1947, submitted by DP camp residents and local physicians for German aides for pregnant or postpartum (and in some cases postabortus) Jewish women. These requests were often written in good German, suggesting that Yiddish-speaking DPs might have asked for help in formulating their applications.

21. Ibid., folder 410, Request for a *Gehilfsfrau*, n.d.

22. Quotations from interview with Frau U. Jaschinski.

23. The literature on trauma and the Holocaust is enormous. For one overview, see Cathy Caruth, ed., *Trauma: Explorations in Memory* (Baltimore, Md.: Johns Hopkins University Press, 1995). On the "fetishizing" of memory, see Marita Sturken, "The Remembering of Forgetting," *Social Text* 16, no. 4 (winter 1998): 102-25; for a critique of our fascination with (and confusion of) individual and collective trauma, see Pamela Ballinger, "The Culture of Survivors: Post Traumatic Stress Disorder and Traumatic Memory," *History and Memory* 10, no. 1 (spring 1988): 99-132. So far historians have either completely ignored these relationships between Jewish mothers and German nannies, mentioned them only in passing, or at best briefly acknowledged, but professed not to understand, them; for example, Dietrich and Schulze-Wessel, *Zwischen Selbstorganisation und Stigmatisierung*, 105, surmise a certain "satisfaction" (*Genugtuung*) but note that it "still seems hard to understand why Jewish DPs would entrust their children to, of all people, Germans" (*erscheint dennoch schwer nachvollziehbar, weshalb jüdische Dps ausgerechnet Deutschen ihre Kinder anvertrauten*).

24. John Borneman, "Reconciliation after Ethnic Cleansing: Listening, Retribution, Affiliation," *Public Culture* 14, no. 2 (May 2002): 282-83.

25. By 1948, the Jewish DP infant mortality rate stood at a "phenomenal low" of 5.3 per thousand live births. Grossmann, *The Jewish DP Problem*, 20. In 1946, for example, the birth rate in Bavaria was 29/1000 for Jews and only 7.35/1000 for Germans. See Wolfgang Jacobmeyer, "Jüdische Überlebende als 'Displaced Persons': Untersuchungen zur Besatzungspolitik in den deutschen Westzonen und zur Zuwanderung osteuropäischer Juden, 1945-1946," *Geschichte und Gesellschaft* 9 (1983): 437.

26. In 1946 in Bavaria, almost a tenth of all live births were to foreign displaced persons; the fertility rate for "foreign" women was two and a half times that of German women. See "Hinweise zu den Ergebnissen der ersten Ausländererhebung des

Bayer. Stat. Landesamtes vom 30 Juni 1948," in BayHStA, Staatskanzlei Akte 14890. (Interestingly, this report was composed by Fritz Burgdorfer, already well known as a *völkisch* nationalist population policy expert during the Weimar Republic who continued his work in the Third Reich and into the postwar Federal Republic.)

27. Quoted in Hyman, *The Undefeated*, 247. In January 1946, the Joint counted 120 children between one and five; in December 1946, 4,431. Not all these babies had been conceived in the DP camps; the high birthrate and numbers of children also reflected the many new arrivals from Poland who had survived with their families in the Soviet Union. In some cases, children who had been born in the Soviet Union were registered, for political or bureaucratic reasons, as having been born in Poland or in DP camps. See Joseph Berger's story in *Displaced Persons: Growing Up American after the Holocaust* (New York: Scribner, 2001), 276–81.

28. U. O. Schmelz, "The Demographic Impact of the Holocaust," in *Terms of Survival*, ed. Robert Wistrich (London; New York: Routledge, 1995), 44, 50.

29. Schochet, *Feldafing*, 160.

30. Personal conversation with Cilly Kugelmann, Berlin, spring 2002.

31. Borneman, "Reconciliation," 282.

32. Meyer Levin, *In Search: An Autobiography* (New York: Horizon, 1950), 398.

33. Ruth Klüger was exceptional in that she studied literature; see her memoir *Weiterleben: Eine Jugend* (Göttingen: Wallstein, 1992), 207–18; revised English version, *Still Alive: A Holocaust Girlhood Remembered* (New York: Feminist Press, 2001), 163–69. In January 1947, 570 Jewish students were enrolled in German universities; over a third were women. See, among numerous sources, Marie Syrkin, *The State of the Jews* (Washington, D.C.: New Republic Books, 1980), 31.

34. Figure from Nicholas Yantian, "Studien zum Selbstverständnis der jüdischen 'Displaced Persons' in Deutschland nach dem Zweiten Weltkrieg" (M.A. thesis, Berlin, 1994), 43. See also YIVO 294.1, Leo W. Schwarz Papers, file 548.

35. Schochet, *Feldafing*, 161–62.

36. Avraham Fuchs, quoted in Gutman and Saf, *She'erit Hapletah*, 532–33.

37. Lucy S. Dawidowicz, *From that Place and Time: A Memoir, 1938–1947* (New York: W. W. Norton, 1989), 283.

38. Pfc. Hans Lichtwitz, "Erlebnisse eines jüdischen Soldaten in Bayern und Oesterreich," *Aufbau*, 10 August 1945, 32.

39. Hyman, *Undefeated*, 75.

40. Lichtwitz, "Erlebnisse eines jüdischen Soldaten," 32.

41. Hyman, *Undefeated*, 35, 393.

42. For example, Mankowitz, *Life between Memory and Hope;* and Abraham J. Peck, "Jewish Survivors of the Holocaust in Germany: Revolutionary Vanguard or Remnants of a Destroyed People?" *Tel Aviver Jahrbuch für deutsche Geschichte* 19 (1990): 33–45.

43. For example, Dr. Samuel Gringauz in his Yom Kippur sermon at Landsberg DP camp on 17 September 1945, quoted in Hyman, *Undefeated*, 16–17.

44. For example, Ira A. Hirschmann, LaGuardia's inspector general for the UNRRA, in his passionate book *The Embers Still Burn: An Eye-Witness View of the Postwar Ferment in Europe and the Middle East and our Disastrous Get-Soft-with-Germany Policy* (New York: Simon and Schuster, 1949), 149, 45.

45. See Jim G. Tobias and Peter Zinke, *Nakam: Jüdische Rache an NS-Tätern* (Berlin: Aufbau, 2003).

46. Susan J. Brison, *Aftermath: Violence and the Remaking of a Self* (Princeton, N.J.: Princeton University Press, 2002), 13.

47. Oscar A. Mintzer, *In Defense of the Survivors: The Letters and Documents of Oscar A. Mintzer, AJDC Legal Advisor, Germany, 1945–46,* ed. Alex Grobman (Berkeley, Calif.: Judah L. Magnes Museum, 1999), 301.

48. Dietrich and Schulze-Wessel, *Zwischen Selbstorganisation und Stigmatisierung,* 311.

49. Quoted in Koppel S. Pinson, "Jewish Life in Liberated Germany: A Study of the Jewish DP's," *Jewish Social Studies* 9 (1947): 114.

50. Posener, *In Deutschland,* 144.

51. Bud Hutton and Andy Rooney, *Conquerors' Peace: A Report to the American Stockholders* (Garden City, N.Y.: Doubleday, 1947), 86.

52. Quoted in Hyman, *Undefeated,* 16–17.

Eleven

Afro-German Children and the Social Politics of Race after 1945

Heide Fehrenbach

I

This essay explores a formative yet understudied moment in the racial reconstruction of postfascist Germany: contemporary responses to the offspring of white German women and Allied soldiers of color after 1945. Four years of military occupation produced some ninety-four thousand occupation children. However, public attention rapidly fixed on a small subset, the so-called *Mischlinge*, or "mixed-bloods," distinguished from the others by their black paternity. Although they constituted a small minority of postwar German births—numbering only some five thousand by 1955—biracial children were invested with disproportionate symbolic significance by West German federal and state officials, social welfare workers, and the press. This essay surveys the extraordinary attention devoted to postwar *Mischlingskinder* from the occupation through the Adenauer years and argues that references to the children figured prominently in postwar reformulations of social policy regarding the regulation of female sexuality, abortion, adoption, and social integration, all of which had been profoundly racialized under the Nazi regime.

Postwar debates about "miscegenation" and *Mischlingskinder* were central to the ideological transition from National Socialist to "democratic" approaches to race. The term *Mischling*, in fact, survived the Third Reich and persisted well into the 1960s in official, scholarly, media, and public usage in West Germany. But its content after 1945 had changed. It was no longer used to refer to the progeny of so-called mixed unions between Jews and non-Jewish Germans. Rather, immediately after the war it came to connote the offspring of white German women and foreign men of color, as it had done prior to the mid-1930s.[1] Thus, *Mischlinge* remained a racialized category of

226

social analysis and social policy after 1945, as before. But its definition of *which races* had mixed, as well as the social significance of such mixing, was fundamentally altered.

A focus on German responses to biracial "occupation children" yields important insights into the processes by which Germans negotiated the transition from Nazi social policy to its democratic postwar variant. What is more, it permits some preliminary conclusions about that surprising lacuna of postwar German historiography, namely, what became of the social politics of race after 1945?

II

For the majority of Germans who were not among the minority groups persecuted by the Nazi state and its accomplices, 1945 initiated a new era that was marked by the trauma of defeat, the shock of contact with enemy troops, and rapid regime change—first to the occupation governments of the American, British, French, and Soviet zones, and then, after 1949, to the cold war states of East and West Germany. In addition to the political revolution accompanying Allied victory, military defeat served to destroy and delegitimate the particular national ideal of a superior Aryan *Volksgemeinschaft* that had been officially advocated and murderously enacted not only in Nazi Germany, but throughout Nazi-dominated Europe. With the demise of the Nazi regime, postwar Germans faced the task of recasting the social and ideological parameters of their national identity. The first decades after World War II were dominated by debates regarding communal self-definition as contemporaries were compelled to grapple with the question of what it would mean to be German after Hitler and the Holocaust.

This process was conditioned by the unique international matrix within which it occurred. Certain political and legal aspects of German national reconstruction and redefinition were, of course, dictated by the victorious powers. However, in addition to alien official directives, Germans proved intent on responding to what they perceived as the negative social and moral consequences of military occupation. 1945 had been experienced by many Germans as a national humiliation. With the influx of foreign troops, the outbreak of rape, and the advent of heterosexual fraternization, it came to be understood as a sexual humiliation as well.

Much of the moral and social dislocation following defeat was attributed to perceived abnormal relations between German men and women, and in particular to the active displacement of native masculinity by foreign troops and the German women who pursued sexual relationships with them. Beginning in the early days of the occupation and persisting for a good decade, public attention in western Germany was drawn irresistibly to relations between native German women and foreign occupiers as symptomatic of the postwar problems confronting Germany. What was at issue for many contemporaries was the very integrity of the German nation as it had been defined prior to 1945, along with its significant correlates of German honor, German manhood, and the German family.[2]

Postwar attempts to address issues of national self-definition necessarily involved confronting issues of race, since defeated Germany was occupied by the multiethnic armies of hostile nations. These former racial subordinates, moreover, now occupied a position of political superiority due to their membership in the Allied forces. The occupation challenged Germans to learn to function within a context that was radically postfascist in its social composition and political authority, if not yet in its ideological disposition or social policy.

In a very real sense, then, military occupation stimulated and shaped the contours of postwar racial ideology in Germany. And this was because the most explicit discussions of race after the war occurred in response to interracial sex and reproduction between German women and Allied soldiers of color. Postwar West German notions of race were intimately connected with notions of proper female social and sexual comportment—as lovers, as wives, as mothers.

Over the course of military occupation, the specific interracial relations most discussed in public venues became those between white German women and black American troops. Although Germans after 1945 continued to operate within the context of a highly differentiated racial paradigm (grounded in hierarchal racial valuation of various populations within Europe), postwar German officials, social scientists, and social workers increasingly focused on distinctions between blackness and whiteness. In part, this may have resulted from Germans' unwillingness to speak openly about Jews in racialized terms, although antisemitic utterances and actions certainly were not uncommon or unrecorded.[3] However, as the Nazi era receded into the past, West German officials gradually learned to adjust their language and censor their public statements on race, particularly, if not always successfully, as they concerned Jews. German racism prior to 1945 was not limited to antisemitism, though because of the Nazis' obsessive murderous targeting of European Jews its history has often understandably been written that way. While antisemitism was an important, even central, ingredient of German racism, it was not the sole one.

Segregated American military forces and Jim Crow practices in occupied Germany helped shape racial ideology in that country after 1945. This is not to argue that postwar Germans learned anti-Black racism from American occupiers. After all, Germans already had a long tradition of such bigotry that predated and was intensified by both Germany's short stint as a colonial power prior to 1918 and its shorter stint as a National Socialist power between 1933 and 1945. Rather, at the level of the street, Germans absorbed the postwar lesson—inadvertently taught by their new American masters—that democratic forms and values were consistent with racialist, and even racist, ideology and social organization.

Informal contacts between occupier and occupied—along with the discriminatory policies of the U.S. military toward its minorities and the tense relations among occupation soldiers of differing ethnicities—affected the ways Germans perceived and received American political and social values after 1945. German understandings of the content of "democratization" were conditioned by the implicitly racialized context within which it was delivered. As a result, military occupation reinforced white supremacy as a shared value of mainstream American and German cultures. Thus the reformulation of race after 1945 was not merely a national enterprise, but an international, and transnational, one as well.[4]

III

During the Third Reich, a litany of laws was promulgated that restricted the social and sexual choices of "Aryan" German women (those deemed racially and eugenically "valuable," whose duty was to reproduce and rear a racially superior German *Volk*) to Aryan male partners. Relations between Aryan German women and "racially foreign" men, whether Jewish, Polish, or Soviet— to name only the most prominent and reviled groups among the millions of forced laborers and POWs quartered in the Greater German Reich during World War II—were strictly prohibited and severely sanctioned. Tellingly, however, Nazi-era laws were not similarly restrictive for German men. Since masculine vitality and military prowess were assumed to be "highly dependent upon sexual gratification," the German military leadership provided brothels for their men and often turned a blind eye to incidents of rape by German soldiers. This was particularly so on the eastern front, because Jewish and Slavic women were considered for racial reasons to be essentially devoid of value or honor.[5] During its twelve-year rule, National Socialism forged a culture predicated on a "thorough racialization of sex"[6] in which the bodies of Aryan women were stringently policed, while the bodies of non-Aryan women were expressly—and often violently or murderously—exploited. In both cases, female sexuality was instrumentalized for national purposes by a regime intent on building a powerful, racially pure state to dominate the European continent.[7]

By opening access—sometimes forcibly—to German women's bodies, military defeat in 1945 represented a radical rupture with the Nazi regime's prescriptions and legislation regarding normative German sexual and reproductive behavior. The influx of occupation forces in 1945 effected a displacement of native masculinity in political, social, and sexual terms. It also ended a decade of prescribed Aryan exclusivity in social and sexual relations for German women. After all, what came home to the Germans after 1945 was not just their former state enemies, but their declared *racial* enemies as well: Blacks, Jews, Slavs, and other so-called Asiatics who served as non-German nationals in Allied armies or were liberated from slave, POW, or concentration camps. The result for German women was that the restrictive, state-mandated, Aryanized sex of the Third Reich gave way to a broader range of choice in social relations and sexual partners.

However, not all sexual contact between the "liberators and liberated" was elective, as the high incidence of rape in the spring and summer of 1945 indicates. Racially inflected tales of rape by the Soviet Red Army played a dominant role in the postwar mythology of the West German state, if not its East German sibling.[8] This retrospective focus has been tellingly myopic and overdetermined by cold war considerations. If one surveys the social experience and mythology of rape outside of Berlin and eastern reaches of the former Reich—the areas that have dominated historical discussions thus far— a somewhat more complex picture emerges.[9] In southern Germany, the zones of French and U.S. occupation, terrifying stories circulated about the violence done to German women by black troops, both French colonial and, to a lesser extent, African American. German reception of black troops after World War II was informed by earlier German responses to the previous French occupation of the Rhineland after the First World War by colonial troops from Algeria, Morocco, Tunisia, Madagascar, Senegal, and Indochina. In 1918, as in 1945, occupation followed military defeat. The German nation and German masculinity were perceived as severely weakened, and sexual relations and reproduction acquired heightened social and symbolic significance. The presence of non-white troops sparked a furor in Germany (and beyond) and was denounced as an intentional French strategy to destroy Germany's racial purity, cultural patrimony, and national pride. Drawing on racial stereotypes, German pamphleteers and the press portrayed the soldiers as a herd of sexually rapacious, syphilitic black beasts, intent on the rape, torture, or murder of German women, girls, and boys.[10]

These gendered stereotypes of national humiliation via foreign black troops were at the ready for rapid remobilization after 1945. The female victims of rape by Soviet and black troops featured in postwar tales were coded German in terms of nationality and ascribed ethnic identity. So, for example, although Soviet soldiers did not always distinguish between privileged "Aryan" women and persecuted ethnic minorities in perpetrating rapes as they moved westward into Germany, West German chroniclers most certainly did when it came to representing mass rape by Soviet troops. As a result, although Jewish women and other displaced persons were subject to "rape and sexual assault at the hand of their liberators," this form of racialized violence did not enter the annals of postwar German history. It remained both undocumented and uncommemorated by West German historians, media, and the state. Thus the victims depicted as deserving public sympathy and recognition were only some of those affected by actual rapes. The female victim of West German historical and commemorative discourse was delineated in ways that were beholden to, and helped perpetuate, notions of cultural and ethnic homogeneity rather than diversity. White, non-Jewish, and German, she implicitly embodied the Aryan ethno-racial ideal.[11]

Sustained attention to racialized rape occurred in spite of the fact that attacks were perpetrated by white Allied soldiers and white German men, as crime reports show. For a short time in mid-1945, German men prowled the streets asking German women whether they could "offer them a little [sexual] abuse."[12] There is little statistical evidence to indicate that rapes by non-white soldiers were more numerous than those perpetrated by whites—unless, that is, all rapes by Soviet soldiers are considered rapes by "non-white" racial others, regardless of the actual ethnic background of the individual.[13] Thus the focus on the racial dimensions of rape derived less from prevalence than from perception. German police classified perpetrators according to nationality and race or a confused conflation of both. So, for instance, police tabulated rapes by "white Frenchmen," "white Americans," and "colored (*farbige*) Americans," but also by otherwise undifferentiated "Russians," who nonetheless came from diverse parts of the Soviet Union, and "French colonial troops," who hailed from Morocco, Algeria, Tunisia, or Indochina.[14] Thus, three racialized categories initially emerged: "colored Americans," "French colonials," and "Russians."

Individual soldier-rapists were infrequently apprehended, since identification of perpetrators depended upon a woman's ability to "recognize" physical and cultural markers such as phenotype, demeanor, uniform worn, or language spoken. To register, "race" had to be something visible or audible. So while many women could likely identify national uniforms, distinctive European languages, and "colored" complexions—and therefore the putative marks of "Slavs," "Mongols," "Moroccans," or "Negroes,"—they would have been hard-pressed to detect among enemy troops that supreme racial Other of the Nazi period, namely Jews, by such methods. As a result, "Jewishness" disappeared almost immediately from popular and official discussions of German women's rape, abortion, sexuality, and reproduction in the spring of 1945. Discussions of "race" in matters of sexuality and reproductive policy contracted to a focus on the Asiatic Russian and the Black.[15]

Such categories convey important information not only about the ways victims "read" and reported their attacker's racial and national attributes, but also about how race was processed and recorded by police bureaucrats. That is to say, they provide clues about how race *as a social category* was already being subtly deployed and redefined in the days surrounding defeat. As social process and in social policy, military defeat both represented, and was represented as, the replacement of Aryanized sex by racialized sex. But after 1945, unlike before, this racialized sex did not involve Jews.

IV

In 1945, German state officials attempted to nullify the reproductive consequences of conquest by temporarily relaxing Paragraph 218, which outlawed abortion. Under National Socialism, a state-sponsored policy of "coercive pronatalism" had emerged in which access to abortion was severely restricted for Aryan women, who were prohibited from terminating pregnancies under penalty of death, unless there were severe attendant medical problems or unless pregnancy had resulted from sexual relations with "racial aliens."[16]

In liberalizing abortion policy, German officials specifically targeted miscegenist rape by enemy soldiers. In early March 1945, the Reich Interior Ministry issued a decree to doctors, health offices, and hospitals to expedite abortions of "Slav and Mongol fetuses."[17] Sometime during the spring the Bavarian *Landesregierung* followed suit, issuing a secret memo expressly encouraging abortions in rape cases involving "colored" troops. State and municipal authorities continued to refer to those orders in authorizing abortions during the months following defeat.[18] So while compulsory abortions and sterilizations ceased in May 1945 because of the nullification of Nazi laws, elective abortions of fetuses continued apace from the first months of 1945 and over the course of the year "became a mass phenomenon."[19]

The majority of abortions in 1945 and early 1946 occurred in response to rape by perceived racial aliens, indicating that a commitment to racial eugenics persisted in the policy and practice of abortion after defeat.[20] In large measure, this was due to the fact that German authorities at the local and state level were left to deal with women's health and medical issues without firm instructions from the Allied powers.[21] A German medical board of three doctors (preferably gynecologists) decided on applications for abortion. Applications by women alleging rape by white Allied soldiers were often denied, since the medical board "doubted that physical or emotional problems would ensue" if the woman carried the pregnancy to term.[22] Thus notions of *Rassenschande*, or racial pollution, continued to inform the language and social policy of abortion in the early years of the occupation. Nonetheless, the rationale for such decisions signaled a shift in racialist thinking after 1945. In transferring the diagnostic focus from the racialized body of the offspring to the emotional state of its mother, it anticipated a crucial postwar development in the rhetoric and rationale of social policy, namely, the transition from emphasis on the biology of race to the psychology of racial difference.[23]

In the first days of occupation, racial stereotypes of sexually predatory black males tipped the balance in favor of women's applications for abortion. Within months of defeat, however, the image of the pathologically pro-miscuous and materialist *Negerliebchen* or "nigger-lover" were propagated and popularized.[24] By early 1946, as the incidence of rape and legal abortions de-clined, the first "occupation children" were born. As a result, public attention and social policy increasingly shifted from a focus on coercive sex to one on consensual sex between masculine occupiers and native women in the West-ern zones. Evidence from southern Germany suggests that in addition to elec-tive liaisons with American occupiers, German women also chose French occupation soldiers—including those from Algeria, Morocco, Tunisia, and French Indochina—as lovers, bore their children, and in some cases married them and emigrated.[25] The social history of relationships and reproduction between the full range of multinational, multiethnic Allied troops and Ger-man women has not yet been written. Nonetheless, despite this broader range of social interaction and experience, when it came to discussing and address-ing consensual heterosexual sex, American soldiers attracted the lion's share of Germans' attention and aggression.

The black GI came to represent a kind of extreme manifestation of Ameri-can materialism and sexuality whose potency—and appeal, it was feared—was enhanced by racial difference. In a survey conducted in the early 1950s, for example, German social workers queried German women to determine why they became involved with black troops. Similar questions were not posed to women involved with white foreign troops. Relations between black GIs and white German women were condemned not because they were per-ceived as coercive—as in the case of "Moroccan" or Soviet troops—but be-cause women willfully embraced them for material advantage, sexual pleasure, and romance (although such emotional "compensations" were rarely recog-nized by contemporaries).[26] Because black American men, unlike their white German counterparts, apparently had so much to offer destitute German women, and the women offered companionship and often more in return, the latter were denounced as selfish and transgressing sirens. And although al-most half of these women expressed their intention to marry their black beaus, German and official American commentators were united in their in-ability to imagine that interracial relationships grew out of genuine mutual love and desire. As a result, the reigning interpretation of women's motiva-tions was moral or mental deficiency, and they were characterized as mentally impaired, as asocial, or as prostitutes.[27]

Such moral assumptions about the women who engaged in interracial frat-ernization lived on after the occupation to color the ways that the "problem" of biracial occupation children was formulated in the Federal Republic of Germany. From their first births in late 1945 through the 1950s, every Ger-man commentator, particularly the most conscientiously liberal among them, insisted that the child should not be made to suffer for the "sins" of the mother. The high number of births in Bavaria rankled state officials there, who sought in vain to negotiate with the American military government regarding the citizenship status of the children. Ultimately, all occupation children—including those of color—were grudgingly extended German citizenship, but only after Allied Military Government officials made it clear that they would neither entertain paternity suits nor grant citizenship to their troops' illegitimate offspring abroad.

After 1949, with the founding of the West German state, German officials unsuccessfully pursued child support from American soldiers for out-of-wedlock occupation children. American authorities would not permit U.S. soldiers to be called before German courts. Moreover, soldiers were more often than not suddenly shipped back to the United States when German women attempted to press paternity suits. Although the suits were cast as economic grievances, official German pursuit of child support from American soldiers also represented an attempt to rein in the underregulated social and sexual behavior of foreign troops on German soil, subject them to German law and custom, and reestablish the prerogatives and privileges of native German men in domestic public and private life. West German responses to occupation children therefore conjoined issues of German political and patriarchal rehabilitation.

V

From the first years of military occupation after 1945, German official and public attention focused insistently upon occupation children of color, the so-called *farbige Besatzungskinder* or *Mischlingskinder*. The children became the nexus around which social, cultural, and scientific debates about the meaning of race—and its implications for postwar German society—whirled. Discussions concerning the children not only invoked, but also reconstituted, German understandings of race by revising racial classifications, often with reference to contemporary American race relations and social science.

The various ways that attention to the children recast postwar approaches to race can be only succinctly summarized here.[28] Over the course of the early 1950s, Afro-German children were subjected to special race-based censuses and anthropological studies beholden to methodologies of interwar *Rassenkunde*, which would have been unthinkable after 1945 if applied to Jews, the Nazis' favorite racial other, or even so-called *Russenkinder*, the colloquial term for children of Soviet soldiers and German women in the first few years after the war. Born out of wedlock, Afro-German children were a juvenile population of German citizens subject to the control—and in some cases under the legal guardianship (*Vormundschaft*)—of West German officials. Their youth and citizenship differentiated them from surviving Jews in postwar Germany who, as predominantly displaced persons under Allied and especially American purview, overwhelmingly were considered—and considered themselves to be—a transitory population in Germany, biding their time while seeking permanent homes in more hospitable lands. Although Jewish DPs had the highest birthrate in Europe after the war, Jewish children were not subject to official German scrutiny or study. Such attention would have been politically—and morally—impossible after 1945.[29]

Postwar Germans' narrow focus on blackness and skin color in censuses and anthropological studies of *Mischlingskinder* articulated a specific post-war taxonomy of race in social policy and scientific knowledge.[30] Through them, the attribution of other racialized identities previously, obsessively, and lethally targeted by the German state—be they Jewish, Slavic, or "Mongoloid/ Asiatic"—were displaced, and ultimately erased, by a preoccupation with blackness in bureaucratic record keeping and official and public discourse.[31] Classifications of paternity elaborated for a federal census of occupation children in West Germany, for example, included "American," "British," "French," "Russian," and "Colored [*farbige*]." In creating one explicitly racialized (yet denationalized) category, the official census in effect de-raced the offspring of Soviet paternity and rendered Jewishness invisible, implicitly coding the occupation children of these formerly racialized groups "white." What remained were distinctions of nationality on one hand, and color on the other.

In official memos and press coverage, moreover, *Mischlingskinder* were rapidly renationalized as children of black *American* soldiers, thus erasing the diversity of national affiliation among Allied soldiers of color. As a result, the problem of race was embodied in "the *Mischlingskind*" and linked to America. A putatively "new" and peculiarly postwar problem of race had been born.

VI

These reformulations of notions of race after 1945 did not occur in a vacuum, but were shaped by transnational influences and interactions between Americans and Germans. One significant example for the postwar period was the creation of the *Gesellschaft für Christlich-Jüdische Zusammenarbeit* (Society for Christian-Jewish Cooperation, SCJC). The SCJC's model was the National Council of Christians and Jews (NCCJ), founded in the interwar United States to fight antisemitism and the racist violence of the Ku Klux Klan and exported to Europe after World War II in response to the murderous racism of National Socialist Germany. By mid-1948, the U.S. Military Government supported NCCJ efforts to recruit Germans to establish branches in Munich, Wiesbaden, Frankfurt, Stuttgart, Berlin, and other German cities in order to fight against racial discrimination and antisemitism in postwar Germany and foster tolerance and interconfessional understanding.[32]

There were a couple of noteworthy consequences of the *Gesellschaft*'s founding. First, it transferred to the Federal Republic the model of "intergroup relations" that had first emerged in the United States in the 1930s and that sought to counter racism by building viable educational and activist communities across confessional, ethnic, and racial lines. Second, it introduced into West Germany the reigning American social-scientific tool for investigating racism, namely "prejudice studies," which had important consequences for how race was discussed and understood in the postwar German context.[33]

The "prejudice studies" approach is evident in the SCJC's engagement with the topic of the *Mischlingskind*. In 1952, the year that postwar black German children began entering German schools, the organization sponsored the publication of a pedagogical pamphlet titled *Maxi, unser Negerbub* (which became recommended reading for all West German teachers) and organized national conferences for state officials and educators on the "problem of postwar *Mischlingskinder*."[34] These initiatives proved crucial in shaping state and school policies regarding the children and in establishing the ways they would be presented to the public at large as they made their way from the privacy of home to the classroom. Furthermore, they pioneered the principles upon which a liberal discourse of race would be constructed in West Germany.

A primary goal of both the conferences and the *Maxi* pamphlet was to domesticate postwar interracial children by recasting them as a German problem, rather than an American import, requiring German compassion and solutions. In order to facilitate that aim, German participants in the first SCJC conference focused on language—what the children should properly be called—and resolved to reject the term *farbige Besatzungskinder*, which emphasized foreign paternity, in favor of *farbige Mischlingskinder*. While this may have nativized the children in terms of nationality, it certainly reproduced earlier taxonomies of essentialized racial difference. Nonetheless, it was consistent with American practices of categorizing individuals on the basis of *any* black heredity.

Viewed in concert, the activities of the SCJC, official censuses, and anthropological studies of *Mischlingskinder* produced a shift in definitions of race by the early 1950s in West Germany: "Negro/Colored" rather than Jewish heredity was labeled, understood, and investigated in racial terms. This is not to argue that antisemitism disappeared from West German life or that Jews and other European minorities were not still perceived as distinct races by postwar West Germans. There is ample evidence that they were.[35] Rather, it is to argue that West German social policy and academic scholarship of the 1950s did not authorize defining those differences as racial.

In this sense, postwar West German definitions of race paralleled those of the postwar United States. For, over the course of the 1930s and 1940s, American social scientists "softened" the difference among whites of European origin (including, in particular, Jews) to a cultural one and conceived of these groups in terms of "ethnicity." Race, as a concept, continued to be employed, but was reduced to the radically simplified terms of the black-white binary—or, at its most articulated, the black–white–yellow triad—thus re-drawing the lines of meaningful difference according to stereotypical pheno-type.[36] There was, then, a confluence of the broad forms of racial taxonomy in both West Germany and the U.S.

Also in keeping with contemporary American practices, the Society for Christian–Jewish Cooperation departed from German tradition by psycholo-gizing the race problem. Racism came to be understood as a virulent psycho-logical malady that, when acted upon, had serious effects for the psychological and emotional health of its target and society's well-being as a whole.[37] If the psychological approach to racism and its effects was an American import, it was one of the few popular ones in the 1950s, precisely because of its value in denationalizing the postwar German problem of race. In other words, this explanation construed racism as a function and pathology of human, rather than a uniquely German, psychology.

Although the stated goal of the SCJC's conference was to facilitate the social acceptance and integration of black German children, the psychological approach to race and racism could as easily authorize a policy of social segre-gation and eventual emigration. Germans who advocated these "solutions" professed to be motivated by concern for the well-being of the children, who were considered too vulnerable, sensitive, or maladjusted to deal in healthy ways and on a daily basis with their difference from white classmates. As Blacks in a fundamentally white society, the children were considered at risk of developing more severe emotional problems, which, it was feared, would culminate in future social alienation or socially pathological behavior, such as licentiousness or criminality, once they approached puberty.[38]

Although in the early 1950s the West German Interior Ministry followed the SCJC's recommendation and integrated German schools, it nonetheless ordered states to collect detailed reports on noteworthy characteristics of school-aged *Mischlingskinder*. In particular it solicited information on the children's intellectual, physical, and moral development, along with any aca-demic deficits or problems of socialization that would hamper their "integra-tion into our social and civil order."[39]

The racial anxieties underlying this initiative are evident once one consid-ers it from a broader demographic perspective. For although white ethnic German refugee children from Eastern Europe entered West German schools in far greater numbers than black German children, the federal Interior Min-istry ordered school and youth officials to investigate the character, abilities, and integration prospects of only the latter. This despite the fact that white expellees and refugees from the eastern reaches of the former Reich "ac-counted for more than 90%" of population growth in the Federal Republic in the 1950s and constituted nearly one-quarter of West Germany's total popu-lation by the end of the decade.[40] Clearly, then, the overriding concern was not to facilitate social integration. Rather, such selective study shows that official anxieties regarding the social and somatic consequences of "race mixing" persisted well into the postwar period.

VII

Concerns about the social and psychological effects of "race mixing," combined with widespread biases regarding Afro-German children's presumed African American paternity, essentialized "black" identity, and mothers' alleged immorality affected official German "solutions" regarding the children's futures. By the early 1950s, calls for the children's adoption abroad—and particularly to the U.S.—had become more forceful and frequent in West Germany and provoked a good measure of interest and support in the United States among African American organizations, prospective parents, and the press. Interested parties, on both sides of the Atlantic, were intent on pursuing the children's most "proper" placement. This engaged issues of national belonging and racial fit, and involved integration into that most intimate social sphere: the family.

In West Germany, *Mischlingskinder* were typically represented as *Heimkinder*, or unwanted institutionalized children, despite the fact that almost 90 percent lived with families. Nonetheless, most West German authorities viewed the children as a "social problem" and international adoption as a preferred "solution." Throughout much of the decade of the 1950s, state officials, educators, and youth workers from across the political spectrum emphasized the myriad forms of discrimination that the children suffered in Germany as a result of their illegitimacy, foreign paternity, and racial characteristics, or referenced these as demonstrating the multiple ways in which they did not belong.

Adoption by African Americans (described as "families of their own kind") struck German social welfare authorities as a fitting solution, since most Germans were unwilling to adopt children from perceived asocial or inferior biological or moral backgrounds. Under the Nazi regime, such adoptions by white "Aryan" Germans had been legally prohibited in 1939 for "offending the public interest," and any "undesirable" adoptions already concluded could also be terminated by the state. Considerations of heredity and racial-biological factors persisted after 1945 and discouraged adoptions of black German children by white couples. Although this cultural bias no doubt predated the Nazi era, it bears noting that the American Military Government did nothing to counter it. Rather, when asked for clarification by German officials, the American Legal Affairs Branch did not abrogate the 1939 law, but declared it "politically and ideologically neutral" (though the British and Soviets ruled otherwise).[41]

By the early 1950s West Germans had mitigated adoption law to allow more ready adoption of white ethnic or orphaned children, but eagerly sought ways to release Germans of duties toward black German children. In 1951, in fact, West German federal Interior Ministry officials pursued negotiations with representatives of the U.S. Displaced Persons Commission to press for the adoption of Afro-German children there. Strikingly, German officials expressed interest in including even children who had *not* been surrendered by their mothers for adoption, even if they were currently living in German families and would wind up in orphanages in the U.S.[42] While thousands of adoptions of Afro-German children to the U.S. did ensue, most, in the end, appear to have been voluntarily arranged by the mothers.

Adoptions of Afro-German children to the U.S. were encouraged and pursued by African American civilians at home and in the American military in Germany. From the late 1940s into the 1950s, the African American press in particular spread the word about the plight of unwanted "half-Negro" children abroad. The *Pittsburgh Courier* and Baltimore *Afro-American* published appeals to their predominantly black readership, urging them to send special CARE packages to black German children residing in German children's homes or with their unwed mothers. The *Pittsburgh Courier* went so far as to print the names and addresses of two hundred German mothers of black children and encouraged readers to contact the women directly and pledge long-distance material and moral support over the long term.[43]

In addition, the National Association for the Advancement of Colored People (NAACP) and the Urban League became interested in the issue, and used it to chastise the American government and military leadership for its reluctance to engage in civil rights reform. The NAACP pointed out that the "problem of the children" was due to prejudicial official policies that did not permit black GIs to marry their white German girlfriends. Nonetheless, both organizations posed the question of whether the children's adoption to the U.S.—into an American culture of virulent anti-Black racism—would be in their best interest. As Lester Granger of the Urban League put it, "There are colored children in . . . Georgia, for example, who are much worse off than the colored children in Germany."[44]

Walter White of the NAACP followed this up in 1952 with press releases praising German efforts to "assimilate" the children into German schools in a policy of "full integration without any kind of segregation on basis of race," and noted the irony of the "democratic" United States' being surpassed in the realm of racial tolerance by its formerly fascist foe.[45] What is more, by the mid-1950s, increasing numbers of American adoptions of Amerasian children from Japan and Korea, along with increased press coverage of these children's appalling living conditions in those countries, made Germany's treatment of Afro-German children appear both beneficent and progressive in comparison. As a result, African American political organizations and social welfare workers increasingly questioned whether intervention on behalf of black German children was necessary or advisable.

African Americans on the ground in Germany saw things differently. Mrs. Mabel Grammer, occasional correspondent to the Baltimore *Afro-American* and wife of a U.S. warrant officer based near Mannheim, observed the miserable economic conditions of some of the children and their mothers in West Germany and actively sought black adoptive parents for them. Publicizing their plight and working closely with local German public and religious youth offices and orphanages, she facilitated up to seven hundred adoptions between 1951 and 1953 and remained active to the turn of the 1960s. During this time, West German state officials and youth workers cooperated gladly with her, even permitting proxy adoptions. They preferred having the children adopted by Americans, and especially African Americans, both for reasons of racial "fit" and because doing so released German taxpayers from the costs of the children's care.[46]

By late in the decade, however, German officials began to have second thoughts. Economic recovery fueled more domestic German requests for adoption, albeit for white children. Since white German "occupation children" were eagerly sought for adoption by white Americans, federal officials began to demand more stringent regulation of international adoptions by state and religious youth welfare organizations, in order to retain such "desirable" progeny at home.[47]

As a result, the late 1950s marked a retreat from transatlantic adoptions by West German federal and state officials. However, when it came to Afro-German children, German authorities articulated a different rationale for discouraging adoptions to the United States. To explain their policy shift, the federal ministries repeatedly referenced the case of "Otto," an Afro-German child sent to the United States for adoption. Charging that the child suffered severe emotional trauma after being placed with an African American family, ministry memos analyzed the placement problem as twofold: first, the child's shock at, and inability to adjust to, an all-black family and neighborhood in the United States; and second, the child's subjection to racial segregation and Jim Crow laws in democratic America. Since white German families were still not adopting biracial children in any significant numbers (apart from a handful of well-publicized exceptions),[48] the preferred destination for the children placed for adoption became Denmark, where, German commentators curiously insisted, racial prejudice was non-existent.[49]

By the early 1960s, adoptions of black German children to Denmark outpaced those to the United States.[50] In contrast to the troubling reports on adoptive black German children in the United States, West German officials and social workers painted a picture of easy integration due to the elevated class background of the parents and their cultural competence in easing the children from a German to a Danish context. Denmark was portrayed in terms of cultural similarity: it was like Germany, only better, since prospective Danish parents seemed "more broad-minded about the children's origins." Moreover, German psychologists concerned with the children's emotional development in the segregated U.S. now described Danish mothers as more culturally compatible and less overbearing than the "black mammies" who, a decade before, had been seen as "natural" nurturers to the children.[51]

By the late 1950s, the West German state cultivated its role as protector and sought for its wards a more suitable and humane destination. Its experience with adoptions of black German children to the U.S. provided a useful comparative perspective on social progress in both Western democracies and permitted a positive public reassessment of the success of postwar German racial reeducation.[52] In the process, the children's identity was reimagined. As the mark of (presumed) black *American* ancestry, which had formerly seemed indelible, now faded in importance, West German officials encouraged a solution that would allow the children to "retain" their essential identity as Europeans.[53]

By the late 1950s, *Ebony* magazine, along with black newspapers in New York, Chicago, and Philadelphia, were reporting the "frictionless" integration of German schools—and later the workforce—at a time when the National Guard was needed to compel compliance in the American South. Given the protracted civil battle over racial integration raging in the U.S., it is not surprising that in 1960 *Ebony*, in a feature titled "Brown Babies Go to Work," would quote with approval Nuremberg youth office official Dr. Dorothea Struwe's speech on the topic to fellow social workers:

> The incidents in Little Rock have caused much indignation in Germany. I hope that no one will ever have to tell us Germans to clean [our own house] . . . It is essential that our colored children can expand and develop their talents and abilities so that they will be firmly rooted in our community and will not some day constitute a source of unrest. They can help us make good some of the guilt we have laden upon us in the past.[54]

In just over a decade since Hitler's defeat, a chastened nation appeared to have surpassed its tutor in the lessons of democracy and was "credentialed" to that effect by the favorable reviews of African American organizations and the press. By the turn of the 1960s, West German officials could point to their treatment of *Mischlingskinder* and claim a moral victory in the area of race relations.

This self-congratulatory assessment was reinforced by a series of publications by West German academics, youth workers, and educators and by the West German press from the mid-fifties onward which touted the overall success of West German efforts to integrate schools and—as the oldest began entering their teenage years—the national workforce.[55] By the close of the 1950s, official and public attention increasingly turned away from the question of where black German children most properly belonged to focus instead on documenting efforts to aid the absorption of resident black German children into the West German economy. For despite the avid efforts devoted to international adoptions of black German children throughout the 1950s, the majority of the children had not, after all, been surrendered by their mothers for shipment abroad but remained in their country of birth.

VIII

By the turn of the 1960s, as the oldest of postwar black German youth concluded their education, the issue of the children's integration into the Federal Republic increasingly became narrowed to a myopic focus on job placement. Thanks to a strong economy and low unemployment—some West German industries had, by this time, begun to import southern European and Turkish "guest workers" to address a growing labor shortage—municipal and state offices reported the ready cooperation of West German employers in providing training and jobs for biracial youth, and generally painted a rosy picture of welcoming co-workers and unbiased absorption into working life.[56]

What received less public attention was the teens' placement into overwhelmingly manual and sometimes menial jobs. In good measure, this was due to German officials' oft-stated conviction that "among *Mischlingskinder* practical abilities predominate over theoretical intelligence."[57] This official bias persisted from the children's early school days, despite evidence to the contrary, and, together with their often depressed socio-economic background, it conditioned their educational trajectory.[58] Thus black German children were disproportionately routed into rudimentary *Hauptschulen,* in which students' education ended by the age of fourteen, rather than into *Gymnasien,* which extended their formal education for another half-decade and prepared students for university study. When it came to job placement, the boys apprenticed or took work as gas station attendants (a common occupation), in laundries or dry cleaners, as cooks, sheet-metal workers, painters, lathe operators, mechanics' helpers, or automobile, truck, or machine mechanics. Girls, on the other hand, tended to take jobs as domestic help (in private homes or institutions), in laundries, or less frequently as office help. Some became salesgirls (typically in small grocery stores or bakeries) or worked as hairdressers. Although a notable number of teenaged girls expressed interest in careers in sales or in hair salons, they were often discouraged from pursuing them. This was due in large measure to negative response from prospective employers who claimed to anticipate hostile customer reaction. One salon owner, for example, suggested that his clients did not want to be touched by black hands. In addition, given the uncertain climate of reception, some teens proved reticent to expose themselves to the possibility of rejection or humiliation on the basis of race and appear to have abandoned their aspirations untried.[59]

By the early 1960s, at the level of social representation if not social reality,

West German press reports, official memos, and academic assessments projected the image of a stable and prosperous postwar nation whose bureaucrats and employers operated in accordance with the principles of social justice and economic rationality.[60] As a result, the specter of racist irrationality was declared banished from the reconstructed West German state, but only because integration was defined and pursued in exclusively economic, rather than broadly social, terms.[61]

IX

After the declaration that the integration of *Mischlingskinder* had been an overwhelming success, the official and media attention devoted both to the children and to the postwar problem of race in general sharply declined. The early 1960s initiated a shift away from the domestic discussions of race and national belonging that had characterized the 1950s. One significant step in this direction was the resistance encountered by the federal Ministry of the Interior when its officials in 1960 ordered West German *Länder* (states) to conduct another survey of the numbers of *Mischlingskinder* in their jurisdictions. The state cultural ministers of Lower Saxony and Schleswig-Holstein refused outright, citing both pragmatic concerns (understaffing) and legal principle (the Basic Law's prohibition of singling out individuals on the basis of race). While it bears noting that these objections issued from states with minute black populations, it is nonetheless significant that their rebuke effectively nullified the federal Interior Ministry's practice, since the Nazi years, of keeping separate statistics on its black citizens.[62]

The disappearance of "the *Mischlingskind*" as an object of social policy has had a profound effect, for it was accompanied by a silencing of official and public discussions of the role of race within German society and national identity. That is, while contemporary Germans, since the 1960s, have recognized an increasing ethnic diversity within their borders as a demographic fact, they have interpreted this as resulting from an influx of foreign laborers and asylum seekers attracted by Germany's strong economy and social welfare provisions. However, membership in the nation in the form of citizenship was culturally imagined and, until 1999, to a large extent legally prescribed as the more exclusive domain of homogenous whiteness. This perceptual racial narrowing of "nation" left little space—social or psychological—for German citizens of color who, to borrow from W. E. B. Du Bois, daily felt the "doubleness" of their lives as Blacks and Germans in a hostile or, at best, indifferent society that was nonetheless their own. The silence that overtook issues of race in West Germany muted discussions of the relationship between blackness and Germanness for two decades, until its reemergence in the 1980s in the form of identity politics and discussions of German multiculturalism.[63]

The number of Black Germans in the Federal Republic is difficult to establish. Ironically, this is due to the success of the "color-blind" liberalism introduced in the 1950s and the subsequent effacement of race as a category of census taking and social analysis, if not social experience. Estimates of the numbers of Black Germans range widely, from a low of thirty thousand (for Black German citizens) to a high of about seven hundred thousand (as a combined total of all citizens and residents of color in Germany). What is clear is that they are a heterogeneous population, ranging from Afro-Germans whose families have held German citizenship since the nineteenth century, to children of troops that occupied the Rhineland after 1918 or Germany after 1945, to children of "guest workers" or international students entering either of the cold-war Germanys since the 1950s, to more recent immigrants and asylum seekers. What is more, they constitute a significant minority in contemporary Germany—yet one that has not received much recognition from German officials or the German public. They are undetected by the radar of German social consciousness.

Nonetheless, white Germans are not unaware of minorities in their midst. For the past couple of decades, and especially since German unification in 1990, minorities living in Germany have found themselves at the center of heated debates regarding immigration and citizenship law, as well as the impact of immigration on the German nation, culture, and economy. There has also been a good deal of attention devoted to displays of bias and violence toward ethnic minorities in German society, due in part to a marked increase in the number of refugees and immigrants from Eastern Europe and the former Soviet Union since the end of the cold war.

As a result, German officials, social scientists, and press have tended to interpret such expressions of discrimination and violence in the Federal Republic as "xenophobia," or hatred of *foreigners,* and have not investigated these behaviors as reflecting a more generalized German racism. The interpretative act of attributing violence to "xenophobia" and identifying its victims as "foreigners" casts the problem as a short-term one: an uncomfortable period of adjustment issuing from the end of the cold war, the demise of socialism and the East German state, and the ensuing civil, social, and economic crises that these circumstances have unleashed. It locates the origins of the problem as external to the German nation and German history, rather than treating the problem as connected to a longer and deeper German history of racism and notions of race.

This response goes a long way toward explaining the absence of official and public awareness of the existence or experience of Afro-Germans. When their presence does register, many white Germans assume that they too are immigrants, African asylum seekers, or even visiting African Americans. Their daily reception in public has been preconditioned by a public policy focused on immigration. What is lacking is a social and historical consciousness.

Blacks have a long history of residence and citizenship within the German nation. For well over a century, they have been part of the German nation. However, their presence has not been sufficient to alter the conception of the German nation as fundamentally homogenous and white.

Nonetheless, there have been moments in German history when their presence was both publicized and perceived as intimately tied to the health and well-being of the white German citizen, family, and nation. That is the story I have tried to tell here—the story of an extended historical moment after 1945 when Afro-Germans attained a highly charged visibility in West German society, only to be rendered invisible once their value for the democratizing nation had dissipated. Afro-German children were integral to West Germans' postwar process of national rehabilitation and social redefinition, albeit as objects of social policy. The challenge for contemporary white Germans— and for contemporary historians of white Germany—is to find a way to reconceptualize the nation and its narratives to include the existence and experiences of its minorities, not on the basis of "difference" but as Germans and equals.

Notes

1. Fatima El Tayeb, *Schwarze Deutsche: Der Diskurs um "Rasse" und nationale Identität, 1890–1933* (Frankfurt am Main: Campus, 2001); and Lora Wildenthal, "Race, Gender, and Citizenship in the German Colonial Empire," in *Tensions of Empire: Colonial Cultures in a Bourgeois World,* ed. Frederick Cooper and Ann Laura Stoler (Berkeley: University of California Press, 1997), 263–86. On this shift, see Heide Fehrenbach, *Race after Hitler: Black Occupation Children in Postwar Germany and America* (Princeton, N.J.: Princeton University Press, 2005), chapter 3.

2. See Robert G. Moeller, *Protecting Motherhood: Women and the Family in the Politics of Postwar West Germany* (Berkeley: University of California Press, 1993); "Remasculinization of Germany in the 1950s," special forum, *Signs: Women in Culture and Society* 24, no. 1 (fall 1998); Atina Grossmann, "A Question of Silence: The Rape of German Women by Occupation Soldiers," *October* 72 (spring 1995): 43–63; Elizabeth Heineman, "The Hour of the Woman: Memories of Germany's 'Crisis Years' and West German National Identity," *American Historical Review* 101, no. 2 (April 1996): 354–95; Heide Fehrenbach, *Cinema in Democratizing Germany: Reconstructing National Identity after Hitler* (Chapel Hill: University of North Carolina Press, 1995), chapters 3–5; and Uta G. Poiger, *Jazz, Rock, and Rebels: Cold War Politics and American Culture in a Divided Germany* (Berkeley: University of California Press, 2000).

3. Frank Stern, *The Whitewashing of the Yellow Badge: Antisemitism and Philosemitism in Postwar Germany* (New York: Published for the Vidal Sassoon International Center for the Study of Antisemitism (SICSA), Hebrew University of Jerusalem, by Pergamon Press, 1992).

4. See Fehrenbach, *Race after Hitler,* chapter 1.

5. Annette F. Timm, "Sex with a Purpose: Prostitution, Venereal Disease, and Militarized Masculinity in the Third Reich," *Journal of the History of Sexuality* 11, nos. 1–2 (January–April 2002): 227.

6. This phrase is borrowed from Dagmar Herzog, "Hubris and Hypocrisy, Incitement and Disavowal: Introduction to the Special Issue on Sexuality and German Fascism," *Journal of the History of Sexuality* 11, nos. 1–2 (January–April 2002): 9.

7. Timm, "Sex with a Purpose," 246. For excellent recent scholarship, see Dagmar Herzog, ed., "Sexuality and German Fascism," special issue of *Journal of History of Sexuality* 11, nos. 1–2 (January–April 2002), particularly the essays by Herzog, Timm, Patricia Szobar, and Birthe Kundrus. Also see Gabriele Czarnowski, "Hereditary and Racial Welfare (*Erb- und Rassenpflege*): The Politics of Sexuality and Reproduction in Nazi Germany," *Social Politics* 4, no. 1 (spring 1997): 114–35.

8. The quotation is a translation of the title of Helke Sander and Barbara Johr's controversial book, *Befreier und Befreite: Krieg, Vergewaltigungen, Kinder* (Munich: A. Kunstmann, 1992). See also Grossmann, "A Question of Silence"; Norman Naimark, *The Russians in Germany: A History of the Soviet Zone of Occupation, 1945–1949* (Cambridge, Mass.: Harvard University Press, 1995); Ingrid Schmidt-Harzbach, "Eine Woche im April: Berlin 1945; Vergewaltigung als Massenschicksal," *Feministische Studien* 2 (1984): 51–65; Annemarie Tröger, "Between Rape and Prostitution," in *Women in Culture and Politics: A Century of Change*, ed. Judith Friedlander et al. (Bloomington: Indiana University Press, 1986), 97–117; Stuart Liebman and Annette Michelson, eds., "Berlin 1945: War and Rape; Liberators Take Liberties," special issue of *October* 72 (spring 1995), especially the essays by Helke Sander, Gertrud Koch, and Atina Grossmann; Heineman, "The Hour of the Woman"; and Robert G. Moeller, *War Stories: The Search for a Usable Past in the Federal Republic of Germany* (Berkeley: University of California Press, 2001), 51–87.

9. See Fehrenbach, *Race after Hitler*, chapter 2.

10. Christian Koller, "Enemy Images: Race and Gender Stereotypes in the Discussion on Colonial Troops," in *Home/Front: The Military, War, and Gender in Twentieth-Century Germany*, ed. Karen Hagemann and Stefanie Schüler-Springorum (New York: Berg, 2002), 144. See also Christian Koller, *"Von Wilden aller Rassen niedergemetzelt": Die Diskussion um die Verwendung von Kolonialtruppen in Europa zwischen Rassismus, Kolonial- und Militärpolitik, 1914–1930* (Stuttgart: Steiner, 2001), especially 249–61; Sally Marks, "Black Watch on the Rhine: A Study in Propaganda, Prejudice, and Prurience," *European Studies Review* 13, no. 3 (July 1983): 297–334; Keith L. Nelson, "The 'Black Horror on the Rhine': Race as a Factor in Post–World War I Diplomacy," *Journal of Modern History* 42, no. 4 (December 1970): 606–27; Robert C. Reinders, "Racialism on the Left: E. D. Morel and the 'Black Horror on the Rhine,'" *International Review of Social History* 13 (1968): 1–28; Reiner Pommerin, *"Sterilisierung der Rheinlandbastarde": Das Schicksal einer farbigen deutschen Minderheit, 1918–1937* (Düsseldorf: Droste, 1979); and Tina Campt, Pascal Grosse, and Yara-Colette Lemke-Muniz de Faria, "Blacks, Germans, and the Politics of Imperial Imagination, 1920–1960," in *The Imperialist Imagination: German Colonialism and Its Legacy*, ed. Sara Friedrichsmeyer, Sara Lennox, and Susanne Zantop (Ann Arbor: University of Michigan Press, 1998), 204–29.

11. See Atina Grossmann, "Victims, Villains, and Survivors: Gendered Perceptions and Self-Perceptions of Jewish Survivors in Postwar Germany," *Journal of the History of Sexuality* 11, nos. 1–2 (January–April 2002): 306–307; also Marlene Epp,

"The Memory of Violence: Soviet and East European Mennonite Refugees and Rape in the Second World War," *Journal of Women's History* 9, no. 1 (spring 1997): 58–87; and Moeller, *War Stories*, 80–87.

12. In Munich between 1 May and 31 December 1945, 152 rapes were recorded. The nationality of the attacker was given in 100 cases; 55 were Americans and 36 were German. Sieglinde Reif, "Das 'Recht des Siegers': Vergewaltigungen in München 1945," in *Zwischen den Fronten: Münchner Frauen im Krieg und Frieden, 1900–1950*, ed. Sybille Krafft (Munich: Buchendorfer Verlag, 1995), 370 n. 11.

13. Moeller makes this point in *War Stories*, noting that "[a]lthough detailed information on the ethnic composition of the Red Army awaits a comprehensive social-historical account of the war's last months, evidence suggests that 'Asiatic' troops were not overrepresented among those responsible for the Soviet army's worst acts against Germans" (66).

14. Myron Echenberg, "Race, Ethnicity, and Social Class in the French Colonial Army: The Black African *Tirailleurs*, 1857–1958," in *Ethnic Armies: Polyethnic Armed Forces From the Time of the Habsburgs to the Age of the Superpowers*, ed. N. F. Dreisziger (Waterloo, Ontario: Wilfrid Laurier University Press, 1990), 50–68.

15. Staatsarchiv Augsburg, Nr. 30: Gesundheitsamt Sonthofen.

16. Atina Grossmann, *Reforming Sex: The German Movement for Birth Control and Abortion Reform, 1920–1950* (New York: Columbia University Press, 1995), 150–52, and in general chapter 6. Also see Gisela Bock, "Antinatalism, Maternity, and Paternity in National Socialist Racism," in *Nazism and German Society, 1933–1945*, ed. David F. Crew (New York: Routledge, 1994), 110–40; and Gabriele Czarnowski, "Frauen als Mütter der 'Rasse': Abtreibungsverfolgung und Zwangssterilisation im Nationalsozialismus," in *Unter anderen Umständen: Zur Geschichte der Abtreibung*, ed. Gisela Staupe and Lisa Vieth (Dresden: Deutsches Hygiene Museum, 1993), 58–72.

17. Grossmann, *Reforming Sex*, 193, also 153; Kirsten Poutrus, "Von den Massenvergewaltigungen zum Mutterschutzgesetz: Abtreibungspolitik und Abtreibungspraxis in Ostdeutschland, 1945–1950," in *Die Grenzen der Diktatur: Staat und Gesellschaft in der DDR*, ed. Richard Bessel and Ralph Jessen (Göttingen: Vandenhoeck und Ruprecht, 1996), 179–80; and Grossmann, "A Question of Silence," 56.

18. Staatsarchiv Augsburg, Nr. 30: Gesundheitsamt Sonthofen, memo from the Bürgermeister des Marktes Sonthofen, regarding "Schwangerschaftsunterbrechung," 7 June 1945. Also Staatsarchiv Augsburg, Nr. 30: Gesundheitsamt Sonthofen, memo of Reichsministerium des Innern, "Unterbrechung von Schwangerschaften," 14 March 1945.

19. Estimates range from 350,000 to one million in a German population of 64.5 million. Poutrus, "Von den Massenvergewaltigungen zum Mutterschutzgesetz," 193, 178–80.

20. Grossmann, *Reforming Sex*, 194–95; Annette Timm, "The Legacy of *Bevölkerungspolitik:* Venereal Disease Control and Marriage Counselling in Post-WWII Berlin," *Canadian Journal of History / Annales canadiennes d'histoire* 33 (August 1998): 173–214; and Fehrenbach, *Race after Hitler*, chapter 2.

21. Grossman, *Reforming Sex*, chapter 8; and Poutrus, "Von den Massenvergewaltigungen zum Mutterschutzgesetz."

22. Staatsarchiv Augsburg, Nr. 30, Gesundheitsamt Sonthofen; Nr. 19, Gesundheitsamt Neuburg; and VA Lindau 1946: Einzelfälle.

23. For an expanded discussion, see Fehrenbach, *Race after Hitler*, chapter 2.

24. Staatsarchiv Augsburg, Nr. 30: Gesundheitsamt Sonthofen, applications for abortions, 1945–46; and Gesundheitsamt (GA), Nr. 19: Neuburg. Also see U.S. National Archives (College Park), OMGUS, Executive Office, Office of the Adjutant General, General Correspondence, box 43, file: Incidents—American. On *Amiliebchen* and *Negerliebchen* see Heinemann, "The Hour of the Woman"; and Maria Höhn, *GIs and Fräuleins: The German-American Encounter in 1950s West Germany* (Chapel Hill: University of North Carolina Press, 2002).

25. Staatsarchiv Augsburg, VA Lindau, 1946, Einzelfälle. Also Luise Frankenstein, *Soldatenkinder: Die unehelichen Kinder ausländischer Soldaten mit besonderer Berücksichtigung der Mischlinge* (Munich: W. Steinebach, 1954), 29.

26. Frankenstein, *Soldatenkinder,* 16–19, 23–24; Höhn, *GIs and Fräuleins;* and Fehrenbach, *Race after Hitler,* chapters 1–2.

27. NAACP, RG 306, USIA, Research Reports on German Public Opinion, box 9, report C-1, "Assessment of Troop-Community Relations," 30–32; Vernon W. Stone, "German Baby Crop Left by Negro GIs," *Survey* 85 (November 1949): 579–83; and Frankenstein, *Soldatenkinder,* 23. Also see Hermann Ebeling, "Zum Problem der deutschen Mischlingskinder," *Bild und Erziehung* 7 (1954): 612–30; Rudolf Sieg, "Mischlingskinder in Westdeutschland," *Beiträge zur Anthropologie* 4 (1955): 9–79; Gustav von Mann, "Zum Problem der farbigen Mischlingskinder in Deutschland," *Jugendwohl* 36, no. 1 (January 1955): 50–53; Hans Pfaffenberger, "Zur Situation der Mischlingskinder," *Unsere Jugend* 8, no. 2 (1956): 64–71; and Herbert Hurka, "Die Mischlingskinder in Deutschland," *Jugendwohl* 6 (1956): 257–75.

28. For a full discussion of these issues, see Fehrenbach, *Race after Hitler,* chapter 3.

29. See the essay by Atina Grossmann in this volume, as well as her "Trauma, Memory, and Motherhood: Germans and Jewish Displaced Persons in Post-Nazi Germany, 1945–1949." *Archiv für Sozialgeschichte* 38 (1998): 215–39; Grossman, "Victims, Villains, and Survivors"; and Yehuda Bauer, *Out of the Ashes: The Impact of American Jews on Post-Holocaust European Jewry* (Oxford: Pergamon, 1989).

30. On anthropological studies conducted on Afro-German children, see Fehrenbach, *After the Racial State,* chapter 3, and Tina Campt and Pascal Grosse, "'Mischlingskinder' in Nachkriegsdeutschland," *Psychologie und Geschichte* 6 (1994): 48–78.

31. Statistisches Bundesamt/Wiesbaden, "Statistische Berichte: Die unehelichen Kinder von Besatzungsangehörigen im Bundesgebiet und Berlin (West)" Arb.-Nr. VI/29/6, 10 October 1956.

32. Josef Foschepoth, *Im Schatten der Vergangenheit: Die Anfänge der Gesellschaft für Christlich-Jüdische Zusammenarbeit* (Göttingen: Vandenhoeck und Ruprecht, 1993), 155–203.

33. For the United States, see Stuart Svonkin, *Jews against Prejudice: American Jews and the Fight for Civil Liberties* (New York: Columbia University Press, 1997).

34. Alfons Simon, *Maxi, unser Negerbub* (Bremen: Eilers und Schünemann, 1952). On the *Gesellschaft's* activities, see Frank Stern, *Whitewashing,* 310–34, and Foschepoth, *Im Schatten der Vergangenheit.*

35. I am not addressing popular attitudes in this argument. For a discussion of these issues at the grassroots level see for example, Stern, *Whitewashing;* Julius H. Schoeps, ed., *Leben im Land der Täter: Juden im Nachkriegsdeutschland (1945–1952)* (Berlin: Jüdische Verlagsanstalt, 2001); Susanne Dietrich and Julia Schulze Wessel,

Zwischen Selbstorganisation und Stigmatisierung: Die Lebenswirklichkeit jüdischer Displaced Persons und die neue Gestalt des Antisemitismus in der deutschen Nachkriegsgesellschaft (Stuttgart: Klett-Cotta, 1998); Wolfgang Benz, *Feindbild und Vorurteil: Beiträge über Ausgrenzung und Verfolgung* (Munich: Deutscher Taschenbuch-Verlag, 1996); and Höhn, *GIs and Fräuleins.*

36. On shifts in U.S. understandings of race, see Matthew Frye Jacobsen, *Whiteness of a Different Color: European Immigrants and the Alchemy of Race* (Cambridge, Mass.: Harvard University Press, 1999); and Matthew Pratt Guterl, *The Color of Race in America, 1900–1940* (Cambridge, Mass.: Harvard University Press, 2001).

37. For the U.S., see Svonkin, *Jews against Prejudice;* Daryl Michael Scott, *Contempt and Pity: Social Policy and the Image of the Damaged Black Psyche, 1880–1996* (Chapel Hill: University of North Carolina Press, 1997); and Ruth Feldstein, *Motherhood in Black and White: Race and Sex in American Liberalism, 1930–1945* (Ithaca, N.Y.: Cornell University Press, 2000).

38. See, for example, Wilhelmine Hollweg, "Ohne Ansehen der Rasse . . . ," *DPWV-Nachrichten* 5, no. 6 (June 1955): 2–3, in Bundesarchiv Koblenz (hereafter BAK), B153/342. Also see "Zur Frage der Aufnahme farbiger Kinder in Heimen," *Unsere Jugend* 5, no. 8 (August 1953): 376–77; Hans Pfaffenberger, "Farbige Kinder im Heim—ein Prüfstein," *Unsere Jugend* 5, no. 12 (December 1953): 533–36; Walter Kirchner, "Eine anthropologische Studie an Mulattenkindern in Berlin unter Berüchsichtigung der sozialen Verhältnisse" (Phil. Diss., Freie Universität, 1952); and Rudolf Sieg, *Mischlingskinder in Westdeutschland: Festschrift für Frederic Falkenburger* (Baden-Baden: Verlag für Kunst und Wissenschaft, 1955).

39. Staatsarchiv Freiburg, F110/1, Nr. 176: Oberschulamt Freiburg; BayHStA, MK 62245, memo from Ständige Konferenz der Kultusminister, Bonn, 27 February 1956, summarizing report results from the Länder.

40. Ulrich Herbert, *A History of Foreign Labor in Germany, 1880–1980: Seasonal Workers, Forced Laborers, Guest Workers,* trans. William Templer (Ann Arbor: University of Michigan Press, 1990), 195.

41. Edmund C. Jann, "The Law of Adoption in Germany," typescript, Library of Congress, Law Library, Foreign Law Section (Washington, D.C., 1955), 4; and Helmut Glässing, *Voraussetzungen der Adoption* (Frankfurt am Main: Alfred Metzner Verlag, 1957). On the U.S. response, see Archiv des Diakonischen Werks (hereafter ADW), CAW 843.

42. BAK, B153/342, "Vermerk" to Dr. Rothe, 25 May 1951.

43. Yara-Colette Lemke Muniz de Faria mentions these initiatives in *Zwischen Fürsorge und Ausgrenzung: Afrodeutsche "Besatzungskinder" im Nachkriegsdeutschland* (Berlin: Metropol, 2002), 102–103.

44. "Meeting of the Committee to consider . . . the Immigration of . . . German orphans of Negro Blood," 29 January 1951, NAACP papers, reel 8: group II, box G11, "Brown Babies, 1950–58."

45. Walter White press release, 18 September 1952, NAACP papers, reel 8: group II, box G11, "Brown Babies, 1950–58."

46. For a detailed discussion of Mabel Grammer's activities, the response of the International Social Service, and the shifting policy of West Germans, see Fehrenbach, *Race after Hitler,* chapter 5; and Lemke Muniz de Faria, *Zwischen Fürsorge und Ausgrenzung.*

47. Heinrich Webler, "Adoptions-Markt," *Zentralblatt für Jugendrecht und Jugend-wohl* 42, no. 5 (May 1955): 123–24. Also see BAK, B153: Bundesministerium für Familien- und Jugendfragen, file 1335, I-II: "Material über Probleme des Internationalen Adoptionsrechts"; Hauptstaatsarchiv Stuttgart, Akten des Innenministeriums, EA2/007: Vermittlung der Annahme an Kindesstatt, Band II, 1955–66; Franz Klein, "Kinderhandel als strafbare Handlung," in *Jugendwohl*, 3 (1956): 95; and ADW, HGSt 1161, "Kurzbericht über die Sitzung . . . dem 12. Juli 1955 im Bundesministerium des Innern; Bayerisches Hauptstaatsarchiv, MInn 81906."

48. ADW, HGSt 3949, Auszug aus dem Bericht über die Tätigkeit der Adoptionszentrale für den Verwendungsnachweise, Zuschuss 1961 and 1963.

49. BAK, B153: Bundesministerium für Familien- und Jugendfragen, file 1335, I-II: "Material über Probleme des Internationalen Adoptionsrechts," HStAStg, Akten des Innenministeriums, EA2/007: Vermittlung der Annahme an Kindesstatt, Band II, 1955–66; Webler, "Adoptions-Markt"; Franz Klein, "Zur gegenwärtige Situation der Auslandsadoption," *Unsere Jugend* 9 (1955): 401–408; and Franz Klein, "Kinderhandel als strafbare Handlung," *Jugendwohl* 3 (1956), 95.

50. ADW, HGSt 3949.

51. Ebeling, "Zum Problem der deutschen Mischlingskinder"; Sieg, *Mischlingskinder in Westdeutschland;* Pfaffenberger, "Zur Situation der Mischlingskinder"; and Klaus Eyferth, Ursula Brandt, and Wolfgang Hawel, *Farbige Kinder in Deutschland: Die Situation der Mischlingskinder und die Aufgaben ihrer Eingliederung* (Munich: Juventa Verlag, 1960).

52. The first quotation is from Hurka, "Die Mischlingskinder in Deutschland," Teil II, S. 275; the second is from "Die USA bevorzugen 'Blonde,'" *Rheinische Post,* 24 July 1952, press clipping in BAK, B106 Bundesministerium des Innern, file 20620. Also see Eyferth, Brandt, and Hawel, *Farbige Kinder in Deutschland,* 90–93.

53. This reclassification of the children as "European" also appears in a serialized novel about a black German girl; see Ursula Schaake, *"Meine schwarze Schwester: Der Roman eines Besatzungskindes,"* *Revue* 42 (Weihnachten 1960)–15 (9 April 1961).

54. "Brown Babies Go to Work: Germany Launches Smooth Integration of 1,500 Negro Youths in Its Work Force," *Ebony* (November 1960): 97–108.

55. Ebeling, "Zum Problem der deutschen Mischlingskinder"; Erna Maraun, "Zehn kleine Negerlein," *Der Rundbrief: Fachliches Mitteilungsblatt des Hauptjugendamtes Berlin* 3, no. 1 (1953): 2–6; Erhard Schneckenburger, "Das Mischlingskind in der Schule," *Neues Beginnen,* no. 1 (1957): 24; and BayHStA, MK 62245, report by the Ständige Konferenz der Kulturminister on the integration of "Mischlingskinder" into West German schools, 27 February 1956.

56. For an overview of the history of foreign workers in Germany, see Herbert, *A History of Foreign Labor in Germany.*

57. This quotation is from Hessische Hauptstaatsarchiv 940/77, draft letter dated 14 July 1960.

58. See the school reports on black German children in BayHStA, Minn 81084; HStAStg, EA2/007 Akten des Innenministeriums, Nr. 1177: "Jugendsozialhilfe"; and Staatsarchiv Freiburg, Bestand F110/1, Nr. 176.

59. Reports in HessHStA 940/77. Also see "Die Deutschen mit der dunklen Haut," *Quick* 46 (3–9 November 1977): 82–89; Ruth Bahn-Flessburg, "Sie haben die gleichen Chancen wie die Weissen: Auf der Suche nach den farbigen Besatzungskin-

dern," *Unsere Jugend* 20 (1968): 295–303; and Ruth Bahn-Flessburg, "Die Hautfarbe ist kein Problem: Farbige 'Besatzungskinder'—Vierzehn Lebensläufe," *Frankfurter Allgemeine Zeitung* (1968; copy in ADW, HGSt 3949).

60. Tolerance, rational argument and practice, humanistic values, and protection of the individual were the historical hallmarks of German liberalism and were enshrined in West Germany's Basic Law. Dieter Langewiesche, *Liberalism in Germany* (Princeton, N.J.: Princeton University Press, 2000); and Konrad H. Jarausch and Larry Eugene Jones, eds., *In Search of Liberal Germany: Studies in the History of German Liberalism from 1789 to the Present* (New York: Berg, 1990).

61. Eyferth remained the exception to this trend. BAK, B149: Bundesministerium für Arbeit und Sozialordnung, Nr. 8679; BayHStA, MInn 81126, press clippings on "Mischlingskinder," 1960–61; BayHStA, MK62245, "Volksschulwesen Negerkinder"; Hessisches Hauptstaatsarchiv, Abt. 940/77; Elly Waltz, "Mischlinge werden jetzt Lehrlinge," *Münchner Merkur* 164 (9–10 July 1960); "Farbige Lehrlinge— wieder sehr gefragt," *Münchner Merkur* 63 (15 March 1961); and Klaus Eyferth, "Gedanken über die zukünftige Berufseingliederung der Mischlingskinder in Westdeutschland," *Neues Beginnen* 5 (May 1959): 65–68.

62. BayHStA, MInn 81094, correspondence regarding the 1960 survey of occupation children and *Mischlingskinder*, 1960–61.

63. For example, Karen Thimm and DuRell Echols, *Schwarze in Deutschland* (Munich: Piper, 1973); Katharina Oguntoye, "Die Schwarze deutsche Bewegung und die Frauenbewegung in Deutschland," *Afrekete: Zeitung von afro-deutschen und schwarzen Frauen* 4 (1989): 3–5, 33–37; May Opitz, Katharina Oguntoye, and Dagmar Schultz, eds., *Showing Our Colors: Afro-German Women Speak Out* (Amherst: University of Massachusetts Press, 1991); Tina Campt, "Afro-German Identity and the Politics of Positionality," *New German Critique* 58 (winter 1993): 109–26; and May Ayim, "Die afro-deutsche Minderheit," in *Ethnische Minderheiten in der Bundesrepublik Deutschland*, ed. Cornelia Schmalz-Jacobsen and Georg Hansen (Munich: C. H. Beck, 1995), 39–52.

Twelve

The Difficult Task of Managing Migration

The 1973 Recruitment Stop

Karen Schönwälder

I

In Germany's post-1945 migration history, 23 November 1973 marks a turning point. On this day, almost eighteen years of organized foreign labor recruitment, and thus a major period of primary immigration, ended. A long phase followed in which West Germany tried to at least partly revise the process of immigration, and it was only in the year 2000 that a new citizenship law marked the official acceptance of the former guest workers and their descendants as regular members of German society.

The reasons behind the government's decision to stop foreign recruitment have until now not been a cause of major controversy. Most accounts assume that the oil crisis prompted the government to act and that politicians were unaware that their decision might encourage migrants—faced with the alternatives of leaving or staying for good—to opt for final settlement in Germany. German politicians were supposedly "blind to the future,"[1] and it was years before they realized that labor recruitment had instigated processes of permanent immigration. Or, as probably the most famous version of this account puts it, they did not realize that "while they had asked for workers, what they had received was human beings" (Max Frisch). Ignorance and the dominance of economic interests are thus seen as the reasons why German politicians allowed settlement but were unprepared for the emergence of a multiethnic German society.

As will be demonstrated in the following pages, at least some of these established assumptions have to be revised. More archival sources have now become available,[2] and they enable us to investigate the real motives and considerations guiding West German government actions. As it turns out, the switch

252

to a restrictive migration policy was no more motivated by the oil crisis than was the German government blind to ongoing immigration processes. In fact, there had even been some discussion about openly acknowledging Germany's transformation to a country of immigration and reforming its citizenship laws. Although this was not done, politicians had nonetheless consciously allowed immigration to proceed, even though permanent settlement on a large scale was generally seen as unwelcome. So what eventually prompted them to stop immigration, and how can we explain a half-hearted policy that was neither consistently for nor against immigration? In seeking to answer these questions, it will become clear that Germany's migration policy was shaped by a complex set of factors and can be understood only against the broad context of West Germany's political and social history.

II

When, in 1969, the reform coalition under Chancellor Willy Brandt came to power, about one and a half million foreigners were employed in the Federal Republic. A brief slowdown of the economy (in 1966–67) had been overcome, and the number of foreign workers had already exceeded the 1966 peak of 1.3 million. Recruitment now expanded at an unprecedented pace. In March 1971, the number exceeded two million,[3] and by mid-1973, German factories and services employed 2.6 million non–German nationals.

In 1969, neither Social Democrats nor Liberals questioned the continuation of foreign recruitment. As Karl Schiller, minister for the economy, explained during the debate on the first government program in the Federal Parliament (*Bundestag*), an expanding labor force was an indispensable prerequisite for sustained economic growth and could be achieved only through further recruitment of guest workers.[4] Two years later, Labor Minister Walter Arendt still publicly emphasized that foreigners were not a burden and that, like their German fellow workers, they contributed to economic growth and "increasing our prosperity."[5] The government believed that not only economic growth in general but more specifically its ambitious program of social reforms depended on this additional supply of labor. If school attendance was to be extended, if more young people were to go to university, and if workers were to be allowed longer holidays and earlier retirement, they had to be replaced in the factories. Otherwise, as German industrialists warned, growth rates would decline and this would endanger the government's reform program.[6]

And yet, while foreign recruitment was still publicly described as indispensable, in autumn 1971 reconsiderations of migration policy began within the government machinery, and by mid-1972 it was widely agreed that the number of foreigners in the Federal Republic should at least not be allowed to rise much further. Important aspects of migration policy still remained unclear or controversial. The exact aim of policy intervention was not yet clear and no strategy had been agreed. Should the main goal be to reduce overall numbers or to prevent the immigration of family members and thus long-term settlement? And, most importantly, what means of intervention were available to the government, and which might succeed? These questions were still unsolved when, in autumn 1973, the oil crisis presented a welcome opportunity to stop all foreign recruitment. The recruitment ban was in reality thus the result of a longer-term debate within the administration about the pros and cons of labor migration and the available policy options. But what were the reasons for the change of opinion? And did the West German government really expect to end or reverse permanent immigration when it stopped foreign labor recruitment?

III

Probably the most important reason for the policy change was the expected cost of providing acceptable housing, schooling for immigrant children, health care, and other social resources to immigrants, an issue which increasingly troubled politicians.[7] Guest worker recruitment had been profitable because foreign workers paid taxes and social insurance contributions but made few claims on the welfare system and other public provisions. But, increasingly, families settled in Germany, children began to attend schools, and patients needed doctors and hospital beds. In the long run it seemed unacceptable to house immigrants in run-down inner-city dwellings and basement rooms and to deny them access to publicly funded housing. While it remained unquestioned that federal and regional governments had to ensure the provision of schools, housing, and health care for German citizens, in the case of immigrants such expenditure was often regarded as an unwanted burden: an "at least implicitly chauvinistic and inhumane" position, as economist Bert Rürup opined in 1973.[8] As these worries illustrate, the government was well aware that it was dealing with long-term immigration and not just temporary guest workers. In 1972, during a time when the enormous expansion of foreign employment saw many newcomers joining the migrant workforce, an official study concluded that 21 percent of all foreign workers had arrived more than seven years before. Another 12 percent had come between 1965 and 1967, i.e., had lived in Germany for between five and seven years.[9] These figures were known to the government, and although the trend toward permanent immigration was often underestimated, it was clearly not ignored.[10]

Worries about social costs were reinforced by a broader reassessment of the economic costs and benefits of labor immigration. Thus the *Bundesbank* in 1972 warned that, given the costs of immigration, it was questionable whether labor recruitment would in the long run contribute to a favorable economic balance.[11] While the recruitment of additional labor, i.e., an expansion of the labor force, had for a long time been regarded as an essential component of economic growth, reorientations of economic policy encouraged different views. In the public debate the idea that there were "Limits of Growth" emerged, and an expansive economic strategy became the target of more fundamental criticism.[12] Negative evaluations of the considerable German export surplus and a new emphasis on containing inflation played a part. Helmut Schmidt, who in July 1972 became finance minister, represented the changing priorities and took a negative stance toward a further expansion of foreign employment.[13] He argued that, as the peak of the boom had been reached, "current overemployment" should be reduced: "It is completely unhealthy that we employ two-and-a-half million foreign workers in order to produce a 30 million Marks export surplus."[14] Views were not uniform, and the Economics Ministry in 1973 still favored a high level of foreign employment.[15] But unhindered access to additional foreign workers was no longer regarded as the more or less unquestioned condition of economic well-being.

It was not money and the economy alone that concerned politicians. Increasingly they began to worry about the consequences of immigration for German society. Partly this was a response to the events of September 1972. During the Olympic Games in Munich a group of Palestinians had taken a number of Israeli athletes and officials hostage and eleven Israelis had been killed. For several weeks the events dominated newspaper headings. *Innere Sicherheit* (domestic security) became a prominent topic of public discussion, and there was a danger—as the Protestant Church and others feared—that migrants in general would be held responsible for Palestinian terrorism.[16] Indeed, already in 1970 the popular newspaper *Bild* had called upon its readers to join in the chase for those who had set a Jewish retirement home in Munich on fire. The paper alleged that some of the guest workers and foreign students in Germany were disguised supporters of the terrorists.[17]

In summer and autumn 1972 Chancellor Willy Brandt had been extremely worried about developments that threatened to undermine public support for his government. Because of the conflicts over *Ostpolitik*, federal elections were to be held in November.[18] For Brandt, rising prices, the unappealing spectacle of a Social Democratic Party torn by internal conflicts, and worries about domestic security all contributed to a dangerous political situation. Against this background, the terrorist attack of 5 September was a particularly devastating shock. Had the elections been held then, Brandt believed, the Conservatives would have won.[19]

In the 1972 election manifesto of the Social Democratic Party (SPD), migration policy was featured under domestic security.[20] Critics who wanted to emphasize social problems were silenced by Willy Brandt himself, who insisted that a major party had to reflect the concerns of the population. Tough measures were required against those who wanted to turn the Federal Republic into a place where violence could flourish (*Tummelplatz von*

Gewalttätigkeiten).[21] Foreigners thus increasingly appeared as a risk to the security and well-being of the German population, and potential German xenophobia and racism increasingly influenced migration policy. In fact, virtually no protests against immigration had erupted so far. If Germans did not exactly welcome the foreign migrants, their presence was mostly accepted. In the media, more hostile articles began to appear from 1972, but foreigners were also often portrayed as victims of exploitation and as people whose miserable living conditions no social-minded German could tolerate.[22] By turning to a more restrictive migration policy, the government thus responded preemptively to potential protest against immigration and—not atypically—to developments that could diminish its future electoral chances.

Furthermore, politicians feared that social unrest could arise from another source. Apart from Germans protesting against further immigration, the immigrants themselves might in future no longer patiently accept their exclusion from much of what German society offered. Speaking before a workers' assembly, the chancellor expressed his concern about the possible emergence of social and political conflicts because of the housing situation and limited educational opportunities for the guest workers and their children.[23] In the Ministry for the Interior, fears existed that a further increase of immigration would lead to the formation of ghettoes and increasing tensions between different population groups.[24]

Thus a number of factors contributed to an altogether changed assessment of foreign labor recruitment to the Federal Republic of Germany. By mid-1972 a consensus existed that some kind of intervention was required. During the 1972 election campaign, Willy Brandt as well as liberal leader Hans Dietrich Genscher, the minister of the interior, publicly announced that the new government would change West Germany's migration policy. In June the chancellor had already informed German industrialists that there were limits to the number of foreign workers Germany could absorb. Probably a critical number had already been reached.[25] Similarly, Genscher publicly emphasized that the limits of Germany's absorptive capacities had been reached and migration policy had to be reconsidered.[26] So what was to be done?

IV

In 1972–73, two main policy options were debated in West Germany, conveniently summarized in the press as "rotation" and "integration." Rotation was favored by the regional government of Bavaria as well as some representatives of the employers' association.[27] This strategy was potentially effective in preventing immigration. A rotation policy would have allowed the number of foreign workers to remain high, thus serving employers' interests, while the workers' stay in Germany would have been strictly limited to a couple of years and families kept out. Social costs would have been kept to a minimum and permanent immigration avoided. Contrary to widespread assumptions in the secondary literature, West Germany never actually practiced such a policy of rotation. Although residence permits were in general only valid for a limited period of time, they were usually renewed, and, before 1974, legally resident foreigners were rarely expelled.[28] In 1972–73, a policy of rotation was briefly considered in internal government circles, but, although in some ways attractive, it was never likely to become official policy.[29] As early as January 1972, the government had committed itself not to use any legal instruments to limit foreigners' stay.[30] In the course of a confrontation with Christian Social Union–governed Bavaria, the rejection of rotation had acquired the status of a key plank of Social Democratic and Liberal policy.[31] The conflict had arisen when, in winter 1971–72, local authorities in Bavaria and Schleswig-Holstein had informed foreign residents that they would soon have to leave Germany, as their stay was approaching a length at which permanent settlement became likely. In a heated public debate, rotation was overwhelmingly branded a brutal concept, incompatible with the social and humanitarian principles of West German society.[32] As Willy Brandt emphasized, "We have to avoid giving the impression that we regard the foreign workers in the Federal Republic as an industrial reserve army that can be invited into the country and driven out again at will. This would be unsocial, it would be inhumane, and, furthermore, it would be uneconomic." Out of a "spirit of social responsibility" the government had rejected a policy of forced rotation.[33]

Additionally, employers were not altogether favorably disposed toward a policy that would have required them to constantly train new employees. The trade unions objected to such harsh treatment of workers, and they also disliked the idea of a constant influx of young and fit competitors for German workers. Furthermore, there were fears that a huge crowd of lonely and discontented male foreigners could become a source of social unrest.[34]

Interior Minister Genscher, a member of the liberal Free Democratic Party, proposed a radical alternative to rotation. Like many of his colleagues, he was worried about immigration and convinced that the government had to intervene in order to limit a further influx. But unlike many other politicians he believed that, as well as stopping recruitment, the government should take courageous steps toward a true integration of those migrants who were here to stay. Could it possibly be right, he asked, to take people in only for a short period of time? Was it not instead necessary to opt for a "true immigration policy with full integration"?[35] When the Interior Affairs Committee of the Federal Parliament in February 1973 discussed the issue, Genscher declared that in his opinion, since Germany was "in fact an immigration country—we have no choice but to implement an immigration policy."[36]

While Genscher was the first top politician to publicly favor a policy of immigration and naturalization, he was not alone. As early as 1971, calls for a new immigration and naturalization policy had been heard from within the churches, in some newspapers, and in other circles. Even the Christian Democrats' Committees for Social Affairs (*Sozialausschüsse*), at the party's 1971 congress, declared Germany a de facto country of immigration.[37] According to a widespread consensus in the newspapers, the government's rejection of rotation and its declared policy of integration could hardly mean anything but the eventual naturalization of the long-term immigrants.[38] What else could it mean, if differences between Germans and immigrants were to be abolished? As these examples illustrate, the idea that Germany was not a country of immigration was, in the early 1970s, not at all generally shared. A number of Germans seem to have accepted the idea of a less ethnically homogenous West German population.

V

Genscher's twofold strategy of closing the doors to new immigration while at the same time taking bold steps toward full-blown integration of those who wanted to stay in Germany did not win much support among his Cabinet colleagues. It was opposed by the Labor Ministry, where fears of competition for jobs and general reservations about immigration were strong. Minister Arendt was not in favor of easier naturalizations.[39] As head of the Miners' Union, Arendt had opposed foreign recruitment and—in a fairly undisguised nationalist statement—claimed that the Turks in particular could never become part of the highly qualified, close-knit German miners' workforce.[40] The trade unions and parts of the Social Democratic Party were, in the early 1970s, clearly not in favor of opening Germany's doors to permanent immigration. As later reactions to the immigration stop illustrate, it was widely believed that when jobs became scarce, immigrants would have to give way to Germans. If the migrants acquired German nationality, it would be impossible to drive them out. Additionally, a more generous naturalization policy could be understood as an invitation to foreigners to settle in Germany and might thus motivate even more of them to stay.

Within the Cabinet, the foreign secretary and the development minister pointed to the interests of the sending countries, who did not want to lose their citizens forever.[41] Willy Brandt took such foreign policy considerations very seriously. For him the labor migrants formed a "fluctuating" minority, not a settled and rooted one,[42] and he described them as "co-citizens with their own status" ("*Mitbürger, die ihren eigenen Status haben*").[43] Asked about naturalization policy, he pointed out that Yugoslavia would respond to a more generous policy by stopping emigration to Germany.[44]

Openly nationalistic objections to a liberal immigration and naturalization policy were rarely voiced—or at least rarely recorded in the files. But there seems little doubt that Germans found it generally difficult to imagine an ethnically plural German nation, and there were fears that naturalizations without assimilation would introduce minority conflicts into West German politics and society.[45]

And, last but not least, the government was probably afraid of negative reactions from the German population if, by declaring the Federal Republic a country of immigration, it openly acknowledged its responsibility for mass immigration and the transformation of West Germany into a multicultural society.

VI

In the end, Genscher's suggestion of closed doors combined with thorough integration of existing immigrants could not win majority support in the Cabinet. But, as rotation was also ruled out, what other strategies and policy instruments were available?

A range of different options were debated in interministerial discussions and within the *Sozialpolitische Gesprächsrunde,* a consulting body on matters of social policy that included major actors in civil society. There were strong objections to any reduction of the foreign workforce. If foreign employment was not allowed to rise any further, the president of the Federal Employment Agency warned in July 1973, annual growth rates would decline by 0.5 or even 1 percent.[46] If the government wanted to stick to its economic targets and to its social reform objectives, including reduced working hours, then more foreign workers would be needed. As late as October 1973, the Federal Economics Ministry regarded a figure of 2.5 million foreign workers (possibly plus a further 0.3 million) as necessary if a reduction of the available labor force was to be avoided. The ministry was confident that the government could rely on economic mechanisms to regulate employment levels.[47] As the minister informed his Cabinet colleague Walter Scheel in March 1973, a noticeable reduction of foreign employment was not intended and a recruitment stop unwanted.[48] Obviously, as the above-mentioned calls for a restrictive anti-inflation policy illustrate, there was no agreement on economic needs. While there were economically motivated demands for a more restrictive policy from some quarters, for its part the Economics Ministry did not call for a recruitment stop.

Further doubts arose out of foreign policy considerations, which—as officials and politicians believed until 1973—made a restrictive policy impossible.[49] Inquiries abroad convinced Foreign Secretary Scheel that a recruitment stop and a noticeable reduction of the number of foreign employees would seriously disrupt the Federal Republic's relations with the main sending countries.[50] West Germany was reluctant to act on its own, and for a considerable time insisted that longer-term solutions could be found only in a European framework.[51] The government's reservations were not solely about regulations within the European Community, among whose members only Italy was, at the time, a major exporter of labor migrants. West Germany, as can hardly be overemphasized, was a state whose policy was largely defined by considerations of its integration in the Western world, its standing as an export-oriented economy, and—during the key phase of *Ostpolitik* in particular—its relations with its Eastern neighbors, including labor-exporting Yugoslavia. Labor migration was never solely an economic affair; it was also an instrument of foreign policy. This has so far been neglected in the literature.

Given these considerations, officials were struggling to find any potentially effective and politically acceptable strategy. A working group of the *Sozialpolitische Gesprächsrunde* and an interministerial committee of officials considered several options. By putting a ceiling on foreign recruitment (as favored by the Interior Ministry[52]), numbers would be limited, but this would not restrict family migration. Additionally, the Labor Ministry and the Federal Employment Agency feared that politically administered restrictions of this kind would require an allocation mechanism reminiscent of the Nazis' forced labor system. And furthermore, selective interventions into economic processes might have unpredictable negative consequences.[53] It seems that no one wanted to be the villain: the Interior Ministry had similarly declared expulsions to enforce a maximum stay—for which it would have been responsible—unfeasible.[54]

Thus, when in June 1973 the Cabinet for the first time debated the issue, a stalemate had been reached. Influential ministers disagreed on important aspects, and no generally agreeable and potentially effective solution had been found.[55] Consequently, only intermediate measures were agreed on, and the Labor Ministry was assigned the task of developing a longer-term migration policy. The announced policy of "socially responsible consolidation" involved cautious measures aiming to make foreign recruitment more expensive and to set quotas for foreigners in some urban areas. Publicly, the government claimed that the latter measures would help adjust the level of foreign employment to the capacities of the social infrastructure.[56] In fact, this was a middle way intended to lead to a reduction of numbers while shifting the difficult tasks, including setting and administering a quota as well as publicly defending it, to the local authorities. Clearly, local foreigner quotas represented a fairly strong intervention into the rights of foreign residents, severely restricting their choice of employment and residence.[57] To honor the government's commitment to a policy of integration, it was agreed that residence rights should be strengthened.[58] The Cabinet's decisions thus represented a compromise between restrictionism and integration which refrained from consistent measures in any direction.

VII

Officials were still struggling to interpret the Cabinet's half-hearted decisions when the oil crisis changed the political framework. Public concern and the possibility of rising unemployment increased pressure on the Cabinet to act. Foreign policy repercussions could now be limited, as the oil-exporting countries could be held responsible for whatever restrictive steps were taken. On 22 November 1973, the Cabinet decided—under the heading of a report on the energy situation—that foreign recruitment would be stopped. Apparently the decision was taken without much discussion or preparation; there was not even a memo considering its implications.[59] Quite probably, Labor Minister Arendt seized the opportunity to enact restrictive policies he had favored for some time but not been able to get through the Cabinet. On the TV news he explained that it had for some time been intended to reduce the inflow—after all, the Federal Republic was not a country of immigration.[60] Now, as bold decisions had been taken, some politicians abandoned their previous caution. "The time of pussyfooting and caution is over," the chairman of the trade union federation, Heinz Oskar Vetter, exclaimed on TV. "Charity begins at home" ("*Hier ist uns das Hemd näher als der Rock*") he argued, and now the priority was to protect the jobs of "our German workers here in the Federal Republic," and after that the jobs of those foreigners already in the country. And Northrhine-Westfalia's economics minister opined that while the guest workers could not simply be sent home, if confronted with the alternative of keeping a guest worker or a German worker, he would opt for the German.[61]

At the time, the recruitment stop was not understood or intended as a decisive policy turn. Officials in the federal ministries continued to devise measures for the time when the recruitment stop would be lifted, and the Cabinet expected the Labor Ministry to draw up a long-term strategic plan. In 1975–76 this idea of strategic planning was given up. It had become apparent that conflicts within the governing coalition on how to deal with the guest worker population could not be resolved. Attempts on the part of the Labor Ministry to introduce harsher measures to enforce the departure of foreigners repeatedly clashed with positions, held by the interior minister and others, which emphasized individual rights.[62] Among the wider public, neither a harsher restrictionist course nor a consistent policy of integration was likely to find unequivocal support, and the government feared major conflicts. Thus it continued to muddle on until, in 1982, the conservative-led government under Helmut Kohl took over.

In hindsight, the recruitment stop marked a policy U-turn, from extensive foreign recruitment and what had been in effect a laissez-faire attitude toward immigration to an effort to reduce Germany's immigrant population and to prevent any further influx. From now on, and for almost two decades, West German governments attempted to counter the trend toward permanent immigration that arose as a consequence of foreign recruitment and denied that significant immigration had already transformed German society. But, at the same time, they shied away—and were prevented by immigrants' legal rights—from effectively intervening in processes of settlement. The result was the policy of "return-oriented integration," as the *Süddeutsche Zeitung* in 1973 described it,[63] a self-contradictory and inconsistent policy which tried to combine the incompatible aims of both integrating and getting rid of the migrants.

In 1973, the West German government's actions were not guided by a clear and agreed-on strategy. Calls for a clarification of longer-term goals were widespread, and surely the immigrants would have welcomed more precise and reliable information about their future in Germany. The political leadership, however, was unable to balance the complex set of factors linked with migration processes and migration policy and was unwilling to face a conflict within German society. Although hopes existed that a considerable number of foreigners would return home, politicians and officials were aware of ongoing and irreversible settlement processes. Foreign policy considerations, humanitarian and social beliefs, the legal position of foreigners, and the influence of a pro-migrants lobby prevented it from moving toward an active anti-immigration policy including more rigorous measures to force foreigners out of the country. But, on the other hand, those hopes that at least part of the immigrant population would leave, together with fears of negative reactions from the German population and foreign policy considerations, prevented the Social Democratic and Liberal government until 1982 from openly recognizing immigration and adopting an immigration policy.

Notes

1. Ulrich Herbert, *Geschichte der Ausländerbeschäftigung in Deutschland, 1880 bis 1980: Saisonarbeiter, Zwangsarbeiter, Gastarbeiter* (Bonn: Dietz, 1986), 234. For a different version, see Karen Schönwälder, Anne von Oswald, and Barbara Sonnenberger, "Einwanderungsland Deutschland: A New Look at Its Post-war History," in *European Encounters: Migrants, Migration, and European Societies since 1945*, ed. Karen Schönwälder, Rainer Ohliger, and Triadafilos Triadafilopoulos (Aldershot: Ashgate, 2003), 19–37; and Karen Schönwälder, *Einwanderung und ethnische Pluralität: Politische Entscheidungen und öffentliche Debatten in Großbritannien und der Bundesrepublik von den 1950er bis zu den 1970er Jahren* (Essen: Klartext, 2001).

2. In particular, relevant government records in the Federal Archives (*Bundesarchiv*), which remain closed for thirty years, have now been opened. Some documents in the Parliamentary Archive and the files of the Trade Union Federation were accessible before 2004.

3. Strangely enough, in March 1972 the president of the Federal Manpower Agency (*Bundesanstalt für Arbeit*) formally welcomed the two-millionth foreign worker, Vera Rimski from Yugoslavia.

4. *Verhandlungen des Deutschen Bundestages*, 7th session/6th electoral period, 30 October 1969, 177.

5. Walter Arendt, "Zum Geleit," *Das Parlament* 21, nos. 34–35 (21 August 1971).

6. *Geschäftsbericht der Deutschen Bundesbank für das Jahr 1971*, 4–5; president of the *Bundesanstalt für Arbeit* to the labor minister, 9 January 1973, re "Zulassung ausländischer Arbeitnehmer in Verdichtungsgebieten," in Archiv der sozialen Demokratie (hereafter AdsD), DGB-Bundesvorstand 5/DGAZ 513.

7. See, for instance, a paper for *Ausländerbeschäftigung*, a working group of the *Sozialpolitische Gesprächsrunde*, dated 25 November 1971, in AdsD, DGB-Bundesvorstand 5/DGCQ 12. The paper stated that a further increase in foreign employment, longer stays, and family reunions would lead to significantly higher social costs because social measures would have to be intensified and oriented toward permanent integration. The *Sozialpolitische Gesprächsrunde* had first met in March 1970 and was meant to support a more integrated approach to social policy and cooperation between state and civil society actors.

8. Klaus Höpfner, Bernd Ramann, and Bert Rürup, *Ausländische Arbeitnehmer: Gesamtwirtschaftliche Probleme und Steuerungsmöglichkeiten* (Bonn: Gesellschaft für Regionale Strukturentwicklung, 1973), 44–46.

9. *Repräsentativuntersuchung '72 über die Beschäftigung ausländischer Arbeitnehmer im Bundesgebiet und ihre Familien- und Wohnverhältnisse, Beilage zu den Amtlichen Nachrichten der Bundesanstalt für Arbeit* 11 (Nürnberg, 1973), 32–33. At the time of the survey, the number of foreign workers was 2.215 million.

10. See, e.g., discussions in the Federal Ministry for the Interior, whose officials met in October 1971 to discuss consequences of foreign workers' staying longer. They noted that, "as a social phenomenon," stay length was not yet fully understood, but that it was unrealistic to introduce a limit. Note on a meeting on 6 October 1971, in Bundesarchiv Koblenz (hereafter BA Ko) B 106/69844.

11. *Geschäftsbericht der Deutschen Bundesbank für das Jahr 1971*, 4–5. The Federal Bank argued that, given the demands on the infrastructure, it was doubtful whether the expansion of employment could, in the long term, still contribute to stabilization of the overall economic balance (*Festigung des gesamtwirtschaftlichen Gleichgewichts*).

12. Donella H. Meadows et al., *The Limits to Growth: A Report for the Club of Rome's Project on the Predicament of Mankind* (New York: Universe, 1972).

13. See the record of a television interview on the ZDF program *Bilanz* on 31 August 1972, in *Kommentarübersicht des Presse- und Informationsamtes*.

14. Helmut Schmidt, interview in *Der Spiegel* 40 (1 October 1973): 44. See also a speech by Schmidt in the *Bundestag*, 59th session/7th electoral period, 23 October 1973, 3430.

15. Federal Ministry for the Economy to Labor Ministry, 30 October 1973, in BA Ko B 106/69847.

16. See Schönwälder, *Einwanderung und ethnische Pluralität*, 531, 595–600.

17. "Jagt sie, bis sie hinter Schloß und Riegel sitzen!" *Bild*, 16 February 1970; see also commentaries on 25 February 1970 ("Bei Leuten, die Bomben sprechen lassen, helfen keine schönen Worte") and on 11 February 1970 ("Heckenschützen!").

18. In April 1972 the government, a coalition of Social Democrats and Liberals, narrowly survived a vote of no confidence in the *Bundestag*. As the government no longer had a majority in Parliament, early elections were called. The vote had been called by the Conservative opposition after the government had signed treaties with the Soviet Union, Poland, and East Germany and accepted the postwar borders.

19. Willy Brandt, *Begegnungen und Einsichten: Die Jahre 1960-1975* (Hamburg: Hoffmann und Campe, 1976), 571.

20. *Wahlprogramm der SPD*, 16–17.

21. *Außerordentlicher Parteitag der Sozialdemokratischen Partei Deutschlands, 12.- 13. Oktober 1972*, 184–85.

22. For more details see Schönwälder, *Einwanderung und ethnische Pluralität*, 585– 90, 545.

23. Willy Brandt, "Ansprache vor der Henschel-Belegschaft am 5.10.1972," in *Bulletin des Presse- und Informationsamtes der Bundesregierung*, no. 140 (6 October 1972), 1694.

24. Draft letter intended to be sent by Genscher to Brandt, February 1972, BA Ko B 106/69844. The letter remained unsent and should be interpreted as expressing not Genscher's opinions but rather those of officials in the ministry. Contrary to occasional assumptions in the secondary literature, there is no indication in the files that the 1972–73 strikes in the metal industry, in which foreign workers played a prominent role, influenced decision making.

25. Willy Brandt, "Ziele und Grundsätze der Wirtschafts- und Finanzpolitik der Bundesregierung," in *Bulletin des Presse- und Informationsamtes der Bundesregierung*, no. 88 (15 June 1972), 1211.

26. See, e.g., his interviews with the *Westdeutsche Allgemeine Zeitung* on 5 October 1972 and with the *Saarländischer Rundfunk* on 8 October 1972; for the latter see the transcript in the *Kommentarübersicht des Presse- und Informationsamtes* of 9 October 1972.

27. See Schönwälder, *Einwanderung und ethnische Pluralität*, 550–53, 618–23.

28. However, in 1966–67 and from 1974 onward, foreign workers were pressured and sometimes forced to leave West Germany when their labor permits had not been renewed. In December 1973, trade unions and employers agreed that foreign workers should be encouraged to return "voluntarily." See the minutes of a meeting of representatives of DGB and BDA (*Bundesvereinigung der Deutschen Arbeitgeberverbände*) on 10 December 1973, in BA Ko B 149/54458.

29. In March 1973 references to a rotation policy were first included in drafts of a cabinet memorandum, but then dropped—apparently because of interventions by the Interior Ministry (see documents in BA Ko B 149/83758). There are indications that Hans Friderichs, the liberal minister for the economy, was in favor of rotation (see his letter to Foreign Secretary Scheel, 27 March 1973, in BA Ko B 106/45163, and his interview with the *Süddeutscher Rundfunk* on 8 April 1973, partly reproduced in the *Kommentarübersicht des Presse- und Informationsamtes*), and this strategy had supporters within the Labor Ministry. The Labor Ministry's cabinet memorandum of 16 May 1973 did say that Germany should actively encourage return and that no barriers should hinder voluntary return (in BA Ko B 106/69846).

30. "Mit ausländerrechtlichen Maßnahmen wird nicht auf eine zeitliche Begrenzung des Aufenthaltes ausländischer Arbeitnehmer hingewirkt," reply to a parliamentary question by Hussing et al., "Politik der Bundesregierung gegenüber den aus-

ländischen Arbeitnehmern in der Bundesrepublik Deutschland," *Deutscher Bundestag, Drucksache* 6/3085, 31 January 1972, 4.

31. See the notes (*Sprechzettel*) for the interior minister's speech at the Conference of the Federal and the Regional Ministers for the Interior (*Innenministerkonferenz*) on 30 November 1973 (dated 19 November 1973), in BA Ko B 106/69847.

32. For more details see Schönwälder, *Einwanderung und ethnische Pluralität*, 612–26.

33. Willy Brandt, "Besuch in Rüsselsheim: Rede vor der Belegschaft der Opel-Werke am 26.6.1973," in *Bulletin des Presse- und Informationsamtes der Bundesregierung*, no. 79 (28 June 1973), 795–97.

34. The Ministry for the Interior listed five arguments against rotation: security concerns, possible accusations that Germany was exploiting foreigners, employers' objections, the liberal spirit of the Aliens Act, and the difficulties of enforcing deportations. See a note for the minister dated 31 January 1973, BA Ko B 106/45163.

35. Hans Dietrich Genscher, interview in the *Westdeutsche Allgemeine Zeitung*, 5 October 1972.

36. Addendum to the minutes of the third meeting on 21 February 1973: "Fortsetzung der Aussprache über das Arbeitsprogramm des BMI in der 7. WP," 20, in Parliamentary Archive, Bonn, Ausschuß für Inneres, 7. Wahlperiode.

37. "Beschluß der 14. Bundestagung der CDA am 3./4.7.1971 in Koblenz," *Soziale Ordnung*, 5 August 1971, 20.

38. See Schönwälder, *Einwanderung und ethnische Pluralität*, 612–19.

39. See the note by Abteilungsleiter V. Fröhlich, Interior Ministry, 9 February 1973, about talks with Abteilungsleiter Baden in the Labor Ministry, BA Ko B 106/69845.

40. *Verhandlungen des Deutschen Bundestages*, 13 November 1964, 7247–48.

41. Foreign Secretary Scheel to Interior Minister Genscher, 28 February 1973, in BA Ko B 106/69845; Federal Ministry for Economic Cooperation to Labor Ministry, 17 April 1973, in BA Ko B 106/69846.

42. Willy Brandt, "Rede bei der Eröffnungsveranstaltung zur 'Woche der Brüderlichkeit' am 21.3.1971," *Bulletin des Presse- und Informationsamtes der Bundesregierung* 43 (23 March 1971): 442.

43. Willy Brandt, "Die Verantwortung der Kommunen für den Ausbau der Demokratie, Rede vor der ersten Mitgliederversammlung des Deutschen Städte- und Gemeindebundes am 5.10.1973," *Bulletin des Presse- und Informationsamtes der Bundesregierung* 126 (6 October 1973): 1240.

44. Willy Brandt, "Interview des Bundeskanzlers mit dem Norwegischen Rundfunk und Fernsehen am 3.6.1973," *Bulletin des Presse- und Informationsamtes der Bundesregierung* 67 (5 June 1973): 665.

45. See, e.g., an internal policy paper by officials in the Interior Ministry dated 23 January 1973 ("Die ausländischen Arbeitnehmer in der Bundesrepublik Deutschland. Möglichkeiten und Grenzen ihrer Integration im Ressortbereich der inneren Verwaltung"), in BA Ko B 106/69845.

46. Josef Stingl, "Gastarbeiter passen sich an," interview in the *Rheinischer Merkur*, 27 July 1973.

47. Letter from the Federal Ministry for the Economy to the Labor Ministry, 30 October 1973, in BA Ko B 106/69847.

48. Minister Friderichs to Foreign Secretary Scheel, 27 March 1973, in BA Ko B 106/45163.

49. Helmut Heyden, "Diskussion über die Ausländerbeschäftigung in Europa," *Bundesarbeitsblatt* 24 (1973): 36. See also Interior Minister Genscher's statements to the Interior Affairs Committee of the Federal Parliament, addendum to the minutes of the third meeting on 21 February 1973: "Fortsetzung der Aussprache über das Arbeitsprogramm des BMI in der 7. WP," 18, in Parliamentary Archive.

50. Foreign Secretary Scheel to Interior Minister Genscher, 28 February 1973, in BA Ko B 106/69845.

51. See the speech of Labor Minister Walter Arendt to the Federal Parliament on 6 June 1973, *Verhandlungen des Deutschen Bundestages*, 2065. The German government suggested joint action on the occasion of the Paris Conference of the European Communities in October 1972; see "Deutsche Initiative für eine europäische Sozial- und Gesellschaftspolitik," *Bulletin des Presse- und Informationsamtes der Bundesregierung* 147 (20 October 1972): 1757.

52. See a letter to the Labor Ministry of 13 April 1973, containing suggestions for the cabinet discussion. The Interior Ministry pressed for annual targets for the number of foreigners while, on the other hand, it favored expanded residence rights and easier naturalization (BA Ko B 106/69846).

53. Heyden, "Diskussion über die Ausländerbeschäftigung in Europa," 36. For the discussion in the working group of the *Sozialpolitische Gesprächsrunde,* see documents in AdsD, DGB-Bundesvorstand 5/DGCQ 12.

54. See, e.g., a note for the cabinet discussion (*Sprechzettel*), prepared for the interior minister by an official, 28 May 1973, in BA Ko B 106/69846.9

55. The cabinet discussion had been planned for March and was then deferred because ministers could not agree on key measures. Brandt himself met with Genscher, Scheel, and Arendt to sort out problems, which was unusual (see a note of 27 March 1973 for the interior minister, in BA Ko B 106/69845).

56. Different versions of the cabinet memorandum and an extract from the cabinet minutes of 6 June 1973 can be found in BA Ko B 106/69846. The cabinet's decisions were explained to the *Bundestag* and published; see Weidenbörner, "Aktionsprogramm zur Ausländerbeschäftigung," in *Bundesarbeitsblatt* 24 (1973), 350–54, with a summary of the cabinet's decisions.

57. For harsh contemporary criticism of the measures and their discriminatory character, see *Journal* G 2 (December 1973): 9–11; and 3 (1974): 4–5.

58. More secure residence rights (*unbefristete Aufenthaltserlaubnis* or *Aufenthaltsberechtigung*) were to be granted after five and eight years of residence in West Germany. In fact, these changes were not introduced until 1978.

59. The cabinet minutes are quoted in Arnulf Baring, with Manfred Görtemaker, *Machtwechsel: Die Ära Brandt-Scheel* (Stuttgart: Deutsche Verlags-Anstalt, 1982), 690. For the recruitment stop, see BA Ko B 149/54458. Shortly before, on 5 November, an interministerial meeting of officials had taken place to discuss the implementation of the cabinet's decisions of June 1973. The minutes (or rather a note [*Vermerk*]) give the impression that ministries basically remained inactive; there is no indication that any decisive measures were to be taken. The next meeting of the working group was fixed for March 1974 (see the *Vermerk* sent by the Labor Ministry to Chancellery and other ministries on 12 November 1973, in BA Ko B 106/69847).

60. He did this on 23 November 1973; see the transcript in the *Kommentarübersicht des Presse- und Informationsamtes* of 26 November 1973.

61. The minister did so on the news program *Heute* on 23 November 1973; see the transcript in the *Kommentarübersicht des Presse- und Informationsamtes* of 26 November 1973.

62. "Ganz ohne Türken oder Griechen geht es nicht," a paper on interministerial discussions and disagreements reprinted in the *Frankfurter Rundschau*, 23 February 1976.

63. "Ein Signal macht das Millionenheer nervös," *Süddeutsche Zeitung*, 7 December 1973.

Thirteen

How and Where Is German History Centered?

Geoff Eley

I

First, a strong distinguishing thesis: Germany's continuity as a national state, far more than that of the other European polities shaped by the constitution-making of the 1860s (including Italy, its exact peer as a newly unified country), has been repeatedly spoiled. Its official borders have been frequently and drastically redrawn; within the claims to nationhood the gaps between territorial integrity and cultural formation have been both variable and extreme; its constitutional forms have run the gamut from centralism to federalism, dictatorship to democracy, monarchy to republic. "Germany" has been an abstract, mobile, contingent, and highly contested political term. It has only ever approximated the postulated unity of territory, language, institutions, high-cultural traditions, and customary heritage which nationalist discourse—and the usages of common sense—would like to assume. Within 150 years, six major ruptures occurred: during 1864–71, 1914–18, 1918–23, 1936–45, 1945–49, and the still unfolding consequences of 1989–92. With each of these territorial-cum-constitutional rearrangements, the languages of nationhood have either cleared a space for democratic experimentation, or else closed it down. Whatever the outcomes of the immediate political contests, moreover, "Germany" has emerged with the playing field of citizenship and democracy fundamentally changed.

Germany's indeterminacy contrasts with the settled constancy of, say, British national history over the same time. Of course, the big disruptions in British history occurred overseas, in the acquisition and loss of empire. *That* turbulence constitutively shaped Britain's domestic political culture and sometimes penetrated closer to home, as in the rural violence of peasant dispossession in the Celtic borderlands from the late eighteenth to late nineteenth centuries, or in Ulster's peripheral instabilities. But in seriousness and centrality this matched neither the territorial upheavals of unification, conquest, invasion, annexation, dismemberment, partition, and reunification nor the constitutional revolutions and revisions experienced by Germany between Bismarck and Helmut Kohl. Among territorialized political identity, citizenship, and the institutional coordinates of the nation form, British national history afforded reliable continuities which German history palpably lacked.

Moreover, these days not only are the indeterminacies and contingencies of the nation, nationhood, and national identity repeatedly invoked in scholarly discussion, but so are those of other key political terms, from *citizenship* to *the state*. We now believe that, rather than being stable or transparent in meaning, or juridically fixed during the later nineteenth and earlier twentieth centuries, these terms were culturally constructed. They rested on explicit, subtle, and disguised languages and mechanisms of inclusion and exclusion. They were subject to disagreement, conflict, counterinterpretation, and contestation. And they could be transformed. Beyond the organized political contest of dominant and oppositional social forces and their parties, moreover, wider differences of meaning also circulated less visibly through the political cultures concerned. Complicated processes of delegitimization and entitlement were involved, privileging some social groups and categories of people over others. Such differences within the national citizenry—or between those who were accorded the full faculties of citizenship and those who were not—were ordered by gender, class, race, religion, sexual orientation, and other logics of centeredness and marginalization.[1]

Given the dramas of the nineteenth- and twentieth-century German past, in which the unities of national and state-centered political reproduction have been broken so many times, German history offers excellent opportunities for getting inside these indeterminacies—that is, for exploring the processes of transformation and normalization involved in the modern histories of citizenship and their imperfectly realized promises of democracy.

II

The inchoateness of national affiliations in the nineteenth century made the boundaries of national categories in Europe during this period anything but stable and mature. Indeed, for current writing on nationalism that lack of fixity has become almost axiomatic, emphasizing rather the indeterminacies, amorphousness, and impermanence in how national identity came to be formed. But within this "constructionist" idiom national affiliations can easily appear far too malleable and free-floating. There is often an unresolved tension between the insights of the new theorizing about nationalism and the analysis needed of national identity in particular places and times. After 1918, for example, national identifications certainly became hardened into continuities in juridical, institutional, ideological, and other ways, whereas before 1914 the full-blown ideal of the nation-people-citizenry as the basis for state-political organization was still only in the process of being formed. Accordingly, if we are to grasp those dynamics of emergence, we need to temper the idea of nationalism's changeability and unfinishedness by seeing the instituted and material finiteness of the resources available for nationalist action, however creative and bold, at any one time.

Here, the passage to statehood marks a key watershed in the life of any nationalist movement. Owning the nation-state, with its juridical machinery of constitutions, legal codes, courts, and police, its centralized administrative systems, its society-wide institutions in governmental, party, and associational terms, and its organized cultural life, enormously alters both the strength of national identifications and the modalities for building them. Under those circumstances the ideal of "the nation," as against other principles of state-political organization, became a source of extraordinary legitimizing power in the centralizing drives of the nineteenth century, enabling demands on people's loyalties quite different from the expectations of earlier forms of government. As Benedict Anderson famously expressed this, the willingness to sacrifice one's own body and die for the nation, that emotionally gripping call on the citizen's deepest loyalties memorialized in poetry and monuments, became the extreme heroic form for this suturing together of the individual and the nation.[2]

It made a huge difference to this discourse of sacrificial inscription—inescapably gendered in its allegories and public symbolics—whether the nationalism concerned was a campaigning or insurgent movement demanding its rights, or a state already wielding its independence. In each case, different temporalities of state formation pertained. On the one hand, deeper-lying infrastructures of national identification in the old states of Western Europe, coming from long-accumulating histories of legal and institutional sedimentation, allowed practical consciousness of national belonging over the much longer term to coalesce; but outside this core domain of the North Atlantic seaboard, on the other hand, purposeful movements of political creation were needed before demands for national independence could condense.

Thus the coordinates of nationalism in, say, England and France profoundly differed from those in Germany and Italy, still more from the moving nationalist frontier of Eastern Europe. Outside the "core" states of Western Europe, nationality lacked the faculty of an established statehood. For early German nationalists of the anti-Napoleonic wars, the *Vormärz*, and the 1860s, for example, the arduous work of instituting the national category—of inventing the nation as a political program—was conducted without benefit of an already established state power. South of the Alps and east of the Rhine the architecture of national identification, and the process of imagining the nation as an organized, proselytizing act, in a politics of continuous nationalist pedagogy, depended on private more than official bodies, on individuals and voluntary associations rather than governments. Further, this process of proposing the German national category was coterminous with the emergence of a public sphere in Habermas's sense, so that "the nation" became conceived simultaneously as a political community of citizens.[3] Indeed, the very virtue of "publicness" in its civic sense, and the associated coalescence of civil society, were entailments of demands that the nation be formed.

The complex interpenetration of these two ideas—*nation* and *citizenry*—in the political languages of the nineteenth century was extraordinarily important. In processes of national unification a vital tension linked the slow coalescing of national consciousness in institutional ways (as an effect of longer-term histories) to the campaigning of the nationalist movement per se. A political identity of Germanness may have cohered institutionally over a longer period in response to state policies, constitutional frameworks, juridical definitions, and political opportunity structures, that is, but German *nationalism* as such required new languages of political subjectivity that called on the inhabitants of this Central European region to restyle themselves in *national* as opposed to other ways.[4]

There was a tension here between the inventedness of national identity and the constraints within and beneath which any inventiveness had to move. On the one side, as I have argued above, the element of political innovation now vitally structures how we think of nations and nationalism: nationality was not a natural consequence or outgrowth of common culture of great antiquity, and nations were not so much discovered or awakened as they were invented by the labors of intellectuals. That is, nationalisms rested on specific political histories and ideals of citizenship far more than they arose spontaneously out of venerable and preestablished cultural communities. Moreover, achieving continuity in national culture required hard, repeated, creative ideological and political efforts by intellectuals and nationalist leaders. It did not occur naturally by itself. Yet, on the other side, nationalists could only work with the cultural materials at hand—not with cultures of their own choosing, but with cultures directly encountered, given, and transmitted from the past. Despite all the power of our contemporary "constructionist" insight, emphasizing the inventedness and contingency of nations, therefore, it was this complicated dialectic of political innovation and actually existing cultures that provided the key to the particular histories nation-building presumed.

The fissiparous and fractured quality of nineteenth-century political cultures —the existing *thinness* of the conscious, affective, and juridical bonds holding the collective affiliations of the whole society together—was critical to the early dynamics of European nationalisms. Eventually, nations certainly attained a presence independent of the political practices that originally proposed them—they acquired an instituted and renewable everydayness, which built them into the underlying framework of collective identification in a society, part of the assumed architecture of political order and its forms of common-sense intelligibility. With the attainment of sovereignty or political self-determination at the latest, the nation became a discursive formation—ideologically, institutionally, culturally, socially, practically in myriad small ways—of immense power, which already prescribed the possible forms of political action and belief, what was thinkable and what was not. In Tom Nairn's words, nationalism turned into "a name for the general condition of the modern body politic, more like the [overall] climate of political and social thought than just another [free-standing] doctrine."[5] But in the nineteenth century, this hard-wiring could not yet be presupposed. Accordingly, the histories of nationalist belief and practice before 1914 need to grapple above all with the complex processes permitting this to happen.

From our own vantage point today, in contrast, nationality and nation-ness—the complex, conscious, unspoken, and inescapable modalities of "being national" inside the territorialized constitutional polities shaped in the period since the 1860s—have come to deliver the generic languages of political identity formation in the public and everyday conditions of life during the twentieth and now the twenty-first centuries. We are "national" when we vote, watch the six o'clock news, follow the national sport, observe (while barely noticing) the endemic iconographies of landscape and history in television commercials, imbibe the visual archive of suggestion and citation in the movies, and perform the nation day by day in the unreflected repetitions of political recognition. We become interpellated in mundane ways as national subjects in that sense. As Lauren Berlant suggests, this is what talk of "a common national character" implies, in which "National Subjects are taught to value certain abstract signs and stories as part of their intrinsic relation to themselves, to all 'citizens,' and to the national terrain." She calls this the "National Symbolic," namely,

> the order of discursive practices whose reign within a national space produces, and also refers to, the "law" in which the accident of birth within a geographic/political boundary transforms individuals into subjects of a collectively-held history. Its traditional icons, its metaphors, its heroes, its rituals, and its narratives provide an alphabet for a collective consciousness or national subjectivity; through the National Symbolic the historical nation aspires to achieve the inevitability of the status of natural law, a birthright.[6]

In defining "the *political* space of the nation," Berlant continues, this National Symbolic exceeds the legal discourse of citizenship, seeking "to link regulation to desire, harnessing affect to political life through the production of 'national fantasy.'" This work of cultural "nationalization," we might argue, makes the vital difference between the *nation* and the *state*. And this is how the idea of the nation eventuates, figuring history and geography into a landscape of familiarity and promise, inciting memories and hopes of citizenship, and bringing its claims and demands into the intimate and ordinary places of daily life. "National fantasy" captures the process by which "national culture becomes local—through the images, narratives, monuments, and sites that circulate through personal/collective consciousness."[7]

III

I spend so much time ruminating on these general questions of nationalism and the nation because they form such an essential starting point for thinking about the relationship of "center" and "margins." The essays in this volume approach "the margins" most obviously via the question of ethno-religious and ethno-cultural minorities (especially Jewish, but also Polish, Catholic, and so on), while also foregrounding treatments of gender and region. The volume also reflects the current turning to cultural history and is broadly organized around the spatial couplet of core and periphery. But our contemporary language of "margins," "frontiers," borderlands," "liminality," "hidden histories," and so forth also contains a wider menu of approaches, and in what follows I will be venturing a few thoughts about the more metaphorical or allegorical uses of that language—about the representational meanings of "the margin" as well as the more practical and material ones.[8]

In suggesting a few broad areas where the "centeredness" of German history might be explored, I need to enter a vital caveat: I have no desire to reestablish the primacy of the center over the margins. On the contrary, the opening up of previously neglected histories seems to me an unqualified good, as does the rethinking of classical or established perspectives from the new vantage points provided by minority history, gender history, histories of sexuality, and so forth. German history as mainly written and taught during most of the twentieth century certainly privileged an interconnected system of dominant approaches which took both the virtue and the necessity of their own state-centeredness for granted, including the various institutionalisms focused on bureaucracy and army, the ineluctable Prussocentrism of most historiography, the relative neglect of Catholicism, and the tardy development of social history. By proposing the "centeredness of German history" in my title, therefore, I have absolutely no wish to relegitimize all of that. My comments will be rather concerned with the dialectic between these two sets of perspectives. That is to say, once we have acknowledged the interest and significance of studying the many new subject matters which the "view from the margins" encourages and connotes, what then are the consequences for how "the center" might be rethought?

The first point to be made, no less vital for its obviousness, concerns the Third Reich's continuing centrality for how we need to think about the German past. There are several aspects to this question. One is simply that the Nazi era was one of the most brutally centered experiences imaginable—measured, that is, by the forms and degree of centralization of state power, by the institutional machineries of the dictatorship, by the priority of coercion over consent, by the concentration of allowable affiliations in the *Volksgemeinschaft*, by the banning and persecution of dissent, by the killing and violence deployed by the center, and by the erasure of the margin as an available place from which Germans were able to speak. The sheer enormity of the Third Reich—the scale of its destructiveness as an exceptional state—justifies the "centering" of German historiographical interest on this particular period and its priorities. In other words, allowing the meanings of the Third Reich to structure our perceptions of what constitutes a significant question to bring to the German past more generally seems to me entirely understandable and appropriate. Given the new centrality of the Holocaust to the consciousness and practice of German historians, this is perhaps even less avoidable than ever before.

What I am doing here, clearly, is taking a deliberately historiographical view of this question of "centeredness" or "centering." In other words, this seems to me in an important sense to be partly a matter of choice, a matter, that is, of the questions we choose to ask. Again, I don't want to be misunderstood. I am not advocating a groundless relativism, as though we had unlimited scope for shaping the German past and any old question will do: both ethically and empirically, the Third Reich's enormity *requires* the attention of specialists working on other periods; it *imposes* a certain order of historiographical business, filtering the kinds of questions it makes sense for us to ask; and in this light choosing one set of questions about, say, the 1920s or the 1950s over another will crucially shape the relevance and usefulness of what we are able to say.

Thus it seems incontrovertible to me that analyses of the "racial state" and "racialization" developed for the context of the Third Reich and pushed back into the *Kaiserreich* by historians like Hans-Walter Schmuhl, Paul Weindling, Pascal Grosse, and others have profoundly reshaped our grasp of the relationship between race, science, public health, eugenics, social engineering, and the larger complex of modernizing reform in the Wilhelmine era before 1914.[9] Similarly, the most recent debates over Nazi "modernity" have enormous and unsettling implications for how we approach questions of planning, technology, population, and national efficiency in the period before 1914, not only in Germany itself but elsewhere.[10] Likewise, to return to the immediate thematics of this volume, an interest in "margins" and "social outsiders" across the different periods of the German past has certainly been driven to a great extent by the ever-increasing centrality of those subjects to how we have come to see the main character of Nazi domination.[11]

In all of these ways, the importance of Nazism appropriately centers our perceptions of the modern German past. I want to cite one further example of this effect in the work of Tim Mason, who devoted most of his career to tackling precisely that question, namely, how could such an aggressively and successfully centered coercive polity ever have been produced: what were its dynamics of emergence, what were its conditions of stability, how was its cohesion secured, and where were its limits?[12] And for Mason, such questions could only be answered by comparison, by setting the logic of National Socialism against the experiences that preceded it. Mason's big question concerned the difference between the end stages of the two World Wars—that is, between the collapse of popular confidence in the imperial state during 1917–18 and the enduring solidity of popular identifications with the state in 1943–45, for whereas the one opened a space for radically new imaginings of the social and political order, the other produced only destruction and demoralized withdrawal. Not only that, the big rupture of 1918, and all the ways in which it continued to widen during 1919–23, opened a new horizon for political action during the 1920s; and the concentrated power successfully invested by the Nazis in the ideal of the *Volksgemeinschaft* after 1933 came in no small degree from the turbulent energies and aspirations unleashed earlier on.

Of course, Mason's larger ambition was to build an analysis of the Third Reich's central dynamism, from the confrontation with the labor movement to the expansionist drive for war, from the ground up, which for him meant starting from the fundamental causalities of class, in an approach that joined the logic of the economic recovery to the unmastered social history which the Nazis could never entirely control. That project of class analysis ultimately failed, and in the meantime the associated commitment defining the social history of the 1970s, the effort to find a separable and intact "society" which the Nazis proved unable to penetrate or command, seems also to have been given up. Instead, historians seem by now largely to have accepted that Nazism wholly suffused the socio-cultural environment during the 1930s, so that no part of German society remained uncontaminated or immune. "Racialization" has become one way of theorizing that generalized societal complicity; and by now "race" seems to have entirely trumped "class" in the thinking of most historians of the Third Reich. But to connect the hegemony of racialized thinking to some underlying developmental dynamism, some alternative overarching framework has also been required; and for that purpose, replacing the "society" of the social historians, "modernity" has now started to emerge as a new master category. In this new framework, to use Peukert's arresting formulation, "the spirit of science" becomes the new primary context for thinking about "the genesis of the 'Final Solution.'"[13]

If "modernity" becomes the new organizing category or compelling metanarrative for the history of the Third Reich in that way, we have a new logic of "centeredness" for German history that neither depends on the state or political history in any narrow and traditional sense nor remains confined to the Nazi era per se. Indeed, we now have a sizable body of research literature and argument that effectively reperiodizes the modern German field into a new schema stressing the unity of the years between the 1890s and the 1940s. Here, I am thinking less of those older and more contentious efforts at claiming the Third Reich for a pattern of "modernizing" or "developmental dictatorship" than of the social planning utopias analyzed by people like Michael Allen, Omer Bartov, Ulrich Herbert, and Götz Aly.[14] Moreover, there is considerable cognate support for this approach in the new literature on Italy, where the "aesthetics of power" and a "therapeutic" model of governmentality are taken to characterize the fascist project, encompassing "an array of social, scientific, and cultural policies designed to encourage the 'regeneration' of the national body."[15] Within this technocratic panacea, in Bartov's words, society was approached as "an organism to be manipulated by means of a vast surgical operation."[16] In Nazi Germany and Fascist Italy, "engineering, medicine, and science provided the paradigms and lexicon of this approach to governance, which offered comfort and an illusion of control to those racked by fears of Europe's imminent decline."[17]

By focusing so relentlessly on modernity's dark side, these analyses possess unmistakably Foucauldian intimations. But what these new studies still mainly lack is some operative appreciation for governmentality's limitations. The emergent paradigm of technocratic racialization implies a totalizing vision of power, which almost entirely dispenses with the earlier social historians' preoccupation with how individuals and subcultures managed to keep themselves marginally intact. Yet this was less of a lack in Foucault's own thinking. His studies of prisons, asylums, sexualities, regimes of knowledge, processes of normalizing and classification, and the general "order of things" simultaneously marked out the places where resistance might result, where domination pressed and bridled against its constraints. In current Third Reich interpretations, I would argue, this further entailment of a Foucauldian approach to power too deserves some careful consideration. For in seeking to explicate power's "micro-physics"—its forms of dispersal and fragmentation— Foucault also exposed the marginal and hidden places where recalcitrance, subversion, or transgression might occur. By taking a Foucauldian view of the Third Reich's functioning as a system of domination, therefore, we endow the idea of "the margin" with a particular and extremely important meaning.

"Marginality" in this sense takes on a doubled implication. It suggests both a cultural condition and a physical space, at the same time a form of identity or consciousness and a type of location or actual place. Quite apart from the historiography of the Third Reich per se, we might see this as one of the emblematic insights of a broad contemporary cross-disciplinary interest among historians, anthropologists, literary scholars, art historians, geographers, and others working in cultural studies, who have claimed "marginality" as the place where relative freedom can be found from power's all-seeing surveillance. This is the meaning of the pervasive metaphor of "the borderlands." Indeed, the far-reaching recession of class-centered forms of social history (and the associated older metanarratives of anti-capitalist critique), which sought to conceptualize the bases of collective agency around the central category of class, has given this new interest in "the margins" much powerful impetus. As Bryan Palmer points out in his remarkable book *Cultures of Darkness,* many historians, including the practitioners of the new cultural history and some of the most creative voices of the contemporary profession, have increasingly preferred an approach "that accentuates fragmentation, difference, and particularistic parochialism." Still more: "In the name of refusing power's master narratives, [such] thought denies the very importance of a systematic center of exploitation's and oppression's causality" altogether, proposing instead a framework of "pluralism and diversity, in which proliferating stories of class, race, and gender" can all coexist.[18]

This metaphorical reading of "the margin," combined with the Foucauldian dialectic of power and resistance, is enormously helpful in seeing how we can move between the important new empirical sites of research encompassed by the framework of "German history from the margins" and the central questions of political and social history affecting German society as a whole, what Foucault himself described as the necessary linkage from "the little tactics of the habitat" to the "grand strategies of geopolitics."[19] In other words, viewing German history "from the margins" involves not simply finding new, original, or neglected standpoints based in minority interests or peripheral locations. It also requires thinking through the conceptual ramifications of the opposition between "centeredness" and "marginality" along a variety of dimensions, including those of subjectivity and selfhood, the local and the national, the "inside" and the "outside," the normative and the "Others." And thirdly, it demands a willingness to argue back from the fascinating new contexts of marginality to the old established center ground of the state, society, and economy to see how the latter might come differently into focus.[20]

Unless we do the latter—unless we bring the insights culled from the margins back to the old big questions—the exhausted and justly superseded grand narratives may well return to life. In taking stock of historiographical developments since the 1980s, for example, Volker Berghahn recently criticized the new cultural historians for "drift[ing] into topics on cultural developments at the grass roots level of German society," because such interests "have distracted" them from the really important questions, including above all "the crucial question of '1914.'"[21] In Berghahn's view, the blame for this misguidedness lies with a larger contemporary trend, namely, "a phase of historical writing in which the past is seen as not only immensely complex and diverse, but also as totally fragmented and decentered."

My question is whether the time has come to ask if, in the midst of all the deconstruction, contingency, agency, and indeterminacy that is being highlighted everywhere, we have lost sight of the forest because we are so firmly focused on the trees. To be sure, we have to have more meticulous research on artistic and scientific developments, on minorities, women, childhood and old age, rural piety, and urban crime. Upper Franconia or local *Heimat* movements in Württemberg, pub-life in Wilhelmshaven and monuments in Koblenz are significant topics. We must also continue to investigate if groups and individuals had agency and *Eigensinn*. But are we not in danger of forgetting that they were equally embedded in socio-economic and political power structures? If women and men made their own history, please could we also think once more about the conditions under which they willy-nilly had to operate?[22]

Now, the short answers to Berghahn's two questions are: yes, we certainly *can* think about the conditions under which particular human histories have to be made, but many cultural historians have never stopped doing so; and yes, there *is* a danger of neglecting the larger "structural" questions, but even if some practitioners of the new cultural history have forgotten them, many others have never stopped arguing their importance. Contrary to Berghahn's implication, many of us turned to a "culturalist" analytic precisely to engage such larger questions more effectively, because the available social and political approaches seemed so unmoved by entire dimensions of the human condition and indeed militantly neglected them. More to the point, these different sites of analysis—the "micro" and the "macro," or the local and the national, the "cultural" and the structural, the many fashionable areas of work listed by Berghahn and the abiding big questions he thinks are being displaced—are not mutually exclusive or part of any hostile dichotomy. Of course, Berghahn leaves us in no doubt as to which kind of history he prefers: the new subjects are all very fascinating, and it is nice somebody is doing them, he is prepared to concede, but the old big questions are still the ones that matter. Clearly, unless we show how working at the margins can change what we know of the center, dismissals like this will be all the harder to counter.

IV

One area where this has actually been happening is in recent studies of *Heimat*. Celia Applegate's pioneering study of that subject showed how images and conceptions of locality could all shift in meaning during the process of national unification, so that the "big question" of the making of the imperial state became vitally inflected by the "little question" of parochial loyalties to the *Heimat*, which embraced deeply embedded social and cultural affiliations tied to landscape, to the built and cultivated environments, to customary practices and oral traditions, to property rights and usages, to family networks, to parochial religion, and to political autonomies. Subsequent work by Alon Confino and others then further extended this argument.[23] Such works are rethinking the meanings of "the local" in their relationship to the emerging imaginary of the new national state, elucidating the dynamic reciprocities between local and regional rootedness on the one side and national identifications on the other. It is now much harder to sustain the old arguments about backwardness and traditionalism where discussions of *Heimat* used to be trapped.

In Applegate's words, "Those who created and promoted *Heimat*, consciously or not, were suggesting a basic affinity between the new, abstract political units and one's home, thus endowing an entity like Germany with the emotional accessibility of a world known to one's five senses."[24] This was precisely the quotidian and sensual suturing of nation-ness to the lived world of individuals which I discussed earlier in these comments. That suturing was essential if the emotional life of citizens was to be harnessed for the needs of a national culture, allowing the national culture in turn to insert itself into the local. The "national" could make itself "local" in that sense, delivering some of the materials for "a collective consciousness or national subjectivity."[25] *Heimat* entailed a kind of spatial hybridity, which joined a grand story of national origins to the forms of lived identity in local and everyday environments. This provincialized grounding of the nation "enlarged local existence to its ultimate imaginary boundaries by transforming local history into national history." It connected "the abstract nation" with local and personal circumstances, thereby "making national history as tangible as local history." In fact, by bringing the national down to the local, the local became nationalized in return.[26]

The conjoining of local patriotisms with the new consciousness of nation also occurred in the old city environments of geographical Germany like Hamburg, Leipzig, Munich, and Berlin, then experiencing breakneck transformation during industrialization precisely in the wake of Germany's national unification. Thus in Jennifer Jenkins's study of cultural politics in Hamburg, bourgeois reformers projected ideals of national unity onto their campaigns of public education and cultural uplift, while seeking to domesticate an unruly mass public and the associated technologies of mass communication. Commercialization of culture and the social disorder of the modern city combined with the deculturing of respectable taste into kitsch to produce huge anxieties not only among the bourgeois notability, but also among the intellectual advocates of the modernity of the new national state. The resulting projects of national/ist pedagogy marked out a key site where the cultural, social, and political coordinates of the new German citizenship were open to be defined. Once again, the local embeddedness of an existing repertoire of affiliations, often guided by a fierce loyalty to geographical place or the longevity of civic traditions, proved no impediment to finding oneself in the new languages of nation.[27]

Once consciousness of belonging to nation became institutionalized via the national state of 1871, the new field of personal and collective recognition extended from locality, region, and city through the intermediate jurisdictions of the prenational states and churches to the emergent meta-identity of Germanness and beyond, where the transnational arenas of Europe and the global economy added further layers of complexity. In the pre-1914 drive to render German goods competitive in the world market, for example, the uses of local tradition received an additional twist in the efforts of architects, planners, designers, and other reformers behind the *Deutscher Werkbund* (founded in 1907) to devise an authentic German style. The result, as Maiken Umbach has recently argued, was a creative encounter between artfully constructed notions of the vernacular and an expanding, globally oriented conception of the modern and the urbane. In that collaboration, the vernacular became a source for the authenticity that delivered the cultural materials serviceable for the self-consciously national and modern project of securing Germany's global competitiveness. Here "rustic" and "traditional" meant the opposite of a reactionary resistance against change—in the rhetoric of the *Werkbund*, as Umbach astutely observes, adjectives like "simple," "rational," "comfortable," "practical," "homely," and *heimatlich* were part of the connotative ballast the new design movement required, encouraging a new synthesis of vernacular authenticity and affirmative modernity.[28]

This argument can also be pushed toward the patently modernizing modalities of a mass-mediated, commercialized, and consumption-oriented public sphere, in which imagery of *Heimat* and nation consorted together in highly mobile and promiscuous ways. The burgeoning historiographies of leisure, tourism, popular entertainment, and mass consumption provide rich evidence for this effect. New forms of packaging, advertising, mass distribution, and sales techniques were all linked to the emerging mass market, as commodified images increasingly circulated via travel guides, posters, postcards, collectable picture cards in packets of cocoa, chocolate, and other goods, commercialized bric-a-brac, and advertisements. The new urban environments became saturated with cultural references and commercial stimuli, in visual languages whose Germanness became more and more automatic.[29] The opposite of a neutral process, this inspired extensive debate over its socio-political implications. While exciting big anxieties about cultural degeneration (via pulp fiction, penny dreadfuls, early films, and all kinds of kitsch), this new mass market and allied commercial entertainments also invited campaigns of uplift and edification, for which nationalist pedagogy became a natural idiom.

This visualizing of the nation was simultaneously unregulated yet profoundly organized. It was on the one hand decentered, involving mass circulation of images in a liberalized public sphere teeming with rival and competing discourses, embracing the full spectrum of party politics. Yet on the other hand the nation was increasingly defined by common representational frames. Inside these frames, some agencies wielded disproportionate social, organizational, and ideological power—most obviously the state in its various guises, but also some interests and political parties over others. That is to say, determined efforts were made to organize and capture this new representational terrain of popular culture by centering it on one set of values as against another. One would think that this process, which Rudy Koshar calls "the formation of a national optics" or "a multifaceted way of seeing the historical nation in the physical environment," was profoundly relevant to the big questions Volker Berghahn would like us still to address. As Koshar argues, within this new economy of representations the national state had an urgent "need to create objectified symbols of national identity that offered a point of contact and easily recognized visual referent for many disparate groups."[30]

V

There are many particular ways of exploring this question of the relation between "the margins" and "the center," and in these brief remarks I have chosen only a few. We might, for instance, probe the meanings of "marginality" within intellectual history by exploring the uses of Deleuze and Guattari's concepts of "minor literature" and "deterritorialization," which Scott Spector puts brilliantly to work in his study of Kafka and the Prague circle.[31] We might also take a more strictly political approach by using an expanded concept of citizenship to explore the mechanisms and processes of inclusion and exclusion within the German polities of the last century and a half. Political historians might explore the centering of organized allegiances and opportunities on continuities or interruptions in the stability of the dominant political blocs; social historians might do the same in relation to civil society. We might even describe politics *as such* as the always incomplete search for workable forms of "centeredness," or the rival efforts at "centering" political identities and allegiances, which encourage varying degrees of democracy or authoritarianism: the Nazi conception of *Volksgemeinschaft* proved one of the most shockingly effective and viciously exclusionary examples of an authoritarian version of the drive to create a center. For social historians, social structure and social relations of class might provide a similar context for studying the "centeredness" of cultural practices and political allegiances and their limits.

To take another specific question, we might explore the possible equivalence for the German past of the role of empire in the history of Britain. If British history during the nineteenth and twentieth centuries has been centered on the colonial relationship and its consequences in some vital ways, particularly on the problematic of race, then what are the analogous dynamics in German history? Were they to be found merely in the finite episode of German colonialism itself between the 1880s and 1918, or in the larger record of Germany's relations with Poles, Czechs, and other Slavic minorities in the East, in the new nationalist imaginary of *Mitteleuropa* at the turn of the century, in the new vistas of eastern empire opened by Brest-Litovsk, or where? Similarly, if "the view from Vesuvius" and the image of "the South" formed the negativity regulating the discourse of Italian nationhood during the drive for unification and after, then what were the analogous negativities for "Germany"?

Each of these questions concerns a powerful logic of nationalist concentration, but some have recently been attracted by the idea that German history can be radically *decentered*. By replicating Pierre Nora's grandiose and remarkably popular multivolume project on *Les lieux de mémoire*, such historians suggest, discussion of German national identity might be shifted decisively away from old obsessions with the national state in a spirit more in keeping with European integration, the postnational future, and the idea of a common European home. But Nora's paradigm of the "sites of memory" markedly depoliticizes the national question, in my view. For the highly centered national consensus of the French Republican tradition, it substitutes a fragmented and discrete mélange of disparate topics, which affirm an aggregated sense of common cultural identity, while erasing entire contexts of the production of "Frenchness" (such as the colonies) and excluding those parts of contemporary French society unable to find themselves in the artfully assembled mosaic of the national past.[32] In a more realist and less metaphorical mode, on the other hand, regional perspectives among German historians have also been experiencing an upswing, and these offer a much steadier context for thinking about the margins.[33]

But in weighing the importance of "the center" and "the margins," my general point is that we need to address *both*—we need to explore minority viewpoints, open up the neglected spaces, and reclaim the marginalized subjects and areas of the German past, while also relating them to the explicit and unconscious ways in which our understanding has been centered. Only by that means will the "centeredness" of German history be properly unsettled and remade.

Notes

1. For the coordinates of citizenship in Germany, see Andreas K. Fahrmeier, "Nineteenth-Century German Citizenships: A Reconsideration," *Historical Journal* 40, no. 3 (1997): 721–52; Andreas K. Fahrmeier, *Citizens and Aliens: Foreigners and the Law in Britain and the German States, 1789–1870* (New York: Berghahn, 2000);

283

Dieter Gosewinkel, *Einbürgen und Ausschliessen: Die Nationalisierung der Staatsangehörigkeit vom Deutschen Bund bis zur Bundesrepublik Deutschland* (Göttingen: Vandenhoeck und Ruprecht, 2001); and Rogers Brubaker, *Citizenship and Nationhood in France and Germany* (Cambridge, Mass.: Harvard University Press, 1992). Against a more strictly juridical definition, my own approach emphasizes the wider forces acting on citizenship (social, economic, cultural, political) and its location in a bundle of shifting capacities and claims. See, especially, Margaret R. Somers, "Citizenship and the Place of the Public Sphere: Law, Community, and Political Culture in the Transition to Democracy," *American Sociological Review* 58, no. 5 (1993): 587–620; Margaret R. Somers, "Narrating and Naturalizing Civil Society and Citizenship Theory: The Place of Political Culture and the Public Sphere," *Sociological Theory* 13 (1995): 229–74; Lauren Berlant, *The Queen of America Goes to Washington City: Essays on Sex and Citizenship* (Durham, N.C.: Duke University Press, 1997); Kathleen Canning and Sonya O. Rose, "Gender, Citizenship, and Subjectivity: Some Theoretical and Historical Considerations," *Gender and History* 13, no. 3 (2001): 427–43; and Kathleen Canning, "Class vs. Citizenship: Keywords in German Gender History," *Central European History* 37, no. 2 (2004): 225–44.

2. Benedict Anderson, *Imagined Communities: Reflections on the Origin and Spread of Nationalism*, rev. ed. (London: Verso, 1991), 7, 9ff.

3. See Jürgen Habermas, *The Structural Transformation of the Public Sphere: An Inquiry into a Category of Bourgeois Society* (Cambridge, Mass.: Harvard University Press, 1993); and Geoff Eley, "Nations, Publics, and Political Cultures: Placing Habermas in the Nineteenth Century," in *Habermas and the Public Sphere*, ed. Craig Calhoun (Cambridge, Mass.: Harvard University Press, 1992), 289–339.

4. See Abigail Green, *Fatherlands: State-Building and Nationhood in Nineteenth-Century Germany* (Cambridge: Cambridge University Press, 2001), for an institutional approach to the growth of German nationhood in the mid-nineteenth century.

5. Tom Nairn, "Scotland and Europe," in *Becoming National: A Reader*, ed. Geoff Eley and Ronald Grigor Suny (New York: Oxford University Press, 1996), 80.

6. Lauren Berlant, *The Anatomy of National Fantasy: Hawthorne, Utopia, and Everyday Life* (Chicago: University of Chicago Press, 1991), 20.

7. Ibid., 5.

8. For extraordinarily fertile general discussion, see the writings of David Morley: "Bounded Realms: Household, Family, Community, and Nation," in *Home, Exile, Homeland: Film, Media, and the Politics of Place*, ed. Hamid Naficy (New York: Routledge, 1999), 151–68; "Belongings, Place, Space, and Identity in a Mediated World," *European Journal of Cultural Studies* 4, no. 4 (2001): 425–48; and *Home Territories: Media, Mobility, and Identity* (London: Routledge, 2000). Also see Arjun Appadurai, "The Production of Locality," in *Modernity at Large: Cultural Dimensions of Globalization* (Minneapolis: University of Michigan Press, 1996), 178–99.

9. Hans-Walter Schmuhl, *Rassenhygiene, Nationalsozialismus, Euthanasie: Von der Verhütung zur Vernichtung "lebensunwerten Lebens," 1890–1945* (Göttingen: Vandenhoeck und Ruprecht, 1987); Paul Weindling, *Health, Race, and German Politics between National Unification and Nazism, 1870–1945* (Cambridge: Cambridge University Press, 1989); and Pascal Grosse, *Kolonialismus, Eugenik und bürgerliche Gesellschaft in Deutschland, 1850–1918* (Frankfurt am Main: Campus, 2000). For the Third Reich itself, see Robert N. Proctor, *Racial Hygiene: Medicine under the Nazis* (Cambridge, Mass.: Harvard University Press, 1988); and Michael Burleigh and Wolfgang

Wippermann, *The Racial State: Germany, 1933-1945* (Cambridge: Cambridge University Press, 1991). Emblematic as ever: Detlev J. K. Peukert, "The Genesis of the 'Final Solution' from the Spirit of Science," in *Reevaluating the Third Reich*, ed. Thomas Childers and Jane Caplan (New York: Holmes and Meier, 1993), 234–52.

10. See, especially, Götz Aly and Karl Heinz Roth, *Die restlose Erfassung: Volkszählen, Identifizieren, Aussondern im Nationalsozialismus* (Berlin: Fischer Taschenbuch Verlag, 1984); Götz Aly and Susanne Heim, *Vordenker der Vernichtung: Auschwitz und die deutsche Pläne für eine neue europäische Ordnung* (Hamburg: Hoffmann und Campe, 1991); Götz Aly, *Macht, Geist, Wahn: Kontinuitäten deutschen Denkens* (Berlin: Argon, 1997); and Götz Aly, Peter Chroust, and Christian Pross, *Cleansing the Fatherland: Nazi Medicine and Racial Hygiene* (Baltimore: Johns Hopkins University Press, 1994). The best introduction to this work is now Götz Aly, *"Final Solution": Nazi Population Policy and the Murder of the European Jews* (London: Arnold, 1999). See also the important new book by Michael Thad Allen, *The Business of Genocide: The SS, Slave Labor, and the Concentration Camps* (Chapel Hill: University of North Carolina Press, 2002). For my own thoughts: Geoff Eley, "German History and the Contradictions of Modernity: The Bourgeoisie, the State, and the Mastery of Reform," in *Society, Culture, and Politics in Germany, 1870-1930: New Approaches*, ed. Geoff Eley (Ann Arbor: University of Michigan Press, 1996), 67–104.

11. See here, most recently, Robert Gellately and Nathan Stoltzfus, eds., *Social Outsiders in Nazi Germany* (Princeton, N.J.: Princeton University Press, 2001).

12. Tim Mason, *Nazism, Fascism, and the Working Class*, ed. Jane Caplan (Cambridge: Cambridge University Press, 1995); and *Social Policy in the Third Reich: The Working Class in the "National Community"*, ed. Jane Caplan (Providence, R.I.: Berg, 1993).

13. See Detlev Peukert's hugely influential essay, "The Genesis of the 'Final Solution.'"

14. See Allen, *Business of Genocide;* Omer Bartov, *Murder in Our Midst: The Holocaust, Industrial Killing, and Representation* (New York: Oxford University Press, 1996); Ulrich Herbert, *Best: Biographische Studien über Radikalismus, Weltanschauung und Vernunft, 1903-1989* (Bonn: Dietz, 1996); Aly and Heim, *Vordenker der Vernichtung;* and Aly, *"Final Solution."*

15. Simonetta Falasca-Zamponi, *Fascist Spectacle: The Aesthetics of Power in Mussolini's Italy* (Berkeley: University of California Press, 1997); and Ruth Ben-Ghiat, *Fascist Modernities: Italy, 1922-1945* (Berkeley: University of California Press, 2001), 5.

16. Bartov, *Murder in Our Midst*, 5.

17. Ben-Ghiat, *Fascist Modernities*, 5.

18. Bryan D. Palmer, *Cultures of Darkness: Night Travels in the Histories of Transgression* (New York: Monthly Review Press, 2000), 4.

19. Michel Foucault, "Questions of Geography," in *M. Foucault: Power/Knowledge*, ed. Colin Gordon (New York: Harvester, 1980), 149.

20. One simplified illustration: during the successive periods of the nineteenth and twentieth centuries, the patriotic imagery and ideals entailed by "Germanness" or "being German" have been fashioned partly through complex interactions with a series of negative counterimages, whose subjects include most of the minorities and outsiders figuring in this volume; and approaching this process "from the margins" provides necessary and illuminating access to the character of the "center." For comparative purposes, see Nelson Moe's excellent new study of the imaginative geography

of Italian nationhood during the mid-nineteenth century, which rested crucially on negative constructions of the "southern borderland" of the *Mezzogiorno*. Nelson Moe, *The View from Vesuvius: Italian Culture and the Southern Question* (Berkeley: University of California Press, 2002).

21. Volker R. Berghahn, "The German Empire, 1871–1914: Reflections on the Direction of Recent Research," *Central European History* 35, no. 1 (2002): 76–77.

22. Ibid., 77.

23. See Celia Applegate, *A Nation of Provincials: The German Idea of Heimat* (Berkeley: University of California Press, 1990); Celia Applegate, "Democracy or Reaction? The Political Implications of Localist Ideas in Wilhelmine and Weimar Germany," in *Elections, Mass Politics, and Social Change in Modern Germany: New Perspectives*, ed. Larry Eugene Jones and James Retallack (Cambridge: Cambridge University Press, 1992), 247–66; Alon Confino, *The Nation as a Local Metaphor: Württemberg, Imperial Germany, and National Memory, 1871–1918* (Chapel Hill: University of North Carolina Press, 1997); Georg Kunz, *Verortete Geschichte: Regionales Geschichtsbewusstsein in den deutschen Historischen Vereinen des neunzehnten Jahrhunderts* (Göttingen: Vandenhoeck und Ruprecht, 2000); Rolf Petri, "Deutsche Heimat, 1850–1950," *Comparativ* 11, no. 1 (2001): 77–127; Jennifer Jenkins, *Provincial Modernity: Local Culture and Liberal Politics in Fin-de-Siècle Hamburg* (Ithaca, N.Y.: Cornell University Press, 2002); Maiken Umbach, "The Vernacular International: Heimat, Modernism, and the Global Market in Early Twentieth-Century Germany," *National Identities* 4, no. 1 (2002): 45–68; H. Glenn Penny, "The Civic Uses of Science: Ethnology and Civil Society in Imperial Germany," *Osiris* 17 (2002): 228–52; Charlotte Tacke, *Denkmal im sozialen Raum: Nationale Symbole in Deutschland und Frankreich im 19. Jahrhundert* (Göttingen: Vandenhoeck und Ruprecht, 1995); and Patricia Mazón, "Germania Triumphant: The Niederwald National Monument and the Liberal Moment in Imperial Germany," *German History* 18, no. 2 (2000): 162–92.

24. Applegate, *Nation of Provincials*, 10–11.

25. Berlant, *Anatomy of National Fantasy*, 20, 5.

26. Confino, *Nation as a Local Metaphor*, 149. "The potency of Heimat as a national symbol lay in its capacity to depict different levels of one's existence, thus allowing the placement of the individual and locality within the context of greater communities, larger territories, and bigger developments—within the context, in other words, of the projects of nationhood and modernity. Ironically, if Heimat succeeded in symbolizing an intimate and closely knit community, it was only because it represented at the same time large territories and impersonal social relations. Had Heimat symbolized only the local place, it would have disconnected the locality from the larger processes around it" (189).

27. See especially Jennifer Jenkins, "The Kitsch Collections and *The Spirit in the Furniture:* Cultural Reform and National Culture in Germany," *Social History* 21, no. 2 (May 1996): 123–41.

28. Umbach, "Vernacular International," especially 49, 53, 64; Penny, "Civic Uses of Science." For an interesting argument contrasting the stronger "centeredness" of taste and style in France with the contested quality of national culture in Germany, based on the longevity versus the recentness of the respective national pasts, see Leora Auslander, "'National Taste?' Citizenship Law, State Form, and Everyday Aesthetics in Modern France and Germany, 1920–1940," in *The Politics of Consumption: Material Culture and Citizenship in Europe and America*, ed. Martin Daunton and

Matthew Hilton (Oxford: Oxford University Press, 2001), 109–28. For detailed analysis of the French context, see Leora Auslander, *Taste and Power: Furnishing Modern France* (Berkeley: University of California Press, 1996); Deborah L. Silverman, *Art Nouveau in Fin-de-Siècle France: Politics, Psychology, and Style* (Berkeley: University of California Press, 1989); and Patricia Mainardi, *The End of the Salon: Art and the State in the Early Third Republic* (Cambridge: Cambridge University Press, 1993).

29. See especially Confino, *Nation as a Local Metaphor*, 158–209; also Rudy Koshar, *German Travel Cultures* (Oxford: Berg, 2000), and the associated collection, Rudy Koshar, ed., *Histories of Leisure* (Oxford: Berg, 2002). For some well-directed skepticism in an analogous context of discussion, see Carolyn Steedman, "Englishness, Clothes, and Little Things," in *The Englishness of English Dress*, ed. Christopher Breward, Becky Conekin, and Caroline Cox (Oxford: Oxford University Press, 2002), 29–44.

30. Rudy Koshar, *From Monuments to Traces: Artifacts of German Memory, 1870–1990* (Berkeley: University of California Press, 2000), 23.

31. Scott Spector, *Prague Territories: National Conflict and Cultural Innovation in Franz Kafka's Fin de Siècle* (Berkeley: University of California Press, 2000), especially 27–35.

32. See Pierre Nora, *Les lieux de mémoire*, 7 vols. (Paris: Gallimard, 1984–92), translated as *The Realms of Memory: The Construction of the French Past*, 3 vols. (New York: Columbia University Press, 1996–98), and *Rethinking France*, 4 vols. (Chicago: University of Chicago Press, 2001–). For the genesis of a German counterpart, see Etienne François, Hannes Siegrist, and Jakob Vogel, eds., *Nation und Emotion: Deutschland und Frankreich im Vergleich 19. und 20. Jahrhundert* (Göttingen: Vandenhoeck und Ruprecht, 1995). For a searching critique: Peter Carrier, "Places, Politics, and the Archiving of Contemporary Memory in Pierre Nora's *Les lieux de mémoire*," in *Memory and Methodology*, ed. Susannah Radstone (Oxford: Berg 2000), 37–57.

33. See especially Helmut Walser Smith, "The Boundaries of the Local in Modern German History," in *Saxony in German History: Culture, Society, and Politics, 1830–1933*, ed. James Retallack (Ann Arbor: University of Michigan Press, 2000), 63–76; James Retallack, "Introduction: Locating Saxony in the Landscape of German Regional History," ibid., 1–30; Thomas Kühne, "Imagined Regions: The Construction of Traditional, Democratic, and Other Identities," ibid., 51–62; Celia Applegate, "The Mediated Nation: Regions, Readers, and the German Past," ibid., 33–50; and Celia Applegate, "A Europe of Regions: Reflections on the Historiography of Subnational Places in Modern Times," *American Historical Review* 104, no. 4 (1999): 1157–82.

Contributors

Frank Bösch is Professor of Media History at the University of Bochum (Germany). He is author of *Macht und Machtverlust: Die Geschichte der CDU* (2002); *Das konservative Milieu: Vereinskultur und lokale Sammlungspolitik in ost- und westdeutschen Regionen, 1900–1960* (2002); and *Die Adenauer-CDU: Gründung, Aufstieg und Krise einer Erfolgspartei, 1945–1969* (2001).

Winson Chu has recently completed his dissertation, "The Politics of Irredentism: Regionalism and the German Minority in Poland, 1918–1939," at the University of California, Berkeley.

Geoff Eley is Professor of History at the University of Michigan, Ann Arbor. His publications include *Reshaping the German Right: Radical Nationalism and Political Change after Bismarck* (1980) and *Forging Democracy: The History of the Left in Europe, 1850–2000* (2002). He has co-authored *The Peculiarities of German History* (1984); co-edited *Culture/Power/History: A Reader in Contemporary Social Theory* (1993) and *Becoming National: A Reader* (1996); and edited *The "Goldhagen Effect": History, Memory, Nazism; Facing the German Past* (2000).

Heide Fehrenbach is Professor of History at Northern Illinois University. She is author of *Cinema in Democratizing Germany: Reconstructing National Identity after Hitler* (1995) and *Race after Hitler: Black Occupation Children in Postwar Germany and America* (2005); and co-editor of *Transactions, Transgressions, Transformations: American Culture in Western Europe and Japan* (2000).

Neil Gregor is Reader in Modern German History at the University of Southampton (UK). He is author of *Daimler-Benz in the Third Reich* (1998) and *How to Read Hitler* (2005); and editor of *Nazism: A Reader* (2000) and *Nazism, War, and Genocide* (2005).

Atina Grossmann is Professor of History at Cooper Union, New York. She is author of *Reforming Sex: The German Movement for Birth Control and Abortion Reform, 1920–1950* (1995) and *Victims, Victors, and Survivors: Germans, Allies, and Jews in Occupied Germany* (forthcoming). She has co-edited *When Biology Became Destiny: Women in Weimar and Nazi Germany* (1989) and *The Crimes of War: Guilt and Denial in the Twentieth Century* (2002).

Dagmar Herzog is Professor of History at the Graduate Center, City University of New York. She is author of *Intimacy and Exclusion: Religious Politics in Pre-Revolutionary Baden* (1996) and *Sex after Fascism: Memory and Morality in Twentieth-Century Germany* (2005); and editor of *Sexuality and German Fascism* (2004).

Katharine Kennedy is Professor of History at Agnes Scott College in Decatur, Georgia. Her publications include "African Heimat: German Colonies in Wilhelmine and Weimar Reading Books," *Internationale Schulbuchforschung* 24, no. 1 (2002) and "Visual Representation and National Identity in the Elementary Schoolbooks of Imperial Germany," *Paedagogica Historica* 36, no. 1 (2000).

Eric Kurlander is Assistant Professor of Modern European History at Stetson University in DeLand, Florida. He is author of *The Price of Exclusion: Race, Nationalism, and the Decline of German Liberalism, 1898–1933* (2006).

Till van Rahden is Assistant Professor in the Department of History at the University of Cologne (Germany). He is author of *Juden und andere Breslauer: Die Beziehungen zwischen Juden, Protestanten und Katholiken in einer deutschen Grossstadt von 1860 bis 1925* (2000); and co-editor of *Juden, Bürger, Deutsche: Zur Geschichte von Vielfalt und Differenz, 1800–1933* (2001).

Gideon Reuveni is Yad Hanadiv Research Fellow at the Department for Jewish History and Culture, Ludwig-Maximilians-University (Munich). He is author of *Reading Germany: Literature and Consumer Culture in Germany before 1933* (2005); and co-editor of *Jüdische Geschichte lesen: Texte der jüdischen Geschichtsschreibung des 19. und 20. Jahrhunderts* (2003) and *Emancipation through Muscles: Jews in European Sport* (2006).

Contributors

Nils Roemer is Lecturer in Jewish History at the University of Southampton (UK). He is author of *Jewish Scholarship and Culture in Nineteenth-Century Germany: Between History and Faith* (2005); and co-editor of *Jüdische Geschichte lesen: Texte der jüdischen Geschichtsschreibung des 19. und 20. Jahrhunderts* (2003).

Mark Roseman holds the Pat M. Glazer Chair of Jewish Studies at Indiana University. He is author of *Recasting the Ruhr, 1945–1957* (1992), *The Past in Hiding* (2000), and *The Villa, the Lake, the Meeting: The Wannsee Conference and the "Final Solution"* (2002); editor of *Generations in Conflict: Youth Rebellion and Generation Formation in Modern Germany, 1770–1968* (1995); and co-editor of *Three Postwar Eras in Comparison: Western Europe 1918-1945-1989* (2002).

Karen Schönwälder is head of the Arbeitsstelle Interkulturelle Konflikte und gesellschaftliche Integration at the Wissenschaftszentrum Berlin für Sozialforschung, and was Guest Professor at the Universities of Freiburg and Haifa. She is author of *Historiker und Politik: Geschichtswissenschaft im Nationalsozialismus* (1992) and *Einwanderung und ethnische Pluralität: Politische Entscheidungen und öffentliche Debatten in Großbritannien und der Bundesrepublik von den 1950er bis zu den 1970er Jahren* (2001); and co-author of *New Democrats, New Labour, Neue Sozialdemokraten* (1998).

Helmut Walser Smith is Martha Rivers Ingram Professor of History at Vanderbilt University in Nashville, Tennessee. He is author of *German Nationalism and Religious Conflict: Culture, Identity, Politics, 1870–1914* (1995) and *The Butcher's Tale: Murder and Anti-Semitism in a German Town* (2002); editor of *Protestants, Catholics, and Jews in Germany, 1800–1914* (2001) and *The Holocaust and Other Genocides: History, Representation, Ethics* (2002); and co-editor of *Exclusionary Violence: Antisemitic Riots in Modern German History* (2002).

Yfaat Weiss is Director of the Bucerius Institute for Contemporary German History and Society and a member of the Department of Jewish History, University of Haifa (Israel). She is author of *Staatsbürgerschaft und Ethnizität: Deutsche und polnische Juden am Vorabend des Holocaust* (2000); and co-editor of *Challenging Ethnic Citizenship: German and Israeli Perspectives on Immigration* (2002) and *Memory and Amnesia: The Holocaust in Germany* (2005, in Hebrew).

Index

291

Index

Index

Index

294

Index

Index

German History from the Margins reshapes our understanding of the role of regional diversity and ethnic and religious minorities in modern German history. Covering the period between the formation of the Second Empire and the consolidation of the Federal Republic and offering a variety of perspectives, the volume illuminates relationships among different ethnic, religious, and social groups, and the relationship of these to the German state. Included are contributions by Frank Bösch, Winson Chu, Geoff Eley, Heide Fehrenbach, Neil Gregor, Atina Grossmann, Dagmar Herzog, Katharine Kennedy, Eric Kurlander, Till van Rahden, Gideon Reuveni, Nils Roemer, Mark Roseman, Karen Schönwälder, Helmut Walser Smith, and Yfaat Weiss.

INDIANA
University Press
Bloomington & Indianapolis

http://iupress.indiana.edu
1-800-842-6796

ISBN-13: 978-0-253-34743-5
ISBN-10: 0-253-34743-2

90000

www.ingramcontent.com/pod-product-compliance
Lightning Source LLC
Chambersburg PA
CBHW050227270326
41914CB00003BA/604